WORLD RELIGIONS AND CULTS

Moralistic, Mythical *and* Mysticism Religions

Volume 2

General Editors

BODIE HODGE &
ROGER PATTERSON

First printing: April 2016

Master Books®, P.O. Box 726, Green Forest, AR 72638
Master Books® is a division of the New Leaf Publishing Group, Inc.

ISBN: 978-0-89051-922-6
Library of Congress Number: 2015910670

Cover by Left Coast Design, Portland, Oregon

Scripture taken from the NEW AMERICAN STANDARD BIBLE® (NASB), copyright © 1960, 1962, 1963, 1968, 1971, 1972, 1973, 1975, 1977, 1995 by The Lockman Foundation. Used by permission.

Scripture taken from the New King James Version (NKJV), copyright © 1982 by Thomas Nelson, Inc. Used by permission. All rights reserved.

Scripture designated KJV is from the King James Version of the Bible.

Please consider requesting a copy of this volume be purchased by your local library system.

Printed in the United States of America

Please visit our website for other great titles: www.masterbooks.com

For information regarding author interviews,
please contact the publicity department at (870) 438-5288

Master
Books®
A Division of New Leaf Publishing Group
www.masterbooks.com

Acknowledgments

Our appreciation to the following for their contributions and help to bring this book to fruition:

Troy Lacey, Ken Ham, Dr. Terry Mortenson, Dr. Corey Abney,
David Wright, Dr. Royce Short, Dr. Dan Anderson, Pastor Don Landis
and Ancient Man Team at Jackson Hole Bible College, Simon Turpin,
Dr. Elizabeth Mitchell, Dr. Joseph Paturi, Dr. Thane Ury,
Michiko Mizumuri, Tim McCabe, Joe Owen, Mark Vowels,
Dr. James Johnson, Dr. Royce Short, Pastor Tom Chesko,
Marcia Montenegro, Steve Fazekas, Dr. Mary Kraus, Dr. Ron Rhodes,
Dan Zordel, and Shonda Snelbaker.

Contents

Introduction

Bodie Hodge

There are only two religions in the world. We reaffirm this in our second volume of *World Religions and Cults* as we continue to look at religious philosophies based on man's ideas and moralistic systems.

The two religions are God's and man's. God has only revealed one religion and it is the true religion because God is the truth and knows all things. So to have a proper understanding of truth and the one true religion would be to look at religion from the perspective of God (by looking at the 66 books of the Bible).

If a religion doesn't come from God, then it comes from man. This can occur in many ways; a group or individuals (e.g., ancient sages over time), a leading religious person (e.g., Confucius, Buddha), a king or ruler, or even through Satan and demons. But in any case, development of a religion requires the involvement of man. Sometimes the religion morphs into something different by later adherents, taking variant forms, or splintering into various sects.

All man-made religions are deviations from God's Word. They have used man's ideas to supersede God's Word. In other words and usually subtly, man is really seen as the supreme god sitting in authority over the true God. These religions of man are dubbed "humanistic" since they go back to the mind of man or a *human*. As Christians, we should not fear them.

> And do not fear those who kill the body but cannot kill the soul. But rather fear Him who is able to destroy both soul and body in hell (Matthew 10:28).[1]

There are a lot of variations of man's religion that can be broken in hosts of smaller religions. We have divided them by types similar to the way Christian philosopher and pastor Dr. Greg Bahnsen has done.

The religious divisions we are using for the book are:

- Counterfeits of Christianity — religions that look or act much like Christianity but deviate from the truth in some way, like Mormonism, Islam, Satanism, etc.

- Moralistic Religions — religions that teach a moral code that have no god, like Buddhism or Confucianism, or if they do have "gods" they are only slightly above humanity, like some forms of paganism and mythologies

- Mystical Religions — Eastern thought like Hinduism, Taoism, Sikhism, or New Age

- Materialistic/Atheistic Religions — secular humanism, atheism, agnosticism, hedonism, Epicureanism, etc.

Moralistic and Mysticism Religions

Volume 2 of *World Religions and Cults* focuses on moralistic and mysticism religions. This volume includes pagan religions like Greek mythology, witchcraft, and Druidism. Each is making a comeback in our Western world as people search for meaning in the world.

Some religions could have been included like Baal (Belus/Nimrod) worship, which was common in the days of the Old Testament. Baal worship was a blight that Israel often suffered when they rejected God's Word.

But this volume includes chapters of several other pagan systems that may be more relevant than Baal worship, like Egyptian mythology, Roman mythology, and Germanic/Norse mythology. These are having more of a comeback than Baal worship, though they have similar pagan styles. If you can refute one, then you can often refute others since they are based on the same false foundation.

---

1. All Scripture in this chapter is from the New King James Version (NKJV) of the Bible.

Other moralistic religions are Buddhism and Confucianism. These are probably the largest forms of organized moralistic religions. However, there are a lot of moralistic religions and many of these are unaffiliated.

One moralistic religion that could have been placed in this volume is secular humanism. It has a famous moral code (the various Humanist Manifestos) but no god. Since many secular humanists identify themselves as atheistic or agnostic, we opted to put it in the materialistic/atheistic section for volume 3.

As mentioned in the previous volume, some religions could rightly be lumped into more than one category. The chapter on Unitarianism that appears in this volume could have fit into volume 1 (Counterfeits of Christianity). There are some forms of Unitarianism (Oneness Pentecostalism, for example) that make it a counterfeit of Christianity. But the Unitarian churches have departed to the extent that they have become a moralistic religion.

Mystical religions include religious thought that often migrate from the East — Hinduism, New Age, Jainism, Taoism, Sikhism, and the like. They tend to deviate from reason, focusing on mystical experiences to understand the truth. These tend to be religions that have much similarity but they are packaged in different ways or have branched off from a common source.

Be sure to read the overview of moralistic and mystical religions at the beginning of each section to gain a better understanding of the types of religions they encompass. The overviews also show how their truth claims are refuted. But keep in mind the big picture as you read this volume: there are only two religions — the right one and the wrong one (that is manifest in many ways). In all of these, they are dependent upon a man or group of people who founded them, maintained them, and modified them. They are ultimately all humanistic religions — the religion of man.

Refutation Style

Refutations of these religions could be done in several ways. Any one refutation is sufficient to disprove a false worldview. Paul writes:

> All Scripture is given by inspiration of God, and is profitable
> for doctrine, for reproof, for correction, for instruction in right-
> eousness: that the man of God may be complete, thoroughly
> equipped for every good work. I charge you therefore before
> God and the Lord Jesus Christ, who will judge the living and

the dead at His appearing and His kingdom: Preach the word! Be ready in season and out of season. Convince, rebuke, exhort, with all longsuffering and teaching. For the time will come when they will not endure sound doctrine, but according to their own desires, because they have itching ears, they will heap up for themselves teachers; and they will turn their ears away from the truth, and be turned aside to fables (2 Timothy 3:16–4:4).

All refutations of false worldviews must be predicated on the Word of God. It is God who does the refuting.

Arbitrariness

The authors have tried to show where each religion is arbitrary, which is not a good thing in debate or philosophical argument. Arbitrariness includes things like opinions or ideas based on the experience of one individual. If someone is of the opinion that the Constitution of the United States is actually an ice cream cone in the sky, then should that position be taken as truth? No. It is just an opinion.

Other forms of arbitrariness are conjecture, relativism, or unargued bias. Though I don't want to get too technical here, these are all forms of arbitrariness. A worldview or religion that is based on arbitrary ideas has no foundation or ultimate source of authority — it can't be shown to be superior to any other system. Arbitrariness is a fatal flaw in any worldview. Only biblical Christianity offers a non-arbitrary worldview with God as its ultimate source.

Inconsistency

If something is inconsistent, then it is a problem for a worldview. This is where logical fallacies come into play when refuting worldviews. If an argument has fallacies (formal or informal fallacies), then it is a bad argument.

Sometimes people are inconsistent by acting in a way that is contrary to what they say they believe. This is called a behavioral inconsistency. For example, if someone says they view all things in the universe as one but then they don't want a thief to steal their car, they are acting in an inconsistent way! After all, they and the thief would ultimately be the same since they are one with the universe, so why oppose the theft if you are just giving something to yourself?

Reduced to Absurdity

Another form of inconsistency could almost be placed in its own section. It is when you show where an argument leads if it were held in a consistent manner and applied to all aspects of reality. If the basic argument used in a worldview leads to absurdity, then it is inconsistent. Let's take the Taoists for example, who hold that all of the universe is one. They argue that Taoism is correct and Christianity is false. But within their own beliefs, all of reality is one, so Taoism and Christianity are one and the same, which is absurd.

Preconditions

Many religions do not realize that their worldview cannot account for the most fundamental aspects of reality. For example, people in many religions do not know why they wear clothes. Christians wear clothes because of the events of the Garden of Eden and the entrance of sin into God's perfect creation. Clothing covers the shame of nakedness introduced when Adam sinned, having his shame covered by the animals sacrificed to cover his sin (Genesis 3:21).

Many religions fail at explaining a host of these basic aspects of reality. A way to test a religion is to ask, within their professed story (worldview), how do we know that logic, truth, knowledge, or love exist? In the Hindu perception, all of reality is masked with illusion (maya). If this is true, all knowledge is illusion. So how can one even know that knowledge exists in the Hindu worldview?

In the materialistic worldview of many atheists, they claim all things are material (some expression of matter/energy). But the laws of logic have no mass or energy — they are immaterial — so logic is impossible to account for in their worldview even though they must use it to argue for their beliefs.

The Bible, with God as its ultimate author, accounts for all of these foundations of reality and gives a basis for such preconditions. Other worldviews fall short of these preconditions. They often *borrow* from God's Word but don't realize it. These refutations will be used from time to time throughout this volume to help you understand how to expose the false foundations.

Understanding the falsehoods can help you point people to the truth of the Bible and the hope that you have in Christ as Creator and Savior. The ultimate goal is not to simply dismantle someone's worldview, but to call them to build on the solid foundation of the triune God of the Bible.

Chapter 1

Eastern Mysticism Religions: The Overview

Bodie Hodge and Roger Patterson

Imagine seeing a person who has no clothes lying along the road, having been beaten, robbed of everything, and left for dead. Christians might recall the parable of the Good Samaritan (Luke 10:30–37) and honor God and their fellow man by helping the helpless. However, many people in mystical religions like Taoism or Hinduism may simply respond by "letting them be." Why?

In many forms of mystical thought, the person is getting what they deserve due to "karma" from a previous life. So it is not acceptable for someone to get involved and disrupt the karmic cycle by interfering with the consequences the person is experiencing. If the destitute person dies, they will be reincarnated for a type of "do over." By this reasoning, death isn't a big deal in the mind of the mystic. This is also the thinking reflected in those who would refuse to associate with or give aid to the "untouchable" caste within Eastern societies — bringing bad karma upon themselves for interfering.

Besides that, in the grand scheme of these mystical religions lies a concept that teaches nothing is real but is actually an *illusion*. It is called *maya* in Hinduism but has similar counterparts in other mystical religions. If we take this thinking to its natural conclusion, there really was no person who was injured, and you don't exist either, since all is an illusion and not the ultimate reality. This adds another level of confusion about the true nature of reality to Eastern mysticism.

Mystical Religions: Beliefs and Types

When people hear of Eastern religions they typically think of yoga, enlightenment, karma, oneness of being, reincarnation, and mystical contemplation and meditation. They may also think of the many gods in these religions. There are quite a few forms of Eastern mysticism, though Hinduism is surely the largest and most commonly seen in Western cultures.

There are also variants like Hare Krishna, which can be considered a "denomination" of Hinduism. In Hinduism, like some others, the gods are really just manifestations of one impersonal, universal force, Brahman (this is why Hinduism is often called Brahmanism in older literature).

Other forms of mysticism include Taoism (also known as Daoism) where their ultimate impersonal god is termed "Ultimate Reality." Another popular mysticism religion is the New Age movement. New Age is now progressing across the Western world much the way secular humanism (think atheism, agnosticism, evolutionism) has spread across Europe and North America.

Even Jainism is based in Eastern thought, having elements of Buddhism while retaining similarities with Hinduism. Any notion of a supreme god in these religions is *impersonal*.

There are similarities and differences among each of these variant mystical religions (as you can read in the chapters following). Mystical religions, unlike moralistic religions that will be discussed later in the book, go beyond human experience and rationality. So what does that mean? It means that they defy human experience and defy logic as fundamental aspects of reality.

Defying logic and experience might seem strange, but it is the norm in this way of thought. But this is apparent when we think of the notion of maya — that everything we experience is an illusion and not the ultimate reality. Even logic is an illusion, as are your experiences, in religions like Hinduism, Taoism, and Hare Krishna.

They teach that the problem with all of us is that we are blinded by this illusion to think there are distinctions, when in fact there is no distinction between anything. The logical person will obviously point out that there are distinctions based on their experiences (i.e., there is a distinction between a cat and a dog).

But the mystical mind would deny this. They would argue that both cat and dog are an illusion and we mistakenly think (based on our experiences) that there is a distinction. The mystic would say these are all just manifestations of the oneness that exists as the true reality (e.g., these are all emanations of Brahman in Hinduism).

This is why yoga and mystical meditation are required to move beyond experience and dive into the ideas that defy reason and experience. Thus, they argue that when you have entered deep enough into the mystical understanding that you can achieve the final state of bliss. The goal of life is to achieve nothingness, moksha, or nirvana[1] as you are spliced back into the oneness of being — "like a drop of water reentering the ocean of being."

If you have not achieved this perfect level at your death, then you are doomed to keep repeating life at a higher reincarnate level (come back as a human again) or lower level (e.g., come back as an animal or plant). This is done through stages of reincarnations, based on your good or bad karma, until you finally reach this state.

So the goal in many mystical religions is to stop drawing distinctions so that you can move up the reincarnation chain to finally get to nothingness. There are variations in the religions mentioned, but in the generalized sense, this is the basic goal of all mystical religions.

Arbitrariness

When we consider the validity of a religious worldview, the first question we need to ask is, "On whose authority do mystics know about their religion and its beliefs?" Did their impersonal god reveal the truth to mankind? No. The very notion of an impersonal god communicating to man is a logical contradiction — communication is an interpersonal act. They *do* have religious books, like the Vedas, Upanishads, Bhagavad Gita, etc. But these are not revelations from God to man as the Bible is.[2]

Instead, these religious books are merely the ideas or wisdom of ancients on the subject. Essentially, they are just the writings of man to recount old

---

1. These are just different names for essentially the same thing, depending on which Eastern religion is being discussed.
2. The Bible is not just written by men but *inspired by God* while using human authors to write the inspired text of Scripture.

philosophies. They often disagree with each other, but that is the flavor of writings of mere men.

These ideas all originate in the mind of man or are expressed through man (if they have a supernatural demonic origin). Thus, they are humanistic in their outlook.[3] The ideas of man are arbitrary next to the absolute standard of the Word of God, the Bible. The Bible comes with the authority of the *absolute authority*, God. The ideas promoted in the Vedas or Upanishads are just opinions of man. These opinions are arbitrary, having no ultimate source of authority.

In bold terms, "*so what*" if these ancients believed this mystical philosophy. Just because they believed it doesn't make it true any more than someone believing George Washington (the first president of the United States) was a green mushroom!

If one argues that these sages of old were exceptionally wise, then by what standard are they wise? The modern mystics? That again would be an arbitrary opinion. If someone came to me and said, "George Washington was a green mushroom," I would merely point out that their assertion is merely arbitrary and has no grounding in reality.

If they retort, "I heard this from someone who was exceptionally wise," does that really hold water? No. It is still arbitrary and thus a false premise upon which to base any argumentation.

If we consider any of the beliefs within these mystical systems, each is based on the opinion or idea of a mere man. For example, how does a Hindu or Taoist *know* he will be reincarnated? He doesn't. It is an arbitrary assumption that forms a belief.

Inconsistencies

There are also many inconsistencies with mysticism religions that allow us to see their false character. Consider just a few. Let's start with knowledge (in technical terms, this is "epistemology"). If all we experience is illusion, then knowledge is too. One can't consistently know anything in this religious system. To claim to know something based on experience would be to affirm that it is not illusory — a self-refuting position.

But it is just gets worse from here. No believer in Eastern mysticism can know anything about their religion if their religion is what it claims to be.

---

3. This reveals that there are indeed only two religions — God's and man's. All forms of mysticism are from the mind of man or part of the variations of man's religion.

Here is why. Their supreme god is *impersonal*. Since their god is impersonal, then it is impossible for that god to communicate to man, who is *personal*. This alleged supreme god couldn't use language, which is based on personal human experience. There can be no revelation *of any sort* to mankind to know anything about this alleged god. It would be inconsistent for any follower of Eastern mysticism to claim to know anything about their professed religion.

The mystic might argue that Brahman is impersonal but has an aspect where he[4] can be able to manifest as personal at certain times or as certain manifestations (as Brahma, Vishnu, or Shiva). But that would be a logical contradiction, as he would be both personal (relating to these other gods who have emanated from him) and impersonal at the same time and same instance as there is ultimately no distinction between Brahman and the personal manifestations. Besides, an impersonal Brahman cannot decide to manifest himself as personal, as decision making is personal in the first place.

The mystic might say that they can learn about their supreme god (Brahman, Ultimate Reality, etc.) based on utilizing the world in which we live. That also proves nothing since it is all supposed to be an illusion.

Another inconsistency is derived on their doctrine of *all being one* — that there is no distinction. Recall that our problem in mystical religions is that we draw distinctions. This is why we remain in the world of maya or illusion instead of entering into a nirvana, Moksha, or blissful state.

But here is the problem: in the Eastern mystical reality, there would be no distinction between the illusory and blissful states. So making the statement that they are distinct is self-refuting. Let's put it this way: if one argues that there is no distinction and that our problem is that we draw distinction, and they argue this by drawing distinctions, then that is illogical.

Just tell the mystical adherents that you are already in the state of bliss — what are they going to do — draw a distinction to say you aren't? Similarly, in Buddhism, and its variations, the goal is to rid one's self of all desires. So, you must desire to rid yourself of all desires to be released from being — a logical contradiction.

When one dies, who is the judge that determines if they had enough good or bad karma to know where and in what condition or form they will be reincarnated? Judging is a personal attribute, so their impersonal god cannot be the judge.

---

4. Brahman is viewed as a genderless force, but we will use a masculine pronoun here for ease of communication.

Another inconsistency is exhibited in the mystical believer's personal life. If *all is one* and *there is no distinction*, do they live in a manner consistent with that claim? No. If a Hindu says that *all is one* and *there is no distinction*, a good thing to ask for is . . . their wallet.

Would they give their money to you? No. But you could respond by staying, "I am you," since "all is one." You could go on and point out that the money is actually yours since the two of you are actually one as part of the principle of Brahman. If the mystic argues, just point out that they should stop drawing the distinction between you and them.

You need to understand that the mystical mind says one thing and lives their life another way. The believer of Hinduism or New Age or Taoism goes home and kisses their spouse as though they were real and distinct from other people's spouses. They handle their money as though it were real and distinct from someone else's money. Their lives are a walking inconsistency.

If a mystic resists the idea of converting to Christianity, ask them to consider this: if all is one and there is no distinction, then the mystic might as well become a Christian, since there is no distinction.

But remember, we pointed out that the Eastern mystical religions are not rational, i.e., they defy logic. As you talk with them, the mystic may respond by saying they are not bound to the laws of logic, so inconsistencies are acceptable in their religion since *all is one* — thus, logic and non-logic are one and the same.

If a mystic like a Hindu, New Ager, or Taoist says such a thing, just contradict them and point out that "they do believe in logic." What can they do? Would they appeal to logic (e.g., law of non-contradiction) to say that you contradicted what they just said (that they don't believe in logic)? That is inconsistent.

Borrowing from God's Word

The mystical mind cannot account for knowledge, logic, or even a single aspect of their professed religion because it is marred with inconsistences and arbitrariness. Even the lives of many mystics are plagued with inconsistencies within their professed religion.

Yet many held captive by these religions *do* believe in logic and that knowledge exists. They believe their wives or husbands are real and have distinction from any random person. They love their kids. But why?

The answer is because they are borrowing from a biblical worldview and don't realize it. Many of these doctrines were passed down from creation, through the Flood and Tower of Babel and are still retained today — even couched in many religions around the globe.

Man is made in the image of a personal God; this is why we are personal. We are made in the image of a logical God who knows all things. Thus, we are in a position to be logical and to know things. The Bible accounts for why things exist and have distinction — God created them.

The Hindu or Taoist understands that shame and love and dignity and honor exist. Yet these things should not exist, as they are merely illusions of experience in their worldview. But they are real concrete entities in the biblical worldview.

Consider memory. If all is illusion, then how can an Eastern mystic trust their memories? According to their worldview, they cannot. They cannot know that morality is a reality either.

Eastern religions cannot account for absolute morality, as there is no absolute lawgiver who communicated to mankind (thus, a personal God) that morality exists. For all the Hindu, Taoist, etc. knows, the correct path may have nothing to do with being *good enough or knowing enough,* as that can be an illusion, and being *bad and not knowing* may be how you move up a caste. In many respects, the adherents hold to some levels of morality. But why? It is because the law of God is written on their hearts. It is from the Christian viewpoint that morality makes sense.

When it comes down to it, the mystical worldviews cannot hold up to a Christian worldview that makes sense of knowledge, logic, truth, morality, memory, dignity, love, honor, and so forth. If the mystic wants to be logical and rational, they must give up mystical religions and move to the biblical position.

Conclusion

The mystical religions recognize there is a problem in the world and have devised all manner of works to seek to bring balance and harmony. We heartily agree. There *is* a problem in the world, but it doesn't have anything to do with drawing distinctions. It has to do with sin. When the mutual ancestors of us all, Adam and Eve, sinned in Genesis 3, the perfect world God had created became corrupt, and death and suffering came into the perfect creation as a result.

But Jesus Christ, who is the personal God (John 20:27–29), stepped into history to become a man (John 1:1–14; Philippians 2:8) to rescue us from sin and death where an eternal death, or second death, awaits (death is the punishment for our sin — Romans 6:23). Christ took the punishment we deserve on the Cross and died the death we deserved for sin (Colossians 2:13–14) and rose from the dead to demonstrate He had overcome death (Acts 10:40). God offers the free gift of salvation through the blood of Jesus Christ alone to attain heaven (Romans 5:15–18) where we will consciously be with God and His goodness and blessing for all eternity (1 Corinthians 2:9).

It is because we have been saved that we take the message of salvation to others. We want to help rescue unbelievers (those who don't believe in Jesus [yet]), even those trapped in mystical thought, in the same way that Christ rescued us.

We must remember that it was the power of the Holy Spirit (1 Corinthians 12:3) and the proclamation of the gospel that brought us (Romans 10:13–17), as Christians, from the kingdom of darkness and conveyed us into the Kingdom of Christ (Colossians 1:13). More than just showing those blinded by mystical ideas where their own thinking is flawed (2 Corinthians 10:4–5), we must point them to the only man who has ever perfectly understood all of life's mysteries — Jesus Christ.

So when Christians pass by those enslaved to mysticism, we should view them as a person who has no clothes lying along the road and has been robbed of everything and left for dead. They are in need of salvation through Jesus Christ and His death, burial, and Resurrection. The unbelievers need to repent (Acts 17:30) and receive Christ (John 1:12). This is why the Christian stops to help, applying the salve of the gospel to their wounds and calling on the Great Physician to bring them spiritual healing.

Chapter 2

The New Age Movement
(Pantheism and Monism)

Dr. Ron Rhodes

Cindy was exposed to the New Age movement through a human potential seminar sponsored by the company she worked for. The teacher of the seminar informed each attendee: "You are your own god," and "You can create your own reality." By embracing these ideas, he claimed, each employee could become much more successful at the workplace, ultimately leading to increased profits for the company.

Cindy was confused. If she was a god, wouldn't she already know it? Why does a god have to attend a seminar to *discover* that he or she is a god? She later found out that this seminar was part of the New Age movement. It didn't sit right with her. She decided to be very cautious in evaluating the New Age ideas she learned at the seminar.

The New Age movement first emerged in the West in the 1970s and then mushroomed in popularity in the 1980s. Even today the movement continues to influence people on the religious landscape around the world. Many no longer use the term "New Age" — they prefer the term "new spirituality," or something similar — but it is all part of the movement that emerged in the 1970s.

A major problem one encounters in discussing the New Age movement is defining it. Some have attempted to categorize it as a single unified cult.[1] It is probably wiser, however, to define it as a loosely structured network of individuals and organizations who share a common vision of a new age of enlightenment and harmony. Those who share this vision typically subscribe to a common set of core religious and philosophical beliefs — that is, they hold to a particular worldview. This worldview centers on *monism* (all is one), *pantheism* (all is God), and *mysticism* (the experience of oneness with the divine).

Despite these core beliefs, the collective body of New Agers around the world is organizationally diffuse. For this reason, we cannot properly categorize it as a unified cult. Cults are typically exclusivistic groups made up of individuals who subscribe to a uniform set of beliefs and operate according to a rigidly defined organizational structure. Movements, on the other hand, have an element of unity (core beliefs) but are also multifaceted — involving a variety of individuals and groups with different emphases. This is the case with the New Age movement. (More on this shortly.)

Factors which Gave Rise to the New Age Movement

There are a number of factors that contributed to the emergence of the New Age movement in the 1970s. First and foremost is 19th-century transcendentalism, a school of thought that was heavily dependent on Eastern scriptures, such as the Hindu Vedas. Transcendentalism emphasized intuition as a means of ascertaining truth. It also held that all religions contain divine truth, and affirmed that the goal of religion is to obtain conscious union with the divine. Such ideas helped set the stage for the eventual emergence of the New Age movement.

From the Vedas
(Shutterstock)

We can also point to the revival of occultism that took place in the late 19th century. This revival took form in the emergence of such groups as the Theosophical Society (1875), the Anthroposophical Society (1912), the Arcane School (1923), and the I AM movement (1930s). We need not investigate the unique teachings and features of each group. It is sufficient to recognize that spiritistic phenomena — that is,

---

1. An example is Walter Martin's book, *The New Age Cult* (Bloomington, MN: Bethany House, 1989).

contact with entities from the beyond, such as "ascended masters"[2] — was common in such groups. This helped set the stage for the emergence of modern New Age psychics and channelers.

Also contributing to the emergence of the New Age movement was a lesser movement called neo-gnosticism. As a backdrop, Gnosticism — from the Greek *gnosis*, "knowledge" — was a heresy that emerged in the second century A.D., purporting to offer knowledge of otherwise hidden "truth" as the indispensable key to human salvation.[3] Though gnosticism with its secret knowledge is long gone, a revival of certain gnostic ideas (called neo-gnosticism) occurred in the late 19th and early-to-mid-20th centuries. These ideas include, (1) Man has the spark of the divine within, (2) Man is ignorant of his divinity, and (3) Jesus came as a way-shower to bring enlightenment to humankind. These ideas eventually became prominent in the New Age movement.

We might also point to the counterculture of the 1960s. Indeed, in the 1960s many people reacted against the West's traditional way of doing things. During the turbulent sixties, people were open to new ideas — religious and otherwise. The counterculture became saturated with fringe ideas. Common were antimaterialism, utopianism, communalism, interest in the occult, and a rejection of traditional morality. All this helped to lay the groundwork for the emergence of the New Age movement.

Typical 1960s hippie look
(Shutterstock)

Also during the 1960s, the West experienced an Eastern tidal wave. The most pervasive interest was in transcendental meditation, reincarnation, chanting, visualization, and the idea that all of reality was divine and sacred. These ideas would soon become pervasive in the New Age movement.

Finally, we must recognize the failure of secular humanism. Cultural observers in the sixties and seventies recognized that human reason had not

---

2. "Ascended Masters" are believed to be formerly historical persons who have finished their earthly evolutions via reincarnation. Now, even as these Ascended Masters continue in their own evolution toward the godhead, they voluntarily help lesser-evolved humans on earth to reach the masters' present level. These masters allegedly give revelations to spiritually attuned human beings on earth.

3. Justo L. Gonzalez, *A History of Christian Thought*, Vol. 1 (Nashville, TN: Abingdon, 1970), p. 129.

been able to solve all of humankind's problems, as had been imagined by its proponents beginning in the Enlightenment. Moreover, with its relentless overemphasis on secularized reason, one's sense of the divine, the sacred, and the transcendent faded. In the New Age movement, people therefore sought a return to the divine and the sacred in all things. This is an example of the cultural "pendulum effect" — that is, there was a swing from the secular to the sacred, a swing from the merely rational to the transcendent and the mystical.

These six factors, among others, collectively provided a rich and fertile soil for the emergence and worldwide growth of the New Age movement. The so-called Age of Aquarius blossomed and flourished.

Maharishi Mahesh Yogi, developer of the Transcendental Meditation technique
(Jdontfight, Creativecommons)

Common Characteristics of the New Age Movement

We've already noted that core beliefs of New Agers include *monism* (all is one), *pantheism* (all is God), and *mysticism* (the experience of oneness with the divine). Along with these primary core beliefs are some secondary characteristics that are true of most New Agers. For example, most New Agers are highly eclectic. By this I mean that New Agers typically draw their religious and philosophical ideas from a variety of religious sources. They consult holy books like the Bible and the Hindu Vedas, but also feel free to consult psychics and channelers, whose "revelations" from spirit guides are considered just as authoritative as those found in holy books. They have no hesitation in consulting astrologers and others who practice the occultic arts of necromancy, palm readings, ball gazing, tarot cards, etc.

Tarot cards
(Shutterstock)

Not surprisingly, New Agers are also syncretistic. By this I mean that New Agers combine and synthesize religious and philosophical ideas from Jesus, the Buddha, Krishna, Zoroaster, alleged "space brothers" aboard UFOs, Ascended

Masters who live on planet Venus, and many others. New Agers believe there is truth in all religions and religious traditions. This willingness to pick and choose what they believe from various sources of enlightenment is a vivid demonstration of the arbitrary and inconsistent nature of the worldview.

Most New Agers are also transformational on two levels. First, New Agers believe that personal transformation takes place when a human being recognizes his or her oneness with all things in the universe. Second, planetary transformation takes place when a critical mass of human beings come into this same awareness. We are allegedly transforming — or *transitioning* — into a New Age with a new consciousness.

Not unexpectedly, New Agers are typically relativistic in their view of truth and ethics. One New Age curriculum that found its way into some school districts in the United States taught students how to discover *their own* values. The idea in this curriculum is that values are not to be imposed from without (such as from Scripture or from parents) but must be *discovered within*. The underlying assumption is that there are no absolute truths or values. New Agers are well known for their view that "you can have your truth and I can have my truth," and that "your truth should never infringe upon my truth." And yet, it is interesting that they are willing to impose (infringe) this alleged absolute truth upon everyone! This is a self-refuting position as it creates an illogical internal inconsistency within the worldview.

We might also observe that most New Agers are open to meditation. I am not referring to meditation on the Bible (e.g., Psalm 119:148). I am referring to an Eastern form of meditation in which one goes into a trance-like state and seeks to attain a sense of oneness with all things. The goal of meditation varies, but the common belief is that it allows one to connect to the divine or the force that permeates the entire universe. Emptying the mind and directing energies

Eastern meditation
(Shutterstock)

within the body allows the balancing of vital energies (present in meridians or chakras) which is used to promote spiritual and physical healing.[4]

4. Ron Rhodes, "Energies of Mind & Body," *SCP Journal,* Volume 21:3 Fall 1997; Ron Rhodes, *Miracles Around Us: How to Recognize God at Work Today,* Chapter 13: " 'Miracles' of New Age 'Energetic Medicine'" (Eugene, OR: Harvest House Publishers, 2000); Marcia Montengero, "The Religion of Life Force Energy," Christian Answers for the New Age, accessed October 30, 2015, http://christiananswersforthenewage.org/Links.html.

The use of crystals, essential oils, body positions (Yoga *asanas*), breathing practices, mantras, and other methods are used to connect to the divine force and release and balance divine energy within the person doing these practices.

Closely connected to meditation is the New Age view of visualization, which basically involves the idea of "mind over matter." One New Ager said, "Your thoughts are always creating your reality — it's up to you to take charge of your thoughts and consciously create a reality that is fulfilling."[5] Another said: "We literally create our reality through the beliefs we hold, so by changing those beliefs, we can change reality."[6] Today, this idea of manipulating reality through focus practices is called "mindfulness" and is commonly taught in arenas from public schools and children's programming to self-help seminars and corporate trainings.

The New Age View of Key Bible Doctrines

If New Agers are eclectic (open to many religious and philosophical sources) and syncretistic (combining and synthesizing religious and philosophical ideas from many different traditions), then one would naturally expect them to have deviant views on the key doctrines of the Bible. This has indeed turned out to be the case.

View of the Bible

The Bible is a good case in point, for New Agers believe it is merely one of many holy books communicating revelation from God, or the divine. New Agers believe it is incorrect to read the Bible in a straightforward way. Rather, they look for truth by seeking hidden, secret, or inner spiritual meanings of Bible verses, especially in the teachings of Jesus. For example, when Jesus said, "seek first the kingdom of God" (Matthew 6:33), He was allegedly teaching people to seek an awareness of their own inner divinity. Such Scripture twisting is common among New Agers.

Moreover, in place of the biblical Creator-God with whom we can have personal relationships is a pantheistic concept which says that God is all and all is God. In pantheism, all reality is viewed as being infused with divinity. The God of pantheism is an impersonal, amoral "it," and not a personal,

---

5. David Gershon and Gail Straub, *Empowerment: The Art of Creating Your Life as You Want It* (New York: Dell, 1989), p. 21.
6. Jennifer Donovan, "Seth Followers Spoon Up Fun in Their Goal to Enjoy Living," *Dallas Morning News,* July 1, 1986.

moral "He." The distinction between the Creator and the creation is completely obliterated in this view.

Views of Jesus

New Agers also have twisted views of Jesus Christ. Notice I said "views," for New Agers set forth many strange ideas about Jesus. Foundationally, New Agers distinguish between the human Jesus and the divine Christ. New Agers agree that Jesus became the Christ, but they have different interpretations as to how that happened. Some say that a divine cosmic Christ spirit descended upon the human Jesus at His baptism. Others say that Jesus underwent seven degrees of initiation — an occultic ceremony — in Egypt, the seventh degree being "the Christ." Still others claim Jesus traveled to India as a child and learned from Hindu gurus, and this eventually led to his Christhood. Regardless of how He became the Christ, New Agers agree that Jesus was an enlightened way-shower for humankind, demonstrating to humans how they, too, can become the Christ.

View of Man and Salvation

Since New Agers hold to monism (all is one) and pantheism (all is God), it is not surprising that they view human beings as divine. Because humans are divine, they are believed to have unlimited potential. Many Fortune 500 companies have sponsored human potential seminars.

The New Age view that humans are divine has powerful implications for the doctrines of sin and salvation. New Agers claim there is no sin, and hence there is no need for salvation. If human beings have any problem at all, it is allegedly an ignorance regarding their divinity. This being so, humankind's need is enlightenment, not salvation. All we need is "God-realization."

View of End Times

With their twisted views of the Bible, God, Jesus, humanity, sin, and salvation, it is no surprise that New Agers have also completely redefined the end times. New Agers offer different interpretations of the Second Coming. Some believe that prophecies of the Second Coming are fulfilled in the coming of a specific individual named Maitreya, who will allegedly take the primary role of leadership in the New Age. In this view, Maitreya has allegedly been living incognito among human beings since 1977 when his consciousness entered a specially created human-like body of manifestation, the Mayavirupa. In the near future, Maitreya will allegedly manifest himself to all humanity and usher in a new era of peace and happiness.

Other New Agers interpret the Second Coming in terms of the "cosmic Christ" (a divine spirit) falling upon all humanity so that human beings around the world come to recognize their divinity. This Second Coming is thus viewed as a "mass coming" involving not just one "Christ," but *all* humans coming to recognize their "Christhood."

Statistics of the New Age Movement

It is difficult to assess how many New Agers there are in the United States and around the world. After all, they are not a monolithic group that keeps membership roles like the Mormons and Jehovah's Witnesses. Moreover, as noted previously, not all who hold a New Age worldview actually call themselves New Agers today.

During the early nineties, it was estimated that around 12 million Americans were active participants in the movement, with another 30 million avidly interested in one or more different aspects of the movement. At present, the New Age tome titled *A Course in Miracles* has sold well over 1,000,000 copies and has spawned over 1,000 study groups in the United States alone. Such statistics point to a broad penetration of New Age ideas in Western culture. This broad penetration has been reflected in Hollywood movies (for example, *Ghost* and *The Sixth Sense*) and TV shows (for example, *Medium* and *Ghost Whisperer*).

Another way to gauge New Age influence is to consider statistics related to specific paranormal beliefs.[7] A Gallup poll reveals that 32 percent of Americans believe in some sort of paranormal activity. This statistic holds true for even graduating college seniors and college professors. Meanwhile, 28 percent of Americans believe we can communicate with the dead.

Among teenagers, some 73 percent have participated in psychic activities. Four out of five have had their horoscopes read by an astrologer. Seven million claim to have personally encountered a spirit entity, such as an angel or a supernatural entity. Two million claim to have psychic powers.

Even the United States government has been interested in the occult and the paranormal. According to government documents that were declassified

---

7. The word "paranormal" generally refers to that which goes beyond the normal — that is, beyond the five senses (sight, taste, touch, hearing, and smelling). In New Age circles, it often refers to attempts to gain secret or hidden knowledge or information outside the use of the natural senses — for example, by consulting a psychic or an astrologer.

in the 1990s, America — during the years of America's cold war with the Soviet Union — spent a whopping $20 million studying extrasensory perception and other psychic phenomena.

Such facts reveal that the New Age movement has indeed broadly penetrated American culture. For this reason, Christians ought to be equipped to answer the primary claims of New Agers.

Debunking New Age Claims

Someone said that the New Age movement is a target-rich environment when it comes to opportunities for critique. In what follows, I will provide a brief biblical response to some of the primary ideas set forth in the movement.

Relativism is not logically satisfying. One might interpret the statement "all truth is relative" to mean it is an *absolute* truth that all truth is relative. Such a statement is self-defeating. Or, one might understand the statement as saying it is *relative* truth that all truth is relative. But such a statement is ultimately meaningless. In contrast to such nonsense, absolute truth and morals are grounded in the absolutely true and moral God of the Bible (see 1 Kings 17:24; Psalm 25:5, 43:3, 100:5, 119:30; John 1:17, 8:44, 14:17, 17:17; 2 Corinthians 6:7; Ephesians 4:15, 6:14; 2 Timothy 2:15; 1 John 3:19; 3 John 4, 8).

All religions do not teach the same truths. One cannot rationally claim that the various world religions are teaching the same basic truths. This becomes evident by examining key doctrines in each religion. The doctrine of God is a good example. The Christian Bible reveals that there is one personal God who is triune in nature (Matthew 28:19; Mark 12:29; Romans 8:15). The Muslim Quran teaches there is only one God, but God cannot have a son, and there is no Trinity. The writings of Confucius affirm polytheism (there are many gods). Krishna taught a combination of polytheism and pantheism (all is god). Zoroaster set forth religious dualism (there is both a good god and a bad god). Buddha taught that the concept of God was essentially irrelevant. Clearly, the world's major religions hold completely contradictory views regarding the nature of God. The same is true in their view of Jesus and their view of salvation. This means that the New Age claim that all the religions teach the same basic truths is wishful thinking.

Pantheism — the view that "all is God" — is fraught with problems. In pantheism, all distinctions between the creation (which is finite) and the Creator (who is infinite) are destroyed. Biblically, God is eternally distinct from what He created (Hebrews 11:3; see also Genesis 1:1; Psalm 33:8–9). Moreover, pantheism contradicts common sense. If everything in the universe is truly God, then there is no difference between myself and anything else (or anyone else) in the world. Such an idea is nonsensical.

The truth is, the pantheistic God is an impersonal force, not a personal being with whom personal relationships can be established (see Mark 14:36; Galatians 4:6). The God of the Bible is infinitely more appealing and is the only source of the existence of everything in the universe (Colossians 1:15–18; Hebrews 1:3).

There are many problems with reincarnation. The concept of reincarnation finds its roots in Eastern religions and has no basis in any real experience. Even the most sophisticated views of ongoing cycles of birth and death are filled with logical inconsistencies and practical evils.

For example:

- Reincarnation is unfair, for one can be punished (via karma[8]) for things one cannot remember having done in previous lives.

- Reincarnation is ineffective. While it is claimed that karma progressively rids humanity of its selfish desires, the truth is that there has not been any improvement in human nature after millennia of reincarnations.

- Reincarnation yields social pacifism, for it urges that one should not interfere with someone else's bad karma (or bad circumstances). Thus, helping the poor and oppressed could yield bad karma for you since the lower classes are receiving what they have earned.

- Reincarnation is ultimately fatalistic, for the law of karma guarantees that one will inexorably reap in the next life what one has sown in the present life. There is no room for forgiveness and grace!

---

8. If one engages in good actions throughout one's life, one will allegedly build up good karma, which means one will be reincarnated in a desirable state in the next life. If, however, one engages in bad actions throughout one's life, one will allegedly build up bad karma, which means one will be reincarnated in a less desirable state in the next life. One might say this is a cosmic law of cause and effect.

- Reincarnation seems inconsistent with the New Age worldview, for if all is one and all is God, how can there be *individual souls* that reincarnate?

- Reincarnation is unbiblical, for every human lives once, dies once, and then faces the judgment (Hebrews 9:27).

Occultism is dangerous. Deuteronomy 18:9–12 warns that all forms of occultism are detestable to God. Exodus 22:18 even instructs that sorceresses were to be put to death — a penalty in Old Testament times that demonstrates how serious the sin of divination was. Leviticus 19:26 commands, "You shall not . . . practice divination or soothsaying." In Acts 19:19 we read that many who converted to Christ in Ephesus rightly destroyed all their paraphernalia formerly used for occultism and divination.

The New Age openness to channeling — consulting psychics in order to contact the dead, or to contact a guardian angel, or to contact "space brothers" aboard UFOs — is an especially heinous sin against God. Deuteronomy 18:10–11 is clear: "There shall not be found among you anyone who . . . [is] a medium, or a spiritist, or one who calls up the dead." Leviticus 19:31 instructs, "Give no regard to mediums and familiar spirits; do not seek after them, to be defiled by them: I am the LORD your God." In 1 Samuel 28:3 we read that "Saul had put the mediums and the spiritists out of the land." Later, we read that "Saul died for his unfaithfulness which he had committed against the Lord, because he did not keep the word of the Lord, and also because he consulted a medium for guidance" (1 Chronicles 10:13; see also Leviticus 20:27).

New Age meditation can be injurious. New Age (Eastern) meditation's stated goal of transforming one's state of mind into a monistic ("all is one"), if not an outright pantheistic ("all is God"), outlook lies in direct contradiction to the biblical view of the eternal distinction between God the Creator and His creatures (Isaiah 44:6–8; Hebrews 2:6–8). Moreover, Christian experts in occultism note that altered states of consciousness (which occurs in New Age meditation) can open one up to spiritual affliction and deception by the powers of darkness. Additionally, some New Agers may use drugs like LSD to enter these altered states, a practice Christians must avoid. Contrary to such Eastern meditation, Christians ought to practice biblical meditation. This involves objective contemplation and deep reflection on God's Word (Joshua 1:8) as well as God's person and faithfulness (Psalm 119, see also 19:14, 48:9, 77:12, 104:34, 143:5).

The New Age method of interpreting the Bible is faulty. The New Age method of seeking hidden, secret, or inner spiritual meanings of Bible verses violates the scriptural injunction to rightly handle the Word of God and not distort its meaning (2 Peter 3:16; 2 Corinthians 4:2). Among New Agers, the basic authority in interpretation ceases to be Scripture, but rather the mind of the interpreter (i.e., man is seen as the supreme authority over God and His Word). They rely on their own inner illumination as opposed to reliance upon the Holy Spirit (see 1 Corinthians 2:9–11; John 16:12–15). More often than not, New Agers superimpose mystical meanings on Bible verses instead of objectively seeking the biblical author's intended meaning.

Contrary to this New Age subjective approach to Scripture, it is better to interpret each verse in the Bible in its proper biblical context. Every word is part of a verse; every verse is part of a paragraph; every paragraph is part of a book; and every book is part of the whole of Scripture. It is wise to pay attention to both the immediate and broader contexts of Scripture. Moreover, one ought to consult history to get a better grasp on the historical milieu in which the biblical book was written. This objective approach will keep one on track in properly interpreting Scripture.

Jesus didn't train in the East as a child. Many New Agers suggest that the man Jesus studied under gurus in India as a child, returning to Israel as a master to perform miracles and spread the teachings He learned. There are many factors that argue against such an idea. First, Scripture explicitly states that Jesus was raised in Nazareth (Luke 4:16). As He grew up, He studied the Old Testament, as did other Jewish boys His age (see Luke 2:52).

Once an adult, those in His community seemed quite familiar with Him as a long-standing carpenter (Mark 6:3) and as a carpenter's son (Matthew 13:55). Had Jesus just returned from India, this likely would not have been the case (see Luke 4:22).

Some in His community were offended that Jesus was drawing such attention. They treated Him with a contempt born of familiarity (see

Matthew 13:54–57). Again, had Jesus just returned from India, this likely would not have been the case.

Consider also the Jewish leaders. They accused Jesus of many offenses throughout His three-year ministry, but never once did they accuse Him of teaching or practicing anything learned in the East. If they *could* have, they *would* have. This would have been excellent grounds for dismissing Jesus as the promised Jewish Messiah. The truth is, though, that Jesus didn't train in the East.

Jesus was the Christ; He didn't become the Christ. Jesus did not become the Christ as an adult, but rather was the one and only Christ (Messiah) from the very beginning. The angel said to the shepherds in the field, "There is born to you this day in the city of David a Savior, who is Christ the Lord" (Luke 2:11). Jesus' beloved disciple John wrote, "Who is a liar but he who denies that Jesus is the Christ? He is antichrist who denies the Father and the Son" (1 John 2:22).

It is noteworthy that the 100-plus prophecies of the coming Messiah in the Old Testament were fulfilled in a single person — Jesus Christ (for example, Isaiah 7:14, 53:3–5; Micah 5:2; Zechariah 12:10). Of course, the New Testament counterpart for "Messiah" is "Christ" (see John 1:41). Jesus was *uniquely* the Christ.

We might also observe that when Jesus was recognized as the Christ, He never said, "You too have the Christ within." Instead He warned that others would come falsely claiming to be the Christ (Matthew 24:5). Today, we see that fulfilled in the writings of teachers like Deepak Chopra, Eckhart Tolle, Edgar Cayce, and others who teach that each person can attain to Christ consciousness as promoted by spiritualists such as Oprah Winfrey and other popular media outlets.

Human beings are not divine. Contrary to the New Age claim that human beings are God, Scripture portrays them as creatures who are responsible to their Creator (Genesis 1–2; Psalm 100:3). Because human beings are creatures, they are intrinsically weak, helpless, and dependent upon God (you may wish to consult 2 Corinthians 3:5 and John 15:5). The recognition of creaturehood should lead human beings to humility and a worshipful attitude (Psalm 95:6–7). They have confused the fact that we are made in the image of the divine God (Genesis 1:26–27, 9:6) with falsely being equated to the divine God.

One cannot avoid asking: if human beings are God, then why do we have to buy and read New Age books to find out about it? Wouldn't we already know it? The fact that a person comes to realize he is God proves that he *is not* God. For if he truly were God, he would never have passed from a state of ignorance to a state of enlightenment as to his divine nature.

Still further, if it were true that human beings were divine, one would expect them to display qualities similar to those known to be true of God. This seems only logical. However, when one compares the attributes of humankind with those of God (as set forth in Scripture), we find more than ample testimony for the truth of Paul's statement in Romans 3:23 that human beings "fall short of the glory of God." Indeed, while God is all-knowing, all-powerful, and everywhere present (Matthew 11:21; Revelation 19:6; Psalm 139:7–12), man is none of these things (Job 38:4; Hebrews 4:15; John 1:50).

Human beings are fallen in sin and need to be saved. Contrary to the New Age claim that human beings are God and merely need enlightenment about this reality, the biblical truth is that human beings have a grave sin problem that is altogether beyond their means to solve. Human beings are sinners (Isaiah 64:6; Luke 15:10), are lost (Luke 19:10), are capable of great wickedness (Jeremiah 17:9; Mark 7:20–23; Luke 11:42–52), and are in need of repentance before a holy God (Mark 1:15; Luke 15:10). Because of sin, human beings are blind (Matthew 15:14, 23:16–26), enslaved in bondage (John 8:34), and live in darkness (John 3:19–21, 8:12, 12:35–46).

Jesus came into the world to offer a salvation based on grace. The word "grace" literally means "unmerited favor." "Unmerited" means this favor cannot be worked for. Grace refers to the undeserved, unearned favor of God. Romans 5:1–11 tells us that God gives His incredible grace to those who actually deserve the opposite — that is, condemnation. Eternal life cannot be earned. It is a free gift of grace that comes through faith in the Savior, Jesus Christ. As Jesus Himself put it, "Most assuredly, I say to you, he who believes in Me has everlasting life" (John 6:47; see also John 3:15, 5:24, 11:25, 12:46, 20:31).

Jesus is the only way. While the Jesus of the New Age is open to all religions, the Jesus of the Bible is God's exclusive means of salvation. Speaking of Jesus, a bold Peter proclaimed: "There is no other name under heaven given among men by which we must be saved" (Acts 4:12). The Apostle

Paul affirmed, "There is one God and one Mediator between God and men, the Man Christ Jesus" (1 Timothy 2:5). Jesus Himself said, "I am the way, the truth, and the life. No one comes to the Father except through Me" (John 14:6). Jesus also warned His followers about those who would try to set forth a different "Christ" (Matthew 24:4–5). Truly, Jesus is the only way of salvation, and only the Jesus who has revealed Himself in the pages of Scripture.

Jesus will come again at the Second Coming. Contrary to New Agers who claim either that the Second Coming has already taken place in the person of Maitreya, or through the cosmic Christ falling upon all humanity, Scripture reveals that the very same Jesus who ascended into heaven will come again at the Second Coming. Acts 1:11 tells us that angels appeared to Christ's disciples after He ascended into heaven and said to them: "Men of Galilee, why do you stand gazing up into heaven? This same Jesus, who was taken up from you into heaven, will so come in like manner as you saw Him go into heaven." This Second Coming will involve a visible, physical, bodily coming of the glorified Jesus, and every eye will see Him (Revelation 1:7). In Titus 2:13 Paul speaks of "looking for the blessed hope and glorious appearing of our great God and Savior Jesus Christ."

Suggestions for Dialoguing with New Agers

Following are some key considerations to keep in mind as you dialogue with your New Age acquaintances.

Befriend the New Ager. Befriending the New Ager means being *friendly* to the New Ager. As 2 Timothy 2:24–25 puts it, "a servant of the Lord must not quarrel but be gentle to all, able to teach, patient, in humility correcting those who are in opposition." The word *gentle* here carries the idea of being kind. When you witness, don't quarrel; instead, be kind.

Don't make false assumptions. Many New Agers use some of the same words Christians do — words like revelation, Jesus Christ, God, resurrection, and ascension. Do not make the false assumption that simply because they use such words, they mean the same thing you mean by these terms. You must be careful to define the terms you use.

Another false assumption to avoid is the idea that all New Agers believe exactly the same things. While they may be united in certain core beliefs, they also hold certain distinct beliefs. In view of this, it is important not to tell a New Ager what he or she likely believes. Ask questions about their views and then let the New Ager verbalize what he or she believes, and then you can accurately address what they've said (Proverbs 18:13).

Try to avoid unhelpful behaviors. For example, try to avoid arrogance and pride. Some Christians tend to carry a "spiritual chip on the shoulder." Acting like a spiritual know-it-all is a real turn-off. It is better to be humble, speaking with grace and truth.

It's also important to be patient. When witnessing, you will likely have to explain the same thing more than once. Expect this. Don't say, "I already told you this," or "Have you listened to anything I've said?" No matter how slow the New Ager may seem in grasping your points, be patient as you tell the truth about Jesus Christ.

Try to find common ground. As you interact with a New Ager, watch for common ground that you can use as a launch pad to dialogue about spiritual matters. (The Apostle Paul used this approach in Acts 17.) For example, if they speak about ecology, you might say that ecology is good, since God created the earth (Genesis 1:1–2) and the earth belongs to God (Deuteronomy 10:14). Or, if you want to talk about Jesus, you might mention how John 1:3 and Colossians 1:16 tell us that Jesus is the Creator of all things. If you watch for opportunities, it is easy to segue to spiritual matters based on something the New Ager said.

Address the inadequacy of mysticism. The truth is, so-called mystical revelations are too uncertain and insufficient as a ground upon which to build our knowledge of God (i.e., they are arbitrary and lead to an arbitrary understanding). Talk to any three mystics, and you will likely receive three different views on the same issue.

The Bible stresses the importance of objective, certain, historical revelation. For example, John 1:18 tells us: "No one has seen God at any time. The only begotten Son, who is in the bosom of the Father, He has declared Him." In the empirical world of ordinary sense perceptions, Jesus was *seen*

and *heard* by human beings on earth as God's ultimate revelation to human-kind. This is why Jesus said, "If you had known Me, you would have known My Father also" (John 14:7).

The Apostle Paul also stressed the importance of objective, historical revelation. According to Acts 17:31, Paul warned religious people in Athens of the objective reality of a future judgment based on the objective evidence for Christ's Resurrection from the dead. Based on how people respond to this objective, historical revelation, they will spend eternity in a real heaven or a real hell.

There is another related matter worth noting. Those involved in New Age mysticism seem blind to the possibility of spiritual deception by the powers of darkness. Second Corinthians 11:14 warns that "Satan himself transforms himself into an angel of light." We are also told that Satan has the ability to blind the minds of unbelievers (2 Corinthians 4:4). Through mysticism, a New Ager might think he or she is having a positive spiritual experience, when in reality they are being deceived by the devil, who is the father of lies (John 8:44). Mysticism is a breeding ground for spiritual deception.

Point to pantheism's failure in accounting for the problem of evil. One great way to show the inadequacy of pantheism is to demonstrate its inconsistency with the problem of evil. If all is one and all is God, then God is evil as well as good, hatred as well as love, death as well as life. In such a view, life becomes an absurdity. How can it be said that Hitler's extermination of six millions Jews was a part of God (pantheism)? As hard as they might try, New Age pantheists cannot satisfactorily deal with the problem of evil.

Talk about the appeal of a personal God. An important component of your dialogue with a New Ager ought to be contrasting the personal God of Christianity with the impersonal "It" of the New Age movement. The idea of an impersonal God is utterly unsatisfying because one cannot have a personal relationship with a force. In this context, a good idea is to share your personal testimony, and speak openly about your own personal relationship with God.

Jesus was not a mere enlightened master. New Agers typically revere Jesus as an enlightened human being who came to help other humans attain enlightenment. Christians, by contrast, worship Jesus as the eternal God (John 1:1), who became a human (John 1:14), atoned for our sins at the Cross (2 Corinthians 5:21), rose from the dead (1 Corinthians 15:3–8), and ascended back to heaven (Acts 1:9–11), far above all other beings (Ephesians 4:10).

Let us be clear: Jesus was not a mere enlightened master. Rather He was and continues to be the Light of the world (John 8:12) who "gives light to every man coming into the world" (John 1:9). True "enlightenment" therefore involves believing in and following Him who is the Light of the world (see John 1:4–5). Note that the word "believe" occurs almost 100 times in John's Gospel. Salvation is found in believing in Jesus Christ, the Light of the world. It is He — as the Light of the World — who has delivered us from the kingdom of darkness (Colossians 1:13–14).

Closing Thoughts

At the top of this chapter, we learned that Cindy was exposed to the New Age movement through a human potential seminar sponsored by the company she worked for. The idea that she was a god who could create her own reality did not sit well with her. After all, why does a god have to attend a New Age seminar to discover that he or she is a god? This dilemma ended up motivating her to search for the truth.

Her search for truth led her to the following conclusions: there is such a thing as absolute truth; New Age mysticism can lead to deception; the idea that all is god is nonsensical; there is a personal and unique Creator-God; she herself is not a god but is rather a creature; her problems stem not from being unenlightened but rather from the sin that plagues all humanity; deliverance from this sin comes only in the person of Jesus Christ, the only true Savior.

Long story short — Cindy became a Christian, and now has a ministry that warns others about the New Age movement!

Summary of New Age Beliefs

Doctrine	Teachings of New Age
God	Most hold a pantheistic view of divinity, denying the Creator-God of the Bible. All of nature is connected to the divine or vital force. Divinity is within every person, though it is veiled in most. Jesus is not the Savior, but merely an enlightened master who can give guidance.

Authority/ Revelation	All spiritual views contain elements of truth, so various holy books (Hindu Vedas, Koran, Bible, etc.) are used to find hidden truths through mystical means. Revelation comes from spiritual guides who communicate those truths to humans through meditation, visualization, and channeling.
Man	All of humanity contains the divine spark within but needs to be awakened or the individual enlightened to the divine within. Some believe each person is bound by the deeds of former lives (karma), and their position in society or circumstances are based on those experiences (reincarnation).
Sin	The biblical idea of sin is denied. Most believe in the ideas of positive and negative forces/energies that need to be balanced for life to be connected to the divine.
Salvation	There is no need for salvation, in the biblical sense, since sin does not exist. The ultimate goal is to attain connection with the divine or vital force that connects all of humanity to the divine, vital force, or "Christ consciousness."
Creation	Various creation myths are seen as viable explanations for the creation of the universe. The common core is of the universe emanating from one source to which all in existence is connected.

Chapter 3

Taoism

Dr. Mary Kraus

Legend tells us that one day around 600 B.C. in the western province of Honan, China, an old man named Laozi (also spelled Lao-Tzu or Lao-Tze), meaning "the Old Boy" or "the Grand Old Master," climbed onto a water buffalo and rode toward Tibet. He had been keeping the imperial archives in his province and was so discouraged by the state of his society that he decided to abandon Honan and live as a recluse for the rest of his days. When he arrived at the Hankao Pass, the gatekeeper, knowing of Laozi's unusual wisdom, persuaded him not to leave before recording something that would help his countrymen. So Laozi turned around, went home, and three days later appeared with a slim little book of very short chapters that for 2,500 years has been a major influence on not only Chinese culture, but on all of Asia and is even now influencing many Westerners. Thus began Taoism (pronounced like Daoism[1]), one of the oldest Eastern philosophies, after Hinduism.

History and Authority

The *Daodejing*,[2] or *The Treatise on the Way and Its Power*, is traditionally regarded as the work of Laozi (604–531 B.C.), who was a contemporary of Confucius. Both lived during a time of social deterioration when their

---

1. For this chapter, we will use the spelling Taoism unless it is quoted from another source with an alternate spelling.
2. This book is also known as the *Tao Te Ching*, Lao Tsu, *Tao Te Ching*, trans, Gia`Fu Feng and Jane English (New York: Vintage Books, 1972).

society was fragmented into many warring factions. Both philosophers, worried about their societies, prescribed different but complementary solutions to social disintegration. Both men wanted people to be good, but while Confucius[3] taught that man can *learn* to be good by applying rational rules to his behavior, Laozi believed that following nature's way would make people good, solving man's troubles. One might regard these two as one regards rationalism and romanticism or reason and emotion — not as mutually exclusive, but as complementary, and still very inadequate solutions for man's unhappiness.

Taoism, along with Confucianism, has been a major underlying influence of Asian thought and now has become popular in the West as well. Zen Buddhism, for example, has adopted many Daoist principles. Many Eastern health practices that have been adopted by the West today have their origin in Taoism. The Mayo Clinic, for example, recommends *Tai chi chuan,* a slow kind of exercise that seems to bring many health benefits. Taoist *yoga* techniques are practiced by many Americans who seek better health or less stressful lives. The New Age Movement in America, which is really thousands of years old, has also adopted many Taoist ideas that will be discussed later in this chapter.

But the original text, *Daodejing,* which may actually be a reflection of many authors and editors, is the root of all the various beliefs and practices of *Taoism.* It consists of 81 short proverbial and paradoxical chapters that invite meditation on three different meanings of the Way or Dao:

1. *The Dao (Way) of Ultimate Reality* — the Source of all existence (no personal God)

2. *The Dao (Way) of the Universe* — the norm, rhythm, and driving power in all nature and the ordering principle behind all life

3. *The Dao (Way) of Human Life in Harmony with the Dao of the Universe* — the way people should live

Philosophical Foundations

1. The Way of Ultimate Reality

An excerpt from chapter 1 of the *Daodejing* begins by describing Ultimate Reality in negative terms:

---

3. See chapter 20 in this volume for a full description of Confucianism.

> The Dao (Way) that can be told is not the eternal Dao.
> The name that can be named is not the eternal name.
> The nameless is the beginning of heaven and earth.[4]

These lines exemplify the first meaning, that there is an Ultimate Reality that lies beyond human ability to comprehend rationally or describe in language. This is an "eternal" reality without beginning or end. It is not irrational, but is beyond human reason to grasp. It is supra-rational. This Reality is the Source of all existence, but it is "nameless" because, unlike the biblical God, it is not personal and has not revealed itself to human reason. Nevertheless, human reason sees the self-evident principle that something cannot come from nothing, and so Laozi correctly concluded that the source of everything must be some kind of uncaused first cause. In practical terms today, Taoism is a panentheistic religion, teaching that the Dao is expressed in everything, but there are also polytheistic aspects to the religious practice of Taoism, which we will discuss later.

The radical difference between the *Daodejing*'s account of the Ultimate Reality and the biblical God is very clear. God's Word says, "In the beginning was the Word, and the Word was with God, and the Word was God. . . . All things were made through Him, and without Him nothing was made that was made. . . . And the Word became flesh and dwelt among us" (John 1:1–14).[5] Language, being a rational skill, is not able to describe the *Daodejing*'s Ultimate Reality adequately. But God revealed Himself in His Son and chose language, "The Word," to show Himself as a *person*, not an *it*. "For in Him [the Person of Jesus Christ] dwells all the fullness of the Godhead bodily" (Colossians 2:9).

In contrast to the "nameless" Ultimate Reality, the next line of the *Daodejing*, chapter 1 reads, "The named is the mother of ten thousand things," suggesting that the physical world which can be rationally investigated and experienced, is merely the manifestation of this Ultimate Reality that is its source, so that what people experience with their five senses, the visible world, points to an invisible reality as Romans 1:20 states: "For the invisible things of him from the creation of the world are clearly seen . . ." (KJV). However, in Taoism, there is no "Him," but only an It, the eternal source of everything.

---

4. Online site for *Daodejing*, http://www.taoism.net/ttc/complete.htm.
5. Unless otherwise noted, Scripture in this chapter is from the New King James Version (NKJV) of the Bible.

> The Dao begot one.
> One begot two.
> Two begot three.
> And three begot the ten thousand things.[6]

These lines indicate that the Dao began a kind of evolutionary process. There was no special creation in six days as the account in Genesis 1 describes: "In the beginning, God created the heavens and the earth." According to Taoism, the origin of the universe and everything in it is contrary to the account of special creation in God's Word.

2. The Way of the Universe

A second philosophical meaning of the *Dao* is the way the universe works, or the way of nature. This may be seen in the following lines from chapter 2 of the *Daodejing*:

> Under heaven all can see beauty as beauty only because there is ugliness.
> All can know good as good only because there is evil.
> Therefore having and not having arise together.
> Difficult and easy complement each other.
> Long and short contrast each other;
> High and low rest upon each other;
> Voice and sound harmonize each other;
> Front and back follow one another.

These lines accurately describe the dual nature of the universe. Everything is interconnected, interdependent, and closely related. Chapter 42 states, "The ten thousand things carry yin and embrace yang; They achieve harmony by combining these [opposite] forces."[7] *Yin* represents passivity while *yang* represents activity.

The yin yang symbol represents the principle of natural and complementary forces, patterns, and things that depend on one another and do not make sense on their own. These may be masculine and feminine, but they could be darkness and light (which is closer to the original meaning of the dark and light sides of a hill), wet and dry, or action and inaction.

---

6. *Daodejing*, chapter 42.
7. Ibid.

These are opposites that fit together seamlessly and work in perfect harmony. You can see this by looking at the yin yang symbol. Each element is pictured as a small circle within its opposite to show the interconnectedness of all things.

Yin yang symbol

The above lines from chapter 2 of the *Daodejing*, represented by the yin yang symbol, also suggest that to limited human intelligence without any outside or supernatural standard, all things are relative, even moral standards. This idea, called "the relativity of distinctions," was developed by the later Taoist philosopher, Zhuangzi (369–286 B.C.). He correctly explained that everyone is limited in his knowledge by his own limited perspectives, concepts, and experiences. No one can know absolute truth unless he identifies with some unlimited source of truth. Zhuangzi believed that true knowledge and happiness requires that one give up the ordinary way of rational understanding and identify with the infinity of the universe, the Way of Nature, which is the Dao or Ultimate Reality. "Forget the passage of time (life and death) and forget the distinction of right and wrong. Relax in the realm of the infinite and thus abide in the realm of the infinite."[8]

Here Zhuangzi correctly saw that human beings, because of their own limitations, needed something beyond themselves for guidance; "the realm of the infinite." But he had no knowledge of the infinite Creator/God or the catastrophe of the Fall, though he could surely see the evidence of it in his own society. However, the consequent damaging blow to all of nature, including human judgment and natural feelings, was somehow hidden from him, and he believed that man could, with his own power, return to the infinite Way of nature, the Dao or Ultimate Reality, and this return would solve man's trouble. All problems could be rectified by man himself.

But the infinite God tells us in His Word about what happened to nature when man first chose his own way over God's clear direction:

> Then to Adam He said, "Because you have heeded the voice of your wife, and have eaten from the tree of which I commanded you, saying, 'You shall not eat of it': Cursed is the ground for your sake; in toil you shall eat of it all the days of your life. Both thorns and thistles it shall bring forth for you, and you shall eat

---

8. Quoted in John M. Koller, *Asian Philosophies* (Boston, MA: Pearson Education, 2012), p. 232.

the herb of the field. In the sweat of your face you shall eat bread till you return to the ground, for out of it you were taken; for dust you are, and to dust you shall return" (Genesis 3:17–19).

So disobedience to the Creator's clear command plunged the entire human race into inescapable suffering and death. Laozi and Zhuangzi died. Attempting to identify with the Way of nature cannot cancel out God's wrath and the result of man's disobedience.

Another description of the way of nature is found in chapter 76 of the *Daodejing*:

> A man is born gentle and weak.
> At his death he is hard and stiff.
> Green plants are tender and filled with sap.
> At their death they are withered and dry.
> Therefore the stiff and unbending is the disciple of death.
> The gentle and yielding is the disciple of life.
> Thus an army without flexibility never wins a battle.
> A tree that is unbending is easily broken.
> The hard and strong will fall.
> The soft and weak will overcome.

These lines describe an important fact of the physical world, and conclude with a paradox that suggests something about the third meaning of *Dao* — humans should live gently and humbly.

3. The Way of Human Life When It Is in Harmony with the Dao of the Universe

Chapter 76 enjoins people to imitate nature by being flexible and gentle instead of rigid and forceful in their dealings with others and all of their surroundings. When on May 29, 1953, after many previous attempts, Edmund Hillary and Tenzing Norgay finally reached the summit of Mt. Everest, the tallest peak on earth, "the exploit was widely hailed as 'the conquest of Everest.' D.T. Suzuki, a Japanese remarked: 'We Orientals would have spoken of befriending Everest, rather than conquering it.' " This is very much in line with the Taoist principle of attuning and adapting oneself to nature. Much Taoist art reflects this principle very clearly. Note the prominence of trees, mountains, and mist in the picture following, while

Painting by Mossolainen Nikola (Shutterstock)

the boat and human dwellings blend into the scene so closely that one must look carefully to see them. This picture is seen as a visual lesson of the way people should live.

A Japanese team that scaled the Himalayan Mount Annapurna, the second highest peak in the Himalayas, climbed to within 50 feet of the summit and deliberately stopped. Why? Because "Taoism seeks attunement with nature and not dominance."[9]

This Taoist principle agrees in part with God's Word in regard to man's relationship with the natural world. People are to respect and care for it, rather than polluting and wasting it. After God had created Adam and planted the garden, "Then the LORD God took the man and put him in the garden of Eden to tend and keep it" Genesis 2:15). But rather than seeking to merely blend in with nature, God gave man dominion over nature, to use the earth and all its fullness for his benefit without exploiting its resources. In the *Daodejing* we read:

> Do not be concerned with loss or gain. . . .
> Surrender yourself humbly; then you can be trusted to care for all things.

9. Quoted by Huston Smith, *The World's Religions* (San Francisco, CA: Harper Collins, 1991), p. 212–213.

> Love the world as your own self; then you can truly care for all things.[10]

Some of the principles of Taoism are in beautiful agreement with Scripture principles because God created all men according to His master plan, and He intends them to see His invisible attributes, "His eternal power and Godhead" (Romans 1:20) by looking at the natural world. Nature has many lessons to teach those whom God intended to "tend and keep it."

Human Relationships

Humble leadership is one of these principles in which Taoism and Christian Scripture agree. In the *Daodejing*, Laozi asks,

> Why is the sea king of a hundred streams?
> Because it lies below them.
> Therefore it is the king of a hundred streams.
> If the sage would guide the people, he must serve with humility,
> If he would lead them, he must follow behind.
> In this way when the sage rules, the people will not feel oppressed:
> When he stands before them, they will not be harmed.
> The whole world will support him and will not tire of him.
> Because he does not compete,
> He does not meet competition.[11]

In God's Word, Jesus advises, "You know that those who are considered rulers over the Gentiles lord it over them, and their great ones exercise authority over them. Yet it shall not be so among you; but whoever desires to become great among you shall be your servant. And whoever of you desires to be first shall be slave of all" (Mark 10:42–44).

Again, regarding human relations, Laozi says,

> A good soldier is not violent
> A good fighter is not angry.
> A good winner is not vengeful.
> A good employer is humble.
> This is known as the Virtue of not striving.
> This is known as ability to deal with people.

---

10. *Daodejing*, chapter 13.
11. *Daodejing*, chapter 66.

> This since ancient times has been known as the ultimate
> unity with heaven.[12]

In considering human relations and "ultimate unity with heaven," one cannot help noticing the much greater intensity and emphasis of the lawyer's answer to Jesus when asked, " 'What is written in the law? What is your reading of it?' So he answered and said, 'You shall love the LORD your God with all your heart, with all your soul, with all your strength, and with all your mind, and your neighbor as yourself.' And [Jesus] said to him, 'You have answered rightly. Do this and you will live' " (Luke 10:26–28). God, the Creator of the universe, is a person, not an impersonal Ultimate Reality, and so God's greatest command to human beings to love Him is not only reasonable, but wonderfully possible. It is actually man's whole reason for being.

The many similarities in biblical and Taoist thinking may come from a common source of truth transmitted through the ages from the dispersion at Babel or from drawing true principles from what we can observe of God's character in nature. Whichever is true, the Taoist ultimately has no true grounding in special revelation from God, but only in general revelation in nature. Because of this, it is ultimately an arbitrary standard. On what grounds is it best to co-exist with nature rather than exercise dominion and control over it? God's Word gives us a consistent foundation while Taoism is based on the opinions of men.

Vitality Cults

In addition to philosophical Taoism with its three meanings, another kind of Taoism arose and has now become popular in both East and West, the vitality cults. The aim of this kind of Taoism is to increase health and longevity. The feeling of vital energy that Taoists felt within themselves they named *chi* (also spelled *qi*). "The Taoists used it to refer to the power of the Tao . . . coursing through them — or not coursing because it was blocked — and their main object was to further its flow."[13] Today, Taoists use various methods in their attempt to increase this physical/spiritual vital force of chi that comes from the Dao. Many believe that chi can be increased nutritionally as it mixes with the innate chi that is generated in the kidney, and so hundreds of medicinal herbs are on the market. Here are just a few claims

---

12. *Daodejing*, chapter 68.
13. Smith, *The World's Religions*, p. 201.

of medicinal herbs (note that "energy" is used to refer to chi, not merely physical energy):

> **Ginkgo** (*Ginkgo biloba*) helps the brain better utilize oxygen, improves mental alertness, and improves peripheral circulation. Is an antioxidant, and kidney tonic.
>
> **Ginseng** (*Panax ginseng*) benefits exhaustion and helps the body deal with stress, adrenal exhaustion, fatigue, immune weakness, and postoperative recovery. Ginseng is an adaptogen, chi tonic, digestive tonic, immune stimulant, rejuvenative, restorative, stimulant, and tonic.
>
> **Hawthorn leaves, flowers, and berries** (*Crataegus species*) help break down fatty deposits in the blood and gently dilates the capillaries so that heart can function more efficiently. Hawthorn improves peripheral circulation and the body's ability to utilize oxygen.
>
> **Licorice root** (*Glychyrriza glabra*) is naturally sweet, helps normalize blood sugar levels and nourishes exhausted adrenal glands. Licorice is nutritive and rejuvenative.
>
> **Schizandra berries** (*Schisandra chinensis*) improve endurance and are an antioxidant. It improves fatigue and insomnia. Schizandra is considered to be an adaptogen, cerebral tonic, immune stimulant, kidney and liver tonic, rejuvenative and restorative.
>
> **Essential oils** can improve physical and psychological energy levels. Essential oils that benefit fatigue include basil, clary sage, geranium, lavender, lemon, orange, peppermint, and rosemary. Simply open a bottle of the pure essential oil and take no more than ten deep inhalations.[14]

The Internet is replete with various foods to boost chi, and various sources make claims about which forms of chi are promoted by various herbs and which organs benefit, with varying degrees of scientific validity. Obviously, foods have the nutrients that humans need to stay healthy, but chi, whose source is the *Dao*, is not at all the same thing as the life and vitality, both spiritual and physical, that the Creator God provides.

---

14. Various pages on the website of a Taoist herbalist and author, Brigitte Mars, brigittemars. com, accessed November 4, 2015.

Tai Chi Chuan

In addition to attempting to extract chi from food, Taoists engage in various kinds of bodily movements such as *tai chi chuan*, which is a kind of slow exercise that combines calisthenics, dance, meditation, yin/yang philosophy, and martial arts. Tai chi chuan is "designed to draw chi from the cosmos and dislodge blocks to its internal flow."[15] This exercise is practiced by many in the West and recommended by numerous health centers. It involves stretching and slow motion graceful dance movements that have a calming influence and help people's physical balance, particularly older people. It is believed that these movements allow the flow of chi through the meridians, invisible energy channels in the body. These benefits, however, are available with many kinds of exercises without depending on the flow of chi and belief in the Dao as its source. A Christian believer who loves God and wants to be loyal to

A group practicing tai chi chuan movements (Shutterstock)

Him will not go to the Dao or any other supernatural entity for spiritual or physical power *even if these activities are physically beneficial.*

The Creator's purpose for human beings is for them to give Him pleasure and glory. At the same time, God pours blessings on His children. But a believer's aim should not be merely to reap benefits from God, but to give Him love and glory. God's Word teaches that there really are "spiritual hosts of wickedness in the heavenly places" (Ephesians 6:12), and the enemy of souls would like nothing better than to entice God's people away from Him. God is a jealous lover and has repeatedly warned His people against idolatry of all kinds. "I am the LORD your God. . . . You shall have no other gods before Me" (Exodus 20:2–3).

Accupuncture

Another Taoist method of removing blockages to the flow of the body's chi is acupuncture. Taoism developed the view of an entire circulatory system

---

15. Smith, *The World's Religions,* p. 201.

of chi called meridians. Acupuncture meridians are called many names, including Chinese meridians, energy meridians, and chi meridians, to name a few. These meridians are believed to carry the life force that vitalizes all life forms and allows them to flourish and grow. Different cultures call this life force by different names like subtle energy, Spirit, Prana, and vital energy. Additionally, these meridians were developed for animals, and there is a modern resurgence of applying acupuncture to veterinary medicine.

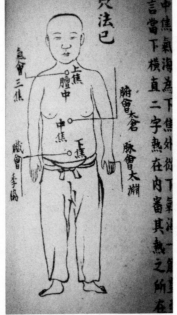

This drawing from an ancient Chinese medical book represents the chi meridians described in ancient Chinese Taoist thinking.
(Shutterstock)

Believed to be similar to electricity, this energy is invisible to the human eye. However, the practitioners claim they can feel and trace these pathways of energy with their hands as they flow like streams through the body.

Western science has neither proven nor disproven the existence of chi meridians, and surely there are mysteries of the human body and mind that man has not discovered; but all that exists comes from the Person of the Creator God, who really is the personal Ultimate Reality. Christians would do well to steer clear of practices that were developed out of a philosophy that denies God as Creator and focuses on mystical healing.

Feng Shui

You may have heard the term on a popular home design show, but feng shui is also an outgrowth of Taoism's yin yang principle. The main idea is to develop environments where humans can interact with the normal flow of chi in the universe to nurture the chi of the individual. This idea comes from the connectedness of everything to the Ultimate Reality. Seeking balance of objects in a space and usage of light are believed to make an environment calming or energizing. There are various schools of thought about the criteria to be used in the design, showing that this concept is really just an arbitrary idea developed by people and reflecting their own opinions and preferences.

In Hong Kong, for example, with its beautiful architecture, buildings have been aligned and spaces created for the free flow of chi. This is again man's effort to exert some control over his life by appealing to what he believes is a natural power without acknowledging the true source of all nature, the Creator God, Yahweh.

Meditation

Meditation is another self-help method of imbibing more of the Dao's vital energy, or chi. "This practice involves shutting out distractions and empty-ing the mind to the point where the power of the Dao might bypass bodily filters and enter the self directly."[16] Trying to create a mental vacuum is not only dangerous, but is directly contrary to the instruction in God's Word to "be *filled* with the Spirit" (Ephesians 5:18, emphasis added). Taoist yoga is much like the psychosomatic exercise of raja yoga in Hinduism. The practi-tioner works through his body to reach the inner recesses of his mind, and eventually to lose all self-consciousness. He begins by trying to rid the body of physical cravings, then finds a posture that is neither too comfortable nor uncomfortable. The famous lotus position seems to be conducive to medita-tion for many. Then he works to control his breathing, "When, for example the yogi [practitioner] is doing a cycle of sixteen counts inhaling, sixty-four holding, and thirty-two exhaling, there is a stretch during which animation is reduced to the point that the mind seems disembodied."[17] This is his goal and allows connection with the Dao.

Divination

Another Daoist practice is using the *I Ching* or *The Book of Changes*. This is a divination manual that is composed of 64 hexagrams. Each one represents a particular tendency to change, and is accompanied with texts that help the user to interpret the hexagram. People use the *I Ching* to foretell the future and also to direct one in making decisions about personal or business rela-tionships and other important matters.[18]

In general, Taoism doesn't make a rigid division between body and spirit, and regards physical activities, such as yoga, meditation, tai chi, and martial arts, as an important way to spiritual growth and a long life. This

16. Ibid., p. 202.
17. Ibid., p. 46.
18. Koller, *Asian Philosophies*, p. 170.

is exactly why believers in Jesus Christ are careful not to commit a kind of spiritual adultery by trusting in something supernatural that does not come from God. His Word repeatedly warns His people about seeking supernatural help from other gods or supernatural powers. "They provoked Him to jealousy with foreign gods; with abomination they provoked Him to anger. They sacrificed to demons, not to God. . . . Of the Rock who begot you, you are unmindful, and have forgotten the God Who fathered you" (Deuteronomy 32:16–18).

In addition to philosophical Taoism with its three meanings of the Dao or Way as Ultimate Reality, as the Way of the universe, and as the Way people should live, Taoism as a communal religion arose around the second century A.D. The Vitality Cults are a part of religious Taoism, but they are also an outgrowth of philosophical Taoism and have been discussed under the third meaning of the Dao, the Way people should live.

Religious Daoism

There is no unified Taoist answer to the question of what happens after this life. However, many Taoists believe that immortality is their main aim. "To attain it [immortality], people have to transform all their chi into the primordial [original] chi and refine it to subtler levels. The finer chi will eventually turn into pure spirit (*shen*), with which practitioners increasingly identify to become transcendent spirit people. The path that leads there involves intensive meditation and trance training as well as more radical forms of diet and other longevity practices. It results in a bypassing of death, so the death of the body has no impact on the continuation of the spirit person. In addition, practitioners attain super-sensory powers and eventually gain residence in otherworldly realms."[19] So immortality is earned by much earnest effort. Some Taoists believe that those who do not work for this goal will live in an eternal condition of suffering. Other Taoists believe that death is a perfectly natural part of the yin yang cycle, so when they die they simply go from the yang being to yin or nonbeing. In general, Taoists place most emphasis on living in tune with the natural way in the present.

This way of earned salvation is quite opposite of the Christian way in which trust in Jesus Christ alone is the single requirement. Jesus said, "I am the way, the truth, and the life. No one comes to the Father except through

19. Livia Kohn, *Health and Long Life the Chinese Way* (Dunedin, FL: Three Pines Press, 2005), p. 7–8.

Me" (John 14:6). All people, the Bible teaches, must live somewhere forever, either in heaven or in hell. But the fact of sin and the need for atonement is nowhere to be found in Taoism. Jesus Christ, the God-Man, is the bridge between sinful man and the righteous God. As the only innocent man, He took the world's sin upon Himself, and gives His divine righteousness in exchange to all those who trust in Him. "He [God] made Him [Jesus] who knew no sin to be sin for us, that we might become the righteousness of God in Him" (2 Corinthians 5:21). Taoists believe that one must work hard "to gain residence in wondrous other-worldly paradises," whereas Christians know that "by grace [unearned favor] you have been saved through faith, and that not of yourselves; it is the gift of God, not of works, lest anyone should boast" (Ephesians 2:8–9).

While the philosophical view of Taoism is panentheistic (teaching that everything is connected to the Dao in essence), Taoism is a polytheistic religion in practice. Unlike Christianity, there is not one single god to worship or honor. Taoist deities are part of the universe, as manifestations of the Dao, and are worshiped or venerated in Taoist temples. Religious adherents often choose one of many gods that is especially useful at a particular time. Taoist deities exist in a great pantheon [all the gods]. Within this pantheon is a structure, with various deities operating under the authority of other deities. The pantheon generally changes over time, and various Taoist sects have differing views of it. But all Taoist sects acknowledge the pantheon's existence. These deities are seen by some as a mixing of pure Taoism with Chinese folk religion and ancestor worship, but there is no formal structure or authority within the religion that would deny that this is an acceptable form of worship.

Some consider the Taoist pantheon as a heavenly bureaucracy that mimics the secular administrations of Imperial China. Since the Imperial administrations and the religious culture of the time were closely intertwined, it is also reasonable to think that the earthly structure was based on the heavenly organization, but there is no clear teaching on which view is true.

One of the sects, the Celestial masters, views Laozi as the chief god, with others organized below him:

> With the Way of the Celestial Masters, Laozi became a principle deity, and he continues to be the personification of Tao for many Taoists. He is usually regarded as one of the Three Pure

Ones, along with the Celestial Worthy of Primordial Beginning, the Celestial Worthy of Numinous Treasure. There are also the three Officials, the Emperor of the South Pole and Long Life, the Emperors of the Thirty-two Heavens, the Emperor of Purple Tenuity and the Northern Pole, and many, many more. All of these deities are divine emanations of celestial energy, pure cosmic qi, and have emerged from primordial chaos.[20]

The existence of this huge pantheon of many gods is an expression of man's instinctive need not only for supernatural aid, but also for *personal* supernatural aid. The impersonal "Ultimate Reality" will not do, and so the pantheon of personal deities arose to meet man's deep need. The very term "religion," which comes from the Latin *re ligare* and means literally "to bind again," indicates that people in all cultures recognize the fact that something that was once right has gone tragically wrong. So they have devised innumerable systems by which they attempt to bind themselves back to their origin and recapture their first condition of immortality, innocence, and bliss. There are 19 major religions in the world that are subdivided into a total of 270 large religious groups and countless smaller ones.[21] In fact, anthropologists have yet to discover a people anywhere who do not have some belief in the supernatural.

Taoism is like other religions — it relies on human effort to attempt to achieve immortality. Everyone wants to overcome death and live forever, as if they sense that man was not born to die. And they are right, for the Creator programmed all humans to know this truth. When the personal God first created the universe and placed man and woman in it, physical death was not part of the scene. He made the first humans with immortal souls like Himself, so they were His image-bearers with moral agency and the ability to love their Creator and one another. When they were tempted to go their own way instead of submitting to God, they gave in, and plunged their race into a condition of suffering and death, a condition that Taoism, along with all other religions, has been trying to change from its beginning until now. Death is the ultimate expression of a righteous God's wrath for the rebellion of His creation.

20. Julia Hardy, "Taoism: Ultimate Reality and Divine Beings," Patheos.com, accessed November 5, 2015, http://www.patheos.com/Library/Taoism/Beliefs/Ultimate-Reality-and-Divine-Beings.

21. http://www.religioustolerance.org/worldrel.htm, accessed November 5, 2015.

But this holy God is not only just and perfectly right, He is infinitely merciful and loving too. So He devised a way to bind man back to Himself. This would happen not by man's most heroic efforts at all, but by God's own action of saving His creatures who are unable to save themselves. The Triune God "so loved the world that He gave His only begotten Son, that whoever believes in Him should not perish but have everlasting life" (John 3:16). His Son is Jesus Christ, both God and man, who satisfied a holy God's justice by accepting death in place of all other sinful people, so that those who choose to trust Him may be with Him forever in heaven.

The Ultimate Reality of Daoism which cannot be named or known, the "unknown god," is actually the person "who made the world and everything in it. . . . He is not far from each one of us for in Him we live and move and have our being" (Acts 17:24–28).

Summary of Taoist Beliefs

Doctrine	Teachings of Taoism
God	Denies that God is a personal being, but refers to a nameless and impersonal Ultimate Reality or Source that has no beginning or end. There is a belief comparable to panentheism in philosophical Taoism, while many religious Taoists worship many gods (polytheism).
Authority/ Revelation	The writings of Laozi in the *Daodejing* are considered the founding principles of Taoism. Other important writings include the *Zhuangzi, I Ching*, and collections by various writers of the years. There is no direct revelation from the Ultimate Reality, but it is drawn from self-evident truths in nature and described by men.
Man	Man is a reflection of the universe and should seek harmony with the universe through pursuing the balance of yin yang.
Sin	The biblical concept of sin is denied, while the Taoist seeks to find balance of yin and yang.
Salvation	Since sin is denied, there is no need for personal salvation from judgment. The ultimate goal is to achieve unity with the Dao by purifying the spirit (shen).

| Creation | The universe is a continually existing force, chi, that is constantly recreating itself through physical emanations of yin and yang. The Dao is eternal, having no beginning or end. There is no clear teaching on when the earth came into existence. |

Chapter 4

Hinduism (with Hare Krishna)

Dr. Joseph Paturi with Roger Patterson

Hinduism (also known as Brahmanism in older writings and as a stage in the development of Hinduism) has ancient roots. It is unquestionably the oldest living major religious tradition not connected to the Bible. However, Hinduism has no known historical founder and has no firm date of its origin. The term *Hinduism* is derived from the word *Sindhu*. *Sindhu* is a Sanskrit word for the great Indus River in northwestern India.[1]

In Sanskrit, *sindhu* simply means a large mass of water. It was first applied to the people living on the Indus River who Alexander the Great, an early invader, called *Indu*, from which the words Hindu and India were derived. Further, the Muslims coming from Arab lands through the northwest side of India used the term *Hindu* to refer to the people who lived east of the Indus River. Hindus, whose history can be traced back for at least four thousand years, came to be known as Hindus on a wide scale only in the 18th century when the British and other Europeans who colonized India began to call them Hindus.

The actual term *Hindu* first occurs as a Persian geographical term for the people who lived beyond the Indus River. The term Hindu originated as

---

1. The reader should be aware that words translated from Sanskrit into English have various spellings in different resources. Some words may have an "aa" rather than a single "a" in their spelling (praana vs. prana), and include extra letters like "h" (astanga vs. ashtanga) that would be pronounced in certain dialects.

a geographical term and did not refer to a religion. Later, Hindu was taken by European languages from the Arabic term *al-Hind*, which referred to the people who lived across the Indus River. This Arabic term was itself taken from the Persian term *Hindū*, which refers to all Indians. By the 13th century, Hindustan emerged as a popular alternative name for India, meaning the "land of Hindus." The term *Hinduism* was introduced into the English language in the 19th century to denote the religious, philosophical, and cultural traditions native to India.

The term *Hinduism,* which was originally a geographic descriptor, presently stands for a singular religious identity of the Hindu tradition that incorporates multiple cultures and a variety of belief systems practiced by the Hindu people.

A Brief Biblical History of the Indian People

The region of India, beginning with the Indus valley, was populated early after the events at the Tower of Babel in Genesis 11. As peoples left Babel, some migrated by land to the subcontinent of India — others likely came by boat.

Some of Noah's descendants who can be traced to India include many of the sons of Joktan through the lineage of Shem. The sons of Joktan were Almodad, Sheleph, Hazarmaveth, Jerah, Hadoram, Uzal, Diklah, Obal, Abimael, Sheba, Ophir, Havilah, and Jobab. They originally settled in the Arabian Peninsula and then, as Arab records afford, 11 of these 13 sons' family groups continued to migrate over to India.[2]

The Coptic name for India is *Sofir* (think *Ophir* with an "*s*") — Ophir (named for one of Joktan's sons) was famous for its gold![3] A Jewish historian from about 2,000 years ago writes:

> Solomon gave this command: That they should go along with his own stewards to the land that was of old called Ophir, but now the *Aurea Chersonesus*, which belongs to India, to fetch him gold.[4]

---

2. Dr. John Gill, *John Gill's Exposition of the Entire Bible*, notes on Genesis 10:26, http://www.biblestudytools.com/commentaries/gills-exposition-of-the-bible/.
3. M.G. Easton, *Easton's Bible Dictionary*, s.v., "Ophir," http://eastonsbibledictionary.org/2796-Ophir.php.
4. Flavius Josephus, *Antiquities of the Jews*, translated by William Whiston, http://lexundria.com/j_aj/8.150-8.175/wst.

India is the source of the famed port of the famous gold of Ophir mentioned in the Bible (1 Kings 9:28, 10:11, 22:48; Job 22:24, 28:16; Isaiah 13:12). Considering that each of these sons (and others who settled here) brought an entire language family with them to India, it would make India a "melting pot" of languages. For those who know India, it is, even to this day!

Demographics

Hinduism has about 900 million adherents worldwide (15% of the world's population), which is just above atheism at 13%.[5] Along with Christianity (31.5%) and Islam (23.2%), Hinduism is one of the three major religions of the world by percentage of population. It is the third largest religion in the world, behind Christianity and Islam. The following are estimated adherents of these religions worldwide.

- Christianity: 2.1 billion
- Islam: 1.3 billion
- Hinduism: 900 million

A great majority of Hindus live on the Indian subcontinent, and India remains the heartland of Hinduism. However, there has been a global diaspora of south Asians that made Hinduism spread to over 150 countries today. About 2.25 million Hindus make North America their home, mostly immigrants.[6]

Defining Hinduism

It is difficult to define Hinduism in a comprehensive manner that would encompass all the facets of its practice. According to Klostermaier, "Hinduism is a state of mind rather an assembly of facts or chronological sequence of events."[7] Because of its relatively tolerant nature and ancient history, Hinduism has assimilated a variety of polytheistic beliefs, traditions, and practices.

> Hinduism ranges from monotheism to polytheism, from monism to materialism and atheism to pantheism; from

---

5. Global Index of Religiosity and Atheism, Gallup International, 2012, http://www.wingia.com/web/files/news/14/file/14.pdf.

6. John L. Esposito, Darrell J. Fasching; Todd Lewis, *World Religions Today* (Oxford, UK: Oxford University Press, 2014).

7. Klaus K Klostermaier, *Hinduism: A Short History* (Oxford, UK: Oneworld, 2000), p. 4.

non-violence to moral system that see blood sacrifices to sustain the world; from supernatural other worldliness which both apotheosizes and marginalizes humans; defend social causes at any cost from critical, and scholastic philosophical discussion to the cultivation of sublime, mystical, and wordless inner experience.[8]

The most common term used by Hindus is *Sanatana Dharma*, meaning ancient or eternal religion, which is a descriptive word for Hinduism. As Christians, we would not believe that this is the eternal religion, holding the Creator God of the Bible, who is the Alpha and Omega (beginning and the end), as the ultimate authority on such matters. Based on God's Word, the Christian views Hinduism as a corruption due to sin since the events at the Tower of Babel as the arbitrary ideas of man are elevated to supersede God's Word, taking people down the wrong path.

Our hope is to bring the truth to those who have bought into Hinduism, giving them good news of great joy through Jesus Christ, the Creator God who has come to save them from sin.

General Beliefs

- Hindus believe in the divinity of their holy books, the *Vedas*, which are among the world's most ancient "scripture," and venerate the *Agamas* as equally revealed. These primordial hymns are assumed to be God's word and the bedrock of Sanatana Dharma, the eternal religion, which has neither beginning nor end.[9]

- Hindus believe in one all-pervasive Supreme Being (Brahman) who is both immanent and transcendent, both Creator and Unmanifest Reality.

- Hindus believe in the cyclical nature of time and that the universe undergoes endless cycles of creation, preservation, and dissolution.

---

8. Esposito, *World Religions Today.*
9. Being that the Hindu Brahman is impersonal, it is unclear how these *personal* books that utilize many *personal* things like human language are from the impersonal god, Brahman. If one argues, as some have, that Brahman is both personal and impersonal, then there is an internal inconsistency that makes his character illogical.

- Hindus believe in *karma*, the law of cause and effect by which each person creates his own destiny by his thoughts, words, and deeds.

- Hindus believe that the soul reincarnates, evolving through many births until all *karmas* have been resolved and *moksha*, spiritual knowledge and liberation from the cycle of rebirth, is attained. Not a single soul will be eternally deprived of this destiny.[10]

- Hindus believe that divine beings (*devas*) exist in unseen worlds and that temple worship, rituals, sacraments, and personal prayers create a communion with these *devas* and gods.

- Hindus believe that a spiritually awakened master, or *satguru*, is essential to know the Transcendent Absolute, as are personal discipline, good conduct, purification, pilgrimage, self-inquiry, and meditation.

- Many Hindus believe that all life is sacred, to be loved and revered, and therefore practice nonviolence and noninjury (*ahimsa*) to show universal compassion.

- Hindus believe that all revealed religions are essentially correct, and no particular religion teaches the only way to salvation above all others, but that all genuine religious paths are facets of God's Pure Love and Light, deserving tolerance and understanding.

These general beliefs are applicable to any Hindu person. However, Hindu beliefs and practices can deviate significantly. But let us pause for a moment and reflect. How can a Hindu know any of this for sure? In other words, how does the Hindu know these nine beliefs are *the truth*? Were they truly revealed from the Ultimate Reality?

How can an impersonal being reveal things in a personal fashion? It would be illogical. The obvious answer is that these beliefs are arbitrary. But what about the ancient wisdom books like the Vedas, Upanishads, Bhagavad Gita, etc.? Are these not like the revelation from God that Christians have?

---

10. If all people will eventually attain moksha, the practice of Hinduism is pointless.

Family performing an act of worship at a family shrine (Shutterstock)

Actually, no. The Bible is the revealed Word of God from a personal God to mankind created in the image of a personal God, which is what makes personal communication between the two possible. At best, these Hindu books like the Vedas are merely the suggested ideas of man about reality, being purely arbitrary compared to the Word of God (the Bible).

General Obligations

- Worship (*upasana*): Hindus are taught daily worship in the family shrine room from childhood — rituals, disciplines, chants, yogas, and religious study. They learn to be secure through devotion in home and temple, wearing traditional dress, bringing forth love of the Divine, and preparing the mind for serene meditation.

- Holy Days (*utsava*): Hindus are taught from childhood to participate in Hindu festivals and holy days in the home and temple. They learn to be happy through sweet communion with God at such auspicious celebrations. *Utsava* includes fasting and attending the temple on Monday or Friday and on other holy days.

- Virtuous Living (*dharma*): Hindus are taught from childhood to live a life of duty and good conduct. They learn to be selfless by thinking of others first; being respectful of parents, elders, and swamis; following divine law, especially ahimsa, which is mental, emotional, and physical noninjury to all beings. By doing so, they can resolve all karmas.

- Pilgrimage (*tirthayatra*): Hindus are taught from childhood the value of pilgrimage and are taken at least once a year for gazing at (*darsana*) holy persons or beings, temples, and places, near or far. They learn to be detached by setting aside worldly affairs and making god, gods, and gurus life's singular focus during these journeys.

- Rites of Passage (*samskara*): Hindus are taught from childhood to observe the many sacraments that mark and sanctify their passages through life. They learn to be traditional by celebrating the rites of birth, naming, head-shaving, first feeding, ear-piercing, first learning, coming of age, marriage, and death.

These general practices are applicable to any Hindu, though the expressions will vary to some degree.

Foundational Concepts

- Worldview: The worldview of a Hindu is based on the concept of karma, reincarnation, and caste. In fact, religion permeates every phase of existence.

- Ontology: The concept of three worlds is popular. It includes the world of the living, of the dead, and of the spirits (supernatural). There is no separation between sacred and secular. Hindus believe in the unity of all creation.

- Time: The concept of time is cyclical in nature. Everything is repeated age after age like seasons.

- Cosmology: The cosmological concept includes that nature is filled with spiritual beings and life forces that are all part of the universal force of Brahman (Gita, 4:35).

- Mankind: Man is brought into existence as *atman*, a spiritual emanation from Brahman. The atman is the essence of the individual, yet is part of the Divine. The self must experience the law of karma and come to realize that it is divine. In this sense, each person is divine and must recognize that the atman and Brahman are one.

- Maya: Reality as we know it is actually a form of illusion because we draw distinctions when there are no distinctions since all is one.

Major Divinities

Hinduism accommodates multifaceted concepts of god. The fundamental theological belief for a Hindu is in Brahman, the Impersonal Spirit, the Changeless and the Universal Force that comprises everything that exists. The Brahman is perceived in two different ways (with and without attributes). The Brahman, who is without attributes (*nirguna*), cannot be known by man. This naturally begs us to ask the question how it is possible for man to know that Brahman, the Impersonal Spirit, even exists!

The Brahman with attributes (*saguna*) demonstrates traits such as truth (*sat*), consciousness (*cit*), and blissfulness (*anand*), and can be known by man. The Brahman with these qualities is also known as *Isvara*, who is the creator of the world. Brahman, veiled with mysterious cosmic creative power known as *maya*, caused the material creation to come into existence. The whole of creation, which actually includes multiple universes, emanates from Brahman as the web that a spider weaves, and returns back into Brahman. Brahman exists in everything and everything exists in Brahman, making Hinduism a pantheistic worldview. Brahman alone is the Ultimate Reality. Maya and its created world is a created illusion and not eternal. Brahman creates this illusion for the purpose of joy or sport (*lila*).

In the functional aspect, Hindus believe in a triad of emanations made up of Brahma the creator, Vishnu the preserver, and Shiva the destroyer. So God is accepted as a person with personal attributes (saguna Brahman) such as being the creator, preserver, and destroyer of the universe. The three personal aspects of the Brahman can be referred to as a Hindu triad (*Trimurti*): Brahma the creator, Vishnu the preserver, and Shiva (Mahesha) the destroyer. In depictions of the triad, Brahma is shown as a multi-headed figure with Vishnu and Shiva.

There are many different incarnations (*avataras*) of Vishnu. *Avatara* is a Sanskrit word that refers to a divine incarnation that literally means "one who descends." Every Hindu believes in ten incarnations of the god Vishnu, of which nine avataras are already manifested and one more avatara is yet to come. The term *avatara* refers to a male or female person having divine powers. The term means an incarnation or appearance of a supernatural being or an illusion of that being. According to the *Bhagavad Gita*, whenever there is a decline of virtue and religious practice, Vishnu himself descends on earth to destroy evil and to uphold or re-establish righteousness. The most popular incarnations are *Rama* and *Krishna*. The final incarnation, *Kalki*, is yet to come into the world. All the avataras can be included in the second line of divinities.

Hindu Trimurti: gold statues of Brahma, Vishnu, and Shiva
(Shutterstock)

The ten avataras of Vishnu assume a prominent place in the Epics (the Hindu mythologies) and more so in the Puranas (a series of texts that describe specific gods).

The first three have a cosmic character and are foreshadowed in the hymns of the Vedas: *Matsya* (fish), *Kurma* (tortoise), and *Varaha* (boar).

The fourth incarnation belongs to a later age when the worship of Vishnu had become established: *Narsimha* (man-lion).

The fifth incarnation, *Vamana* (dwarf), whose three strides deprived the *asuras* of the domination of heaven and earth, follows the fourth avatara, and the three strides are attributed to Vishnu in the Vedic text as *Urukrama*.

The next three incarnations, *Parasurama, Ramchandra,* and *Krishna,* are mortal heroes whose exploits are celebrated in poems so fervently as to raise the heroes to the rank of gods.

The ninth avatara is the deification of any great teacher, known as *Buddha.* This is not a specific name, but a title. Most know this as the title taken by Siddhartha Gautama who achieved enlightenment and was known as Gautama Buddha. He is now a revered figure in Buddhism and various forms of Hinduism. According to the theory of the avataras, the Buddha himself was adopted as an avatara. In this way, Hinduism as the Vedic religion was able to enfold Buddhism under its large umbrella. Jainism also became, in essence, a doctrinal modification and adaptation of the Vedic religion.[11]

The final avatara is *Kalki*, who is yet to come and whose arrival will signal the end of the present age before the universe is annihilated and reborn. The idea resembles the manifestation of Jesus referred to in the Book of Revelation in the Bible. Jesus rides a white horse with a flaming sword (see Revelation 19:11–12) at the end of the world to usher in the new heavens and earth. It is possible that this is merely a corruption of early Christian teachings that have made their way into Hinduism since the Apostle Thomas and others (e.g., Luke 24:46–47; Acts 2:5; Romans 16:26) first brought the gospel into India nearly 2,000 years ago. What we supposedly know about Kalki is written primarily in the Puranas, which were written after the New Testament.

Popular Divinities

Many people have heard that there are millions of Hindu gods who are worshiped in various ways. This is due to the fact that there are so many popular deities and gurus who are worshiped and that individuals, families, and clans can create a deity to help with specific aspects of their lives.

Every Hindu family is supposed to have a family god or a personal deity to whom they show strong allegiance and worship by observing correct rituals, prayers, and festivals. The deities can be worshiped in public temples or shrines installed in homes. Certain sacred persons, living or dead, can be accepted as divine due to the miracles attributed to them before or after death. Popular Hindu deities include children of the major deities such as *Ganapati* (the elephant-headed god also known as *Ganesha*), who is a son of Shiva and Parvati. Ganapati is considered the god of knowledge and the obstacle remover. *Hanuman* or *Maruti* (the monkey-headed god), an associate of Rama, is believed to give health and strength.

Without the concept of female divinity, Hinduism would not be complete. A person, family, or a clan often worships female deities with great

---

11. See chapter 5 in this volume for a description of Jainism.

Hindu God Ganesha
(Shutterstock)

Illuminated statue of Hanuman
showing Rama and Sita in heart
(Shutterstock)

allegiance. Most female deities are mothers or consorts of major deities believed to have power (*shakti*) to protect a faithful devotee from evil powers. *Kali Mata* (Black Mother) of Calcutta is the most well-known female deity in India and is believed to have power to destroy evil and to protect and bless. She is believed to have seven sisters who are worshiped in different parts of India with different names such as *Durga Mata* or *Bhavani*.

Fertility cults are popular in rural India, and Shiva and *Parvati*, his consort, are associated with the male and female generative powers (similar to Priapus, the Roman god of generative power, who is worshiped in priapic or phallic symbolism). In addition to the above, there are 330 million gods traditionally accepted in Hinduism.

Spirits

Ancestral spirits are historical persons who are cultural, mythical, or religious heroes whom individuals may have experienced in dreams, visions, and miracles for benevolent results. These also include saints, gurus, and family heads. Recently deceased persons are remembered and honored through family rituals and family events. These are generally believed to be able to benefit the family.

A man killed in an accident or an unexpected mysterious death of a youth is often believed to exist as a bad spirit. Similarly, female malevolent spirits are created from unexpected deaths. However, ancestors can be both good and bad spirits and are ritually appeased by family members.

Demons and ghosts are believed to be living in abandoned houses, cemetery objects, trees, mountains, rivers, or strange places. Protection from these forces is sought from family gods, diviners, gurus, rituals, and magic.

Nature worship includes totem spirits of sacred trees, animals, birds, and imagined creatures. The cow is often considered the most sacred animal in the Hindu mythology. The Western expression "holy cow" comes from this bovine veneration. Since there is no meaningful distinction made between creator and the creation (or natural and supernatural), the whole cosmos is a sacred entity generally deserving reverence and worship.

The Living

Gurus (spiritual teachers or masters) have an important place in the Hindu tradition. A family or a person may have a guru according to their experience, sect, or background. A guru is also like a medium, a medicine man, an arbitrator, and a diviner who is believed to have power over human desires with supernatural abilities.

Saints or monks who live an ascetic life reside in the mountains, temples, or monasteries. Some are itinerant saints who travel from place to place and live on alms. This group of leaders generally stays away from social activities.

Magicians, though not very popular, are believed to have the ability to handle witchcraft, demons, and diseases in rural expressions of Hinduism.

Bhagats (self-taught priests) and priests born in a priestly family are the conductors of rituals, sacraments, and socio-religious events in temples or at homes. Magicians and Bhagats are very much a part of social life and participate in all community activities.

Concept of Karma

Karma simply means good or bad deeds considered as one of the paths to earn salvation. Whatever man receives or loses in life (including caste, spouse, children, family, and material things) and after life is believed to be the result of karma. It broadly describes the universal law of cause and effect. It is on a principle: "as you sow, so shall you reap." This means that what a man is now, is the result of what he has done in his past lives, and what he is doing now will determine what he shall be in the future life.

One of the arbitrary aspects of karma relates to determining what is good and what is bad. Since the individual experiences the world in an illusory form (maya), there is no ultimate standard of what is right or wrong. Additionally, there must be some form of accounting for good and bad deeds by a supreme being, but Brahman is supposed to be an impersonal force. This leaves the Hindu in a place of seeking to be judged by an impersonal force to determine his or her fate in a future incarnation — a logical inconsistency.

Scriptures

The Hindu scriptures can be categorized into two sections. The first category is *shruti* ("what is heard") and the second is *smruti* ("what is remembered"). *Veda* means "knowledge." The Vedas were oral traditions eventually written in ancient Sanskrit language and viewed as the most authoritative sacred texts. They are believed to have been developed from 1200 B.C. on.

The Vedas are considered shruti (heard) and have four parts: *Rig Veda, Sam Veda, Yajur Veda*, and *Atharva Veda*. All other scriptures are considered smruti (remembered).

The *Upanishadas* (dated from 600 B.C.), also called *Vedanta* ("final knowledge"), are philosophical discussions. These are written by gurus, and each of the vedas includes a section of Upanishadas at the end.

The most well-known epics are *Ramayana* and *Mahabharata* (fourth century B.C. to second century B.C.). The *Bhagavad-Gita* (200 B.C.) is a section from *Mahabharata* that has the story of *Krishna* and is considered the most popular book for Hindus to study and follow.

Many Christians reading this may immediately assume that the Hindu scriptures are like the Christian Scripture (the Bible). However, these are not in the same category. The Bible was inspired by God, who created man in His own image. God used chosen men to write His Word by the power of the Holy Spirit.

So when reading the Bible, we are reading what God has revealed to man. Thus, the Bible comes with the authority of God. The Hindu scriptures are not like this. They are merely the ancient writings of ancestors. Some are poems, prayers, and hymns; some contain history that reflects practices and beliefs; some have brilliant literary pieces, but not *inspired* or *inerrant* words by their god, Brahman.

So what is the source of authority of these Hindu scriptures? They are not authoritative like the Bible, but merely arbitrary writings of man (brimming with contradictions, no less). The Hindu may protest, "But this is the wisdom of the ancients," to which we might respond, "By what standard?" There is no greater standard than the true God.

The opinions of ancient people about various gods, Brahman, reality, and nature have no weight in an argument when compared to the Word of the personal Creator God in the Bible, who is the absolute authority on all issues. This is actually good news! The many peoples of India and elsewhere who have bought into Hinduism through the opinions of ancient peoples can be set free by the truth that only comes from the true Creator God.

Temples and Worship

India is famous for old Hindu temple architecture and its elaborate worship rituals. Temples, unlike churches or mosques, are not really meeting places but are the places of gods. The temple is built according to a sacred diagram that is described in the ancient sacred books. Much of a temple building is selected according to a divine sign and not according to human will.

A temple may be dedicated to a deity, and an icon of the presiding deity is placed in the sanctum. However, it is not surprising to see icons (many times formless objects) of many other gods and goddesses placed in different parts of a temple. Generally, a priest who presides over rituals may sit in the sanctum area. Icons in Hinduism are believed to have life or power of the divine. Devotees visit the temple for darsana (sacred gazing), to offer food or other items to the god, or to view and feel a sense of holiness.

A personal prayer or ritual in a temple may include facing a deity with folded hands; ringing a temple bell; offering water, fruits (especially coconut), food, or flowers; burning incense sticks; applying ash or red powder on the forehead; and circumambulation (*pradakshina*; walking around a shrine or temple). Congregational prayers could include group singing, dance, rituals, food in the temple hall, and preaching by learned gurus or monks during sacred days.

Pilgrimage in Hinduism is not mandatory, but the benefits are elaborately outlined in the Hindu texts: benefits such as healing, good karma, and personal purification. Kashi, also known as Banaras or Varanasi, is the most important center of pilgrimage for Hindus. It is believed that every religious act done in Kashi is multiplied good karma, impacting several life-times compared to the same act done elsewhere.

The largest human gathering on earth, called the *Kumbha Mela* ("pot festival"), happens every 12 years at Prayag ("the place of sacrifice") near modern Allahabad at the confluence of the Ganges, Yamuna, and the invisible Saraswati rivers. It also occurs at three other sites on a rotating basis. It is believed that immortal nectar (*amrita*) drips from a pot carried by Vishnu at each of these locations. About 30 million Hindu pilgrims gather to bathe ritually during Kumbha Mela time. This act of bathing in the river is believed to wash away the person's sins. There is also a procession of saints and blessings by various gurus and saints offered to the pilgrims. Here we can see a shadow of what the Bible teaches about baptism, but twisted in a way that denies the need for Christ's sacrifice to wash away sins.

Social Practices

While life for a Hindu is certainly colored by the particular culture they live in, there are certain aspects of Hindu life that cross borders of states and nations. Just as various Christian sects have different worship practices formed by their culture and the Bible, so Hindus vary in their personal expressions of worship.

Social Life

According to the scriptures, four divisions or castes (*varna*) regulate Hindu social life. Both Krishna (in the *Bhagavad Gita*) and a supernatural person's sacrifice in a creation myth in *Rig Veda* are considered the origin of the caste system.[12] A *Brahmin* caste has priestly duties, and *Kshatriya* is the warrior caste. *Vaysha* is the business caste, and *Shudra* is the lowest or servant caste. Those in the low castes are to serve the high caste and have been treated in the past as "untouchables." The detailed duties of the castes are mentioned in a controversial Hindu book called the *Laws of Manu*.[13] For centuries, the low caste community lived outside the Hindu socio-cultural circles. However, people are not allowed to observe the caste divisions in India today according to the constitution.

---

12. *Rig Veda*, tr. Wendy Doniger (New York: Penguin Classics, 1981).
13. James Fieser and John Powers, *Scriptures of the World's Religions* (New York: McGraw Hill, 2004).

Religious Life

Hindus believe in rebirth or innumerable births according to one's deeds. Every person is subject to the law of karma (cosmic law), and everything happens according to the law of karma. Salvation (moksha) is to liberate oneself.

While Hindus believe in a supreme force, most have individual or family gods and depend on them for daily needs. Observing strict rituals and customs related to deity is the mark of allegiance. Generally, a family consecrates a separate place for a deity that serves as a shrine in the house. An image of the presiding deity is placed in the center with multiple images of deities surrounding the centerpiece. The shrine orientation depends on the god of the household or family. Ritual or prayer times are common during daytime, sacred days, and special family or personal events.

Many perform daily *puja* (worship), especially the elderly. With folded hands, one stands or sits in front of a small family shrine. The shrine may contain the main family deity along with other preferred images, generally made of clay, wood, brass, copper, silver, or gold. The most popular deities in the central part of India are *Krishna, Rama, Ganapati, Durga,* and *Maruti.*

Other aspects of worship are the various *yogas* ("yoking") or *margas* ("paths") that an individual may perform. Various schools of thought will dictate an individual's practices, including acts of service, devotion, meditation, and seeking wisdom.

Festivals

Festivals are religious, cultural, and social events. Most are based on mythological stories of gods and goddesses such as *Ramanavami* that celebrates the birthday of the god Rama. The birth of the god Krishna is celebrated during *Gokulasthami*, and *Ganeshchuthrthi* celebrates the birth of the popular deity Ganesha.

The most popular Hindu festival is *Diwali* or the Festival of Lights. It is one of the most colorful and is a week-long community event. Families light earthen lamps throughout their homes, keeping them burning day and night. They put on new clothes and visit their extended families sharing sweets and gifts. Families pray to family deities at home or in temples and especially worship *Lakshmi*, the goddess of wealth, in hope of a prosperous year to come.

Family Life

Families usually live together under the authority of the family elders such as parents or grandparents. Marriages are typically arranged, though some of the cultural practices are changing in urban sections of India. Daily life is immersed with prayers, fasts, offerings, and rituals. Every Hindu — especially a person from the high caste group — needs to go through more than 70 *sanskaras* (sacraments).

Individual devotional elements and meditation are common in the Hindu community. A person who spends time in prayer, meditation, singing, and scripture chanting may be called the devotee of a deity. Devotional practices may include acts such as regular fasts, festivals, and observance of dietary laws and pilgrimages. Committed Hindus may practice meditation at home or in temples. These devotional and meditational aspects are perhaps the unique contribution made by India to the world religions, especially Buddhism and New Age.

Salvation as Liberation

Hindus believe in the concept of reincarnation (*punarjanma*), the idea that the soul is reborn in another body after death, and the quality of the future existence or next birth depends on one's current life lived or doing good deeds (karma).

When a Hindu dies, there is only one place he can go to, that is, back into Brahman. But since man and Brahman are so vastly separated, one must work his way up to Brahman through a *Samsara* (cycle of death and rebirth).

Striving to liberate (*moksha/mukti*) oneself from the Samsara cycle of death and rebirth called *karmabhadhan* (bound by the principle of karma) is the aim of a Hindu person. According to *Bhagavad Gita*, various paths to liberate oneself are: *karma marga* — the path of selfless action; *bhakti marga* — the path of devotion (personal worship); *astanga/raja marga* — the path of physical discipline and meditation; and *jnana marga* — the path of wisdom. As mentioned above, these paths to enlightenment are also called yogas. As a group, these can be seen as the religious salvific practices of Hindus, the ultimate goal being to escape all of the connection to the material world, achieving enlightenment and being united to Brahman, the universal reality.

Bahkti marga, total devotion to a god or avatara, is a popular path in India and depends on studying the religious texts and gurus. Many would agree that it is impossible to do only good deeds or live a perfect life, and thus assurance of liberation is impossible due to bad karma. *Jnana marg* (the path of wisdom) releases a person from the bondage of ignorance (*ajnana*) through inner enlightenment and finally unites the soul with Brahman forever. Various physical exercises, cleansings, and meditation allow one to realize the divinity of the soul revealed in the wisdom of the gurus by overcoming the distinctions produced through maya. Once the inner self realizes its divinity, laying aside all connections to the material world, the soul can escape the samsaras and be united with Brahman. As such, there is no notion of a heaven in Hinduism, but a form of annihilation of the soul as a distinct entity.

The Hindu caste system makes salvation harder for some. According to the *Laws of Manu,* a low caste person should attain high caste birth by serving the high caste community, and then the person may get the high caste birth and finally may get liberated if they are eventually able to live a good life and reach enlightenment.

Hare Krishna

Hinduism finds many different expressions and sects, but the development of specific systems is seen in Jainism, aspects of Buddhism, and Hare Krishna. You may know Hare Krishna practitioners as the saffron-robed men peddling flowers at an airport, but their religious views are Hindu at root. Officially known as the International Society of Krishna Consciousness (ISKCON), this group was formed in 1965 in America by a Hindu guru out of a devotion to Krishna, an avatar as the supreme god. This makes them a monotheistic expression of Hinduism (though they still hold pantheistic views). Hare Krishna followers see the stories of the warrior Arjuna's encounters with Vishnu in the Bhagavad Gita as the key texts to follow. Using Bhakti yoga practices of selfless devotion, meditation, physical postures, and song and dance, they believe they can achieve salvation through Krishna-consciousness, realizing their own divinity.

Krishna followers may lead normal lives as part of a society or be dedicated to living an ascetic lifestyle in a temple where they would abstain from various foods, alcohol, gambling, and illicit sexual activity. Vegetarianism is esteemed as the sanctified form of eating, and meat, fish, and eggs are avoided as to treat animals with reverence. The popularity of Hare Krishna increased when Beatles member George Harrison adopted the religion.

The main distinction of Hare Krishna comes from the mantra they believe to voice the supreme names of Krishna, Hare, and Rama. This chanting is believed to promote purification and connection with the true self, promoting peace and well-being. Using a string of 108 beads (*japa*; similar to a rosary), the chant is repeated 16 times each day for a total of 1,728 recitations. It is done in quiet meditation, aloud, or in groups with dancing. The chant states: Hare Krishna, Hare Krishna, Krishna Krishna, Hare Hare, Hare Rama, Hare Rama, Rama Rama, Hare Hare.

> The prayer or mantra that ISKCON devotees repeat is called the Maha Mantra, or the "great mantra for deliverance." It is made up of three words Hare, Krishna and Rama. Hare refers to God's energy. Krishna and Rama refer to God as the all-attractive and all-powerful one who is the source of all pleasure. Repetition of this mantra awakens the soul and brings strength, peace and happiness. It ultimately connects us with Lord Krishna and reveals our original spiritual life of eternal bliss and knowledge.[14]

In this we see the same goal of salvation through good deeds and realizing the divinity that lies within. While we can commend the Krishna followers for their care for creation and their desire to promote peace among all people, they are ultimately pursuing salvation through vain means — denying Jesus as the Savior and only source of salvation for fallen men.

Influence on the West

Hinduism's influence on the West can be seen in two major areas. The first is in the prominence of transcendental meditation. This practice was introduced to the West during the period of British imperialism. It gained traction among those who were looking for alternatives to traditional Western religious understanding of human consciousness. The modern view was popularized by Maharishi Mahesh Yogi in the mid-20th century. Meditation is prominent in Eastern religions, but the broad acceptance of this practice in various forms spread to the West as it was popularized by his disciples, especially the Beatles, Beach Boys, and many prominent entertainers.

---

14. http://www.iskcon.org/meditation/.

During the 1960s and '70s, many traveled to India to study under various gurus, yogis, and swamis, bringing those ideas back to the West, influencing cultural practices and beliefs. The New Age movement adopted many of these practices, seeking to empty the mind and connect with the inner divinity that was connected to the cosmos.[15]

Eastern meditation practices stand in stark contrast to biblical meditation. Biblical meditation focuses the mind on truths revealed by God with the goal of being conformed to His character. It is focusing on a truth that is outside of the self and revealed by a personal God. Eastern meditation attempts to clear the mind, using breathing techniques, repeated mantras or sounds, and looking within the self to recognize the inner divinity that is connected to Brahman.

The second major influence has been through what most Westerners would call yoga. Yoga means "to yoke" and is understood to be one of the paths to connect to the divine reality. The typical practice of yoga in the West involves various forms of Hatha or Ashtanga yoga — the physical exercises and meditative practices intended to be forms of Hindu worship and enlightenment. While there are many different schools of yoga, the postures and practices can be traced back thousands of years and are included in the Vedas and other writings.

Beginning in the mid 1800s, as Hindu philosophy was being introduced to the West, the practices of yoga were brought by Swami Vivekananda. He toured Europe and the United States, teaching yoga philosophy. Many other swamis and gurus have promoted their own versions since then. Rather than merely the postures and meditation, yoga encompasses an entire philosophy tied to the pantheistic view of Hinduism. Believing that each person is part of the Divine, having a divine spark within them, the popular schools of Hatha and Astanga yoga employ an eight-fold path to liberating the soul — the enlightenment of moksha that is the equivalent of salvation in Hinduism. These aspects of yoga include everything from purification, to controlling the body's vital force and senses, to meditation and absorption with the Divine force.

The various poses used in yoga, called *asanas*, are postures that are intended to bring relaxation. Many are based on various Hindu gods and aspects of nature, imitating them in a pose of worship. To strike the poses

---

15. See chapter 2 in this volume for a full description of New Age beliefs.

and meditate on them is to acknowledge the individual's connection with all of the cosmos and to remove thinking that makes distinctions. One common yoga progression is the sun salutation, a series intended to connect the inner self to the sun in an act of worship and meditation on how the sun expresses divinity. Additionally, these poses are intended to be practiced in concert with the other aspects. The breathing focus is intended to influence the vital force (*praana*) that flows through the body in channels called *nadi*. The use of focusing on objects, breath control, chanting mantras or sounds, and emptying the mind are all part of the practice. The postures facilitate this balancing of inner energy as well as moving inner focus through the various *chakras* in the body where the inner self can achieve enlightenment. This focus on the chakras progresses from the base of the spine up to the mind where the self recognizes its divinity. Many people report ecstatic experiences and spiritual connections during yoga.

Some refer to this as opening the third eye, by which the self is able to see past the illusions of the cosmos and approach moksha. The Tantric and Shaktic schools connect this flow of the force through the ascending chakras as the snake goddess, Kundalini, is awakened within and brings enlightenment. The Christian cannot miss the echoes of the promise of the serpent in the garden, promising Eve she could become like God. Several of these schools use various sexual expressions to achieve enlightenment, again showing a perversion of God's good gift and provision for new life through children.

The popularization of yoga practice in illustrated books and the philosophies that accompany it accelerated in the 1970s and continues today.

One modern proponent of yoga as a path to self-healing and self-realization writes:

> First and foremost, yoga is a systematic process of spiritual unfoldment. Yoga is a 5,000-year-old system of self-knowledge and God-realization, the aim of which is to unleash our full human potential — including our physical, ethical, emotional, mental, intellectual, and spiritual dimensions.
>
> The eight limbs are
> 1. Yama — Rules of Social Conduct
> 2. Niyama — Rules of Personal Behaviour
> 3. Aasana — Physical Postures
> 4. Praanaayaama — Control of Vital Force

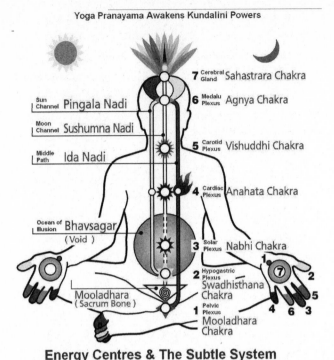

Yoga Pranayama Awakens Kundalini Powers

7 Cerebral Gland — Sahastrara Chakra

6 Medalu Plexus — Agnya Chakra

Sun Channel — Pingala Nadi

Moon Channel — Sushumna Nadi

5 Carotid Plexus — Vishuddhi Chakra

Middle Path — Ida Nadi

4 Cardiac Plexus — Anahata Chakra

Ocean of Illusion — Bhavsagar (Void)

3 Solar Plexus — Nabhi Chakra

2 Hypogastric Plexus — Swadhisthana Chakra

Mooladhara (Sacrum Bone)

1 Pelvic Plexus — Mooladhara Chakra

Energy Centres & The Subtle System

Modern books, websites, and classes offer teaching on the utilizations of the eight aspects of yoga to achieve health benefits, supernatural powers, and salvation. (http://www.kentonbell. guru/what-is-kundalini/)

5. Pratyaahaara — Control of the Senses

6. Dhaarana — Right Attention or Concentration

7. Dhyaana — Meditation

8. Samaadhi — Absorption

The first five limbs (from Yama to Pratyaahaara) make up the outer aspect of Yoga and the last three (Dhaarana, Dhyaana, Samaadhi) are called Samyama or Integration. Yama and Niyama refer to the right attitudes, values, and lifestyle practices necessary for Yoga, its ethical foundation. Aasana, Praanaayaama, and Pratyaahaara are the means to control the outer aspects of our nature as body, breath, and senses. Attention or concentration naturally leads to Meditation, which in time results in Absorption or the Unification of the Perceiver, the Perceived and the process of Perception. We get the knowledge of our true Self.[16]

---

16. Sangeetha Rajah, "Ashtanga Yoga," accessed March 28, 2016, http://www.hindupedia. com/en/Ashtaanga_Yoga..

Both meditation and yoga practices have been embraced by the popular culture, integrated into government school systems, and used by individuals and corporations to promote inner peace and general well-being. While often cloaked in scientific and health-related terminology, these are both part of the Hindu paths to salvation and should not be practiced by Christians, despite their promotion by some churches. Doing so opens one to the influences of false teachings and even demonic activity and influence. Rather than looking inside the self (a self with a nature that is irreparably corrupted by sin) through yoga practices to find union with the Divine, looking to Jesus Christ in repentance and faith is the only way God has made available to be united with Him for eternity.

Hindu Attitudes

While it is difficult to describe the attitudes of such a large and diverse group of people, the Hindu religious beliefs color the thoughts and actions of the followers, just as any worldview does.

Theological

All paths lead to the same goal (Gita).[17] Hinduism is viewed as sufficient enough for salvation, and all people are free to take a suitable path, investing differently toward the afterlife.[18] Hindus generally claim that no one religion has the monopoly on the truth.[19]

Socio-political

Conversion to another religion is considered similar to denying one's own mother, and denial of one's religious heritage is denial of a great treasure. Conversion is a great form of violence against Hinduism. (This would seem to contradict the idea that "all are free to take a suitable path.")

Those who turn away from Hinduism can expect being disowned by the convert's family, friends, and society. Ridicule, persecution, and even death can be expected, especially by those who turn to Christianity. Though Hindus claim to be nonviolent, religious fervor often expresses itself in

---

17. Once again, this would render Hinduism as pointless.
18. By what standard? Impersonal Brahman has not revealed this, so it is arbitrary. But for the sake of argument, even if this statement were true, then it makes Hinduism meaningless.
19. In saying this, the Hindu is making an absolute religious truth statement to which he is imposing what he believes as an absolute truth, assuming his religion is the absolute truth; thus it is self-refuting.

violence against those who leave Hinduism or seek to convert others from Hinduism.

Doctrinal Differences between Hinduism and Christianity

Concept	Hindu Belief	Christian Belief
Brahman	Nirguna Brahman is impersonal, unknowable, relationless, and without personal attributes.	God is triune, personal, knowable, holy, loving, and man can enter into a personal relationship with Him.
Isvara	Saguna Brahman is personal, knowable, with attributes, though he never revealed himself in a written form.	God has revealed Himself as a personal being with personal attributes: the Father speaking to man as recorded through prophets; the Son coming in flesh, dwelling among us, and revealing words recorded in the Bible; the Holy Spirit inspiring the writings of the prophets and dwelling in believers.
Avatar	There are ten incarnations of Vishnu in various human and animal forms. The final incarnation will destroy the wicked and annihilate the universe.	There has been one incarnation of God, Jesus the Son, taking on flesh to bring redemption to the wicked and restore the universe to perfection.
Trimurti	Triad: Brahma as creator; Vishnu as preserver; Shiva as destroyer.	Trinity: Father, Son, and Holy Spirit — three persons but one God.
Maya	Maya veils Brahman from mankind, giving the illusion of distinction in the cosmos that is actually all united.	God creates a real, perfect world that is corrupted through man's sin.

History of the Creation	Cyclic: Everything is repeated in cycles of life and death, from individual lives to different universes.	Linear: Time moves forward from the point of creation, through corruption, and forward to a final consummation and restoration.
Atman	Man's spirit emanated from Brahman and is eternal.	God created man in His own image with an eternal spirit.
Ajnana	"Sin" is defined as ignorance and making false distinctions, but there is no revelation that describes this concept.	Sin is disobedience or unfaithfulness to God's revealed law.
Karma	An impersonal reckoning of "good" and "bad" deeds determines one's future state of reincarnation; dependent on one's own works; no possibility of forgiveness.	After death, individuals are judged based on their obedience to God's law; forgiveness is available through Christ's substitutionary atonement.
Samsara	Cyclical: Birth, death, and rebirth dictated by karma and the individual's deeds.	Linear: Born with a sin nature and born again by God's grace through faith in Christ's atonement apart from individual deeds.
Moksha	Release from samsara through enlightenment, recognizing self as deity, and eventually being absorbed into Brahman.	Redemption from sin as a gift of God through repentance and faith in Christ's atonement.

Arbitrariness and Inconsistency

The Hindu doctrine of maya presents a powerful point of discussion. The Ultimate Reality is supposed to be hidden behind the illusion of the physical reality while all is really united and emanates from Brahman. But do Hindus really live in a way that is consistent with the teaching of maya?

If they are honest with themselves, they do not. A Hindu can only live in the real world by acknowledging the distinctions between light and dark, love and hate, waking and sleeping. If the Hindu were truly consistent with the belief system, he would not be bothered if you took the money from his wallet — there is no difference between rich and poor, after all.

If clothes are not real but illusion, then why wear them? If there is no distinction and *all is one*, then why is there a caste system? If there is no distinction in Hinduism, then why should a Hindu follow Hinduism rather than follow Christ? If the Hindu were to respond and say, "But that is a different religion," then ask, "Why do you draw the distinction if all is one?"

If, as Hinduism teaches, our problem is that we continue to draw distinctions when we shouldn't, then we are all already in a state of moksha! To say otherwise is to draw distinction between the current state and the future potential state.

Notice the violations of logic inherent within the Hindu worldview. Some might argue that that is the point of Hinduism — to move *beyond* logic to the "transcendent" — so logic is not helpful when dealing with Hinduism. What can the defender of Hinduism say? Would they use a logical appeal to say that it was illogical to contradict their claim that logic isn't applicable? If so, they have used logic to argue that logic isn't useful in the Hindu worldview — this creates a self-refuting argument.

The point of this is to show that, when honestly and carefully considered, Hinduism is internally inconsistent. It is illogical. We've shown it to be arbitrary, being built on the opinions and writings of men rather than direct revelation from God. So having both internal inconsistency and arbitrariness logically reduces Hinduism to a false belief. Our hope though is to point Hindus to the truth of Jesus Christ.

Doctrinal Bridges to Reach Hindus

Common concepts shared between Christianity and Hinduism are the ideas of God, incarnation, sin, salvation, good deeds, and life beyond this present state. Hindus normally conclude by saying that Hinduism has the same basic teaching as Christianity or that things sound very similar. This should not close the doors but form bridges for sharing the gospel. We can reach out to the Hindu by asking them to carefully compare the differences between the doctrines — especially the person and work of Jesus Christ.

1. Brahman: As we have seen, Brahman, the ultimate reality, is the one behind many gods of Hinduism. This supreme Brahman is in the nature of spirit and remains unchanged. Likewise, in Christianity, God is One. He is Spirit and never changes.

2. Isvara: Isvara, the creator is similar to the Christian concept of Creator God. We can point to the Bible and explain how all three members of the Trinity were involved in creation (Genesis 1; Colossians 1; John 1).

3. Avatara: Since the Hindu accepts avatars, there is no problem accepting the fact of God taking on flesh in the person of Jesus Christ. In fact, some Hindus already accept Jesus as an avatar of Krishna or a yogi. It is always helpful to stay focused on the life and teaching of Christ when presenting the gospel to Hindus.

4. Trimurti: The triad of Hinduism paves the path to explain the Christian doctrine of the Trinity.

5. Cyclical History: In Hinduism, history is cyclical. Everything is presented age after age. History in Christianity is linear. The present world order is to be destroyed and a new one created which will continue forever. It is difficult for a Hindu to grasp the Christian affirmation that God is a God of history and entered into history as Jesus Christ. The centrality of historical facts of the Incarnation, the Cross, and the Resurrection of the Lord Jesus must be emphasized.

6. Atman: Both Hindus and Christians believe that the Atman (spirit) is eternal and comes under the bondage of sin. The Lord Jesus came to deliver people from the bondage of sin.

7. Karma: This doctrine of karma is similar to the biblical concept of "as you sow, so shall you reap." This can serve as a bridge to point Hindus to God's judgment of our sins. The Hindu has to be told how the Lord Jesus took upon Himself the

sins of the world on the Cross of Calvary as a substitute. The law of karma is the immutable law that a person pays for the evil he has done. There is no concept of forgiveness of sins for a Hindu. The Cross shows that God is not only a God of law (judging sin), but also a God of love. In the Cross of Christ, justice and love met and together granted forgiveness of sins. No amount of good works gives assurance of salvation. God alone has the power to save a person by grace through faith in Christ Jesus who paid the price for sins (Ephesians 2:8–9).

8. Samsara: The Hindu seeks to be free from the cycles of samsara. This keeps recurring until one finds liberation from samsara. The grace of the Lord Jesus Christ can deliver one from the clutches that bind one to the false wheel of samsara.

9. Moksha: Salvation is release from the wheel of karma-samsara. The Hindu longs for release from the cycle of births and deaths and from karma itself. When he is liberated, he wants to be united with Brahman. The Lord Jesus presents in Scripture how He can break the power of sin and satisfy the longing of those who search for liberation. Rather than being united to Brahman, we can be united to Christ and receive all of the benefits of being true children of God in this life and in eternity (Galatians 2:10–21).

As a gospel messenger, look for open doors and connecting bridges, prayerfully presenting the hope in Christ in a relevant and loving manner (Colossians 4:2–6). At the right time, communicate the difference between the two faiths and allow the Holy Spirit to work, trusting in the power of the gospel.

Practical Points for Communicating the Gospel to Hindus

Witness

Be the salt and the light that will help to earn the trust of Hindu friends and neighbors. As a follower of Christ, it is a lifelong commitment through word and action before, during, and after sharing Christ. Pray for specific families and rely on the Holy Spirit at every stage. Let your life and conduct reflect the change that Christ has worked in your life. As you speak, do so with grace and truth, not avoiding hard truths, but speaking in a winsome way.

Friendship

Hindu friends and neighbors are open to hear the gospel when facing critical situations such as sickness, failure, or death of loved ones. Most of the time they are open for prayer for healing because of fear, which can be a good opening to share Christ. Friendship allows them to see how Christians deal with trials and difficult situations.

Hospitality

Invite friends and neighbors for family events such as birthdays, anniversaries, or even Christian festivities like an Easter dinner. Try to avoid culturally offensive practices, foods, or expressions accordingly to make them feel at home. Some may be vegetarians or avoid certain foods. Don't be afraid to ask what things you should avoid serving in order to eliminate unnecessary offenses. This will show respect and keep the door open for future communication of the gospel.

Remove Hindrances

Most common objections against Christians in India are that church-going people discard Indian practices or become Westernized. This refers to dietary habits, dress, music, and language. Such hindering practices could be easily addressed by the believers for the sake of the gospel. In the West, Hindus may be more open to adopting various customs.

Christ Likeness

Christians can be sensitive to neighbors' lifestyles in order to keep the door open for the communication of the gospel. Some committed believers have sacrificed consumption of certain foods for the Kingdom cause. Most of all, neighbors will listen to the message through a Christ-like life lived by the believers and the message that accompanies it.

Conclusion

Jesus Christ is the true answer to the fervent prayer of Hindus as expressed in the Vedas:

> From untruth, lead me to the truth;
> From darkness, lead me to light;
> From death, lead me to immortality.

Finally, Jesus Christ is the fulfillment of the noble aspirations of Hinduism. He says to the Hindus (John 14:6):

> I am the Way — The Karma Marg
> I am the Truth — The Jnana Marg
> I am the Life — The Bhakti Marg

God loves the whole world, including Hindus, irrespective of any national, language, or cultural background: "For God so loved the world that He gave His only begotten Son, that whoever believes in Him should not perish but have everlasting life" (John 3:16; NKJV). Innumerable Hindus have come to the saving knowledge of Jesus Christ over the centuries; their lives were beautifully transformed by the power of the gospel and were used by God as mighty witnesses for Him in India and around the world. Even today the same continues to happen. Glory to God as the gospel message brings sinners to repentance and faith in Jesus Christ — even Hindus!

Summary of Hindu Beliefs

Doctrine	Teachings of Hinduism
God	Deny the existence of the biblical God. See Brahman as the supreme expression of the divine impersonal force that is in all of creation. There are many expressions of lesser gods known as avatars. The trimurti represents a triad of Brahma, Vishnu, and Shiva. Millions of popular and personal gods are worshiped for various protections and benefits. Some may view Jesus as a guru, but not as God.
Authority/Revelation	The Bible is rejected. The *Vedas*, *Upanishadas* (*Vedanta*), and the epics, *Ramayana* and *Mahabharata*, are seen as scriptures. The *Bhagavad-Gita* is often studied as a key text.
Man	All men are part of Brahman, individually as atman, which is bound to the laws of karma and samsara. The atman experiences the physical reality as false distinctions, maya, which must be overcome to realize that the atman is divine. Each person is divine, though flawed. The atman is reincarnated in various forms based on the law of karma and dharma. Bad karma results in reincarnation as lesser life forms or in a lower social caste.

Sin	Sin is vaguely identified as bad deeds. The law of karma relates good and bad deeds done during an individual's lifetime. There is no ultimate standard, though lists appear in the various scriptures as dharma.
Salvation	Escaping the cycles of samsara is the goal, achieving moksha as a state of oneness with Brahman. Moksha is achieved through yoga practices and creating good karma by doing good deeds and living a virtuous life.
Creation	There are many universes, each bound in a cycle, that emanate from Brahman. All of creation is an expression of Brahman (pantheism). There are many variations of creation myths in Hinduism, some of which would embrace evolutionary ideas as part of the process of the universal cycles.

Chapter 5

Jainism

Dr. Daniel Anderson

There lived a family in a farm house. They were enjoying the fresh, cool breeze coming through the open doors and windows. The weather suddenly changed, and a terrible dust storm set in. Realizing it was a bad storm, they got up to close the doors and windows. By the time they could close all the doors and windows, much dust had entered the house. After closing all of the doors and windows, they started cleaning away the dust that had come into the house.[1]

This brief illustration has been used as an analogy to capture the essence of life as a follower of the religious system known as Jainism. What is the meaning of the recounting of this rather ordinary event? How does this analogy portray a spiritual concept or a religious system? To fully grasp how this "farmhouse" illustration summarizes spiritual ambition, it is necessary to explore the history, doctrine, and practices of Jainism.

Historical Background

Jainism (jī·nih·zəm), traditionally known as Jain Dharma, is a religious system originating in India during the sixth century B.C. as a reformation

---

1. Jainism Global Resource Center, "Introduction," accessed February 2, 2016, www.Jain-world.com/philosophy/fundamentals.asp.

movement within Hinduism.[2] The adherents of Jainism follow the religious teachings of Vardhamana Mahavira who, according to Jain tradition, was the last of a succession of 24 Tirthankaras (saints). In addition to liberating their own souls, these Tirthankaras spent their lives teaching others the path to *moksha* (salvation).

Mahavira was also known as the "Jina" (Victor), from which the term "Jainism" comes. The concept of victory describes the conquest of one's self over inner enemies such as pride or anger, as well as the conquering of any worldly passions through the practice of a rigid asceticism and a life of extreme self-denial. Motivating this life of denial is the hope that the cycle of rebirth can be broken by overcoming the consequences of the rule of karma.

Essential to the practice of Jainism is the emphasis upon observing a life of nonviolence (*ahimsa*) to purge the soul (*jiva*) of karma. This exercise of ahimsa is fanatically observed in the avoidance of killing any living creature to the point of refraining from activities such as wearing silk, picking flowers, swatting at bugs, or eating honey, as it is the food of bees. Thus, the followers of Jainism are characterized as being one of the strictest vegetarian communities of any religious sect. Observing these strict guidelines is seen as essential to achieving the spiritual enlightenment that leads to moksha.

The Founder of Jainism

Vardhamana Mahavira (ca. 599–527 b.c.) was born in Bihar, India.[3] According to tradition, he lived in the same general area as the Buddha during approximately the same time period. Some will even note comparisons between the two religions and the two persons.[4]

Mahavira was particularly revered because of his life of denial and self-imposed hardship. According to Jain tradition, Mahavira grew up in a life of comfort and ease, abandoning it all at the age of 30 to wander throughout India for 12 years in silence and nakedness, enduring deprivation and abuse. His dedication attracted a following of disciples.

---

2. See chapter 4 in this volume for a full description of Hinduism.
3. Western scholars differ from the traditional Jaina dates, suggesting Mahavira lived from 480 to 408 b.c. See Charles Taliaferro and Elsa J. Marty, eds. *A Dictionary of Philosophy of Religion* (New York: The Continuum International Publishing Group, 2010), p. 126.
4. Our earliest accounts of either person (Buddha and Mahavira) were written hundreds of years after they lived. Some have proposed that variations of these two developed in the oral accounts. Others argue that Buddha and Mahavira go back to the same person because they have many recorded similarities. Though interesting, it is still unlikely due to the recorded differences.

Claiming to have achieved the state of infinite knowledge (*kevala*), Mahavira began to promote his beliefs through an organized brotherhood of monks who took oaths of celibacy. Completely opposed to the idea of a supreme being, he even denied any gods existed to be worshiped. However, his disciples exalted him as a deity, with later Jain writings describing him as descending from heaven, free from sin and from all earthly desires. They present him as an ideal model for all to follow.

The Basic Structure and Tenets of Jainism

The followers of Jainism are part of a four-fold congregation of adherents composed of monks, nuns, laymen, and laywomen. The basic tenets of the corporate body are identified as the three jewels (*triratna*):

- right faith (*samyagdarshana*)
- right knowledge (*samyagjnana*)
- right conduct (*samyakcharitra*)

Observing these jewels is believed to lead one to a liberation from the bondage of karma. Both monastic and lay followers take solemn vows to comply with these basic beliefs. Jains believe that observing the strictest of ethical behavior restructures one's karma, expelling dark materiality (*pap*) and nurturing light (*punya*), thus advancing one's progress toward the release from the cycle of rebirth.

While the founder of Jainism was noted for his life of solitude, monks and nuns today typically live in a collected setting (*gana*) where they may benefit from the counsel and instruction of those deemed to be superiors among the brotherhood. A formal system of ordination is carried out for those joining the gana, which requires the departure from one's home, the abandonment of all property, and the shaving of one's head. The initiate then receives the "equipment" of a monk, which includes an alms bowl, a broom, a napkin, and loincloths.

Central to the practice of all Jains, whether lay or monastic, is the taking of vows. The Mahavratas (five great vows) of monastic Jains mandate abstaining from:

1. the killing of any living things, frequently referenced as non-violence (*ahimsa*)
2. false speech (*satya*)

    3. taking what is not given (*asteya*)

    4. sexual pleasure (*brahmacarya*)

    5. worldly attachments (*aparigraha*)

The 12 Anuvrata (lesser vows) of a layperson are similar to the Great Vows but are less demanding and allow for a family life while still observing strict vegetarianism, diligent honesty, fidelity in marriage, and regular donations to religious persons and organizations. Additionally, both sets of vows forbid the taking of food or drink at night to minimize the risk of injury to insects, which might go unnoticed in the darkness.

Jain literature defines explicit guidelines for a monk's religious conduct on a daily basis involving such activities as begging, confession, and study. Compliance with the five great vows govern all of these activities. Beyond these five great vows, monks and nuns must comply with five rules of conduct known as *samiti*. Intended to increase awareness of the soul, both personally and in others, these five rules of conduct are:

- care in walking
- care in speaking
- care in accepting things from others
- care in picking up and putting down objects
- care in the performance of excretory functions[5]

In the first century A.D. a major division developed within Jainism leading to the formation of two distinct sects: the Digambaras and the Svetambaras. The primary issue was controversy over the practice of nudity as an evidence of ultimate deprivation and self-denial. Mahavira, the founder of Jainism, had practiced nakedness as a mark of rigid asceticism; loyal followers of Mahavira believed that they should do the same, determining that their nudity was in no way an act of moral impropriety. These Jains formed the Digambaras sect and were known as the "sky-clad" or "space-clothed."

The Svetambaras sect believed they should wear white robes and became known as the "white-clad." Because the basic tenets of Jainism had been well established by the time of this division, the Digambaras and Svetambaras adherents fundamentally agree in their primary beliefs.

---

5. John Cort, "Singing the Glory of Asceticism: Devotion to Asceticism in Jainism," *Journal of the American Academy of Religion*, vol. 70, no. 4 (December 2002): 83.

Ornate Jain temples exist around the world, including this one in Ranakpur, India.
(By Nagarjun Kandukuru, https://commons.wikimedia.org/w/index.php?curid=33434794)

The Growth and Spread of Jainism

Spread in India

Jainism originated in the northern state of Bihar, India. The ascetic life of Mahavira limited the extent of its influence during the early years of its existence. However, after Mahavira's time, the Jain community spread along the caravan routes from Bihar to the west and to the south where the teachings of Jainism were accepted by various princes and rulers. The Digambaras sect became particularly influential in the Deccan region with numerous variations of the sect being founded. The Svetambaras sect was especially successful in the Gujarat region with several of the kings of that area converting to Jainism. Adherents erected ornate worship centers such as that on Mount Abu, now in Rajasthan, during this period as well. Opposition resulting from Muslim invasions eventually led to the decline of Jainism in these locations.

Colette Caillat has noted that "although the Jain community never regained its former splendor, it did not disappear entirely; nowadays, the Digambaras are firmly established in Maharashtra and Karnataka and the

Svetambaras in Panjab, Rajasthan, and Gujarat. Jain businessmen are generally active in all the main cities of India, and many also outside India."[6] Currently, the Jains of India could be described as a small but influential and comparatively prosperous community engaged largely in commerce and finance. Many of India's prominent business leaders, financial leaders, and some political leaders are Jainists.[7]

Spread beyond India

Jainism has significantly spread outside India within the last 150 years. Prominent locations of Jains include the United Kingdom, the diamond business of Belgium, Singapore, Japan, Hong Kong, Kenya, Canada, and throughout the United States. In North America alone there are over 20 Jain Temples and 70 Jain Centers.[8]

Jainism first came to the United States in 1893 when Virchand Raghavji Gandhi delivered an address in Chicago at the World's Parliament of Religions (now identified as the Parliament of the World's Religions). In 1933, Champat Rai Jain gave a speech entitled "Ahimsa as the Key to World Peace" at the World Fellowship of Faiths. During the years following these initial occasions there was a small immigration of Jains. Turmoil in Kenya, Tanzania, and Uganda in the 1960s led to a significant increase in Jains fleeing those countries and eventually coming to the United States. They would often share worship areas with Hindus during these years. The Jain Center of New York was started in 1966, and the first designated Jain temple was opened in Boston in 1973. Additional temples and centers have been constructed in such prominent U.S. cities as Washington, DC, and Chicago. Every two years a major convention of Jainists sponsored by the Federation of Jain Associations in North America (JAINA) convenes. At the present time, JAINA estimates there are over 100,000 Jains living in North America.

Jainism has attracted significant attention in the United States in two ways related to their strong emphasis upon nonviolence (*ahimsa*). Because one of the prominent forms of charity practiced by Jainists is the provision of care facilities for diseased and disabled animals, such as the Jain Bird

---

6. Colette Caillat, "Jainism," *The Encyclopedia of Religion* (New York: Macmillan Publishing Co., 1987), p. 508.
7. *Columbia Electronic Encyclopedia*, s.v. "Jainism," 6th edition (2015): 1, accessed November 7, 2015.
8. According to JAINA: Federation of Jain Associations in North America in their JAINA/Jain Vision 2020. www.jaina.org.

Hospital in Delhi, animal rights groups have become increasingly interested in and supportive of Jainism.

The second evidence of attraction is the inclusion of Jain ethics in thousands of yoga studios.[9] Yoga teachers are incorporating the ethics of Patanjali's Yoga Sutra, which is related to the five vows of Jainism. In fact, this blend of yoga and Jainism has even begun to include environmental concerns as illustrated by the following "Green Affirmations of the Yamas" adopted and promoted by prominent yoga instructor Clayton Burns Horton (shown here in a reduced form).[10]

- I observe the results of my actions so that I may discontinue my tendencies that are hurtful to myself, other human beings and all of creation.

- By eating a plant based diet, I am minimizing global warming and world hunger.

- As I recognize divinity in all of creation, I recognize the sacredness of fragile ecosystems, all beings and myself.

- I give thanks for the food I eat, the water that I drink and for the blessings that I receive from the material world.

- Acknowledging that I consume and receive so much from our Mother Earth, I try to give back something, however I can.

- I look inwards, study yogic texts and commune with nature so that someday the nature of reality will be revealed to me.

- I wake early to do my Yoga practice with the rising Sun so that I may connect with and be in harmony with the natural diurnal rhythms of the Earth and Sun.

Basic Doctrines of Jainism

Jainism is a religion of demanded legalism that requires extreme asceticism to achieve one's own salvation. This belief leads to a system of doctrine completely derived from human reasoning and dependent upon human endeavors.

9. Christopher Key Chapple, "Jainism, Ethics, and Ecology." *Bulletin for the Study of Religion* 39, no. 2 (April 2010): 5.

10. Clayton Horton, "Green Affirmations of the Yamas & Niyamas," accessed January 11, 2016, http://www.greenpathyoga.org/article_affirmations.html.

View of Scripture

Beginning shortly after the establishment of their religion, Jains were prolific writers, composing a wide variety of literary works intended to both serve the followers of Jainism as well as provide an apologetic for their beliefs. The oldest texts were written in the Prakrit language, reflecting their origin in northern India.

Later literary works made use of Sanskrit, which became the primary language used in scholarly discussion. "From the first to the fifteenth century [A.D.] an enormous mass of literature was produced, covering a wide range of topics: dialectics and logic, politics and religious law, grammar, scientific subjects, epico-lyric poems devoted to 'universal history,' narratives on the Jain law, short stories illustrating the doctrinal teachings, gnomic poetry and hymns."[11]

While these writings serve as a source of direction and influence for Jains, they are not seen as canonical in the way that Christians view the Bible. Jains believe there were 14 *Purvas* (ancient knowledge) taught by Mahavira which contained all the knowledge available in this universe. These texts were eventually lost, though Jains claim that parts of the material were incorporated into various treatises. The two sects differ on which parts of the Purvas were preserved and which books contain the information. However, Umasvati's writing from around A.D. 100, known as *Tattvarthasutra*, is accepted as the authoritative text on Jain philosophy and teaching by both sects.

View of God

Claiming that the world as we know it is made of living souls (*jiva*) and nonliving matter (*ajiva*), "Jainism believes that [the] universe and all its substances or entities are eternal. It has no beginning or end with respect to time. [The] universe runs [on] its own accord by its own cosmic laws. All the substances change or modify their forms continuously. Nothing can be destroyed or created in the universe. There is no need of some one [sic] to create or manage the affairs of the universe. Hence, Jainism does not believe in God as a creator, survivor [sustainer], and destroyer of the universe."[12] God, in the Jain theology, is ultimately the term used to describe the person

---

11. Caillat, *The Encyclopedia of Religion*, p. 508.
12. Pravin K. Shah, "Concept of God in Jainism"; *Jainism Literature Center*, Jain Study Center of North Carolina; The Pluralism Project at Harvard University (online compilation accessed January 14, 2016).

who has reached perfection by destroying all of his karmas, achieving liberation of the soul (moksha). Once the karmas are destroyed, the person is described as possessing infinite knowledge and power and ultimate bliss.

Because of this view, every living being has the potential to become a god. Therefore, it is accurate to say that Jains do not have one god. In fact, they believe the number of gods continuously increases[13] as more souls (*jivas*) attain moksha, receiving the status of *siddhas*.

View of Salvation

As has been repeatedly stated, Jainism is a religious system of self-imposed afflictions for the purpose of achieving release from the bondage of karma. Karma consists of miniscule karman particles floating throughout the universe which attach to souls (jivas). These particles can be either good (*punya*) or bad (*pap*). The amount of karma depends upon the nature of the activity as well as the depth of passion associated with the activity.

Passions are like glue which bind the karma to the soul; an unintentional action (whether physical, verbal, or mental) or an action without passion will be easily separated from the soul. The greater the vigor of activity and intensity of passion the longer the bondage of karma — up to thousands or millions of years. Once the accumulated karma matures (produces its results), the soul experiences either good things such as happiness and material comfort from the punya, or suffering and poverty from the pap. Karma can be dealt with passively by waiting for the results to conclude or actively by following austerities such as fasting, isolation, meditation, charity, atonement, or spiritual study. After death, the complete and final liberation of the soul from karma is called *moksha*. It is important to note that this process of eradicating karma is only possible as one places firm faith in the commands, primarily the five vows, of Mahavira, the founder of Jainism.

To stop the flow of karma particles, one must practice a synthesis of exercising care, restraint, sufferings, and contemplations. Care is demonstrated in such ways as avoiding injury to any living being as one walks, or avoiding any speech that may incite responses like violence, gossip, flattery, or condemnation. Care even encompasses the proper disposal of trash or bodily excretions so that no harm is done to any living being.

---

13. According to Jain tradition, the last person in this time cycle to reach moksha was Jambu, who was only two generations removed from Mahavira; he was a disciple of Mahavira's disciple Sudharman. Therefore, no souls have attained moksha for almost 2,500 years. Padmanabh S. Jaini, *The Jaina Path of Purification* (Berkeley, CA: University of California Press, 1979), p. 46.

Restraint describes the disciplining of the mind to restrict expressions of extreme emotions such as grief, anger, joy, or anxiety. Speech may be restrained to the point of taking a vow of silence. Sufferings include enduring hardship such as hunger, thirst, celibacy, cold, heat, or even ragged clothing while demonstrating a sense of serenity and contentment.

Contemplations refers to a process of meditating and reflecting upon 12 specific categories called *bhavanas*, where one must "contemplate" subjects to eliminate or discard in order to advance in the removal of karma. There are many types of karmas, but they have been broadly classified into eight categories:

1. Mohniya karma — it generates delusion in the soul in regard to its own true nature, and makes it identify itself with other external substances

2. Jnana-varaniya karma — it covers the soul's power of perfect knowledge

3. Darsana-varaniya karma — it covers the soul's power of perfect visions

4. Antaraya karma — it obstructs the natural quality or energy of the soul as charity and will power. This prevents the soul from attaining liberation. It also prevents a living being from doing something good and enjoyable.

5. Vedniya karma — it obscures the blissful nature of the soul, and thereby produces pleasure and pain

6. Nama karma — it obscures the non-corporeal existence of the soul, and produces the body with its limitations, qualities, and faculties

7. Gotra karma — it obscures the soul's characteristics of equanimity, and determines the caste, family, social standing, and personality

8. Ayu karma — it determines the span of life [at one's] birth, thus obscuring the soul's nature of eternal existence[14]

A Jain's ambition is to eradicate all eight karma categories before death. The destruction of the first four (called *ghati karmas*) results in achieving the

---

14. Shah, "Concept of God in Jainism."

status known as *arihant*, whereby the restoration of the original attributes of the soul (perfect knowledge, perfect vision, perfect power, and perfect bliss) are attained. While still a human being in this status, the arihant has achieved a level of perfection which will never be tarnished by an influx of karma.

Once a person has destroyed his ghati karmas, he will definitely destroy the remaining four karmas, called *aghati* karmas, before his death. The accomplishment of this stage of destroying karma provides complete liberation and results in a status called the siddha. Siddhas are totally free from the birth and death cycle. They do not possess a physical body but rather enjoy everlasting bliss at the top of the universe. They have achieved moksha.

The removal of karma through various practices is believed to bring about liberation (moksha) of the soul.

Summary Illustration of Jain Doctrine

We began our discussion of Jainism by using an analogy that we can now interpret. The analogy stated the following:

> There lived a family in a farm house. They were enjoying the fresh, cool breeze coming through the open doors and windows. The weather suddenly changed, and a terrible dust storm set in. Realizing it was a bad storm, they got up to close the doors and windows. By the time they could close all the doors and windows, much dust had entered the house. After closing all of the doors and windows, they started cleaning away the dust that had come into the house.

The interpretation of this illustration incorporates some of the primary terms and beliefs of Jainism. That interpretation is as follows:

1. Jivas are represented by the people.

2. Ajiva is represented by the house.

3. Punya is represented by worldly enjoyment resulting from the nice, cool breeze.

4. Pap is represented by worldly discomfort resulting from the sand storm, which brought dust into the house.

5. Asrava is represented by the influx of dust through the doors and windows of the house, which is similar to the influx of karman particles to the soul.

6. Bandh is represented by the accumulation of dust in the house, which is similar to bondage of karman particles to the soul.

7. Samvar is represented by the closing of the doors and windows to stop the dust from coming into the house, which is similar to stoppage of influx of karman particles to the soul.

8. Nirjara is represented by the cleaning up of accumulated dust from the house, which is similar to shedding off accumulated karmic particles from the soul.

9. Moksha is represented by the clean house, which is similar to the shedding of all karmic particles from the soul.[15]

It obviously takes a great deal of understanding of Jainism to comprehend this analogy to its fullest degree. However, this succinct illustration, with its parallel meanings, quickly demonstrates the essence of the doctrine of Jainism which is dominated by a philosophy requiring a self-imposed abdication of fleshly gratification and devotion to the avoidance of harming others in order to achieve eternal "bliss." Tragically, one can never be certain of obtaining this bliss.

The Jain Symbol

Adopted by all sects of Jainism in 1975 in commemoration of the 2,500th anniversary of the death of Lord Mahavira, the official Jain emblem contains much symbolism.

---

15. Jainism Global Resource Center, "Introduction."

The hourglass outline symbolizes the shape of the universe as described in Jain literature.

The text below the hourglass reads, "All life is bound together by mutual support and interdependence."

The upraised hand includes the symbol for "ahimsa," the fundamental teaching of Jainism. This hand is intended as both a warning and a blessing — a warning to stop and consider one's actions so as not to perpetrate violence on another or on oneself, as well as a gesture of blessing for the soul who practices ahimsa. The circle further warns that the cycle of reincarnation awaits the soul who violates ahimsa.

The swastika's four arms (left figure above) represent the four primary types of souls: heavenly, human, animal, and hellish. During the cycle of reincarnation, faithfulness to ahimsa and diligence in austerities will determine into which of these four categories a soul may be reborn. In addition, the four arms represent the four classifications of Jain followers: monks (sadhus), nuns (sadhvis), and male and female laypersons (shravaks or shravikas).

Because of the swastika's association with Nazism, Jains in America have replaced that figure in the design with one that combines the word "Om" with the symbol for the Federation of Jain Associations in North America (JAINA) (figure on right above).

The three parallel dots at the top of the hourglass represent the "Three Jewels of Jainism" or what Jains consider to be the threefold path to moksha (liberation): Right Faith, Right Knowledge, and Right Conduct.

The crescent at the top of the hourglass stands for Siddhashila. In Jain cosmology, this upper part of the heavens is the final resting place for all liberated souls. The single dot above the arc represents a siddha (liberated soul).[16]

---

16. Information gathered from jainworld.com and pluralism.org; Illustrations: Official Jain Symbol clip art created by Mpanchratan as posted in Wikimedia Commons; Variant Jain Symbol clip art created by Etienekd as posted in Wikimedia Commons.

Primary Errors in Jainism

Jainism as a religious system has created its own terms and definitions. Part of the challenge of evaluating Jainism is understanding these terms so as to fairly assess their meaning and implications.

As has been noted, Jainism holds to a view of God that denies His very existence, instead defining "god" as humans who have destroyed all karma and have become gods. Jivas who have attained enlightenment are essentially seen as *god* in both existence and authority. There is no personal or separate person absolutely existing as God in Jainism.

Furthermore, there is no belief in a creation of the world by God. That denial of creation is further expressed as a rejection of any possibility of divine intervention in the history of the world, as seen in a Noahic universal Flood. Jainism claims that as humans we are the sole reason for suffering or happiness, both as an individual and on a corporate level.

A striking observation in all of the material about Jainism is their absence of any reference to Jesus Christ. They make no attempt to incorporate Him, even historically, into their religious system. Likewise, they make no inclusion of the Bible in their teachings.

Jainism will acknowledge the need for faith in order to reach the soul's intended destination of bliss. That faith, however, is placed in its founder, Mahavira, a mere man, and his teachings.

Concepts of heaven and hell are likewise erroneous in Jainism. Not only do souls exist on this earthly level, depending on the amount of good or bad karma accrued, a soul could also be punished in hell (infernal) until the bad karma is burned off and they are reincarnated into another body, or, for a time, a soul could enjoy a level of heaven (celestial) though not the complete liberation of moksha. The eradication of all karma and liberation from the reincarnation cycle would be equivalent to the classical definition of "heaven," but this destiny is never assured and certainly lacks any substantive hope. Hell as a place of punishment is not seen as an eternal reality; being trapped in the cycle of reincarnation because of the failure to destroy karma would be the equivalent to the classical view of "hell." Even at that, there is always the possibility in Jainism to eventually overcome the cycle of reincarnation and thus be freed from "hell."

The glaring error of Jainism in many ways is the utter hopelessness that exists in this religious system. There is no assured means of salvation, nor anyone to intercede for you. Any reference to salvation is usually identified with the word "liberated" and refers to the liberation from the reincarnation cycle. Without question, salvation to a Jainist is the performance of good works. One can never be certain that they have adequately achieved the necessary steps to eradicate karma and thus enter into eternal bliss. The depth of this hopelessness is powerfully illustrated in the description of what is called the "wise man's death," that is, the exalted fast-unto-death experience (*samlekhana*).[17]

Another question that arises is who judges the soul for good and bad? Judging is a specific action based on a standard of good and bad, and yet there is no true and absolute standard of good and bad or an absolute personal judge in the Jain view of the universe. If one is just to take someone's word for it (e.g., Mahavira or his early followers), then the definitions of good and bad are arbitrary, based on the opinions and writings of mere men.

Witnessing to Jains

While the religion of Jainism is relatively small in numbers, the followers of Jainism are widely scattered. This is somewhat due to the nature of occupations prevalent among Jainists that take them into cities all around the world. Therefore, it is important to be prepared to witness to these precious souls who need to trust Jesus Christ, since one never knows when an encounter with a Jain may occur.

As is true in any witnessing setting, it is imperative that a Christian prayerfully approach any opportunity to share the gospel with a sensitivity to the Holy Spirit's guidance. Likewise, a witness for the Lord must always rely upon the innate power of the Word of God, remembering that faith comes by hearing, and hearing by the Word of God (Romans 10:17).

One of the difficulties in reaching Jainists with the gospel is their tendency to restrict engagement with persons outside of their religious community. One of the primary reasons for that limitation is their strict vegetarian practices. That introduces one of the most important considerations in attempting to evangelize these people. Great caution must be exercised to avoid trespassing their vegetarian lifestyle. It is important to remember that the reason for their dietary practice is due to their dominant religious tenet of nonviolence (ahimsa). This tenet, more than any other, is central to their religious beliefs and is an intrinsic part of their culture.

---

17. Caillat, *The Encyclopedia of Religion*, p. 511.

This presents another important consideration when witnessing to a Jain. Because of their commitment to nonviolence, they are characteristically known for their gentle and contrite demeanor. Effective evangelization to Jains must be done with a spirit of gentleness and meekness. Simply stated, it is essential to demonstrate the fruits of the Spirit if one is to reach these souls with the gospel (Galatians 5:22–23).

At the same time, one must be careful not to amplify a Jain's tendency toward the promotion of wholesome, moral behavior. Moral conduct is a prominent component of their religion. Caution must be taken to avoid emphasizing the behavior of a Christian as though that is a part of becoming a Christian. Most dedicated Jainists are already well aware of and committed to a moral lifestyle. Care must be given instead to emphasizing the unique blessing of the grace of God as one shares that salvation is not by works of righteousness which we have done, but according to His mercy (Titus 3:5).

In seeking to witness to a Jain, one effective method to nurture a relationship is to regularly visit their shops. By engaging them in their area of business, it is possible to demonstrate the genuine love of the Lord to them in a way that is enviable to their desire to achieve moral goodness. There are ways to identify a business as owned by a Jain. First, many Jains take the name "Jain" as their last name. Second, the Jainists have a distinct symbol to identify their religion (as shown above). Observing either of these is a good indication that the individual is a Jain.

When seeking to introduce conversation about the gospel, it is valuable to identify Scriptures to relate to their concerns and interests. One passage which has proven effective when witnessing to Jains is the Sermon on the Mount, especially the Beatitudes, which emphasize the importance of moral behavior. Transitioning from interest in moral living to the One who gave these principles allows one to introduce Christ. Here one could also introduce them to the teaching of Jesus in Matthew 11:28–30, calling them to forsake their striving for perfection and accept that Jesus has accomplished our liberation on the Cross. Point them to the rest you have found in Christ.

Another effective avenue for witnessing is to discuss the meaning behind their word "Jaina," meaning "conqueror." Jains use that term to describe their founder who went to extreme measures attempting to conquer personal passions and sins. Presenting the message of the gospel and Christ's supreme example of sacrifice to assure us victory over sin can be used in an impacting way to a Jain.

Without a doubt, reaching Jains with the gospel can be a tedious and challenging task. May God give followers of Jesus Christ a dedication to living and giving the gospel that surpasses the dedication of those who have given themselves to the deception of Jainism. May each jiva come to know the true moksha as they realize that whoever calls upon the name of the Lord shall be saved (Romans 10:13).

Summary of Jain Beliefs

Doctrine	Teachings of Jainism
God	Deny the God of the Bible, including the possibility of a divine Savior. No mention of Jesus whatsoever. Each living soul (*jiva*) can progress to godhood by eradicating karma, thus achieving first enlightenment as a human (*arihant*) and then liberation after death (*moksha*) as a siddha. Jains consider both arihants and siddhas gods.
Authority/ Revelation	Fourteen original *Purvas* were recorded by Mahavira's disciples, but were largely lost. The later *Tattvarthasutra* writings are generally accepted as the authoritative text regarding Jain practices.
Man	All men are born carrying the karma from their previous life. There is no concept of an innate sin nature, but each individual must follow strict rules to avoid attracting additional karma.
Sin	Sin could loosely be defined as activities that attract bad karma. However, both good and bad karma are undesirable. The effects of karma can often be seen immediately in either suffering or enjoyment but may also carry over into the next life.
Salvation	Salvation is liberation from the effects of karma and the cycle of reincarnation. Karma is eradicated by austerities and keeping the 5 great vows or 12 lesser vows, the central tenets being nonviolence (*ahimsa*) and non-attachment. After death, liberated souls having achieved moksha ascend to the top of the universe (*siddhashila*).

Creation	The universe is eternal and uncreated, consisting of living souls (*jiva*) and nonliving matter (*ajiva*). There is no creator god. Evolutionary ideas are generally rejected, though some may accommodate them. Souls themselves may be seen as "evolving" as they progress through the karmic cycle, with the possibility that life may even exist within the most basic elements of nature.

Chapter 6

Sikhism

Steven Fazekas

Sikhism is a strange religion to people in many parts of the world. It has elements of Eastern religions like Hinduism and yet aspects of Middle Eastern thought like that of Islam. So what do we make of this?

The famous "duck test" is a humorous way of reasoning which asserts, "If it looks like a duck and swims like a duck and quacks like a duck, chances are it's a duck."

When it comes to the Eastern religions, there is a galaxy of gurus and a plethora of messiahs. Despite the things that differ, there is a consistent, almost monotonous sameness that, more times than not, gives the proverbial duck its "duckness," even though the respective beaks and webbed feet may appear a little bit different.

It is difficult to accept that the Sikh religion is a faith completely independent from Hinduism, Islam, or any other Eastern systems of belief. At some point, all of the foxes are joined at their tails.

In other words, Sikhism is a type of mixture between two religions — Hinduism and Islam. By the way, one might be tempted to argue, "Isn't this *sameness* found in the glut of Christian cults which are choking the Western mind as well?" Unfortunately, the answer is yes.

To the affirmative, there is a breathtaking surplus of mind-numbing views which have comfortably found a home in our Western culture where many groups borrow much of the Bible, then mix it with some other view to dilute to man's word.[1] Generally speaking, we might say that the heart of man worldwide is incurably religious.

What Is a Sikh?

Let's let the Sikh tell us what the Sikh is and does. The Rehat Maryada is the Sikh statement of beliefs and code of conduct. Article 1 states:

> Any human being who faithfully believes in: (1) One Immortal Being, (2) Ten Gurus, from Guru Nanak to Guru Gobind Singh, (3) The Guru Granth Sahib, (4) The utterances and teachings of the ten Gurus and (5) the baptism bequeathed by the tenth Guru, and who does not owe allegiance to any other religion, is a Sikh.[2]

The discerning mind, with a small amount of careful reading, will discover nothing unique in this definition. We have a call to belief in a supernatural Being, surrounded by a brotherhood of prophets who are devoted to a collection of prophetic writings, given to ritual, and devoted to no other worldview. We conclude, by way of definition, there is nothing unique that is not found in a hundred other religions.

Where Do I Find a Sikh?

The answer is "anywhere and everywhere." There are over 20 million followers of Sikhism, many of them having originated largely from the Punjab region of India, a highly cultural and religious area at a crossroads between areas dominated by Hinduism and Islam. In the day in which we live, Sikh communities are found in major population centers all over the world. Guru Nanak, who was born in 1469, was the founding apostle of Sikhism. We might say with a degree of accuracy that we are discussing a world religion that is comparatively young yet exceedingly well established.

The Sikh and the Nature of God

The Sikh view of God is distinctly different from the biblical view of God. They say:

---

1. These counterfeits of Christianity are explored in volume 1 of this work.
2. "Rehat Maryada," Sikhs.org, accessed November 19, 2015, http://www.sikhs.org/rehit.htm.

In Sikhism God is conceived in two forms i.e., in Nirguna form and in sarguna form. 'Ik' (meaning one) in Ikoankar defines Nirguna state of God. It is that state of God when He had not created the universe as yet. He was one and the only one at that time. He was in himself. There was no universe, no suns, no planets, no satellites, no living or non-living creatures, no good or bad deeds, no light, no days or nights. In fact there was total darkness at that time. God had not created in Himself His own powers, including the power of creation and the power of destruction. He was thus devoid of any characteristics or any qualities. He was one and only one. The ancient Hindu books describe this period of darkness, when God was one and only one, extending to 36 yugas (one yug is variously described as 1,000 years, 10,000 years or even more).

Once, Guru Nanak Dev Ji was asked by learned saints (Sidhas) to describe the "Nirguna" state of God. Guru Nanak Dev Ji replied that "Nirguna" state of God is a divine wonder. A man is too little a creature to even think of that state, let alone to describe that state. When God Himself had not acquired His power of creation, how can a created one, the human, think of that state of God? Everyone and everything is created by God. How can a created one think of the state of a creator when there was nothingness, no creation, only the creator. He, the creator, only knew about Himself of that state.[3]

Take note that God, in Sikhism, had to figure out how to create his own power and that man cannot comprehend this God.

Sikhs believe in one God who has gone by many names such as Ram, Rahim, Allah, Pritam, Yar, Mahakal, and Waheguru. To the Sikh, God is known by the inward eye of faith. Much like Islam, the Sikh God is omnipresent, timeless, universal, fearless, silent and self-existent, incomprehensible, genderless, and inaccessible with no form nor feature. Like Hinduism, communication between God and human beings can only take place through rigorous meditation, although you still can't really know God.

3. Sujan Singh, Guru Nanak Ki Bani website, "Concept of God in Sikhism," accessed 9/16/2015, http://www.gurunanakkibani.com/index.php/concept-of-god-in-sikhism.

These things being understood, many a devout Sikh has said, "We are all children of the same Universal Divine Love."

This concept of the Sikh God presents several internal problems. If this God is incomprehensible and inaccessible, then how can anyone know anything about the Sikh God? Since their God has not revealed truth, any human assertion about this God is unverifiable. This provides a logical refutation of the existence of the Sikh concept of God. For example, how can it be known that this God is loving if he is impersonal and incomprehensible?

Considerer that the Sikh God is not a *personal* God like the God of the Bible. This being the case, how then can anything in personal experience describe this God? There cannot be a personal revelation from an impersonal God; thus any alleged prophets claiming to speak for this impersonal Sikh God cannot be doing so.

The God of the Bible is a personal God who made us in His image (Genesis 1:26–28). Thus it is possible for personal revelation to exist through prophets and apostles by the power of the Holy Spirit revealing God to man.

The Word: Written and Living

The written authority for the faithful Sikh is their own version of the authoritative text called the *Guru Garanth Sahib*. It contains the writings of their designated holy men along with large portions of hymns and poetry claimed to have been passed down to them directly by God (see the explanation of this inconsistency above).

Guru Nanak (1469–1532), as the first guru and self-proclaimed prophet, was a prime contributor to this collection of writings; however, there were others who were highly esteemed in the Sikh community over the centuries whose works were added. The writing of the Sikh canon closed with the last guru (1709) making ten final prophetic voices, nine embodied as gurus in the flesh and one as written text. The *Guru Garanth Sahib* is considered the ultimate written source of spiritual encouragement for the devout Sikh.

Of course, we can ask, by what standard is this ultimate written source judged? By God's standard, revealed in the Bible, the alleged Sikh scriptures falls tragically short as the ultimate standard.

In contrast, the Christian holds the Bible as the only judge in all matters of faith and practice. For the Christian, the era of God revealing Scripture to men has ended. The Book of Jude teaches that the faith *was once for all delivered to the saints* (Jude 1:3). Thus, there was no need for further revelation after the New Testament was completed and no need for more prophets. Any alleged prophets after the New Testament must be considered false prophets.

The authority of the Old and New Testament is sufficient. The preface of the Chicago Statement on Biblical Inerrancy clearly states:

> The authority of Scripture is a key issue for the Christian Church in this and in every age. . . . To stray from Scripture in faith or in conduct is disloyalty to our Master. Recognition of the total truth and trustworthiness of the Holy Scripture is essential to a full grasp and adequate confession of its authority.[4]

In other words, this Christian truth claim also sets forth a revealed document (understood to be 66 unified books comprising the Old and New Testaments) that is inerrant, infallible, free from falsehood, duplicity, and deceit, and totally trustworthy in all that it asserts, as the dominant worldview. Unlike the Sikh God, the God of the Bible is personal and knowable, having made us in His image and revealed Himself to us because He loves us.

> Knowing this first, that no prophecy of Scripture is of any private interpretation, for prophecy never came by the will of man, but holy men of God spoke as they were moved by the Holy Spirit (2 Peter 1:20–21).[5]

Further, when examining other worldviews, the believing Christian is exhorted from the pages of the Bible to be clothed with a cautious discernment.

> Beloved, do not believe every spirit, but test the spirits, whether they are of God; because many false prophets have gone out into the world. By this you know the Spirit of God: Every spirit that confesses that Jesus Christ has come in the flesh is of God (1 John 4:1–2).

The caution in this text points to the "pseudo-prophet," the one who pretends to have special gifts from God and who invites the sincere seeker of the

---

4. http://storage.cloversites.com/gracechurch2/documents/CHICAGO%20STATEMENT.pdf.
5. Scripture in this chapter is from the New King James Version (NKJV) of the Bible.

truth to embrace a message which may sound enticing but will ultimately fail the test. Here are a few brief examples.

The Sikh teaches there are numerous pathways which lead to God.	The Christian embraces the words of Jesus: "No one comes to the Father except through Me" (John 14:6).
The Sikh denies being specially chosen by God.	The Christian claims an exclusive divine sonship rooted in faith: "To them He gave the right to become children of God, to those who believe in His name"(John 1:12).
The Sikh says that members of all religions share the same rights and privileges and liberties.	The Christian embraces the words of Scripture: "If we, or an angel from heaven, preach any other gospel to you than what we have preached to you, let him be accursed. As we have said before, so now I say again, if anyone preaches any other gospel to you than what you have received, let him be accursed" (Galatians 1:8–9).

The Christian faith teaches that God Himself has come to earth, clothed in flesh (which is purportedly to Eastern thought a bad thing), and having spoken to us through the prophets, has in these last days spoken to us through His Son, Jesus Christ (Hebrews 1:1–2). The difference, to all other claims, is found in the Son of God.

It is really against the truth claim of the Christian Scriptures as both the written and the living Word that we will attempt to address some of the components of the Sikh religion, its doctrine, philosophy, and spiritual claims.

Sikhism as Religion

The word "religion" itself is sometimes difficult to explain. Webster defines it as "beliefs embracing the cause, nature, and purpose of the universe and containing a moral code for the human race usually with a ritual observance of faith." This definition seems to work for our purposes, though a proper definition would involve much more than this.

There is disagreement among Sikh scholars with regard to its roots. However, Sikhism appears to be the product of a number of strong influences, such as the Sant tradition blended together with elements of Hinduism,

Jainism, and Islam. Sikhism appears to be a syncretism of Eastern religious ideas. Emerging from this milieu is the coming together of polytheism and monotheism, that is, one God manifesting himself in many different ways.[6]

The historic Christian confessions of faith, regardless of denomination, with one voice and without embarrassment proclaim the nature of God as three divine persons (Father, Son, and Holy Spirit) sharing one divine essence. Here is both unity and diversity blended together. Contrary to most Eastern religions is the Christian worldview that God is not a solitary unity but a composite unity. The words *Trinity, triune,* and *Trinitarian,* are not in the Bible, but they are necessary descriptive units indicative of both the mystery and reality of the God we love and serve and the things most surely believed among us who look to the Bible as the source of truth about God.

Sikhism as Philosophy

The underlying philosophic basis for most Eastern religions, including Sikhism, is what is known as "monism."

Monism can be illustrated in this way: Even as the river flows endlessly toward the ocean and becomes assimilated into that broad liquid expanse by finally "coming home," so the *self* enters its own journey, ever seeking, ever searching for home by way of a lifelong pilgrimage. Full liberation becomes "salvation" when the *finite* becomes one, merging with the *infinite*. This, to the Eastern mind, is redemption. It is the struggle of a good soul trapped inside an evil body of flesh wrestling to escape until full liberation takes place. In a sense, the human body to the Sikh is viewed as the prison house of the soul.

Monism is basically the idea that all is one, and our problem is that we don't realize that all is one! The human flaw is in continuing to draw distinctions that separate us from the "oneness of reality" rather than seeking unity of all things. Some claim that Christianity carries the same basic teaching since we are to "merge" with the Divine. The Christian "merging" may on the surface appear the same, but in fact is radically different. Hear the words of Jesus.

> . . . that they all may be one, as You, Father, are in Me, and I in You; that they also may be one in Us, that the world may believe that You sent Me (John 17:21).

---

6. Sean O'Callaghan, *The Compact Guide to World Religions,* "Sikhism" (Oxford, England: Lion Hudson, 2010), p. 129.

For the Christian, to be united with the Divine is permeated with sonship, as we are united to Christ as adopted sons and daughters and have the Spirit of God living within us.

The "Light" in All of Us

> Deep within the self is the Light of God. It radiates throughout the expanse of His creation. Through the Guru's Teachings, the darkness of spiritual ignorance is dispelled. The heart-lotus flower blossoms forth, and eternal peace is obtained, as one's light is merged into the Light.[7]

In 1974, a country and western song by Donna Fargo hit the charts:

> You can't be a beacon if your light don't shine.
> There's a little light in all of us by God's design.

It's a catchy little tune. However, the only problem with it is . . . it simply isn't true. The Sikh claim that men are all endowed with the same divine potential, that divinity permeates everyone and everything, is simply not true. It's a nice thought but totally opposite to the teaching of the Bible.

The Bible tells us that man's problem from the very beginning is the overwhelming desire to *be* the light of deity on earth.

> Then the serpent said to the woman, "You will not surely die. For God knows that in the day you eat of it your eyes will be opened, and you will be like God, knowing good and evil (Genesis 3:4–5).

As optimistic as this quest for inner light sounds, the Bible does not paint an overly optimistic picture of the heart of man. According to Jesus, who happens to be the One who exhaustively knows the human condition, we consider His words carefully.

> For out of the heart proceed evil thoughts, murders, adulteries, fornications, thefts, false witness, blasphemies (Matthew 15:19–20).

The Bible also speaks of the heart in other passages:

---

7. Guru Amar Das, Majh, p. 126, http://www.sikhs.org/english/eg1.htm#p13.

The heart is deceitful above all things, and desperately wicked; who can know it? (Jeremiah 17:9).

And the LORD smelled a soothing aroma. Then the LORD said in His heart, "I will never again curse the ground for man's sake, although the imagination of man's heart is evil from his youth; nor will I again destroy every living thing as I have done" (Genesis 8:21).

Today's Western society practices self-deification of the individual (i.e., man is the ultimate authority, not God). The promotion of the "self" is also highly significant in the Sikh worldview. All men, to some degree, are practical Sikhs when it comes to their inner passions for deification and cosmic recognition. Frankly put, we all want to be the God of our life in one way or the other, which is contrary to the Bible.

Basic to Christian thought is the Fall of man and his rebellion toward his Maker. Whatever shines from man, it's hardly the "light of God" shining forth from the inner self.

As it is written: "There is none righteous, no, not one; there is none who understands; there is none who seeks after God. . . . there is none who does good, no, not one. . . . destruction and misery are in their ways. . . . There is no fear of God before their eyes (Romans 3:10–18).

Sin has corrupted the human race, mind, will, and emotions. We have been affected, not only in our actions but also in our basic disposition toward sin. The Bible tells us we are slaves to sin (Romans 6:20) and our inner disposition is revealed with these words: Men love darkness rather than light because their deeds are evil (John 3:19).

The Six Badges of Sikh Identity

There are six insignias which the devout Sikh (Khalsa) wear as an outward sign of recognized piety.[8]

- KESH — uncut hair, kept in place by a turban (dastar), and a beard (for men) symbolizing dedication and a connection to other Khalsa

---

8. "The Khalsa," Sikhs.org, http://www.sikhs.org/khalsa.htm.

- DASTAR — a turban to signify dignity and self-esteem

- KANGHA — a comb worn in the hair symbolizing hygiene and discipline

- KIRPAN — a short sword indicating the desire to help the defenseless

- KARA — steel bracelet showing God's unity and as a reminder to show restraint

- KACHHAS — baggy shorts showing readiness to action and chastity

These six symbols are parts of the attire identifying Khalsa, "The Pure Ones," as a kind of righteous standard of initiation.

Under the Old Covenant, the Bible teaches the badge of Abraham's descendants as circumcision. This was a ritual ceremony of cutting the flesh performed on the male child usually around eight days of age.

It is made clear in the coming of Messiah that there is a New Covenant, and in Christ Jesus neither circumcision nor uncircumcision means anything,[9] but rather a new creation (Galatians 6:15). In other words, the significance of an external badge of distinction and identity is removed when Messiah comes and a new heart is given. Those with the "pure heart" are those with a spiritually circumcised heart. All the outer trinkets and symbols and gadgets and items of attire of Sikhism are insignificant when Jesus Christ grants a new heart, because along with it comes the power of a changed life.

There is an answer, and it is found in the absolute incomparable uniqueness of the Son of God Himself. The difference is in the Son!

The Things Surely Believed Among Us

To the Christian, every truth claim, including Sikhism, is held up against the incarnate Son of God in His life and death on behalf of a fallen race, and without exception, each claim is found woefully wanting.

The historic Westminster Confession of Faith sets forth one of the most marvelous statements on Jesus Christ in language worthy of committing to memory by every confessing believer in the gospel. Lofty language? Maybe.

9. Circumcision was a physical shadow of the *spiritual circumcision of the heart* for those who are descendants of Abraham who love the Lord their God with all their heart and all their soul (Deuteronomy 30:6; Luke 10:27–28; Romans 4:16, 9:6–8).

But we have here set forth to us a magnificent, majestic God who does not hide His glory, but has revealed Himself to the world in great humility and breathtaking condescension in the Person of the Son.

> The Son of God, the second person in the Trinity, being very and eternal God, of one substance and equal with the Father, did when the fullness of time was come take upon him man's nature, with all the essential properties, and common infirmities thereof, yet without sin; being conceived by the power of the Holy Ghost in the womb of the virgin Mary, of her substance. So that two whole, perfect, and distinct natures, the Godhead and the manhood, were inseparably joined together in one person, without conversion, composition, or confusion. Which person is very God, and very man, yet one Christ, the only Mediator between God and man.[10]

There is something radically life changing in the marketplace of world religions. There is something that has been elevated high above the "monotonous sameness" of world religions. It is God in Christ reconciling the world to Himself by the gospel.

Unlike Sikhism, in Christianity God became a man (the God-man) to suffer and die on our behalf to make salvation possible. Sikhism recognizes there is a problem of evil, but doesn't offer its origins or the way to escape it. According to God's Word, man (in Adam) sinned against God, bringing death, suffering, and evil as a punishment for sin (e.g., Genesis 2:17, 3:19; Romans 5:12).

Since we are all descendants of Adam, we are all sinners. God, being perfectly holy and just, must punish sin. The punishment for sin is death, and the power behind it is infinite in its force, being that God is infinite in His nature. This death would thus result in an eternal punishment for high treason against God.

Yet God did the unthinkable. God stepped into history in the person of His Son, Jesus the Christ, to become a man to take the punishment (on our behalf) from the infinite God in the person of the Father. The infinite Son took that infinite punishment. This then satisfied the wrath of God upon

---

10. Westminster Confession of Faith, "Of Christ the Mediator," chapter 8, par. 2, http://www.reformed.org/documents/wcf_with_proofs/index.html.

sin, and the Lord offers the unmerited free gift of salvation through the shed blood of Jesus Christ alone.

The Central Philosophy of Monism

Again, the overarching premise of most Eastern religions, including Sikhism, is what is known as *monism*.

Monism can be illustrated in a number of different ways. Even as a river flows endlessly toward the ocean and becomes absorbed and liberated into the wide expanse of waters, so the self enters a kind of lifelong pilgrimage whereby the individual becomes set free by merging with some impersonal God or ultimate source of reality.

This, of course, brings to mind a simple question: How can one know this? An impersonal God cannot communicate with man in a *personal* way to reveal this alleged truth. After all, language and communication is personal. A leading Sikh guru states:

> He who created the worlds, solar systems and galaxies —
> that God cannot be known.[11]

If the Sikh God cannot be known, then how can anyone know anything about him or even know that he cannot be known? When monism is mixed with monotheism it becomes inherently illogical.

Over time and through striving, the finite supposedly achieves unity with the absolute. Without some form of revelation, this idea becomes a mere arbitrary assertion.

Another way of explaining monism might be in a kind of migration of the soul as it goes through cycle after cycle of birth and death until it attains the form of humanity. A basic tenet of Eastern thinking is, "God is all, and all is God." Therefore, in some mystical metaphysical way, all of reality including man himself is, in a sense . . . deity. This is problematic logically. If all is already one, then there is no distinction, and if distinction really exists, then there cannot be an ultimate form that is pure unity.

Sikhism teaches that ultimate salvation is thus achieved by living an exemplary life, virtuous and truthful, frugal and honest until one may finally experience the merging of the Infinite with the finite.

---

11. SriGranth.org, "Sri Guru Granth Sahib," p. 907, http://www.srigranth.org/servlet/gurbani.gurbani?Action=Page&Param=907&english=t&id=38944#l38944.

The soul goes through cycles of births and deaths before it reaches the human form. The goal of our life is to lead an exemplary existence so that one may merge with God.[12]

But why? If there is really no distinction in the ultimate oneness that is monism, then lying and truth have no distinction. What real difference is there between an exemplary life and a miserable life?

Lamentably, there is an absence of grace in Sikh teaching. Here is where the Son makes the difference. How does the Sikh know for certain that he or she has lived a life that is commendable enough to gain assimilation into the One? How does the devout Sikh come to full knowledge that there are enough good works accrued to one's account to assure final peace with God? Assurance is virtually unknowable without the Son.

> For by grace you have been saved through faith, and that not of yourself, it is the gift of God; not of works, lest anyone should boast. For we are His workmanship, created in Christ Jesus for good works, which God prepared beforehand that we should walk in them (Ephesians 2:8–10).

The Sikh life of absorption into Oneness through good works is totally contrary to grace and the work of Christ on the Cross. While Christians pursue a virtuous life, it is not *for* salvation, but *because of God's grace in their life.* While the life of a Sikh and a Christian may appear similar on the outside, the motivation could not be more different.

Man in Creation

The Bible teaches the uniqueness of God's creation, especially His crowning achievement, man, whom He made in His own image.

> What is man that You are mindful of him, or the son of man that You take care of him? You have made him a little lower than the angels; You have crowned him with glory and honor, and set him over the works of Your hands. You have put all things in subjection under his feet (Hebrews 2:6–8).

---

12. "Introduction to Sikhism," Sikhs.org, accessed November 30, 2015, http://www.sikhs.org/summary.htm.

Sikhism has a low view of man and can never achieve the freedom found in Jesus Christ because it has a faulty, pessimistic view of humanity. To the Eastern mind, man is a good soul trapped in evil flesh trying to escape. The ultimate goal of man is the absorption of the human soul into the Great Divine Spirit. It might be called "the great escape."

This enslavement to the evil world (maya) is a product of the creation and is ultimately attributed to the divine, not man's actions in rebelling against the Creator. Man has been enslaved to evil since his creation rather than created perfect and experiencing a fall from that state.

Sikhs view the creation as having no ultimate beginning, but the physical aspects had a beginning and resulted from the will of the Creator. Describing the nature of creation, they say *the Lord is in his creation and the creation is in the Lord as all are in the One and the One is in all.* So the creation is the Creator, which is ultimately absurd. A Sikh apologetics website, Real Sikhism, states that the Sikh God created the entire universe and earth and life, though there is a twist. They write:

> Sikhism states that God created the entire Universe and the Universe including the Earth has been evolving since then. Earth while being in the Universe is a creation of God and all the life on the Earth is a creation of God. However, Sikhs respectfully disagree with Christians that the Earth was created 6000 years ago. Sikhism instructs that the Universe has been going on for billions of years. The Universe, including billion of stars, planets and the moons revolving the planets were created by God and it has been evolving since. In addition, this is not the first time God has created the Universe; He has done it many times.[13]

The Sikh God has allegedly made many universes over time! Universes include the *time dimension.* In light of this, their God must have created *time* more than once. Again we see how the arbitrary claims create internal contradictions. Sri Guru Granth Sahib Ji states:

> (Before the creation of the world) for endless eons, there was only utter darkness. There was no earth or sky; there was

---

13. Real Sikhism, "Sikh Views on Christianity: Do Sikhs believe in creation or evolution?" accessed November 30, 2015, http://realsikhism.com/index.php?subaction=show-full&id=1226710464&ucat=7.

only the infinite Command of His Hukam [will]. There was no day or night, no moon or sun; Vaheguru sat in primal, (like) in profound undisturbed meditation.[14]

If God existed in time, then time is superior to the Sikh God and he is bound by time. Os Guiness notes,

> Monism does not see man's dilemma as moral (in terms of what he has done) but as metaphysical (in terms of who he is). Monism thus leads to the notion that a man cannot be helped as an individual because it is his individuality which is the essential problem. He must be helped from his individuality; he must merge with the Absolute to reach salvation.[15]

Monism implies that human individuality must be lost or absorbed or assimilated into a larger whole in order to attain true freedom. In other words, to the Sikh it is a freedom *from* individuality. But how do they know this is really freedom? Did one rise from the dead to prove Sikhism was correct in the afterlife? No.

This idea of being absorbed into the Divine holds true in many Eastern religions. In contrast, the Bible sets forth the opposite. Man is amazingly complex, made in the image and likeness of God, and endowed with individuality, personality, mind, will, and emotions, all as an expression of the One who created him. The real problem is moral in its apostasy and expressed in rebellion toward a good and gracious Creator. The Sikh's problem is not finitude but sin.

Illusion of the Five Thieves

Chaucer had his Seven Deadly Sins. The Apostle Paul devastatingly cites what he calls the works of the flesh in Galatians 5:19–22. Sikhism has its "Five Thieves." All of these are simply variation on a theme and nothing new. "The Five Thieves," so called, are not just five bad acts, but rather they are the five bad acts from a bad heart. These acts come from the perception of reality and attachment to it, known as *maya*. To the Sikh, reality is a perceived illusion that must be escaped by avoiding the five forms of

---

14. Sikh Answers "How was the world created, according to Sikhi?" accessed November 30, 2015, http://www.sikhanswers.com/god-and-his-universe/creation-of-world/.

15. Os Guiness, *The Dust of Death*, "The East: No Exit," out of print; http://www.str.org/articles/reflections-on-hinduism#.VsysURh4yoI.

attachment. Whether these be *ego, anger, greed, worldly attachment, or lust,* "relentless devotion" cannot be the Sikh antidote to the things which so easily cause us to stumble. While the Christian can agree with the Sikh that these are vices, we know that they are sinful because they are contrary to the will of God and His character (revealed in the Bible). The cure is found in Paul's letter to the Romans 8:13–14.

> For if you live according to the flesh you will die; but if by
> the Spirit you put to death the deeds of the body, you will live.

The larger context of Romans chapter 8 will disclose the Trinitarian nature of the real antidote to these "Five Thieves," and many others that plague all of humanity. The "putting to death" of these five deadly sins are really the activities of the Father (Romans 8:15), the Son (Romans 8:3), and the Holy Spirit (Romans 8:9), and require so much more than mere "relentless devotion." The work of the Son on the Cross was not only relentless, but it was also thorough enough for Him to cry out, "It is finished."

There truly is no escape through any religion, Eastern or otherwise, which does not recognize the absolute uniqueness of the Son of God.

> O Christ our hope, our heart's desire, redemption's only spring,
> Creator of the world thou art, its Savior and its King.
> How vast the mercy and the love which laid our sins on Thee
> And led Thee to a cruel death to set Thy people free.
>
> O Christ be Thou our present joy, our future great reward,
> Our only glory may it be to glory in the Lord.
> All praise to Thee ascended Lord, all glory ever be,
> To Father, Son and Holy Ghost through all eternity.
> (Seventh to Eighth Century, Author Unknown)

Summary of Sikh Beliefs

Doctrine	Teachings of Sikhism
God	Deny the existence of the biblical God or a personal God, but are monotheistic. Deny that Jesus was God. View God as the Supreme Lord who created the universes and is described by many names. Their God is timeless, formless, fearless, universal, and self-existent.

Authority/ Revelation	The Guru Granth Sahib is a collection of sayings of the gurus and is viewed as the authoritative scripture of Sikhs.
Man	Men are conscious souls created by the Divine with attachment to the physical creation. All men are seeking to escape the cycle of births and deaths that attach them to the "unreality" of the physical world (maya).
Sin	Sin is viewed as five vices (ego, anger, greed, worldly attachment, and lust) that proceed from a bad heart and failure to realize that the world is not the ultimate goal.
Salvation	Salvation is equated with merging into the Divine of the universe. Salvation is achieved by following the guru's commands and meditating on the Divine Name. There is no concept of hell, but of returning to the cycle of births and deaths until achieving unity with the Divine.
Creation	The Creator created all of the universe and souls of living things with an attachment to the physical, evolving aspects of the creation. Life was created on many worlds. Many universes have been created.

Chapter 7

Moralistic and Mythological Religions: The Overview

Bodie Hodge and Roger Patterson

Does morality exist? If you don't want to get shot and killed, raped and tortured, stolen from and lied to, you are probably going to say yes! But why? *Why* does morality exist?

In the Christian worldview, morality exists because God is the *ultimate* lawgiver and the *supreme* basis for what is right and wrong. Thus, God's Word, the 66 books of the Bible, defines morality as a direct revelation of God's will for His creatures. Morality exists because God exists. Apart from God, there is no consistent grounding for determining what is true and holy.

But there are many people who believe in morality and yet do not hold the Bible as authoritative. Nor do they particularly hold to any God or gods in their worldview. Sometimes they hold to a vague notion of a universal force similar to a god or gods, but this god or force does not inform their morality. Morality comes strictly from man's experience and rationality in these systems. These are immanent moralistic religions, taking their cues of right and wrong based on what they immediately experience through nature or natural law.

Moralistic religions are *humanistic* by nature because they have elevated man's authority (human authority) to be greater than God and His Word on the issue of morality. In other words, people set their own morality or merely appeal to other people as those who define morality. Moralistic religions deny God's Word on morality and, by default, must appeal to their authority as absolute. Man is the ultimate standard of right and wrong in a moralistic religion.

Moralistic Religions

Moralistic religions encompass religious types that rarely have theistic elements but preach that there is some sort of code of behavior that needs to be adhered to. These sorts of religions basically believe there is some type of overarching code of morality that exists and should be followed but often do not include absolute morality.

Some of the more popular forms of this religion come from the East, such as Confucianism or Buddhism. In these, Buddha or Confucius (or other ancient sages) are seen as the ones who set the moral code to follow. Moralistic religions have appeared all over the world.

Even secular humanism could be classed as a form of this religion since there is a type of code of behavior, though it constantly changes and varies by individual. Although, we are placing secular humanism with the humanistic/atheistic religions in the third volume of this book series, it could rightly be in this volume. We have included Unitarian Universalism in this volume, though it aligns strongly with secular humanism. As mentioned elsewhere, with the classification system we are using, several of the religions could be placed in several categories.

Most of the adherents of moralistic religions might surprise you. They are individuals who often insist they have no religion or embrace multiple religious ideas! Of course, this is still a humanistic religious view that reflects one's morality and way of thinking about the world. This is why there are so many different forms of moralistic religions, since many are unaffiliated.

Moralism Invading the Church

This view has become a fixture of churches in the Christianized West. Sadly, it affects unsuspecting persons even in church pews. Often, many people consider themselves moral and believe this is good enough to be right with God. In other words, people walking on the street or attending churches may think that they are good enough for something better in the afterlife because they view themselves as "good people," often comparing themselves to some murderer or terrorist. Their moral code says, "As long as I am better than those wicked people, God will accept me." This is moralism and is a grave error — a damnable error.

Jesus dealt with a person who was a moralist. Consider Matthew 19:16–22:

> Now behold, one came and said to Him, "Good Teacher, what good thing shall I do that I may have eternal life?"
>
> So He said to him, "Why do you call Me good? No one is good but One, that is, God. But if you want to enter into life, keep the commandments."
>
> He said to Him, "Which ones?"
>
> Jesus said, " 'You shall not murder,' 'You shall not commit adultery,' 'You shall not steal,' 'You shall not bear false witness,' 'Honor your father and your mother,' and, 'You shall love your neighbor as yourself.' "
>
> The young man said to Him, "All these things I have kept from my youth. What do I still lack?"
>
> Jesus said to him, "If you want to be perfect, go, sell what you have and give to the poor, and you will have treasure in heaven; and come, follow Me."
>
> But when the young man heard that saying, he went away sorrowful, for he had great possessions.[1]

This person speaking to Jesus had the *basic* morality as he claimed to have kept the commandments, held to the concept of good coming from God, and wanted to do a good work to enter into heaven. But this man could not part with his possessions to follow Christ. He was focused on obeying a system and had deceived himself into thinking he had perfectly obeyed every command.

But he was missing something. He did not understand that the commandments pointed to Christ who fulfilled the law and is the epitome of good. Yet in his heart of hearts, this man chatting with Jesus realized he needed more. His hope was not in Christ, but in obeying a moral code to be good enough to be fit for heaven. What he did not realize is that the one who had already obeyed on his behalf was standing right in front of him. His own works, stained with his own sin and self-righteousness,

---

1. Scripture in this chapter is from the New King James Version (NKJV) of the Bible.

could never satisfy God's standard of perfect obedience. Only through Christ can we find the means to be good enough to inherit eternal life. This example shows how moralism invades even godly religion and makes it of no effect.

We find moralism influencing many unsuspecting people in church congregations. They often buy into this idea that if they are a "good person" or do some good works, then they will be saved in the end. But they are not good enough if they have committed even one sin. To go to heaven, you must be perfect — a standard none of us can achieve given our inherited sin nature and our individual choices to sin.

So is it impossible to go to heaven? One would think, but in steps, the Lord God helps us to do the impossible (Luke 18:27). Jesus, who is God, became a man and took our punishment upon Him through His shed blood. In doing so, Jesus was without sin and perfect. Those who receive Christ share in Christ's righteousness. His perfection is imputed (transferred) to us, so that we are seen as spotless and without blemish to enter heaven for eternity with God where we can share in His blessing and goodness (2 Corinthians 5:20–21).

Many within the Church mistake morality's role. They try to use morality to get to heaven or to find favor with God when the opposite is in order. It is because of our faith in Christ and the forgiveness we have received that we strive to be moral.

> Therefore gird up the loins of your mind, be sober, and rest your hope fully upon the grace that is to be brought to you at the revelation of Jesus Christ; as obedient children, not conforming yourselves to the former lusts, as in your ignorance; but as He who called you is holy, you also be holy in all your conduct, because it is written, "Be holy, for I am holy" (1 Peter 1:13–16).

Arbitrariness

Immanent moral religions like Buddhism, Confucianism, and any form of moralism, are *based on* human experience (man's ideas) unlike religions such as Hinduism, Taoism, Sikhism, etc., which go *beyond* human experience and rationality to establish a moral framework.

Any religion that comes from man (man's ideas) is arbitrary — man is simply not the absolute authority on any matter. Just because man says something is right or wrong doesn't mean it is. Many reading this may not realize how devastating this arbitrary nature is to an argument, but it shows it has no foundation beyond the changing opinions of men. Arbitrariness proves that something is without warrant (i.e., not a feasible defense).

It is as simple as that — moralistic religions are based on man's fallible opinions. When a moralistic religion states there is a moral code by which people should live, it is merely their *opinion*. How do they know that one person's opinion is absolute? They don't.

This is why moralistic religions have different rules and claims by which they make people (perhaps themselves) abide. Where one moral religion says not to murder or have multiple wives, another could say that murder and polygamy are acceptable within their allegedly moral religion. It is merely based on opinions and leads to the inconsistencies within a false worldview and between competing worldviews.

Some religions that are moralistic might claim that the sages of old (e.g., Confucius) or ancestors (mythological religions where ancestors became their gods like Oden, Zeus, Baal, etc.) have developed the code by which we are to live — but why trust their opinions? A potential response from those holding to moralistic religions might be, "But these ancients were exceptionally wise." To which we might respond, "By what standard? Your fallible *opinion*?"

Any way you slice the cake, moralistic religions are based on mere opinions. Furthermore, this is why there are so many of them — people's opinions vary. Having a lot of moralistic religions *is* a refutation of the underlying philosophy since they cannot all be right.

You need to understand that man's opinions are ultimately meaningless. If someone is of the opinion that 2+2=-3, who cares? Opinions have no merit in a debate or in determining truth from error. The only "opinion" that matters is the one that is grounded in ultimate reality. But in the moralistic religions, there is no absolute authority, creating a self-refuting position.

One might be tempted to say that this is a reversible argument to Christianity by *stating opinions* that Christians are also just offering arbitrary assertions for their theology, though they do not understand the Christian account.

In the Christian worldview, we have an absolute authority, God, who is not arbitrary by His very nature. That would be God's "opinion," which is the ultimate authority. He is not arbitrary but final and absolute. To object to this would be to appeal to a lesser, *arbitrary* authority and to claim to know more than God Himself.

God is the only one in a position to set true religious doctrine and moral standards. That perfect morality is demonstrated fully in Jesus Christ — and God said in Mark 9:7, "This is My beloved Son. Hear Him!" The point is that in the biblical worldview the reasoning is consistent and based in an ultimate authority and His revelations to us, but in the moralistic religious view we find inconsistency and arbitrary ideas, which produce a self-refuting worldview.

Inconsistency

The concept of inconsistency has to do with adhering to the law of non-contradiction — something cannot be both true and false at the same time in the same context. Why would moralistic religions hold to one person's opinions on matters of morality and not also take another person's opposing opinions on morality into account? When they allow these contradictions to exist, they become inconsistent, the second fatal flaw in these worldviews.

Inconsistencies within and between the Systems

Moralistic religions are inconsistent in two ways. First, there is no unity within the systems — they contradict themselves. Consider the words of Confucius:

> True wisdom is knowing what you don't know.[2]

Of course, if you are wise to know what you don't know, then you do know it. These are glaring inconsistencies that result from fallible men expressing ideas without full knowledge. Other moralistic religions also have inconsistencies. Consider when someone adheres to a moral code that says not to murder children and then turns around and supports abortion (the killing of children in the womb!).

The second inconsistency comes when we compare the systems to one another. While many of these systems will claim that other systems have a valid way of knowing truth, they wind up contradicting one another in significant ways. The boldest expression of this is the modern Unitarian Universalist Association, which allows its members to be atheists or polytheists and everything in between.

---

2. Confucius, Sayings of Confucius, http://www.goodreads.com/quotes/497572-true-wisdom-is-knowing-what-you-don-t-know.

The most important type of inconsistency is the failure to conform to the truth of the Bible. Any worldview that is not consistent with the revelation in the Bible is inherently false. If a worldview denies the Trinity or the fact that Jesus died to pay for the debt of sinners, they are false, contradicting the truth.

How Can One Be Perfected to Live Up to the "Code"?

We are told that we must live up to a particular code in moralistic religions like Confucianism or Buddhism. Of course, the problem is that no one lives up to that code. Thus, everyone is guilty of breaking that code and will continue to break that code. Therefore, everyone needs help to be able to live up to that code.

But this is not offered in these religions beyond looking inside yourself or seeking guidance from another imperfect person. What can make a person perfect and able to live up to the code? Nothing. And even if they could, that is not God's standard for redemption from our sinful nature and acts. We can never obey enough laws to be seen as righteous in God's eyes. There is truly no hope in these systems. These systems have no source of redemption, only a call to work harder and do more, even making up for wrongs done in past lives.

Hope for the Christian comes in the doctrine of redemption and union with Christ. Rather than trying to earn a righteous standing by following a moral law, Jesus Christ stepped into history as God in the flesh to take the punishment for our sin, rising on the third day for our justification. For those who repent and place their trust in Christ, God no longer sees them as failing to meet the standard, but as righteous through Christ (Isaiah 61:10). His blood and the work of the Holy Spirit are making us perfect (e.g., Galatians 3:3; Colossians 1:28, 4:12; Hebrews 12:23). The growth in holiness and the ability to do what is pleasing to God comes as a result of our redemption, not to gain it (Romans 8:1–8). This holiness arrives in its finality with a new heavens and new earth.

No Help for Past Wrongs

Another inconsistency is related to this. Even if one is able to live up to the code at some point, how have past wrong actions been dealt with? Let's use an extreme example here. Imagine that you murdered someone years ago. Now you try to live up to a code that says not to murder (and other positive actions).

How do you deal with the guilt for this past murder? How does justice work for the family of the murdered victim? What code of morality provides and satisfies for past wrongs? None. Moralistic religions just cannot consistently satisfy their own demands. Not doing wrong cannot make up for having done wrong.

Laws and Morality

Many try to follow the laws of a nation, believing they are "morally okay." But this is also inconsistent. There is a large difference between man-made laws and moral law as given by the absolute standard of God. Upon death, all will be judged by God's standard (Hebrews 9:27). They will not be judged based on the laws of the countries they lived in or the laws of the time they lived in. Christ will judge them based on His absolute Word and the standard of perfect righteousness.

Consider morality in Nazi Germany in the 1930s and 1940s. They had laws too, and what the leader Adolf Hitler did was *legal*, when he murdered millions and attacked nations in the hope of conquering the world. You see, the Nazis set the laws in their country and then they held these to be the standard of morality, murdering millions. They attacked all who held different sets of morality — particularly God's standard.

We observe similar things in our own Western countries today where certain government officials have passed laws to murder children (they call it abortion, but it simply means to end the life of a child) and impose the acceptance and promotion of homosexuality upon their respective realms. They even attack people who oppose such things as being immoral. The examples of governments promoting a false morality could be multiplied. Following man-made laws does not meet God's standard in the end. Apart from being found holy in Christ, the most obedient citizen of an earthly kingdom will not inhabit the heavenly kingdom.

Borrowing from God's Word (Openly or Inadvertently)

Moralistic religions have no valid basis for determining morality or offering hope for eternity. But we want people to realize something. Morality does exist, but it has nothing to do with moralistic religions and the wisdom of the sages. Morality exists because God exists and He determines morality. Any moralistic religion is therefore borrowing from God — whether they realize it or not.

Some might argue that Buddhists (or whomever) had no access to God's morality and yet they came up with some decent morals, so you can't say that they "borrowed it" from God. But this is false. In many cases, the moral codes agree with biblical morality. We would generally all agree that it is wrong to steal, murder, and rape. These things might in some cases encourage humanity to flourish for a short term in community, but if they are done for pragmatic reasons they are not pleasing to God (Romans 8:7–8). In other words, being good for goodness' sake is just arbitrary and does not please God. People have had access to God's Laws going back to early Genesis, and God made man in His own image with a knowledge of right and wrong (e.g., Genesis 1:26–27, 26:5).

Man has had knowledge of good and evil since the Garden of Eden (Genesis 3:22), being passed on from Noah after the Flood. Since God's Curse, man's fallible codes of behavior fail to perform properly, and men unrighteously suppress what they know to be true about God and His character (Romans 1:18–20). True morality is predicated on a true lawgiver, and that lawgiver is God alone.

Conclusion

If a religion is *moralistic*, they aren't hurting anyone so why oppose them? Actually, a moralistic religion is not moral, but immoral by God's standard. Redefined morality is not moral. As an example, consider marriage. Redefining marriage, which is a man and a woman by God's created standard, as anything else is endorsing what is immoral. But every man-made moral standard itself will be judged by God, and it will fall short of His perfect standard.

Many who have been entrenched in moralistic faiths (or one in particular) need to understand that they likely did it out of ignorance, as did their teachers before them. But the Lord has commanded those captured by a moralistic religion to repent and be converted that their sins may be blotted out. This is great news, as it can bring refreshment form the Lord and escape from the guilt of past sins, offering hope and redemption through the Lord Jesus Christ.

Chapter 8

Paganism

Pastor Tom Chesko

We Love Sin!

A young girl named Rachel decided to serve as a counselor at a Christian camp in the summer of 2014. She expected the usual mix of Christians who wanted to grow in their faith in an exciting environment, others undecided about what to believe who were there mainly for the fun, and some who were forced to go but didn't really want to be there at all.

What Rachel didn't expect was a few professing Wiccans (modern day pagan witches) who decided to make their beliefs known in a rather disturbing way. Acting in unison one night, they refused to obey the rules and began to shout, "We love sin." Campus security had to be called to quell the disturbance. The church group that brought the girls to camp was hoping to give them an exposure to the Christian way of life, not knowing what they truly believed.

This might be easy to write off as a few young girls seeking nothing more than attention, but their aberrant behavior was disturbing and frightening to other campers. Were they really part of the pagan community attracted to witchcraft? Probably not, because Wiccans do not believe in sin by Christian definition, but these young girls may have been familiar with Wicca to some extent and could very well adopt it as their personal expression of spirituality in the future.

Out of the Shadows

Paganism is a religion that has been experiencing growth in America since the 1960s, although the number of pagans is difficult to track. Many people don't openly admit to their belief in paganism, and pagans don't belong to denominations or structured religious groups. There are loose associations that cooperate, but paganism is an eclectic worldview that encompasses many specific views. You won't see a recognizable pagan meeting place like a church or synagogue, and pagans don't go door-to-door seeking converts like the Mormons and Jehovah's Witnesses.

Paganism is not as concerned about the growth and spread of their beliefs as much as the personal growth of the individual in what some simply refer to as "the craft." As a prelude, paganism can be expressed as ancient spiritism, Wicca, Druidism, witchcraft, polytheistic mythologies of the past, and a host of other variations.[1] In a practical sense, pagans value their own experience above all else. The majority of pagans are solitary and prefer to keep their religion to themselves. "Learning the craft" is being schooled in the beliefs and literature of the pagan way of life.

In a certain sense you don't become a pagan; you are a pagan. It is more of an inner discovery than a conversion. However, the Internet has helped pagans make their beliefs better known in a "try-before-you-buy" approach. It has moved paganism out of the closet — or should I say, the broom closet. Yes, brooms still have their place among the pagans, and not just at Halloween. They are used to symbolically sweep a place clean for certain rituals and in Wiccan handfast ceremonies.[2] In a handfast ceremony, two Wiccans make a binding commitment to each other for a certain period of time as a prelude to marriage, or the ceremony can be incorporated into an actual marriage ceremony. Sometimes the participants will jump over the broom at the end of the ceremony. When the bride and groom jump the broom at the end of the ceremony, they are sweeping the past away and jumping into their future together!

---

1. For specific information on groups referred to broadly as pagan, see the other chapters in this volume on Wicca, Norse and Germanic Mythology, Egyptian Mythology, and Greek and Roman Mythology.
2. The term may have come into English from the Old Norse word *handfesta*, which means "to strike a bargain."

Symbolism

Paganism employs many different symbols and symbolic actions like jumping the broom, but there is more to it than mere symbolism. Pagans will use various types of incense and candles on an altar to achieve certain objectives. Incense is believed to have therapeutic properties and is used in rites of purification. The same is true of essential oils, and various fragrant flowers and herbs are likewise employed to manipulate energies. An advertisement for a female human figure candle on the products page of a pagan online store called The Magickal Cat reads as follows:

> This reversible candle is made with black wax over red wax. Charged with reversing magic, it is intended to aid in returning negative energies and attentions to their source, leaving your enemies tasting what they have served. The female image in this candle can be particularly helpful if you are also calling upon the Goddess, using the candle to help protect a woman, or returning the negative energies in question to a woman.[3]

The Magickal Cat also sells a basic "Wiccan/Pagan altar set," scrying bowls, tarot cards, pendulums, spell-casting supplies, wands, gemstones, and your very own crystal ball, in addition to many other enchanting and exotic items to fill your pagan toolbox. It's kind of like an all-in-one, do-it-yourself pagan version of a home improvement store con-  veniently located on your computer. Pagans also use black cauldrons as pots to hold fire in which to brew potions. The witches' spell in Shakespeare's *Macbeth* contained the lines, "Double, double toil and trouble; Fire burn, and cauldron bubble."

Moving toward Paganism

The move out of the shadows by pagans can be seen by Christian apologists as a good thing in some ways, because it also reveals the darkness of paganism masquerading as light. The Bible gives repeated warnings about Satan's strategy to deceive in this manner (2 Corinthians 11:14). He is the "father

---

3. The Magickal Cat, accessed October 21, 2015, http://www.themagickalcat.com/Candle-Human-Figure-Female-Reversible-p/chrevf.htm.

of lies" (John 8:44). The world of false religion has many different shades of deception, and the lure of a powerful personal experience is a particularly attractive hue. Satan's first great lie to Eve in Genesis 3:5 included the promise of power and great enlightenment: "For God doth know that in the day ye eat thereof, then your eyes shall be opened, and ye shall be as gods, knowing good and evil."[4] This is what makes paganism so dangerous and attracts so many people to the New Age movement.

In addition, people are gullible by nature and tend toward sinful desires, especially those who are more open-minded to spiritual matters and personal growth apart from the wisdom and discernment that come from God's Word. Just witness the constant bombardment of products that the average person is subjected to every day. The advertisers know that if they can offer you something to enhance your life, it will probably sell. Highlight the benefits of a certain product and put it in an attractive package and people will buy it. It's a basic sales pitch, and Satan has a great marketing strategy to enlarge his kingdom of the cults and the occult.[5] Infomercials work because the claim is "Here is what I can do for you now." Paganism has the same message: "Here is what I can do for you now." The payoff is in this world, not a world to come.

People who have been disenchanted with organized religion constitute another class of potential pagans. They have tried other religious products, so to speak, and they did not work for them. These spiritual dropouts from the more traditional faiths may find the paganism packaging attractive, and when they buy it, they also find acceptance and encouragement to express their own beliefs rather than conform to a standard. They no longer feel like *outsiders*; they have become *insiders*. It's like belonging to a special club with all kinds of nice perks without the baggage of membership standards and dues.

Furthermore, the pagan man or woman can climb the ladder of paganism as high as they desire to go. There is no "top rung," and there is nothing like the clergy-laity separation they likely experienced in organized religion. Each person belongs to the priestly class in paganism, although advancement in the pagan covens (esbats) may take time. The prominent American pagan witch

---

4. All Scripture in this chapter is from the King James Version (KJV) of the Bible.
5. In general, the occult refers to gaining secret knowledge through spiritual practices. In paganism, this comes through channeling energies and spirits as well as entering altered states of consciousness. The occult is generally viewed by Christians as dealing with the supernatural realm of Satan and demons influencing humans through religious practices and rites.

Starhawk defined the coven as "a Witches support group, consciousness-raising group, psychic study center, College of mysteries, surrogate clan, and religious congregation all rolled into one."[6] On her personal web page under the listing "About Starhawk" we find the following:

- Starhawk is one of the most respected voices in modern earth-based spirituality. She is also well-known as a global justice activist and organizer, whose work and writings have inspired many to action.

- Starhawk is perhaps best known as an articulate pioneer in the revival of earth-based spirituality and Goddess religion. She is a cofounder of Reclaiming, an activist branch of modern Pagan religion, and continues to work closely with the Reclaiming community. Her archives are maintained at the Graduate Theological Union library in Berkeley, California.

- Starhawk is a veteran of progressive movements, from anti-war to anti-nukes, and is deeply committed to bringing the techniques and creative power of spirituality to political activism.

- Starhawk travels internationally teaching magic, the tools of ritual, and the skills of activism. She lives part-time in San Francisco, in a collective house with her partner and friends, and part-time in a little hut in the woods in western Sonoma County, California, where she practices permaculture in her extensive gardens, and writes.[7]

Like many traditional religions, paganism does not discriminate on the basis of age or gender, and women constitute the majority of pagans overall. This should not come as a surprise given the fact that in a masculine-dominated society, there are women seeking liberation and empowerment. Among the open-minded, the young spiritual explorers often dabble in some form of paganism often influenced by its prevalence and positive portrayals in popular media. Catherine Sanders notes, "The book *Teen Witch: Wicca for a New Genera-*

6. Helen A. Berger, "The Coven: Perfect Love, Perfect Trust," *A Community of Witches Contemporary Neo-paganism and Witchcraft in the United States* (Columbia, SC: University of South Carolina Press, 1999), p. 54.

7. "Starhawk," Transition United States, accessed October 21, 2015, http://transitionus.org/starhawk.

tion has sold more copies for occult publisher Llewellyn than any other in its 95-year history."[8] Ruth La Ferla writes of two teenage witches:

> Ms. Trayer and Ms. Haddad-Friedman are members of a movement gaining an ardent following among teenagers, mostly girls, who are in part captivated by the glossy new image of witches portrayed on television shows and in the movies. No longer the hideous, wart-covered crone of folklore and fairy tale, witches in hit television shows like "Charmed," starring Shannen Doherty, and the 1996 movie "The Craft," a favorite with teenagers at video stores, are avatars of glamour, power and style. Other youthful adherents of Wicca, seeking an alternative path to spirituality, are attracted by the craft's lack of structure and dogma.[9]

Paganism and the Wiccan Connection

The term *pagan* comes from a Latin word for "country or village dweller" and was first used in the early Christian era in a broad sense to refer to the unconverted. In current usage, the word *pagan* is often associated with someone who behaves contrary to established norms. We often envision pagans as people with multiple body piercings, brightly colored hair, strange tattoos, and strange music. That stereotype does an injustice to the true nature of paganism; it's not about a certain outward appearance. You might find pagans fitting that mold, but you will also find them dressed in casual clothes or a business suit. They are typically middle class, educated, and come from all walks of life.

In the religious or spiritual sense, modern paganism, often referred to as neo-paganism, is more concentrated in Britain, North America, Australia, and New Zealand, according to author Barbara Jane Davy.[10] Although paganism is definitely not a mainstream religion like Protestantism, Catholicism, Buddhism, Islam, or Hinduism, pagans see it differently. They believe that paganism is the original religion from which all other religions eventually developed. This is not the case (as various forms of paganism are actually a

---

8. Catherine Sanders, "The Hidden Traps of Wicca," Focus on the Family, accessed October 21, 2015, http://www.focusonthefamily.com/parenting/teens/hidden-traps-of-wicca.
9. Ruth La Ferla, "Like Magic, Witchcraft Charms Teenagers," *New York Times,* February 13, 2000.
10. Barbara Jane Davy, *Introduction to Pagan Studies* (Lanham, MD: AltaMira Press, 2007), p. 3.

Cadet Chapel Falcon Circle, located on the hill top between the Academy Visitors Center and the Cadet Chapel, is dedicated May 6, 2011.
(Wikimedia Commons, U.S. Air Force/Photo by Mike Kaplan)

corruption of the truth as it was passed down since Noah), but there is an association of the word *pagan* with ancient religious traditions and heritage.

Some Wiccans refer to Wicca as the "Old Religion." Gerald Gardner, an Englishman, is considered the man who did the most to popularize modern Witchcraft and establish the Wiccan traditions beginning in the late 1930s. He said that the "Old Religion" had followers who preceded him, the religion having survived from the Middle Ages. However, Gardner's credibility is not without its doubters. In an essay titled, "History of Wicca in England: 1939 to the Present Day," author Julia Phillips, a Wiccan high priestess writes:

> Of course we can never really know the truth about the origins of the Wicca. Gardner may have been an utter fraud; he may have actually received a "Traditional" initiation; or, as a number of people have suggested, he may have created the Wicca as a result of a genuine religious experience, drawing upon his extensive literary and magical knowledge to create, or help create, the rites and philosophy. What I think we can be fairly certain about is that he was sincere in his belief. If there had been no more to the whole thing than an old man's fantasy, then the Wicca would not have grown to be the force that it is today.[11]

---

11. Adapted from a talk Phillips gave at the Australian Wiccan Conference in Canberra, 1991.

Gerald Gardner

Gardner's book, *Witchcraft Today*, published in 1954, was instrumental in the growth of American paganism, although he certainly leaned on others in his writing. He borrowed some of the rituals, which he incorporated into Wicca from a variety of sources including a Rosicrucian group, Kabbalah (a mystical offshoot of Judaism), the works of Aleister Crowley, and Free Masonry. For example, Gardner adopted the three-degree initiation rite of the Masonic order in his witchcraft.

Two of Gardner's followers, Rosemary and Raymond Buckland, established a coven in New York in 1964. In 1968, Buckland opened the Museum of Witchcraft and Magick on Long Island, New York. He has authored over 50 books, both fiction and nonfiction, the majority of them about witchcraft and magic. Wicca now had a foothold on American soil and would eventually spread westward. The first large gathering of pagans in the United States occurred in 1979 at the Pan-Pagan Festival in Indiana. These festivals provide a place and time for pagans to come together in a supportive environment to learn from one another and develop their individual skills in the craft.

Pagan Origins and Diversity

Wiccans comprise just a slice of the diverse pie of paganism that is composed of many different strands and elements of ancient and modern beliefs, some of which are identified in the Bible. When the Israelites entered the land of Canaan (the Promised Land), they saw an agriculturally prosperous region inhabited by people who worshiped nature gods and goddesses. The Canaanites attributed their agricultural success to these gods and goddesses who had power over the land.

Cuneiform tablets describing the Canaanite gods, including the chief god Baal ("lord" or "master"), were discovered in the Canaanite city of Ugarit (Ras Shamra), located in modern Syria.[12] Baal was a god who was believed to control the weather.

---

12. Excavations at Ras Shamra began in 1929.

The Ugaritic tablets credit Baal with sending the rains that make the land fruitful. He is called, "Prince, the Lord of the Earth," and "Baal, the Mighty One." In the texts Baal is also connected to the morning dew. 1 Aqht I, 42–46 says,

> Seven years shall Baal fail,
> eight the rider of the clouds.
> There shall be no dew, no rain;
> no surging of the two depths,
> neither the goodness of Baal's voice.[13]

Baal was sometimes pictured with a horned helmet that symbolized power and strength but is not to be equated with the image of a horned devil. If the Israelites could compromise their faith and worship these heathen deities, perhaps the ground would bring forth a plentiful harvest and they too would prosper economically as the Canaanites had. It was a strong temptation they could not resist.

The Book of Judges is a testimony to the apostasy of Israel during this early time in their history. During the lifetime of Joshua, the children of Israel followed the Lord, but things changed for the worse after his death:

> And Joshua the son of Nun, the servant of the LORD, died, being an hundred and ten years old. And they buried him in the border of his inheritance in Timnathheres, in the mount of Ephraim, on the north side of the hill Gaash. And also all that generation were gathered unto their fathers: and there arose another generation after them, which knew not the LORD, nor yet the works which he had done for Israel. And the children of Israel did evil in the sight of the LORD, and served Baalim: And they forsook the LORD God of their fathers, which brought them out of the land of Egypt, and followed other gods, of the gods of the people that were round about them, and bowed themselves unto them, and provoked the LORD to anger (Judges 2:8–12).

Elijah's dramatic confrontation with the false prophets of Baal was a divine rebuke and judgment of Baal worship; it was actually the God of Israel who brought rain to the land (2 Kings 18). Although many things have changed

---

13. Allen Ross, "The Miracles of Elijah and Elisha," Christian Leadership Center, accessed October 21, 2015, http://www.christianleadershipcenter.org/elijah.htm.

in the world since the Canaanites disappeared from history, paganism continued in the polytheism of the Greco-Roman gods/goddesses and their Celtic, Nordic, and Druid counterparts. The gods of Greece and Rome, which New Testament Christianity encountered, were all based on pagan mythology, rather than divine revelation. In the -isms of the world, animism, shamanism, Shintoism, and occultism all have their roots in religious beliefs going back a long time.

Other offshoots of the stream of paganism would include Native American religions, pantheism, and Totemism. Totemism is a system of belief in which humans are said to have kinship or a mystical relationship with a spirit being, such as an animal or plant.[14]

In an abstract on Canaanite Religion published in 2006, K.L. Noll from Brandon University states the following:

> Religion in an ancient Near Eastern context consisted of (1) acknowledgment of a supernatural reality usually defined as a god or gods, (2) reverence for objects, places, and times considered sacred, that is, separated from ordinary objects, places, and times, (3) regularly repeated ritual activities for a variety of purposes, including ritual magic, (4) conformance to stipulations alleged to have been revealed by the supernatural reality, (5) communication with the supernatural through prayer and other activity, (6) experience of feelings described by participants as awe, fear, mystery, etc., (7) integration of items 1–6 into a holistic, though not necessarily systematic, worldview, and (8) association with, and conformity of one's own life priorities to, a group of like-minded people.[15]

Noll's analysis, while true of many religions to some degree, fits well with neo-paganism as well. Sacred altars and shrines, places, days, ritual magic, meditation, divination, a sense of mystery, etc., all have a part in the lives of those who practice some expression of paganism. At the heart of it all is the attempt to make contact with the divine or essential world surrounding the practitioner. Immanence rather than transcendence is a key concept of paganism. The divine is seen as nature (pantheism) or in nature (panentheism) rather than a god/being that exists apart from nature. This idea of

---

14. For more information on these specific views, see chapter 12 in this volume.
15. K.L. Noll, "Canaanite Religion," *Religion Compass* 1/1(2007):61–92.

immanence is the foundation for the experiential nature of pagan beliefs — connecting to nature is connecting to the divine.

Back to Nature

In paganism, nature is the temple of the sacred, so pagans, ancient and modern, attach deep reverence to the natural world, which leads many of them to be active in environmental causes today. In Greek mythology, Gaia (or Gaea) was the earth goddess who originated, or created herself, out of primordial chaos. According to some legends she gave birth to Pontus (the sea) and Uranus (the sky). Hesiod the poet wrote, "She [Gaia] bore also the fruitless deep with his raging swell, Pontus, without sweet union of love."[16] Earth Day, which has been celebrated in America since April of 1970, has become a pagan holiday of sorts.

> The spirit of Earth Day 1970 did not just happen; its roots could include the gradual stirring of environmental consciousness that accelerated in the 1960s, but that stirring itself had deeper roots in an American consciousness of a special relationship with the land, even if that relationship was often abusive. Still, if there was a year when Wicca (in the broad sense) became "nature religion," as opposed to the "mystery religion" or "metaphorical fertility religion," labels that it had brought from England, that year was 1970.[17]

Neo-pagan Gus di Zerega states:

> I think Earth Day is a particularly important moment for contemplation and commitment by us Pagans. Often American Christian critics accuse us of "pantheism," and in an important respect they are right. We do find the sacred, most of us, in the earth without reference to any transcendental spiritual force. In my mind there is a transcendental dimension as well, but it is not needed at all for us to honor the earth as sacred.[18]

16. "The Theogony of Hesiod," translated by Evelyn-White, accessed October 21, 2015, http://www.sacred-texts.com/cla/hesiod/theogony.htm.
17. Chas Clifton, *Her Hidden Children: The Rise of Wicca and Paganism in America* (Lanham, MD: AltaMira Press, 2006), p. 43.
18. Gus DiZerega, "Earth Day and the Sacredness of the Earth," *A Pagan's Blog*, Beliefnet, April 1, 2012, accessed October 21, 2015, http://www.beliefnet.com/columnists/apagansblog/2012/04/earth-day-and-the-sacredness-of-the-earth.html#more-1346.

Former Vice-President Al Gore is an environmental crusader and "prophet" of a global ecological crisis, who holds the view that earth does not belong to man, man belongs to the earth. This is the very opposite of what we find written in the first book of the Bible:

> And God said, Let us make man in our image, after our likeness: and let them have dominion over the fish of the sea, and over the fowl of the air, and over the cattle, and over all the earth, and over every creeping thing that creepeth upon the earth (Genesis 1:26).

Christians must be good stewards of God's creation, but the earth was made for man, not man for the earth. To be a good steward of the earth is to care for it as a gift and responsibility given to mankind from God. But Al Gore sees things a little differently. For him, there is a spiritual connection to the earth that was lost. He envisions a revival of interest in the belief that the earth is our Mother. In his *New York Times* best seller, *Earth in the Balance: Ecology and the Human Spirit*, Gore wrote:

> We feel increasingly distant from our roots in the earth. In one sense, civilization itself has been on a journey from its foundations in the world of nature to an ever more contrived, controlled, and manufactured world of our own imitative and sometimes arrogant design. . . . At some point during this journey we lost our feeling of connectedness to the rest of nature. We now dare now to wonder: Are we so unique and powerful as to be essentially separate from the Earth?[19]

Here Gore emphasizes the idea of regaining a "connection to nature." Our separation (distance) from the earth must be bridged. This is pagan thinking in a thinly veiled disguise.

It is similar to the New Age belief that "only the unity of all can bring about the well being of all."

In his speeches, Gore frequently reminds his audience of the need to seek the diversity and spiritual wealth that can be gleamed from the teachings and traditions of many different faiths. Paganism does not claim to be

---

19. Al Gore, *Earth in the Balance: Ecology and the Human Spirit* (New York: Houghton Mifflin, 1992), p. 1.

the one true way, just another way leading to some divine source. This is the syncretism of paganism, but their "openness" only goes so far. Pagans have no fondness for Christianity! Article X of The Principles of Wiccan Belief drawn up by the American Council of Witches in 1974 stated that Wiccans object to Christianity's claim to be the only way. But Jesus unapologetically made that very claim in the Gospel of John, and we find it essentially reiterated in Acts:

> I am the way, the truth, and the life: no man cometh unto the Father, but by me (John 14:6).

> Neither is there salvation in any other; for there is none other name under heaven given among men, whereby we must be saved (Acts 4:12).

Pagans would vigorously deny this assertion by and about Jesus Christ.

May the Force Be with You

Unlike systematized religions, paganism is primarily rooted in personal experience and power utilizing various forces of energy and nature to create beneficial changes in self, the life of fellow human beings, and the planet. Some shamans (spiritual mediators) identify this as a luminous energy field consisting of four layers: the spirit, the soul (psychic), the mental (emotional), and the physical (the body). As a form of paganism, the shaman works on the energy field to bring about a state of well-being. Anthropologist Michael Harner, a practicing shaman, describes his role in this fashion:

> The shaman moves between realities, a magical athlete of states of consciousness . . . a power-broker in the sense of manipulating spiritual power to help people, to put them in a state of equilibrium.[20]

To be a pagan is to be in charge of individual spiritual transformation through a variety of means at your disposal. There are chants, charms, spells, rituals, drumming, meditation, dance, and other such practices that all can be customized for the individual or group. These are the sacred rituals of

---

20. Michael Harner, *The Way of the Shaman* (New York, NY: Bantam New Age Books, 1982), p. 56.

paganism. They also have their holy days (sabbats) and seasons (of feasting and magic).

Pagans tend to believe that if things can be changed on an individual level, they can ultimately be changed on a universal level by "skilled practitioners" who collectively seek to improve mankind and the universe itself. It sounds far-fetched, and it is, but before you dismiss paganism as an insignificant system of beliefs (i.e., a religion), remember that just as the blind religion of evolution supposedly requires lots of time to bring about changes, the cosmic flow of positive energy takes time to redirect for the good of all. This is pagan thinking that borrows from a variety of sources from New Age to animism to Greek mythology.

The earth is supposed to have been around for a long time, so the pagan sees his religion more in the long term. He or she is just part of the circle of life occupying a sacred place on a planet in a vast universe for a certain amount of time and making the best of it. And for many, the pagan lifestyle is entertaining in the short term. It's like Halloween every day. They take their paganism seriously but have fun doing it. Just think of how many children and adults were spellbound by J.K. Rowling's *Harry Potter* books with sales totaling in the hundreds of millions. Fantasy yes, but some Potter fanatics delved deeper and deeper into the pagan, occult world of spiritual darkness.

According to a 2011 census, "Jedi" is now the most popular faith in the Other Religions category in England and Wales, taking seventh place among all the major world religions.[21] It is a church inspired by George Lucas' *Star Wars* films. The website of the Jedi Church states:

> The Jedi church believes that there is one powerful force [energy field] that binds all things in the universe together. The Jedi religion is something innate inside every one of us, the Jedi Church believes that our sense of morality is innate. So quiet your mind and listen to the force within you.[22]

---

21. Henry Taylor, " 'Jedi' religion most popular alternative faith," *The Telegraph*, December 11, 2012, http://www.telegraph.co.uk/news/religion/9737886/Jedi-religion-most-popular-alternative-faith.html.
22. Description on the Homepage at http://www.jedichurch.org, accessed October 21, 2015.

As the familiar saying goes, "buyer beware" — the Jedi religion is paganism pure and simple. The Jedi Church even warns its members to be cautious of the dark side of the force. It's territory that no Jedi should dare to enter. But how is someone to know when he crosses over from the light side of the force to the dark side by simply listening to the voice within? By what standard can good and bad be judged in this pagan belief? It would be arbitrary to assert some absolute good or evil in a religion where no absolutes, like the claims of Jesus Christ, are tolerated! In truth, there is no such thing as a light side of paganism. It's all darkness and it is a consuming darkness, like voodoo, which originated in sub-Saharan Africa that claims to be used to heal or to harm.

Pagan Polytheism

Paganism has some lofty spiritual goals, but it amounts to false worship based on teachings that are contrary to the Christian faith. It is both polytheistic (a belief in many gods) and pantheistic (all is god). It sprang from the seeds of polytheism sown in many different soils as people spread across the globe after the dispersion at Babel (Genesis 11). The pagan pantheon is composed of a variety of gods and goddesses, and the pagan may establish a close relationship with one or more of these gods. The spread of Hinduism in the West has also contributed much to the development of pagan thought and practice. An article on the history of modern paganism on the British Broadcasting Corporation website highlights this fact:

> The 1960s and 1970s were times of radical social change. Hinduism and Taoism helped shape contemporary Paganism as the hippy trail led people to become interested in Eastern religions and philosophies. North Americans rediscovered Native American traditions and the Afro-American traditions of Santeria, Candomble, and Vodoun. Paganism found an ally in the ecological and feminist movements of the 1960s. Pagan philosophies appealed to many eco-activists, who also saw Nature as sacred and recognized the Great Goddess as Mother Nature. The image of the witch was taken up by feminists as a role-model of the independent powerful woman, and the single Great Goddess as the archetype of women's inner strength and dignity.[23]

23. "History of Modern Paganism: Renaissance and Revival," BBC Religions, accessed October 21, 2015, http://www.bbc.co.uk/religion/religions/paganism/history/modern_1.shtml.

Thou Shalt Have No other Gods

The first commandment that God gave to Moses on Mount Sinai was: "I am the LORD thy God, which have brought thee out of the land of Egypt, out of the house of bondage. Thou shalt have no other gods before me" (Exodus 20:2–3). The Israelites were also warned about the diverse occult practices of the nations they would encounter:

> When thou art come into the land which the LORD thy God giveth thee, thou shalt not learn to do after the abominations of those nations. There shall not be found among you any one that maketh his son or his daughter to pass through the fire, or that useth divination, or an observer of times, or an enchanter, or a witch. Or a charmer, or a consulter with familiar spirits, or a wizard, or a necromancer. For all that do these things are an abomination unto the LORD: and because of these abominations the LORD thy God doth drive them out from before thee (Deuteronomy 18:9–12).

Rather than obey God, the Israelites failed to heed the Word of the Lord and fell into pagan idol worship and spiritism — the very thing God had warned them against in Deuteronomy 4:15–19. King Saul even went so far as to seek counsel from a medium called the witch of Endor (1 Samuel 28:1–8). In the New Testament, we read about Paul's trip to ancient Athens and the grief he experienced over what he saw: "Now while Paul waited for them at Athens, his spirit was stirred in him, when he saw the city wholly given to idolatry" (Acts 17:16). In Romans 1, we learn that when people fail to worship God as their Creator, they begin to worship the creation:

> For the invisible things of him from the creation of the world are clearly seen, being understood by the things that are made, even his eternal power and Godhead; so that they are without excuse: Because that, when they knew God, they glorified him not as God, neither were thankful; but became vain in their imaginations, and their foolish heart was darkened. Professing themselves to be wise, they became fools, and changed the glory of the uncorruptible God into an image made like to corruptible man, and to birds, and fourfooted beasts, and creeping things (Romans 1:20–23).

Christian author A.W. Tozer put it well: "Wrong ideas about God are only the fountain from which the polluted waters of idolatry flow; they are themselves idolatrous. The idolater simply imagines things about God and acts as if they were true."[24] The irrationalism of paganism is the belief in the multiplicity of gods, or no gods at all. Not all pagans believe the same about deity and divinity. Some make a distinction between the terms. Davy writes:

> "Deity" is a nonspecific word for divine beings, goddesses and gods, and The God and the Godess. Divinity is a more generic word for the sacred, not necessarily quantifiable as a distinct class of beings. Practitioners generally feel that belief in divinity is not a useful way of looking at Pagan religious practice, pointing to the strangeness of the idea one must "believe" in something to relate to it.[25]

Norm Geisler notes:

> Some neopagans debate about the ontological state of their "gods," assigning an idealistic or aesthetic role to them. But as one put it, "All these things are within the realm of possibility. It has been our nature to call these 'god.' "[26]

The confusion over the reality and nature of the gods in paganism is not a matter of confusion in the Scriptures. There is only one true God who created all things; all other gods and goddesses are false gods. They have no existence:

> For though there be that are called gods, whether in heaven or in earth, (as there be gods many, and lords many,) But to us there is but one God, the Father, of whom are all things, and we in him; and one Lord Jesus Christ, by whom are all things, and we by him. Howbeit there is not in every man that knowledge (1 Corinthians 8:5–7).

---

24. A.W. Tozer, Tozer Devotional, "The Essence of Idolatry," accessed October 21, 2015, https://www.cmalliance.org/devotions/tozer?id=1301.
25. Davy, *Introduction to Pagan Studies*, p. 14.
26. Norman Geisler, *Baker Encyclopedia of Christian Apologetics*, 1st ed., "Neopaganism" (Grand Rapids, MI: Baker Books, 1998), p. 523.

This is the pagan's real problem. They have no knowledge of the truth found in God's revelation of Holy Scripture and so they have opened themselves up to lying spirits posing as ancestral spirits, gods, goddesses, or other entities. "Now the Spirit speaketh expressly, that in the latter times some shall depart from the faith, giving heed to seducing spirits, and doctrines of devils" (1 Timothy 4:1). Christian researcher Dave Hunt sounds the warning:

> In all pagan/nature religions there is a presumed cause-and-effect relationship between the ritual or ceremony performed and the obtaining of the power or healing or other blessing sought. The whole idea of pagan ceremonies — the rites of the shaman or witch, the burning of candles, the making of potions, the use of fetishes, etc. — is that they will (if done correctly) elicit a response from the gods or spirits.[27]

The further one goes down the path of spiritual deception, the harder it is to escape because paganism is one of Satan's strongholds — it is a lie masquerading as enlightenment (2 Corinthians 11:4). The only hope for someone lost in its maze is the truth concerning Jesus Christ. He is the true light of the world who promised that those who follow him will not walk in darkness, but shall have the light of life (John 8:12).

The Pagan View of Jesus

One of the tests of a lying spirit is what it professes about Jesus:

> Who is a liar but he that denieth that Jesus is the Christ? He is antichrist, that denieth the Father and the Son. Whosoever denieth the Son, the same hath not the Father: he that acknowledgeth the Son hath the Father also (1 John 2:22–23).

Many pagans believe that Jesus did live at one time and was skilled in magical arts, which he passed on to his disciples, but that's as far as most pagans take it. Ultimately, the answer to the question "who is Jesus?" would invoke a variety of opinions depending on the pagan you talk to (i.e., each may have a different opinion). For the most part, Jesus hardly appears on the pagan radar screen. He is not part of their belief system. But I must ask, "How can He be so ignored by so many pagans?" The

---

27. Dave Hunt, "Native, Indigenous, and Nature Religion," *Occult Invasion* (Eugene, OR: Harvest House, 1998), p. 145.

American statesman Daniel Webster wrote: "All that is best in the civilization of today, is the fruit of Christ's appearance among men."[28] And Webster is not alone in recognizing the significance of Jesus Christ:

> I find the name of Jesus Christ written on the top of every page of modern history. (Historian George Bancroft)[29]

> I am an historian, I am not a believer, but I must confess as a historian that this penniless preacher from Nazareth is irrevocably the very center of history. Jesus Christ is easily the most dominant figure in all history. (Author H.G. Wells)[30]

> As the centuries pass by, the evidence is accumulating that measured by its effect on history, Jesus is the most influential life ever lived on this planet. (Historian Kenneth Scott Latourette)[31]

> All history is incomprehensible without Christ. (Historian Ernest Renan)[32]

> As a child I received instruction both in the Bible and in the Talmud. I am a Jew, but I am enthralled by the luminous figure of the Nazarene. . . . No one can read the Gospels without feeling the actual presence of Jesus. His personality pulsates in every word. No myth is filled with such life. (Albert Einstein)[33]

One thing that can be said for certain is that no pagan myth has the power to give life like Jesus did. In their defiance, pagans do not acknowledge Jesus as the Divine Son of God who came into the world to give them spiritual life. To possess spiritual life is what it means to be born again (John 3:5–7; 1 Peter 1:23; James 1:18).

---

28. Martin Manser, *The Westminster Collection of Christian Quotations,* 1st ed. (Louisville, KY: Westminster John Knox, 2001), p. 351.

29. J. Gilchrist Lawson, *Greatest Thoughts about Jesus Christ* (New York: George H. Doran, 1919), p. 122.

30. P.J. Clarke, *Lives That Made a Difference* (Cork: Publish on Demand Global LLC, 2012), p. 10.

31. Josh McDowell, *The New Evidence That Demands a Verdict* (Nashville, TN: Thomas Nelson, 1999), p. 321.

32. Britton H. Tabor, *Skepticism Assailed* (New York: S.S. Wood, 1895), p. 49–50.

33. George Viereck, "What Life Means to Einstein," *Saturday Evening Post,* October 26, 1929, p. 117.

Rejecting Christ, pagans stumble into their own destruction because Jesus said: "If ye believe not that I am he, ye shall die in your sins" (John 8:24). If you die in your sins, pagan or otherwise, you will spend eternity separated from the God in the lake of fire (Revelation 20:14).

Hell is not a state of mind; it's a place that was prepared by God for the devil and his angels (Matthew 25:41). Pagans may scoff at the idea of a literal hell and eternal punishment, but Jesus didn't. And if they refuse to repent (turn from their sin) and receive Jesus as Lord and Savior, they will ultimately learn of hell's awful reality. Most of what we know of hell in the New Testament comes from Christ's lips. In Revelation 1:18, Jesus said he had the controlling keys of death and hades (hell): "I am he that liveth, and was dead; and, behold, I am alive for evermore, Amen; and have the keys of hell and of death."

Notice that the one who holds the keys of hell and death is the one who conquered death. Jesus was not a wise sage, or spiritual teacher who came on the scene and died like all men. Though He died on a Roman Cross, He rose from the dead and presently sits in the position of all authority at the right hand of His Father in heaven on the throne of God (Ephesians 1:17–20). All authority is His (Matthew 28:18). Christ's Resurrection from the dead was proof that He is the eternal Son of God (Romans 1:4) and the foundation upon which the Christian faith rests. Without the Resurrection of Christ there would be no Christianity (1 Corinthians 15:13–19). One day the resurrected, historical Jesus is coming to judge the living and the dead.

The biblical case for the deity of Jesus is easy to make from Scripture (e.g., John 1; Colossians 1; Hebrews 1; etc.), but church history also affirms the fact. Quote after quote from Christian writers following the death of Apostles could be cited in this regard. Even some non-Christian sources testify to the Resurrection (e.g., the Jewish historian Josephus). I will not make the effort to do that here.

The belief in Jesus as divine was a fundamental doctrine of the early church and remains so today. Only those who were called heretics denied that Jesus was God manifest in the flesh. He suffered and died on the Cross as Savior of the world, rose again on the third day, ascended into heaven, and sits at the right hand of the father, waiting for the time He will come to judge the world in righteousness and establish His Kingdom. Contrary to some pagans' claims, the Council of Nicaea in A.D. 325 did not invent the doctrine of the deity of Christ. Rather, the Council affirmed the apostolic teaching of who Christ is, "The one true God and the Second Person of the Trinity." The proclamation states:

> We believe in one God, the Father Almighty, Maker of heaven and earth, and of all things visible and invisible.
>
> And in one Lord Jesus Christ, the only-begotten Son of God, begotten of the Father before all worlds; God of God, Light of Light, very God of very God; begotten, not made, being of one substance with the Father, by whom all things were made.
>
> Who, for us men for our salvation, came down from heaven, and was incarnate by the Holy Spirit of the virgin Mary, and was made man; and was crucified also for us under Pontius Pilate; He suffered and was buried; and the third day He rose again, according to the Scriptures; and ascended into heaven, and sits on the right hand of the Father; and He shall come again, with glory, to judge the quick and the dead; whose kingdom shall have no end.[34]

There Is No Salvation in Paganism

> God so loved the world, that he gave his only begotten Son, that whosoever believeth in him should not perish, but have everlasting life. For God sent not his Son into the world to condemn the world; but that the world through him might be saved (John 3:16–17).

Many people have seen John 3:16 on a placard at a sporting event, but, like the general population, have become so accustomed to the message that it is largely ignored. But it should not be ignored; it is a message about the grace of God to pardon sinners so they can become the heirs of salvation. However, since pagans do not recognize the biblical view of sin — an offense against a Holy God for which he or she is accountable — they believe there is no need for salvation. So where does that leave them? All dressed up in pagan garb and nowhere to go?

Do they depart this life for another state of consciousness? Will they face another life on earth as taught in reincarnation? Once again, pagans are free to decide for themselves what happens *when*, not *if*, they die, and some

34. Philip Schaff, *The Creeds of Christendom*, 6th ed., Vol. 1. (Grand Rapids, MI: Baker Book House, 1996), p. 27–28.

of them put the afterlife in the category of useless speculation that detracts from the joy of living. But how do they really know? Any answer they give is merely *arbitrary* and hence, logically fallacious. To the pagan, dying, after all, is just as natural as living; it is for the human what it is for a tree. It's part of sacred evolution; death as a return to the nature of one's elements. This is a pagan postulate. But what does the Scripture say?

> It is appointed unto men once to die, but after this the judgment (Hebrews 9:27).

Death is not an end to all existence as individuals, and there will be no second chances after death for those who die without Christ. Right now, pagans, as well as all people alive, are in a "grace period," if you will. We all deserve to suffer eternal separation from our Creator for the sins we have committed against His divine law. The good news is that Jesus bore the punishment for our sins on the Cross, and salvation is freely available to all who believe. This is why Christians are missionary minded: "Knowing therefore the terror of the Lord, we persuade men" (2 Corinthians 5:11). We want people, including pagans, to be saved!

The terror of the Lord is real, but for the Christian, death holds no uncertainty or apprehension: "We are confident, I say, and willing rather to be absent from the body, and to be present with the Lord" (2 Corinthians 5:8). Death has lost its power over those who belong to Jesus Christ (1 Corinthians 15:55–56). It will be a wonderful day of rejoicing when faith in Christ is turned into sight:

> But as it is written, Eye hath not seen, nor ear heard, neither have entered into the heart of man, the things which God hath prepared for them that love him. But God hath revealed them unto us by his Spirit: for the Spirit searcheth all things, yea, the deep things of God (1 Corinthians 2:9–10).

In paganism, since no single belief in the afterlife is normative, nobody knows for sure what will occur. This uncertainty comes from a lack of an authoritative revelation. Pagans think they have an ultimate spiritual destination in mind, whatever they may call it, but they have no reliable map to get them there. Christian philosopher Gordon Clark underscores the dilemma of pagan religion:

The beclouding effects of sin upon the mind as it tries to discover God and salvation in nature may best be seen in the divergent results obtained among the pagan religions. The ancient Babylonians, Egyptians, and Romans looked on the same nature that is seen by the modern Moslem, Hindu, and Buddhist. But the messages that they purport to receive are considerably different.[35]

Who Is in Charge?

Neo-paganism has no single authoritative book like the Bible. Therefore, they have no written creed, or standards acceptable to all pagans, which dictate what they do. This is an important distinction between paganism and Christianity. Unlike Christianity, paganism makes few absolute truth claims, but there are some basic beliefs that most pagans would generally hold to. One key view is the postmodern belief that truth is relative (it may change depending on the circumstances).

Pagans prefer situational ethics to moral absolutes. What might be right for one pagan could be wrong for another. An example of this would be in the diets pagans follow. Some are strict vegetarians while others are not. Some are heterosexual and others homosexual. Many are dedicated feminists; others are not. Paganism delights in personal choice and diversity. Oddly enough, pagans tend to think that the lack of written dogma unites them more than a universal statement of beliefs. It gives birth to self-expression, and pagans love to borrow techniques from one another. The more learned are still quick to teach the beginners the pagan way.

For many pagans, the lack of an ultimate authority is what made paganism attractive to them. Why become a disciple of some religious teacher when you can be your own spiritual master? Whatever it takes to be a good pagan and work for human enlightenment and progress is acceptable so long as it does no harm. Pagans are not interested in following a list of commandments like those found in Judaism or Christianity. Pagans do not like to feel guilty about anything. The closest thing one can find to a code of conduct would be the Wiccan Rede (counsel). There are long versions of the Rede and short versions that embody the idea of doing whatever you desire so long as you do not harm anyone. But in a relativistic religion (no absolute right and wrong), how do you determine what is harmful?

35. Carl Henry, ed., *Revelation and the Bible* (Grand Rapids, MI: Baker Book House, 1958), p. 27.

Some Wiccans also hold to a three-fold law that basically teaches that whatever you do will come back upon you magnified many times over. This is close to the Hindu concept of cause and effect stated in the law of karma.

> Even as I have seen, they that plow iniquity, and sow wickedness, reap the same (Job 4:8).

Instead of using a God-given conscience or revealed truth, the neo-pagan determines right and wrong for himself or herself, albeit with certain self-imposed restraints — do no harm. This is their golden rule, but it is a very subjective method of morality. What constitutes harm? Is abortion harmful to an unborn baby? Is it permissible to take recreational drugs without harming the body? Is lying with good intention permissible? The problem is that an undefined moral law is no moral law at all. It is why some witches' covens can perform certain rituals while they are naked. *Skyclad* is the term for ritual nudity. Starhawk believes that nudity establishes a bond among conveners. Gardner believed performing rituals in the nude was a sign of true freedom. It may be the freedom to do as one pleases, but it is condemned in the Bible as a sin of the flesh when it defies God's Word. When Adam and Eve sinned in the garden, they hid themselves from God and covered their shameful nakedness:

> And when the woman saw that the tree was good for food, and that it was pleasant to the eyes, and a tree to be desired to make one wise, she took of the fruit thereof, and did eat, and gave also unto her husband with her; and he did eat. And the eyes of them both were opened, and they knew that they were naked; and they sewed fig leaves together, and made themselves aprons. And they heard the voice of the LORD God walking in the garden in the cool of the day: and Adam and his wife hid themselves from the presence of the LORD God amongst the trees of the garden (Genesis 3:6–8).

For the Christian, the conscience is not a reliable guide. God has given man much more than a three-fold law. God has given his Word in the 66 books of the Bible. The Word of God tells the Christian what is right and what is wrong. "Thy word is a lamp unto my feet, and a light unto my path" (Psalm 119:105).

In Romans 3:20, Paul spoke of the law of God as that which brings the knowledge of sin. Psalm 119:11 reads: "Thy word have I hid in mine heart, that I might not sin against thee." Because paganism lacks spiritual insight from the source of all wisdom and knowledge, the Lord Jesus, it lacks moral judgment. Therefore, pagans feel free to live without a doctrine of sin to inhibit them.

Christians live by the Word of God, which gives the true perspective on sin because God's perspective is the only one that has *not* been tarnished by sin (e.g., Romans 1:28–32; 1 Timothy 4:1–3; 2 Timothy 2:24–26). But it also points us to the power to live a life pleasing to God through the Holy Spirit. The Christian has present joy and pleasures forevermore in the presence of God. "But as it is written, Eye hath not seen, nor ear heard, neither have entered into the heart of man, the things which God hath prepared for them that love him" (1 Corinthians 2:9). The pagan has myths and magic. Belief in magic among pagans is based on the idea that changing one thing can change other things because all things in the universe are connected. But no pagan magic can ever change the fate that awaits them if they continue in their present darkness. No magic spell or potion can make restitution for their sins or give them the hope of eternal life.

Final Analysis

In the end, paganism takes its place among the religions of the world, most of which lack inspired revelation, a clear path to God and His righteousness, and the certainty of final salvation. These things are found *only* in the inspired Word of God, the way of the Cross, and the promises of God:

> All scripture is given by inspiration of God, and is profitable for doctrine, for reproof, for correction, for instruction in righteousness: That the man of God may be perfect, thoroughly furnished unto all good works (2 Timothy 3:16–17).

> For the preaching of the cross is to them that perish foolishness; but unto us which are saved it is the power of God (1 Corinthians 1:18).

> For all the promises of God in him are yea, and in him Amen, unto the glory of God by us (2 Corinthians 1:20).

The true father of paganism is the prince of darkness who comes to steal, kill, and destroy. Jesus came to give life, and life more abundantly (John 10:10). Everyone must choose whom they will follow. It's one or the other.

I conclude this study on paganism with the exhortation of Joshua to the children of Israel as they were about to enter a land filled with pagan nations who practiced things God called abominations. They had a choice to make and so do each of us:

> And if it seem evil unto you to serve the LORD, choose you this day whom ye will serve; whether the gods which your fathers served that were on the other side of the flood, or the gods of the Amorites, in whose land ye dwell: but as for me and my house, we will serve the LORD (Joshua 24:15).

To God be the glory!

Summary of Pagan Beliefs

Doctrine	Teachings of Paganism
God	Pagans deny the existence of a supreme God. Various views are common, but worship or connection with various gods and goddesses (polytheism) are common, as well as worship of nature and the spirits of nature (pantheism or panentheism).
Authority/ Revelation	The Bible is rejected as authoritative. Individual experience is esteemed above any form of authority. Various forms of spiritual meditation and altered states of consciousness are used to gain secret spiritual knowledge.
Man	Man is seen as a self-defining and self-determining individual who is part of the whole of nature. Details about the nature of man vary widely among pagans.
Sin	The idea of absolute moral truths is denied, especially as related to the Bible. Each individual pagan determines morality by practicing the general guideline of "do no harm."

Salvation	There is no concept of salvation from a sinful nature. Various views on the nature of the afterlife are held by pagans.
Creation	The biblical account of creation is denied. Various views, including ancient pagan mythologies and various forms of evolution, are held by pagans.

Chapter 9

Voodooism

Dr. Corey Abney

Hollywood screenwriters and practitioners in New Orleans have shaped the modern perception of Voodooism, at least in Western culture. Movies depicting witch doctors, zombies, or voodoo dolls often shape the way people think about the religion. Major events like Mardi Gras draw attention to the city of New Orleans. There, voodooism has a significant presence and ongoing promotional opportunities, but partygoers often dismiss or overlook the number of people who practice voodoo.

The result of this Hollywood/Mardi Gras effect is that many people in our culture do not take voodooism seriously as a world religion, although millions of people around the world practice it, enslaved to its teaching. Voodooism powerfully influences many places around the world and can only be overcome by the gospel of Jesus Christ.

History

The modern term for voodooism comes from the African tribal word *vodu*, which means "god," "worship," or "fear of the gods." Voodooism originated in West Africa as a tribal religion,[1] and came to Haiti and eventually the United States as the result of the 16th-century slave trade that began in 1517. Many tribes in Sub-Saharan Africa claim exclusive rights to the origins of voodoo, but the specific origins of the religion cannot be verified.

---

1. See chapter 12 in this volume for more information on animistic religions.

The country of Benin (West Africa) is generally regarded as the birthplace and capital of voodooism, as voodoo remains the state religion of Benin to the present day.

The slave trade that launched in 1517 brought multitudes of Africans to the West Indies (Caribbean). When these African slaves settled in their new land, they possessed almost nothing beyond their deeply held religious convictions.

Their European masters, however, forced the Africans to embrace Roman Catholicism, which resulted in a mingled belief system that combined major tenants of Catholicism with traditional African rituals. Moreover, similarities existed between the two religions that allowed for faster integration. For example, Catholicism allows for the worship of saints, while voodooism promotes the worship of "lesser deities" and ancestors. Catholicism uses sacramental objects in worship, while voodooism uses charms. Many followers of voodooism added components of Catholicism to their religious practices, leading to a different brand of voodooism than was practiced in West Africa. Over time, Catholicism influenced voodooism in a profound way, especially in the New World.

Thus, modern voodooism has numerous variations and practices that reflect the geographical location of the practitioners. Additionally, modern voodoo practices continue to illustrate the influence of Roman Catholicism. For instance, many voodoo followers integrate Catholic rituals, prayers, and liturgies with old African animistic observances. Some voodoo places of worship have statues or pictures of Catholic saints and the virgin Mary. This modern version of voodooism is seen most profoundly in Haiti, a country that is said to have been dedicated to Satan over 200 years ago[2] and still has significant voodoo influences. Voodooism is also practiced in Trinidad, Jamaica, Cuba, and parts of North and South America, but its most significant following remains in West Africa and Haiti.

Beliefs

Voodooism is based on the idea that spirits in the spirit world interact with humans in a harmonious relationship. Humans provide various items to help the spirits make their way in the spirit world, while the spirits provide health, protection from evil, and good fortune to humans on earth. The

---

2. While this claim is popular, the details of the event are disputed. Regardless of its historicity, voodoo remains a strong influence in the country.

spirit beings are understood to be lesser gods, and the interaction between human beings and voodoo spirits is based largely on ritual ceremonies led by a voodoo witch doctor.

The core beliefs are difficult to nail down in a systematic way because of significant variations that exist around the world, with various tribes using different terminology to reference similar beliefs and concepts. Most voodoo followers share similar beliefs about god, authority, and salvation, however, which provide a starting point for understanding and engagement.

God

Voodoo practitioners believe in a supreme being who is responsible for creation and who possesses ultimate authority over the world. They do not believe that a person can know this god, however, because the "supreme being" is far removed from people (reminiscent of a deistic view of God).

Voodoo tribes use different names for the spirit world, but *loa* is the standard name for the spirits. These spirits take many different forms and fall ultimately under the con-trol of the chief deity. Voodoo practitioners focus primarily on these spirits (loa) because they participate in the lives of individuals and are knowable. According to voodoo teaching, some loa are the souls of deceased ancestors who protect the family. Not all ancestors become loa, although every soul lives forever even if it does not become a lesser deity. Pre-existing spirits choose the spirits who become loa.

Some spirits have been present since the creation of the world and control all aspects of life. These spirits are typically associated with the magic aspects of voodooism. No detailed hierarchy of deities exists within voodooism, although

Voodoo charms, talismans, and idols are used in various ceremonies and in everyday life.
(Wikimedia Commons, by user: Doron, own work)

these "creation spirits" are considered to be the heart of the universe. Moreover, these spirits communicate their desires by possessing individuals and tormenting them, so voodoo worshipers appeal to loa in order to receive blessings and to avoid curses. One of the ways voodoo practitioners appeal to these deities is through the use of relics and charms.

Voodooism employs many rituals that are designed to invoke the help of loa. These rituals are held for securing help in times of difficulty, celebrating a holiday or significant event such as a marriage or the birth of a child, for healing, or to provide a smooth transition into the afterlife. During various ceremonies, loa take possession of individuals to act and speak through them.

A witch doctor presides over all ritual ceremonies as the priest of the community. The rituals include singing and dancing to the beat of drums in order to invoke the presence of the spirits. Offerings may be given and animals sacrificed. In some cases, worshipers may fall into a trance and manifest the spirit of loa by speaking, singing, or offering healing. These rituals are a necessary and important part of voodoo culture because of the impersonal nature of loa. Voodoo spirits participate in the lives of its practitioners without maintaining an ongoing, personal relationship. Additionally, various forms of divination are used to answer questions and give direction.

Authority

Voodooism does not possess a holy text that guides belief and practice. Key doctrines and practices are passed down orally from one generation to the next. This is the most significant reason that so much variation exists within voodooism. The lack of an authoritative text allows for wide variations of voodoo worship rituals and practices that vary greatly from one culture to another. For example, in many voodoo contexts, symbolic animals and plants represent certain elements of spirituality, with snakes (especially pythons) serving as a universal sign of voodoo power. In other contexts, people have a fear of ocean or river water because of the belief that evil spirits reside there.

Another example of variation within voodooism due to the absence of a holy text is the role of witch doctors. Witch doctors assume positions of great authority in many tribes of voodooism due to the absence of a holy text, especially in countries like Haiti. Many voodoo practitioners believe that witch doctors are chosen by loa, with selection often following family tradition as authority is passed down from generation to generation. Existing loa either confirm or deny an ancestor to take the mantle of a deceased witch doctor. In Haitian voodoo, male witch doctors are known as *houngan* and females as *mambos*. Additionally, *bokors* are involved in the practice of magic and sorcery.

Technically, anyone can be chosen to become a witch doctor by loa, even if an individual's family does not have a history of witch doctors, but the majority of witch doctors come from family units. They begin as apprentices who serve with more experienced witch doctors, start their own "practice," and achieve higher rank by gaining more knowledge of the spirit world. Witch doctors in contexts like Haiti place flags on top of their places of operation, with the most powerful witch doctors displaying more flags than their subordinates.

While Voodoo has no central authority, holy text, or governing body, witch doctors serve as authoritative voices and community leaders in many contexts. Haitian society, for instance, views witch doctors as men with the most understanding and wisdom. People seek them out for leadership, spiritual guidance, and even medical treatment. Witch doctors allegedly discern if people

Flags with various symbolism are used in voodoo rituals in the community.
(Wikimedia Commons, Voodoo banner by Valris, Sam Fentress, author)

suffer from physical maladies or something related to a spiritual cause. Their approach to attempted healing will differ based on whether or not "spirits" are involved. Typically, in cases that are determined to be physical in nature, witch doctors will use herbal remedies and organic "medicines" such as tea leaves and roots. In cases that are spiritual in nature, they turn to rituals and ceremonies that are designed to invoke direct action from loa. Ultimately, witch doctors are judged on their effectiveness to heal people and to lead their communities, and they can be replaced if the community determines that they are unable to heal and/or lead in a consistent manner.

Salvation

Voodooism does not articulate a doctrine of salvation where sin is forgiven or defeated. The focus of the religion is how to endure this life with as little trouble as possible. The Lao are called on to help voodoo followers navigate the present life and to move smoothly into the life to come. Fear is a motivating factor for voodoo practitioners and a reason that most followers demonstrate a high degree of morality. Many people are scared to do anything that may draw the ire of their Lao. In short, superstition rooted in fear trumps any notion of salvation rooted in love. In this way, voodooism is a religion that keeps its followers bound with fear and anxiety.

Engaging Followers

Engaging followers of voodoo begins with a description of the Creator God as the one, true, and living God of the Bible. Voodooism teaches that a supreme being created the world but is unknowable and removed from the world he made. Christians agree that a sovereign Creator made the world and that He is far greater than anyone or anything on the earth. Christians also believe, however, that God is personal and knowable. Therefore, the doctrines of transcendence and immanence are key starting points of Christian engagement with voodoo practitioners.

Transcendence

God's transcendence refers to His separation from all that He has made. He is infinitely exalted above all creation. God is set apart from everything else and in a class by Himself. God is not like man; rather, He is holy, sovereign, infinite, independent, all-knowing, ever-present, and perfect in all of His ways. Mankind is fully and completely dependent upon Him.

> Yours, O LORD, is the greatness, the power and the glory, the victory and the majesty; for all that is in heaven and in earth is Yours; Yours is the kingdom, O LORD, and You are exalted as head over all (1 Chronicles 29:11).[3]

> For You, LORD, are most high above all the earth; You are exalted far above all gods (Psalm 97:9).

> Who is like the LORD our God, who dwells on high, who humbles Himself to behold the things that are in the heavens and in the earth? (Psalm 113:5–6).

> "For My thoughts are not your thoughts, nor are your ways My ways," says the LORD. "For as the heavens are higher than the

3. Scripture in this chapter is from the New King James Version (NKJV) of the Bible.

earth, so are My ways higher than your ways, and My thoughts than your thoughts" (Isaiah 55:8–9).

God, who made the world and everything in it, since He is Lord of heaven and earth, does not dwell in temples made with hands (Acts 17:24).

The Scriptures present a clear picture of God's transcendence: He is greater than all that He created and separate from it. God is exalted above everything that exists in the universe and is not dependent upon anything or anyone.

Immanence

Thankfully, God is not only transcendent, He is also immanent. God is near to His people, present with them, active on earth, and involved in the world. He is present and involved in history and in the lives of individuals. He interacts with His people and assures them of His power and presence. He promised to never leave or forsake His own:

Be strong and of good courage, do not fear nor be afraid of them; for the LORD your God, He is the One who goes with you. He will not leave you nor forsake you (Deuteronomy 31:6).

Go therefore and make disciples of all the nations, baptizing them in the name of the Father and of the Son and of the Holy Spirit, teaching them to observe all things that I have commanded you; and lo, I am with you always, even to the end of the age (Matthew 28:19–20).

The ultimate demonstration of God's immanence and involvement in this world is the incarnation of Jesus Christ. The Son of God took on human flesh, was born of a woman, lived on the earth, interacted with others, and died among His people. God became what mankind is so that people can know Him and be like Him.

The Bible teaches that God's work of redemption is motivated by love for His people: "God demonstrates His own love toward us, in that while we were still sinners, Christ died for us" (Romans 5:8). Jesus came, died, and rose from the dead in order to reconcile men and women to Himself. God could have remained detached from His creation and left human beings without a way to know Him, but He initiated a relationship with them through His Word, His prophets and, most significantly, His Son.

Hebrews 1:1–2 says, "God, who at various times and in various ways spoke in time past to the fathers by the prophets, has in these last days spoken to us by His Son, whom He has appointed heir of all things, through whom also He made the worlds." The incarnation is the greatest manifestation of immanence and of God's desire to have a personal relationship with His people. John 1:14 notes that "the Word became flesh and dwelt among us, and we beheld His glory, the glory as of the only begotten of the Father, full of grace and truth." Literally, God "set up a tent" among His people so that He could have a personal relationship with them.

Balance

Scripture is clear that God is both transcendent (far from man) and immanent (near to man). Both truths must be affirmed and kept together in balance in order for a person to perceive God correctly. Only Christianity has a proper understanding and balance of God's immanence and transcendence.

> Therefore know this day, and consider it in your heart, that the LORD Himself is God in heaven above and on the earth beneath; there is no other (Deuteronomy 4:39).

> For thus says the High and Lofty One who inhabits eternity, whose name is Holy: "I dwell in the high and holy place, with him who has a contrite and humble spirit, to revive the spirit of the humble, and to revive the heart of the contrite ones" (Isaiah 57:15).

> "Am I a God near at hand," says the LORD, "and not a God afar off? Can anyone hide himself in secret places, so I shall not see him?" says the LORD; "Do I not fill heaven and earth?" says the LORD (Jeremiah 23:23–24).

Voodooism distorts God's transcendence and misunderstands God's immanence. Followers of voodoo maintain that the *supreme being* is unknowable, distant, and unconcerned about people on earth. If such were true, however, then how can they know anything about this god, even his existence? Moreover, they believe arbitrarily in lesser spirits that interact with human beings, mostly to possess them, harm them, or repay them for acts of wickedness.

Charms and relics are used, with blind hope, to appease the spirits and to persuade them to heal or bless voodoo practitioners. Voodoo practitioners participate with their gods without the comfort or confidence of a personal relationship. This stands in sharp contrast to the teaching of Christianity, which emphasizes that God is both the supreme Creator who is independent from man, but also the nearby Savior who stands ready to forgive anyone who calls on Him for salvation.

Philippians 2:5–8 says:

> Let this mind be in you which was also in Christ Jesus, who, being in the form of God, did not consider it robbery to be equal with God, but made Himself of no reputation, taking the form of a bondservant, and coming in the likeness of men. And being found in appearance as a man, He humbled Himself and became obedient to the point of death, even the death of the cross.

Jesus is both God and man. He came in both glory and humility. He is both the suffering servant and the sinless Savior.

The God of the Bible is both transcendent and immanent. Followers of voodooism need clarity concerning the nature of God that will bring together their view of a supreme being and the spirits who are present on earth (Deuteronomy 32:17; 1 Corinthians 10:20–21; Hebrews 1:14). Christians know the Creator God as the same God who is with us in a personal way. One God in three persons: Father, Son, and Holy Spirit.

The Ministry of Jesus Christ

Voodooism does not have a doctrine of salvation, so the need for a savior is glaringly absent. The presence of a mediator, however, is a significant part of voodooism, with witch doctors fulfilling the role of mediator within the religion. They invoke the presence of Lao, offer wise counsel to the people, and provide healing for spiritual and physical problems. Christians can engage voodoo followers with the concept of mediation, showing ultimately that Jesus Christ is the true mediator between God and man. Jesus is the only person who can reconcile mankind's relationship with God. He alone fulfills the roles of prophet, priest, and king that are so often fulfilled by the witch-doctors of voodoo culture.

Prophet

Followers of voodooism understand the concepts of good and evil, but they cannot know for sure that such concepts exist. Their distant god does not inform them of what is good or evil. Christians have the capacity to know good and evil, however, because of God's revelation, and one of the most significant ways God revealed Himself to His people was through His prophets. The Old Testament prophets communicated a clear standard of right and wrong to God's people and they spoke with a unique authority and clarity. Ultimately, this prophetic ministry was fulfilled by Jesus Christ, who came into the world as the divine Word of God.

As prophet, Jesus pronounced an end to all our sin. Prophets in the Old Testament served as God's mouthpiece to nations and individuals. Prophets spoke words of judgment when people sinned against God, and called them to repentance in order to be reconciled:

> Alas, sinful nation, a people laden with iniquity, a brood of evildoers, children who are corrupters! They have forsaken the LORD, they have provoked to anger the Holy One of Israel, they have turned away backward. . . . "Come now, and let us reason together," says the LORD, "Though your sins are like scarlet, they shall be as white as snow; though they are red like crimson, they shall be as wool" (Isaiah 1:4, 18).

Jesus is the greatest prophet who speaks God's Word because He is the very Word of God (John 1:1–4). Moreover, He fulfills the prophetic role by exposing sin and the need for repentance and saving faith. Jesus proclaimed pardon and forgiveness for all who believe. He speaks truth to all who will receive it and guides His people in wisdom and understanding. Unlike the witch doctors who are often wrong and unable to discern what is true, Jesus gives us a sure and perfect word.

Priest

Witch doctors presume their role as mediators and "priests" of their religion, yet their priests are not connected to their distant, unknowable god.

As priest, Jesus offered Himself as the ultimate sacrifice for the sins of His people. Priests in the Old Testament served as mediators between God and man. The high priest entered the Most Holy Place once a year on the Day of Atonement to offer a sacrifice to God on behalf of His people (Leviticus 16:34). The high priest sprinkled the blood of the sacrifice on the mercy seat "because of the uncleanness of the children of Israel, and because of their transgressions, for all their sins" (Leviticus 16:16).

Other sacrifices were made throughout the year as well, and these sacrifices were made on an annual basis. Jesus, however, is the true high priest who offered Himself as a sacrifice once and for all. Hebrews 9:12–14 states:

> Not with the blood of goats and calves, but with His own blood He entered the Most Holy Place once for all, having obtained eternal redemption. For if the blood of bulls and goats and the ashes of a heifer, sprinkling the unclean, sanctifies for the purifying of the flesh, how much more shall the blood of Christ, who through the eternal Spirit offered Himself without spot to God, cleanse your conscience from dead works to serve the living God?

Not only did Jesus offer Himself as the true, perfect sacrifice for His people, He continues to intercede on their behalf.

> Who is he who condemns? It is Christ who died, and furthermore is also risen, who is even at the right hand of God, who also makes intercession for us (Romans 8:34).

> But He, because He continues forever, has an unchangeable priesthood. Therefore He is also able to save to the uttermost those who come to God through Him, since He always lives to make intercession for them (Hebrews 7:24–25).

Jesus fulfills perfectly the priestly role described in the Old Testament, and He is the only one who can bring God and man together. His death, Resurrection, and ongoing intercession provide all that is required for mankind to draw near to God. Unlike the witch doctors who demand constant sacrifices and produce faltering results, Jesus' sacrifice was perfect and complete.

King

As King, Jesus conquers sin and death, securing an everlasting Kingdom of peace for His people. Monarchies in the Old Testament existed for the peace, prosperity, and welfare of nations. People looked to their kings for righteousness and justice. King David, for example, was a beloved king who ruled with equity and strength. Second Samuel 8:15 says, "So David reigned over all Israel; and David administered judgment and justice to all his people." David's reign served as a type of Christ, who rules with true righteousness, justice, equity, and power. Jesus came in the line of David to rule and reign over David's throne so that He is both David's son and David's Lord (Matthew 22:42–45). Jesus is "the ruler over the kings of the earth" and our "King of kings and Lord of lords" (Revelation 1:5, 19:16). His reign will never end and He will never be defeated. Followers of Christ can rest in His Kingdom of righteousness and peace.

Voodoo practitioners look to witch doctors, sacrifices, and rituals for what Jesus alone can provide. Jesus is infinitely wise, powerful, and loving. He offers salvation, healing, intercession, and comfort that bring peace, love, joy, and contentment. Followers of Jesus have no need for relics, charms, sacrifices, or spells, because the blood of Jesus grants access to God, and His ongoing intercession maintains the relationship. Ultimately, followers of voodooism don't need better education, an improved economy, or a more civilized religious system; rather, they need a mediator who can atone for their sin debt and satisfy the righteous demands of a holy God. They need a Savior who is present with them as prophet, priest, and King.

Those who are trapped in voodooism by the devil can know the true God and have a relationship with Him — particularly a God who destroys sin and evil. Furthermore, those who have been witch doctors and convert to Christ through repentance and faith can point people to the *true mediator* between God and man.

The Indwelling of the Holy Spirit

The Holy Spirit indwells every Christian from the moment of conversion (Acts 2:37–38). The nearness of God is so profound that God is not only *with* His people, He resides *in* them as well. The Apostle Paul writes, "But you are not in the flesh but in the Spirit, if indeed the Spirit of God dwells in you. Now if anyone does not have the Spirit of Christ, he is not His"

(Romans 8:9). The Holy Spirit stirs the conscience, enables understanding of the Scriptures, comforts God's people, guides into truth, cheers the soul, and convicts of sin. He interacts constantly with believers in such a way that God's Word is applied and Christ is glorified. Therefore, followers of Christ are commanded to walk in the Spirit and His many fruits. Galatians 5:16 states, "I say then: Walk in the Spirit, and you shall not fulfill the lust of the flesh."

Followers of voodoo long for their gods to be near them and act favorably toward them. Charms, relics, and sacrifices are offered to appease the gods and to provide some measure of assurance. Christians can engage voodoo practitioners with the hope of the one, true, and living God, who draws near to His people through Christ and indwells them with His Holy Spirit. God's Spirit will never withdraw from His own.

Furthermore, Christians do not live in fear and anxiety, striving to appease God constantly, because Jesus has already satisfied the righteous demands of the Father. The presence of the Holy Spirit in the life of a believer is a guarantee that he or she is loved by God and assured of everlasting life. People who are trapped within a culture of voodooism under the whims of a witch doctor and unseen dark spiritual forces need the confidence and assurance that can only come through the blood of Jesus and the indwelling of the Holy Spirit. As the Apostle Paul told the people of Athens, God "is not far from each one of us; for in Him we live and move and have our being" (Acts 17:27–28).

The Authority of the Bible

The nature and character of God as revealed in the Bible are the foundation of faith and morality for the Christian. The Scriptures provide a clear moral standard by which followers of Christ must live. Voodooism, however, does not possess a standard of doctrines, which leads to the loss of an ethical standard for voodoo followers and communities. Although a concept of law-breaking or wrongdoing exists in their culture, such "ethics" are sanctioned primarily by the specific community in which a follower of voodoo resides. No concept of sin is present within voodoo communities, nor is a clear moral standard taught throughout the religion. Evil magic can be applied to people or objects, and property can be destroyed for personal vengeance. The lack of an authoritative doctrinal foundation or moral standard is a source of tension within voodoo communities. Witch doctors assume authoritative roles with little accountability.

Christians should equip voodoo converts with the authority of the Bible, which provides a moral and doctrinal foundation for faith and practice. The Word of God is the foundation of faith, obedience, and Christian community. Followers of Christ have confidence knowing that in the Bible, God has spoken, revealed His nature and character, and provided clear principles of Christian conduct.

Converts from voodoo need the firm foundation of God's Word, which is always profitable to those who receive it:

> All Scripture is given by inspiration of God, and is profitable for doctrine, for reproof, for correction, for instruction in righteousness, that the man of God may be complete, thoroughly equipped for every good work (2 Timothy 3:16–17).

After all, God himself testifies that His Word "shall not return to Me void, but it shall accomplish what I please, and it shall prosper in the thing for which I sent it" (Isaiah 55:11).

Conclusion

Christian engagement with followers of voodooism should emulate the Apostle Paul's approach in Athens, where he stood at the Areopagus and made known the God who was previously unknown to the people. Paul speaks to the Athenians with appeals to the preeminence of God as Creator and the glory of God in general revelation. He finds a point of agreement in the Athenian belief in a supreme, unknown God. Paul then appeals to the authority of the one, true, and living God as Creator and Sustainer. Moreover, he points to the glory of God in general revelation and implies that people in Athens made an appropriate judgment based on general revelation about the presence of a Creator from whom man originates.

> Then Paul stood in the midst of the Areopagus and said, "Men of Athens, I perceive that in all things you are very religious; for as I was passing through and considering the objects of your worship, I even found an altar with this inscription: TO THE UNKNOWN GOD. Therefore, the One whom you worship without knowing, Him I proclaim to you: 'God, who made

the world and everything in it, since He is Lord of heaven and earth, does not dwell in temples made with hands. Nor is He worshiped with men's hands, as though He needed anything, since He gives to all life, breath, and all things. And He has made from one blood every nation of men to dwell on all the face of the earth, and has determined their preappointed times and the boundaries of their dwellings, so that they should seek the Lord, in the hope that they might grope for Him and find Him, though He is not far from each one of us; for in Him we live and move and have our being, as also some of your own poets have said, "For we are also His offspring." Therefore, since we are the offspring of God, we ought not to think that the Divine Nature is like gold or silver or stone, something shaped by art and man's devising. Truly, these times of ignorance God overlooked, but now commands all men everywhere to repent, because He has appointed a day on which He will judge the world in righteousness by the Man whom He has ordained. He has given assurance of this to all by raising Him from the dead' " (Acts 17:22–31).

Paul exposes the Athenians' mistake of crediting pagan gods with a power they do not possess. Thus, Paul appeals repeatedly to God's creative power and the subsequent implications manifested through general revelation as a point of agreement and as a launching pad for gospel proclamation.

Paul's method of evangelism in Athens is a helpful one for those who engage followers of voodooism. A point of agreement can be established with the belief in a Supreme Being who created the world. Mankind lives, moves, and has their being in the Lord of heaven and earth. But contrary to voodoo teaching, the true God is knowable and near to His people.

Moreover, He is not confined to temples made by human hands, nor is He shaped by art and man's devising. He is one God in three persons who extends grace and mercy to those who receive it. He commands that people repent of their sin because He has appointed a day on which He will judge the world in righteousness. This judgment will come at the hand of "the Man" whom God ordained and is the same Man who saves people from their sins. He is not a lesser deity or a voodoo priest; rather, He is the sinless Son of God who died for His people as an atoning sacrifice and rose from the dead as the victorious King of kings. Thus, the only hope for eternal life is found not in a witch doctor, but in a Savior, who is Jesus Christ the Lord.

Summary of Voodoo Beliefs

Doctrine	Teachings of Voodooism
God	Deny the God of the Bible, but believe in a creator god who is detached from his creation. Lesser gods (loa) and ancestral spirits are seen as ruling the affairs of man. Jesus is not acknowledged.
Authority/ Revelation	There are no standard writings. Oral traditions exist and vary by region. Syncretism with other religious views (e.g., Roman Catholicism) exist. Witch doctors are seen as the sages and priests in a community.
Man	All men are spiritual beings seeking to avoid trouble in this life and enter safely into the afterlife. There is no notion of a sin nature, though moral codes are to be followed.
Sin	Sin is based on local traditions and brings trouble in the present life. There is no notion of mediation or forgiveness of sins.
Salvation	There is no view of salvation apart from achieving a trouble-free life and entering the afterlife. All souls enter the afterlife, but some are able to become lesser gods (loa).
Creation	The creator god is responsible for creating, but not sustaining the creation. Evolutionary views vary, but are generally rejected.

Chapter 10

Wicca and Witchcraft

Marcia Montenegro

Author's Disclaimer: Since Wicca and Witchcraft are not centralized or monolithic, the disparities in beliefs and practices are widespread. Additionally, given the history of these beliefs, it can be challenging to sort fact from fiction. Therefore, some may dispute portions of the material given here due to these variations. For the sake of brevity, the words Wicca and Wiccan are used interchangeably with Witchcraft and Witch when possible, with the understanding that these terms are not always equated with each other by their followers. Since there are numerous and ever-evolving forms of Wicca and Witchcraft, this chapter gives a broad overview and cannot address all forms of Wicca and Witchcraft. To distinguish the generic use of the term "witch" and "witchcraft" from the modern religion of Witchcraft, "Witch" and Witchcraft" will be capitalized when referring to the contemporary religion.

You are in a circle. Protection from the Goddess and various spirits are invoked. The elements of earth, fire, air, and water are called in. You begin to dance slowly around the circle, then faster. There is chanting. The pace increases; the group is "raising energy." Or you are around a fire and each person, one by one, comes to the fire and throws something in while stating a personal truth or desire. In many such scenarios, a ritual will be performed, whether to call for protection, healing, a special favor, world peace, etc. The rituals vary from group to group, even person to person.[1]

Teen Witch, by Silver RavenWolf, a how-to manual for teens, came out in 1998 and sold so many copies that bookstore shelves were cleaned out, and several printings were required to fill the demand. Eventually, a small spell kit was sold alongside the book. It has become common to find books for children and teens featuring heroes who are Witches or cast spells and save the day by their magic arts (e.g., Harry Potter series, Disney's *Wizards of Waverly Place*). For adults, there are movies and television shows such as the popular series, *The Good Witch*, on the Hallmark channel or the classic *Bewitched*. These instances only indicate society's growing acceptance of Witchcraft and "good" Witches.

There are many myths and misunderstandings about Witchcraft, arising from sources as divergent as the entertainment industry, the early founders of the modern Witchcraft movement themselves, elaborate tales stemming from the European Inquisition, and dubious Internet data. Because of this, erroneous perceptions abound, and the result is a conflation of fact and fantasy. Christians, however, should make efforts to know the truth for the sake of those who need Christ, who is the way, the truth, and the life, so that our witness is both credible and compassionate.

History

The modern religion of Witchcraft, also known as Wicca, has drawn an increasing number of adherents for the last several decades in Europe and in the United States. The word "witchcraft" is a word of later origin than when the biblical canon was written; therefore, words in the Bible translated as "witchcraft" arise from Hebrew and Greek words that refer to sorcery, enchantment, or divination, and not to the modern concept of "Witchcraft"

---

1. These activities were open to outsiders; Wiccan rituals are normally closed and for adherents only. The author participated in these when she was an astrologer and New Ager.

as a religion. It is also useful to keep in mind the distinction between the generic term "witchcraft," which refers to occult practices and folk magic in many cultures today, and the contemporary Western religious terms "Witchcraft" and "Wicca" that describe a modern religious practice.

Witchcraft and Wicca are a subset of neo-paganism, the alleged revival of ancient practices of worshiping and invoking gods (polytheism), belief in nature spirits, rituals to honor the cycles of nature, and occult practices such as divination[2] and spell casting. In the Old Testament, there are references to paganism that include the worship of false gods, rituals in the "sacred groves" or under trees with thick foliage, and ritual prostitution.[3]

Neo-paganism today exhibits itself as polytheism, seasonal rituals honoring nature and moon phases, worship of the Goddess (by some), and occult practices such as casting spells and the practice of divination. Neo-paganism is an umbrella term which covers Witchcraft, Wicca, modern Druidry, the worship of Norse and Germanic gods in Asatru and Odinism,[4] the worship of the ancient Greek and Roman gods, Italian witchcraft (*Stregheria* or *Strega*), and a number of other modern neo-pagan movements. Although neo-paganism includes modern Witchcraft or Wicca, they are not equivalent. Witches and Wiccans are pagans, but not all pagans are Witches or Wiccans. Wicca is also categorized by some as a subdivision of Witchcraft.

Wicca is a modern term for what is declared to be the religion of Witchcraft, particularly as it relates to Gerald Gardner (1884–1964), a native of England. Gardner, the main person responsible for initiating the modern Wicca movement, claimed he was reviving an ancient religion, a theory since discredited.[5] Gardner stated he was initiated into a Wiccan coven[6] by a

---

2. Divination in a pagan or an occult context is gaining information and advice through occult techniques and reading hidden meanings in esoteric symbols or omens. Divination is forbidden throughout the Bible (Leviticus 19:26; Jeremiah 14:14; Acts 16:16; Galatians 5:19–21; Revelation 21:8).

3. Deuteronomy 12:2, 16:20, 23:17; Judges 2:11–13, 3:5–7; 1 Kings 14:23; 2 Kings 16:4, 17:10; 2 Chronicles 28:4; Jeremiah 3:6, 13; Ezekiel 6:13, 20:28–29; Isaiah 1:29–30, 57:5; Hosea 4:13.

4. See chapter 14 for more information on Norse mythology.

5. The two most well-known works on this are Ronald Hutton, *The Triumph of the Moon: A History of Modern Pagan Witchcraft* (NY: Oxford University Press, Inc., 1999) and Margot Adler, *Drawing Down the Moon* (NY: Penguin Group, 1986); also Encyclopedia Britannica, http://www.britannica.com/EBchecked/topic/225915/Gerald-Brousseau-Gardner.

6. A coven is a small group of Wiccans or Witches that varies in number, usually anywhere from 3 to 20, although 13 is the usual limit. However, the number required will vary from coven to coven. The number 13 is thought by many to derive from anthropologist Margaret Murray's works; Murray's writings have since been largely discredited.

woman in the New Forest area of England, but there is only Gardner's word for the existence of this coven.

Gardner adapted many of the rituals and spells based on materials from occult sources and from the secret societies he joined and researched. Influences on Gardner include Margaret Murray (1863–1963), an Egyptologist, folklorist, archaeologist, and anthropologist, whose works on Witchcraft have been largely discredited;[7] the controversial 1899 work, *Ariada, or the Gospel of the Witches* by folklorist Charles Leland; James Frazer's *The Golden Bough*, published first in 1922; the 1948 book by Robert Graves (1895–1985), *The White Goddess*; and the writings of ceremonial magician and occultist Aleister Crowley (1875–1947).[8] Many enduring myths about a pre-Christian religion of Witchcraft and practices, as well as a supposed organized universal pagan religion, arose from these works and persist today.

In the 1960s, a Gardner initiate, Alex Sanders (1926–1988), started his own Witchcraft group in England, known as Alexandrian Wicca, a branch of Wicca still practiced today. The seed for Wicca was planted in the United States when Gardner follower Raymond Buckland (b. 1934) came to the United States and introduced Gardnerian Wicca in 1964. From that beginning, groups began to spread forms of Gardnerian and Alexandrian Wicca.

The late author and Wiccan priestess Margot Adler (1946–2014), in her landmark work on the modern neo-pagan movement, wrote, "The majority of Pagan scholars no longer accept Margaret Murray's theory of the witch cult, and they have come to accept that the persecution, torture, and killing of people accused of witchcraft in Europe involved a relatively small number of people accused of witchcraft."[9]

No matter what may be claimed, there is no historical evidence for an ancient religion of Witchcraft, or for the claim made by some present-day Goddess worshipers (some of whom who are Wiccans) that an ancient

---

7. Hutton, *The Triumph of the Moon*, p. 194–201; additionally, other portions of Hutton's book discuss the investigation of Murray's works on Witchcraft and resulting conclusions about its invalidity; Adler, *Drawing Down the Moon*, p. 45–46; "Margaret Murray's Unlikely History," http://wicca.cnbeyer.com/murray.shtml.

8. "Wicca and Neopaganism," Sacred Text Archives, http://www.sacred-texts.com/pag/.

9. Adler, *Drawing Down the Moon*, p. 235, also, Ellen Evert Hopman and Lawrence Bond, *People of the Earth: The New Pagans Speak Out* (Rochester, VT: Destiny Books, 2006), p. 349. The phrase used in Adler's title, *Drawing Down the Moon*, refers to a ritual during which the Wiccan priestess invokes the Goddess into herself so that while in a trance state the Goddess will speak through her.

matriarchal Goddess-worshiping culture existed.[10] There are Wiccans who admit that Wicca is a recent innovation but nevertheless choose to view the idea of an ancient religion as a useful metaphor, while others adamantly believe and claim it is humanity's oldest religion.

It is not that pagan practices did not exist in the ancient world, but rather that there is no evidence for a pre-Christian Witchcraft religion as practiced today, for ancient matriarchal societies that primarily venerated a Goddess distinct from the role as consort for a god, or for organized pagan religions such as described by Frazer, Murray, Gardner, and others. Interestingly, scholar Ronald Hutton writes in his highly respected work, *Triumph of the Moon*, that Frazer wrote *The Golden Bough* in part to discredit Christianity.[11]

Some Witches have divided modern Witchcraft into branches, such as Classical, Familial (passed down or inherited through a family line), Immigrant, Ethnic, and Feminist.[12] To this list can be added Natural, Eclectic, Dianic, Green, Neo-Shamanic, Hedge, and Faery (or Fari). Such divisions, and others, are still made by Wiccans and Witches.

Wiccans in cremonial dress

Authority

There is no monolithic organization or central authority in Wicca with a stated creed or dogma (i.e., personal or self-authority). In fact, it is precisely this lack of structure that draws many to these groups. Each group or

---

10. Cynthia Eller, *The Myth of Matriarchal Prehistory* (Boston, MA: Beacon Press, 2000). This book is highly recommended as a scholarly work exploring the myth of ancient Goddess cultures and matriarchal societies.

11. Hutton, *The Triumph of the Moon*, p. 114. Frazer's work also influenced others, such as Margaret Murray and Gerald Gardner, and still holds sway today.

12. Adler, *Drawing Down the Moon*, p. 40. Adler attributes some of these classifications to Isaac Bonewits (1949–2010), an American Druid who wrote books on neo-paganism and magic, and founded a Druidic organization. Bonewits extensively researched the history of Witchcraft, concluding that there was no Witchcraft religion until the 20th century, and that the term "witchcraft" alluded to sorcery and other occult practices until the 14th century when baseless allegations of organized witches practicing a religion were made by those heading the Inquisition in Europe; Adler, *Drawing Down the Moon*, p. 65–67. This conclusion agrees with the research of others as well.

One of the *Book of Shadows* owned by Gerald Gardner
(Wikimedia Commons, Midnightblueowl)

person can form his own version of Wicca so that it can be a highly personal spiritual path; this is also an attraction.

For most who follow the Gardnerian teachings and British Traditional Witchcraft,[13] Gardner's *Book of Shadows*, first used in Gardner's coven in the 1950s, is the guide and instructions for rituals. Gardner's book included contributions from Gardnerian Wiccan, Doreen Valiente (1922–1999), who wrote many of the rituals, chants, and liturgies, including the well-known and well-used "Charge of the Goddess." The latter is an alleged discourse from the Goddess given through the high priestess after she invokes the Goddess in a ceremony known as "drawing down the moon." As is often true concerning Gardner, there is controversy about the sources Gardner used for this work. Valiente herself rewrote some of the material because she recognized that part of the content was from Crowley's writings, as well as that of others.[14] Although Valiente later broke with Gardner, she continued to accept some of Gardner's stories about his initiation into a coven despite the later exposés.

---

13. British Traditional Wicca also may refer to Alexandrian Wicca.
14. A detailed discussion of *The Book of Shadows* and the working relationship between Gardner and Valiente is found in Hutton, *The Triumph of the Moon,* p. 206–207, 226–236, 338–339, and Adler, *Drawing Down the Moon,* p. 79–81.

Others also criticized Gardner's claims about *The Book of Shadows,* noting that Gardner used modern writings as sources for the rituals.[15] Aidan Kelly, a neo-pagan who authored a book on the history of Witchcraft, explained that "the Gardnerian style deals with *The Book of Shadows* and the degree of adherence to it. At least the orthodox Gardnerians do it that way. The Liberal Gardnerians take the attitude that Gerald rewrote all the rituals, and if you truly want to follow Gerald, then *do what he did, rewrite the rituals.*"[16]

Indeed, there is no definitive *Book of Shadows* at present, since each Wiccan group or tradition have tailored their own to match their specific practices, and individuals may add material or write their own.[17]

Wiccans and Witches often follow a tradition from whatever teachers they learned from, and these teachings themselves may have been pieced together with others. Practices and beliefs can vary widely and do not have to be aligned with any specific teaching or doctrine. It is normal for followers to change groups or teachers. Solo practitioners, called Solitaires or Solitary Witches, practice alone and are not part of a particular group and may or may not adopt a particular lineage.

However, most Wicca and Witchcraft today incorporates aspects of the teachings of Gardner, Sanders, and Raymond Buckland, as well as influences from teachers and writers Stewart (d. 2000) and Janet Farrar (authors of the prominent work *A Witches Bible*); Wiccan teacher and writer Starhawk (b. 1951; real name, Miriam Simos); Margot Adler, Witchcraft teacher and popular author Scott Cunningham (1956–1993); and Wiccan High Priestess Selena Fox (b. 1949, founder of Circle Sanctuary in Wisconsin).[18]

Other notable voices include Z. (Zsuzsanna) Budapest (b. 1940), founder of the first documented women-only coven oriented to Goddess worship, called Dianic Wicca;[19] and Dion Fortune (1890–1946), who, although not a Witch, was an occultist and practitioner of ceremonial magic whose books influenced practices in Witchcraft.

15. Adler, *Drawing Down the Moon*, p. 61, 79, 115.
16. Hopman and Bond, *People of the Earth*, p. 272 (italics in original).
17. Rosemary Ellen Guiley, *The Encyclopedia of Witches, Witchcraft, and Wicca* (NY: Checkmark Books, 2008), p. 35.
18. According to the Circle Sanctuary website, Circle Sanctuary was founded in 1974 and is a "Wiccan church" that is "dedicated to networking, community celebrations, spiritual healing and education," https://www.circlesanctuary.org/. Fox is also a psychotherapist, https://www.circlesanctuary.org/index.php/organization/about-rev-selena-fox.
19. "Famous Witches: Zsuzsanna Budapest," Witchcraft and Witches, accessed October 15, 2015, http://www.witchcraftandwitches.com/witches_budapest.html.

Starhawk

Cunningham wrote a book on practicing as a Solitary, and this book was one of the top best-selling books on the topic, although many Wiccans thought he watered Wicca down.[20] Starhawk, whose book *The Spiral Dance* is considered a key source for modern Witchcraft practices and Goddess worship, has had a major impact on the Witchcraft and neo-pagan cultures. Starhawk has also authored other popular books on Witchcraft and neo-pagan practices.[21]

"Wicca" is allegedly an old English term for "witch" which originally meant to "bend," as in the use of magic[22] to alter reality, though there is dispute as to the word's true origins.[23] Many Wiccans refer to Wicca simply as "the Craft" or sometimes as "the Old Religion." Terms such as "Earth Religions" or "Earth Spirituality" are also used for neo-pagan, Witchcraft, and Wiccan beliefs, including by those outside of the religion.[24]

In fact, there is an organization of neo-pagans within the Unitarian-Universalist Church called The Covenant of Unitarian Universalist Pagans

---

20. Cunningham's book is *Wicca: A Guide for the Solitary Practitioner*. The criticism of some teachings being watered-down or being "fluffy Witchcraft" is not uncommon in the world of Wicca.

21. Some Witches may consider Starhawk, who is an activist in pagan, feminist, and ecological movements, too polemical. However, her influence on modern Witchcraft cannot be discounted.

22. "Magic" in this chapter refers to occult magic and not to stage magic, such as taking a rabbit out of a hat. Some spell it as "magick" to make the distinction between the two. Occult magic involves working with spirits, forces, or alleged gods using certain rituals and often various tools as symbols and aids in the ceremonies. There is disagreement among Christians as to whether there is any real power in this magic and if so, how demonic powers may be involved.

23. Adler, *Drawing Down the Moon*, p. 10; Starhawk, *The Spiral Dance* (NY: HarperCollins Publishers, 1999), p. 29. Some claim the word means "wise," referring to "wise women" who healed with herbs.

24. The following statement is from a Unitarian-Universalist website in reference to the UU churches: "Found in today's churches are humanism, agnosticism, atheism, theism, liberal Christianity, neo-paganism and earth spiritualism. These beliefs are not mutually exclusive — it's possible to hold more than one. While we are bound by a set of common principles, we leave it to the individual to decide what particular beliefs lead to those principles," http://www.uucnc.org/100q.html#q18. From the official UU website as part of a statement about the traditions from which they draw: "Spiritual teachings of earth-centered traditions which celebrate the sacred circle of life and instruct us to live in harmony with the rhythms of nature," http://www.uua.org/beliefs/principles/.

(CUUPS), which "is an organization dedicated to networking Pagan-identified Unitarian Universalists (UUs), educating people about Paganism, promoting interfaith dialogue, developing Pagan liturgies and theologies, and supporting Pagan-identified UU religious professionals."[25] The adoption of this group in the Unitarian-Universalist Church is arguably an indication of the mainstreaming of Witchcraft and other neo-pagan religions in the United States.

Wiccans may use the term Wiccan or Witch for themselves. Those who follow Wicca may reject the terms Witch or Witchcraft since they consider the term "Witchcraft" to be connected to black magic or casting evil spells, or worry that others view it that way.[26] Wiccans ordinarily perceive their religion to be white Witchcraft or white magic, which is deemed good. Some Wiccans, however, consider Wicca to be neutral in terms of good or bad. On the other hand, those who identify as a "Witch" may deny that Wicca is true Witchcraft, being only a recent innovation and not an ancient authentic religion such as the Witchcraft they follow. Their position may be that Wicca lacks depth or historic validity.

Many classify Wicca as Celtic Witchcraft and therefore different from non-Celtic forms. Then there are those who claim to practice paganism but may call themselves a Witch, and some Wiccans may also use that term. Many are apathetic about which label is used, and others disagree on the meanings, so it is wise to be cautious about applying such terms.

To summarize the view of authority among Wiccans, a person is their own absolute authority on matters of faith and practice within Wicca and Witchcraft, which is actually arbitrary.

Foundations and Beliefs

Doctrine is not primary for Wiccans or Witches.[27] They are more interested in experiences and practice, and they value their Wiccan community as well as the wider community of Wiccans and neo-pagans.

Wiccans "consider themselves priests and priestesses of an ancient European shamanistic nature religion that worships a Goddess who is related to

---

25. From the CUUPS website at http://www.cuups.org/.
26. Guiley, *The Encyclopedia of Witches, Witchcraft, and Wicca*, p. 371–372. This was also the author's experience with Wiccans as her astrological clients.
27. For the difficulty, if not impossibility, of defining Wicca and Witchcraft even among its practitioners, see Adler, *Drawing Down the Moon*, p. 95–103.

the ancient Mother Goddess," writes Adler.[28] Starhawk concurs, declaring that "Witchcraft is a shamanistic religion, and the spiritual value placed on ecstasy is a high one. It is the source of union, healing, creative inspiration, and communion with the divine — whether it is found in the center of a coven circle, in bed with one's beloved, or in the midst of the forest."[29]

"To be a witch," claims another, "means tapping into an ancient energy of wild nature. And also peaceful nature energy."[30] Because nature is sacred, rituals involve calling on spirits and hidden forces of the material creation. Nature spirits, "guardian beings that exist in all life forms in the plant, animal and mineral kingdoms," are called on in rituals for "cooperation and guidance."[31] It is worthwhile noting that using an inner force to cast spells or to summon gods or spirits is typically not seen as a supernatural activity, but as a natural one.

Eight seasonal rituals, called Sabbats, are celebrated throughout the year. Two are at the Summer and Winter Solstices, and two are at the Spring and Autumn Equinoxes. The others are midpoints between those four: February 2, May 1, August 1, and October 31.[32] The phases of the moon are also significant and normally merit a ceremony or ritual.

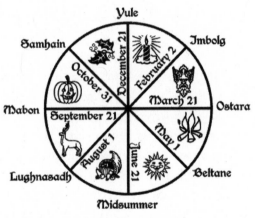

The Wheel of the Year

Divinity

Many Wiccans and Witches hold that Earth is the Goddess and consider Earth to be the source of life, calling the earth "Mother" of all life. Nature is the model and standard for life's principles. An example of this is found in the words of neo-pagan activist and Witch Starhawk: "The store-bought

28. Adler, *Drawing Down the Moon*, p. 10.
29. Starhawk, *The Spiral Dance*, p. 49.
30. Hopman and Bond, *People of the Earth*, p. 65.
31. Guiley, *The Encyclopedia of Witches, Witchcraft, and Wicca*, p. 244.
32. This is called the "Wheel of the Year." Normally Celtic names are given to these celebrations, although other terms can also be used, depending on the group and their tradition.

squash is an object, a dismembered part of the dead world, while the one in my garden is a whole process in which I have participated, from the composting of my garbage to the sense of wonder evoked when I find the vine still producing in November. . . . Our sense of self-worth is dependent on some direct contact with the broader cycles of birth, growth, death, decay, and renewal that do, in reality, sustain our lives."[33]

Male Wiccans and Witches use the same term as females. Although some men may identify as a "Warlock," it is normally used to refer to one who practices black magic, though some Wiccan men may be reclaiming the label.

The one core principle that most Wiccans agree on is what is called the Wiccan Rede: "An ye harm none, do what ye will."[34] Many believe Gardner adapted this from ceremonial magician Aleister Crowley's Law of Thelema, which states, "Do what thou wilt shall be the whole of the law."[35] The stand against doing harm leads Wiccans to think that they are practicing a good religion.

Basics of Wiccan belief about the divine typically include Pantheism or Panentheism, Duotheism, Polytheism, and regarding nature as sacred.

> **Pantheism** is the view that all is God(dess), and that God(dess) is all and thus assumes divine forces within oneself and in nature.

> **Panentheism** holds that all is in God(dess), and god(s), and God(dess) and god(s) are in all. This allows for the Goddess or gods to transcend creation.

> **Duotheism** is the belief in two gods, commonly found in Wicca. In the case of Wicca, it is the Goddess and her consort, a male god. They are customarily referred to as the Lord and the Lady.

---

33. Starhawk, *Truth or Dare* (NY: HarperCollins Publishers, 1987, paperback edition, 1990), p. 200.

34. Adler, *Drawing Down the Moon*, p. 97; Guiley, *The Encyclopedia of Witches, Witchcraft, and Wicca*, p. 371–373.

35. Adler, *Drawing Down the Moon*, p. 97; Hutton, *The Triumph of the Moon*, p. 247–248. Aleister Crowley's Thelemic Law, "Do what thou will shall be the whole of the law" is routinely cited by modern-day Satanists as their creed, leading to the mistaken belief that Crowley was a Satanist. He was actually a ritual magician involved in many secret occult groups and activities, and notorious for debauched practices, though it is difficult to know what he actually did and did not do since he seemingly enjoyed his infamous reputation.

Polytheism is the belief there are many gods, or that many gods and goddesses are multiple separate manifestations of one god.

Wiccan Lady and Lord statues

The Goddess is also known as the "Great Mother" or "Queen of Heaven." The focus on the Goddess comes in part from Robert Graves, poet Robert Bly, and others, positing that "matriarchy was not a historical state but a psychological reality with a great power that is alive and generally repressed in human beings today,"[36] This Goddess focus has created a feminist-oriented religion for many followers of Wicca.

The consort is usually referred to as the "horned god," who is the male principle of the creative force, sometimes identified with the mythical Greek god, Pan.[37] Starhawk writes that the horns of this god are the "waxing and waning crescents of the Goddess Moon, and the symbol of animal vitality."[38] Another asserts that the horns are antlers, standing for the animals killed by the hunter for the tribe.[39] This god is a hunter and a creature of earthy passions, representing the untamed woods and wildlife. The sun is one of his symbols, and the seasons symbolize his dying and rebirth.[40]

For some, the Goddess and/or gods are actual beings or forces of creation; for others, they represent the inner Goddess or god within each person. Still others may see the gods as psychological metaphors or illustrative of nature's powers. Additionally, there is belief in nature spirits and in forces or gods that inhabit and guide creation. A number of Wiccans and Witches

36. Adler, *Drawing Down the Moon*, p. 196.
37. Guiley, *The Encyclopedia of Witches, Witchcraft, and Wicca*, p. 169–170.
38. Starhawk, *The Spiral Dance*, p. 120. Starhawk often cites the discredited Margaret Murray or Robert Graves as sources.
39. Ashleen O'Gaea, *Family Wicca* (Franklin, NJ: The Career Press, 2006), p. 215.
40. Ibid. The "dying and rising" gods are ascribed to ancient pagan cults. Claims that Jesus is a "copycat Savior" based on these gods has been thoroughly refuted. Many online websites address this issue, such as Christian Think Tank at http://christianthinktank.com/copycat. html and Tektonics at http://www.tektonics.org/copycathub.html.

are non-theists or are even atheists, discounting belief in God or denying that God (or any god) exists.[41]

Many Wiccans revere what is known as the Triple Goddess.[42] She is maiden (or virgin), mother, and crone, the three aspects of the Goddess and the feminine nature, corresponding respectively to the new, full, and waning cycles of the moon. As maiden, she is youth, vitality, and pleasure. "Virgin" in this case is not sexual purity, but rather exemplifies that she is not possessed by anyone. The mother aspect is in her prime as nurturer and protector.

Image of Triple Goddess

This archetype is often related to the veneration of Earth as mother, nurturer, and healer. The last stage, crone, is considered the culmination of wisdom, representing independence and power. The stereotyped witch of an old woman with pointed chin and wart is, according to Witchcraft, a perverted version of the crone. Some Witches may even claim that the Trinity was a copy of the Triple Goddess.[43]

The Christian God is regularly stigmatized as patriarchal and oppressive to women, and the Bible is seen as the work of men who were toeing the line for those in charge of what is called "organized religion" (viewed as patriarchal, rules-based, and unjust to minorities).

---

41. The fact that there are agnostic and atheist Witches may be surprising. However, in Wicca and Witchcraft, the Goddess and gods are often metaphors or symbols and not always accepted as having substantive reality. Those who have this view may therefore decide that there is no actual Goddess or god.

42. Some believe the ideas of the Horned God and Triple Goddess came from Robert Graves' writings; Hutton, *The Triumph of the Moon*, p. 188, 194; or from Margaret Murray's works; Guiley, *The Encyclopedia of Witches, Witchcraft, and Wicca*, p. 238. Hutton touches on earlier (but later invalidated) prominent ancient goddesses or three-fold goddesses proposed by various scholars, p. 36–37.

43. In 1995, during a talk to a youth group at a church, the author was told by an eighth-grader that he was told by a Wiccan student at school that the Trinity was copied from the Triple Goddess, which predated it. He did not know how to respond to this. Although the author had known Wiccans and neo-pagans in her past as an astrologer and New Ager, this incident indicated that Wicca was in secondary schools in her area. This led the author to write her first article on Wicca, and to start speaking on it.

Jesus

There are differing assessments of Jesus Christ among Wiccans and Witches. Some reject Him as a symbol of Christian oppression of Witchcraft and/ or women while others regard Him as an enlightened spiritual teacher. Still others may consider Him another god and incorporate Him into their pantheon of pagan gods and goddesses. A few may deny Jesus existed. There is even a branch of Wicca called Christian Wicca that attempts to combine the ethical teachings of Jesus with Wiccan ethics (this is an example of syncretism, mixing two different religions together). Like many beliefs in Wicca and Witchcraft, there are spectrums with wide ranges. Most Wiccans I have encountered in my ministry experience are open to discussion about Jesus and generally are positive about Him.

Satan is rejected as real, and assessed to be an invention of the Christian church authorities in order to keep people subjugated. Although there can be individual crossovers from Witchcraft into Satanism, and though some Satanists might call themselves Witches, these two groups are separate (see chapter 13 on Satanism in volume 1). The line between the two groups becomes more blurred among those younger people who dabble in and mix several belief systems, but it is crucial to recognize that Witches and Wiccans are not Satanists, and, in fact, they do not generally like or get along with Satanists.[44]

Nature of Man

People are born basically good, but if hurt or damaged in life they may become out of balance within themselves and with nature. This can lead to the desire to do harm or to do wrong. Since there is no concept of a righteous God, there is no acceptance of the concept of sin, and thus there is no belief about being born with a desire to do harm or wrong. Wiccans and Witches will admit that they have flaws and make mistakes, and state this is why they need to adhere to the Wiccan Rede and strive to be better. The idea of being in balance is thought to bring harmony and to remedy potentials to commit harm.

Symbolism and Practices

Due to the experiential nature of Wicca, the use of symbols is important. The most well-known symbol is the pentacle or pentagram, a five-pointed

---

44. Nor do Satanists like Witches. Satanists regard Witchcraft and Wicca as a "white-light religion," whose followers attempt to hew to a moral code and do good, something for which Satanists have contempt.

star with the top point normally facing up, represent-ing the four elements of earth, air, fire, and water, plus Spirit.[45] Other symbols include the Ankh (an Egyptian cross-like symbol associated with the worship of Isis and topped by a noticeable loop, representing immor-tality and the union of male and female) and the cres-cent moon (symbol of the Goddess). Crystals, believed to contain healing and spiritual properties, are frequently worn as jewelry, on clothes, or even carried in small pouches.[46]

Pentagram

Meditation, visualization,[47] invocation,[48] calling on the four directions of north, south, east, and west for rituals, chanting, burning candles, and special rituals trigger a sense of the mystical, thus reinforcing the core belief system. Practicing these techniques over a period of time can lead to ecstatic or even what appear to be paranormal experiences because of the subjective expectation, and there are demonic forces that will respond to those who open themselves to such influence (1 Corinthians 10:19–22).[49]

Wiccans view magic and power as neutral, and it is in the intentions of the Wiccan in use of such magic where good and evil lie. Most Wiccans would agree with Aleister Crowley's definition of magic: "the science and art of causing change to occur in conformity to the will."[50] Starhawk writes that power is "the subtle force that shapes reality" and "is raised through chanting and dancing and may be directed through a symbol or visualization."[51] This is a common outlook of the use of magical power in Wicca.

Magic and rituals are inexorably linked in Wicca. Doing magic is done in the context of rituals, and magic is invoking power from external gods or forces through ritual and/or raising energy from within through ritual.[52] Magic is perceived as a natural force, sometimes called a psychic force, resulting from

---

45. Typically, a pentagram with the two points up and the one point down is used by Satanists to represent the carnal (the two points) over spirit (the one point), although some Witch-craft groups use the pentagram with the two points up, according to a few Wiccan sources.
46. This is common also in the New Age.
47. Visualizing something for the purposes of bringing it into reality.
48. Summoning supernatural forces or gods/goddesses.
49. This is the personal belief of the author.
50. Guiley, *The Encyclopedia of Witches, Witchcraft, and Wicca*, p. 216.
51. Starhawk *The Spiral Dance*, p. 38.
52. For neo-pagan and Wiccan views of magic, see Adler, chapter 7, "Magic and Ritual," p. 156; also see lengthy entry on magic in Guiley, *The Encyclopedia of Witches, Witchcraft, and Wicca*, p. 215–220.

the beliefs and the will of the practitioner done in concert with the ritual. As one Wiccan writes, "Magic at its most basic is energy collected from life's reservoir, shaped, and directed towards a goal. Wiccans work magic in particular ways, with certain words and gestures, because over generations, these forms have acquired power of our understanding-in-common."[53]

The state of mind achieved in this practice is considered to be an "altered state," that is, a state similar to a hypnotic or trance state. The person is still aware of one's surroundings but becomes receptive and open to another dimension of knowledge or understanding.[54] Starhawk writes extensively of "the trance state," and, while admitting it makes the mind more suggestible, extols it for opening the self to creativity, insight, growth of psychic powers, and revelation.[55]

Individual Wiccans may set up altars at home, consisting of representations of the Goddess and the god, items standing for the four elements, candles, a book in which to record spells, magical objects, and items with personal meaning. The altar serves as a base for ceremonies, rituals, and spells.

Wiccan altar

53. O'Gaea, *Family Wicca*, p. 99.
54. The author of this chapter is familiar with altered states, as she herself entered altered states during Eastern forms of meditation, past life regression exercises, and when reading astrological charts for clients during her years in the New Age. Seen as valid by those in the occult and New Age, this state is actually dangerous as it renders the mind more suggestible to outside influences, including from the demonic realm.
55. Starhawk, *The Spiral Dance*, p. 171; chapter 9 in this book, "Trance," is devoted entirely to this topic.

Wiccan and Witchcraft groups may combine their beliefs with or base their beliefs on cultural mystical traditions such as Celtic or Norse paganism, the Greek/Roman goddesses, ancient Egyptian spirituality, Eastern shamanism, or Native American spirituality. As an astrologer, I knew one group that was very involved in Native American rituals (or what they perceived to be) such as vision quests, sweat lodges, the wearing of a medicine pouch,[56] ritual dancing, having a totem animal, and other related practices. I had been on a retreat with them, and participated in what was called a "vision quest" to discover my "totem animal," a spirit animal that is a guide but also symbolizes the seeker's path in this life.

After a few years of knowing this group, the leader told me one day that what they thought were aliens were hovering over them and would not leave. I recall the leader showing real fear when relaying this. He said that he thought they were there to take over their bodies. At the time, I did not know how to process this information, especially since the whole group had experienced this. I knew the leader was sane and no one seemed unstable or deluded. Now, as a Christian, I believe that this was clearly the presence of demons who were drawn there due to the group's occult practices. Most in the group ended up leaving shortly after and went to another state.

Divination techniques[57] such as tarot cards, astrology, runes (stones with symbols connected to Norse pagan religions), the I Ching (from Chinese Taoism), clairvoyant or psychic readings, candle magic, and other occult practices are not only common but encouraged as well (though not practiced by all).

Many Witches and Wiccans are initiated via a ritual into covens, or they initiate themselves if they are solo practitioners. Opinions on initiation and when and how it is done vary widely. Traditionally, one is initiated after one year and one day of study, though this is not always followed.[58]

It is important to keep in mind that Wicca and Witchcraft are fluid systems, and can incorporate new ideas and discard old ones, although the

---

56. These pouches can contain bits of nature, such as stones or sticks, or anything representing something special or powerful to the wearer, sometimes something associated with the person's spirit animal, a guide from the spirit world in the shape of an animal. The pouch and its contents are considered an amulet, something which allegedly attracts protection.

57. Divination in a pagan or an occult context is gaining information and advice through occult techniques and esoteric symbols or omens. Divination is forbidden throughout the Bible.

58. Starhawk, *The Spiral Dance*, p. 188.

focus on earth, nature, and rituals remain. Also, many practitioners incorporate New Age beliefs.[59]

Although there are ritual magicians who cast spells, they follow another occult system and beliefs, and do not normally align themselves with Witchcraft.

Wicca has been around long enough now to have been passed down in families to younger generations; thus, there are more books and materials on Wiccan parenting and books for children in Wiccan families, such as *Family Wicca* by Ashleen O'Gaea (who also authored *Raising Witches: Teaching the Wiccan Faith to Children*, a book on how to organize religion classes for pagan children).[60]

Morality

Wiccans and Witches tend to disbelieve in absolutes, so there is no absolute good or evil, and no standard for it. Wiccans determine good and evil subjectively. Naturally this is a problem since they can't be *absolutely* sure that there is no absolute good or evil, which means this view is fallacious. Some adhere to the "Law of Three," which is the belief that what you do comes back to you threefold.

Many hold to a principle of opposites called Polarity. Polarity is based on a view of tension and balance between opposites. As one puts it, "The most crucial polarity is that between the life force and the death force, Eros and Thanatos if you will."[61] This latter notion has appeared to become more widespread since the initial days of the popular "white Witchcraft" standpoint.

Witches Janet and Stewart Farrar explain it this way: "The Theory of Polarity maintains that all activity, all manifestation, arises from (and is

---

59. The New Age, although some of it overlaps with neo-paganism, has a different worldview than that of neo-paganism. The New Age is more transcendent, future-oriented, God and Christ-oriented (though it is not the biblical God or Christ), and Gnostic in nature than neo-pagan beliefs like Wicca or Witchcraft; and the New Age regards mankind differently. The New Age is more apt to quote the Bible and use Christian terminology. Some Goddess-worshiping New Agers combine beliefs with neo-paganism; this could be considered a feminist-based Goddess religion existing apart from Wicca and the New Age, and is often called Goddess spirituality. But there are no objective, clear lines of demarcation apart from those drawn by the followers themselves or those who study these belief systems.

60. O'Gaea, *Family Wicca*, p. 79. O'Gaea admits to strong influences from Adler's *Drawing Down the Moon* and Starhawk's *The Spiral Dance*, p. 18.

61. "Why I Don't Like Scott Cunningham," Michael Kaufman, http://www.wildideas.net/temple/library/letters/cunningham1.html.

inconceivable without) the interaction of pairs and complementary opposites ... and that this polarity is not a conflict between 'good' and 'evil,' but a creative tension like that between the positive and negative terminals of an electric battery. Good and evil only arise with the constructive or destructive application of the polarity's output."[62]

They further state that monotheists are trapped in the belief that good versus evil is a polarity and that "under the unchallenged rule of a non-polarized Creator, nothing can happen."[63] This is a misconception of the God of the Bible; I will discuss this in more detail in a moment. Furthermore, three essential ideas relevant to morality are stated here: (1) an all-good Creator is static, (2) the basis for polarity is not good versus evil, and (3) good cannot exist without evil.

Yin yang symbol

The Farrars use the Yin-Yang symbol to explain this concept. One side is black with a white dot in it, and the other side is white with a black dot in it. Most people think that this symbol represents opposites, but it actually represents the concept of polarity.[64] The dark and light sides are polarities that need to be balanced. Why does each side have a dot of the other color in it? It is because although they appear to be opposites, in actuality they are constantly changing and merging with each other, thus becoming each other. The dark becomes light and light becomes dark. There is no absolute dark or absolute light.[65]

Even the Goddess and gods are not viewed as absolutely good and are said to have a "dark side" to them. This stands in stark contrast to God who is good by His very nature (Psalm 100:5, 145:9). The natural result of this is that there is no final judgment on actions, certainly not from a divine source. In the book *Family Wicca*, while admitting that bad behavior should not be tolerated, the author writes that there is no "divine punishment for evildoing," only "the healing, only the learning."[66] Consider the

62. Janet and Stewart Farrar, *A Witches' Bible*, Part 2 (Custer, WA: Phoenix Publishing, Inc., 1996), p. 107.
63. Ibid., p. 111.
64. The Yin and Yang symbol arose from the ancient Chinese religion of Taoism (see chapter 3), and the idea expressed by the Farrars is very much like that in Taoism. In Taoist belief, the forces of Yin and Yang were produced by the morally neutral source of all, the Tao.
65. From a discussion of the New Age and occult stances on good and evil in the writer's website article, "The Dark Side: Beyond Good and Evil," http://christiananswersforthenewage.org/Articles_DarkSide1.html.
66. O'Gaea, *Family Wicca*, p. 129.

implications of this — without an absolute standard, an individual could justify any act by having good intentions. This is an example of the arbitrary nature of this worldview.

Although belief in evil entities or spirits is not uncommon among Wiccans, outside evil may be considered to be a psychological metaphor, representing a difficult or negative aspect within, which the Wiccan must confront and accept. In fact, Starhawk describes a ritual designed for this confrontation.[67]

Evolution, Death, and Salvation

Wiccans and Witches are very much oriented to the present, so issues about the origin of the universe or life on Earth, as well as ultimate destinies, are not of much concern. Individuals may have their own outlooks, but there are no prevailing beliefs on evolution or any scenario about the end of the world, although some hold to accounts from pagan mythologies as a creation story.[68] Some may regard the existence of Earth as part of a larger cycle that will end and then repeat, as is found in the natural world through the seasons.

Death is seen as part of life and is neutral, or is seen as the opposite polarity of life. "Death is not an end; it is a stage in the cycle that leads on to to rebirth," and "an immanent spirituality cannot deny death. Death is part of life. When we embrace life, we must also embrace the sorrow at its ending,"[69] writes Starhawk.

In email contact with a 13-year-old Wiccan over a period of several months, I once asked this young lady, who believed nature to be sacred, how she would understand it if she were in a forest and lightning hit a tree that fell on her, bringing death. She replied that death was natural, and had to be accepted. Death is not bad or evil.

Time may be seen as a series of cycles, and reincarnation is popular.[70] However, unlike in Hinduism, Wiccans see reincarnation as a "gift of the

---

67. Starhawk, *The Spiral Dance*, p. 166–167.
68. For example, see Starhawk, *The Spiral Dance*, p. 41–42.
69. Ibid., p. 51; Starhawk, *Truth or Dare*, p. 45.
70. Adler, *Drawing Down the Moon*, p. 109. Author's note: Reincarnation is a Hindu and New Age belief that one has many lives; that is, living, dying, and returning in a different body, and doing this repeatedly for thousands or tens of thousands of years. The person supposedly is learning lessons this way, ultimately leading to enlightenment and liberation from this cycle of reincarnation.

Goddess, who is manifest in the physical world. Life and the world are not separate from Godhead."[71]

Others believe in a place called Summerland where the dead are reunited with deceased loved ones in a beautiful place, an idea also found in Theosophy and Spiritualism.[72] One Wiccan states that in the Summerland, "we realize ourselves and our Self."[73] Those who accept reincarnation may see Summerland as the resting place between incarnations where one is "refreshed" and prepared for rebirth on Earth.[74]

Death is a "healing, a loving restoration rather than a punishing destruction" and mortality is sacred.[75] Writing further, the same Wiccan, who worships the Wiccan Goddess, declares that "Death's path to rebirth is the adventure for which all mythical and legendary quests are metaphors."[76]

Atheists and agnostic Wiccans generally hold that life ends at death, and their bodies go back to the Earth. The Goddess or gods are only symbolic for them. However, there are many Wiccans who think the Goddess and gods are merely symbolic but who, nevertheless, believe in life after death.

Since Wicca and Witchcraft reject the concept of sin, the teaching that death is a result of sin or is something to be eradicated is an alien concept, as is the idea of salvation. One must learn lessons to be a better person, but the need for salvation is foreign to Wicca.

The Christian Response

The worldview of Wicca and Witchcraft is remarkably different from the Christian one. It is best to be informed before speaking with those involved in these groups. Because there is such a wide array of beliefs, do not assume what someone claiming to be a Wiccan believes or attempt to refute ideas they may not hold. Asking questions is a good way to find out what the

---

71. Starhawk, *The Spiral Dance,* p. 51; Hinduism views the physical world as an illusion and an impersonal, transcendent force directs reincarnation.
72. Theosophy is an Eastern-based occult group started in the 1800s by Madame Blavatsky, who claimed to have learned secret teachings, mostly in India and Tibet. Theosophy was a major influence on the New Age Movement. Spiritualism is a religious practice and denomination based primarily on contacting the dead for guidance.
73. O'Gaea, *Family Wicca,* p. 129. O'Gaea refers to Irish paganism, and states that Summerland "encompasses the Underworld, Fairyland, and other realms, several astral planes, and a variety of states of mind and being," p. 221.
74. Ibid., p. 221; Starhawk, *The Spiral Dance,* p. 51.
75. O'Gaea, *Family Wicca,* p. 140–141.
76. Ibid., p. 142.

person believes and to direct the conversation in a way that deals individually with that person's views (Colossians 4:2–6).

Basic Wiccan Beliefs

- The natural world and experience are the basis for truth and ethics.

- There is a Goddess, a Goddess and god, many gods, or no gods.

- Power/magic is neutral.

- Good and evil are determined subjectively.

- Although there may be deceptive or even evil spirits, Satan does not exist as an actual, personal being.

- Nature is sacred and there should be a relationship with it.

- Death is not bad nor necessarily final.

Biblical Responses

In contrast, there is the truth as revealed by God, including responses to some assertions made in Wicca.

Absolute good and evil is taught in both the Old and New Testaments. God is absolutely good: "This is the message which we have heard from Him and declare to you, that God is light and in Him is no darkness at all" (1 John 1:5). God is described in 1 Timothy 6:16 as the one "who alone has immortality, dwelling in unapproachable light, whom no man has seen or can see, to whom be honor and everlasting power." Be fervently aware that non-Christians usually do not have the concept of what "righteous" means, much less the concept of a holy God who judges sin. Therefore, do not assume any understanding of these views. Be patient in explaining the nature of God and His righteousness without using theological words.

Satan is real, a fallen spiritual being, in total rebellion against a righteous God who created him, and is evil. Referring to Satan as a personal being, Jesus asserts, "When he speaks a lie, he speaks from his own resources, for he is a liar and the father of it" (John 8:44). Satan can disguise himself as something beautiful, as an angel of light, and in this guise, he is more deadly since he is not easily recognized (see 2 Corinthians 11:14–15).

The concept of polarity regarding good and evil is at odds with what God has revealed. Evil is not necessary for good, nor should we seek balance between light and darkness. Evil is the corruption or rejection of good. As Romans 12:21 puts it: "Do not be overcome by evil, but overcome evil with good." While current culture denies absolute good and evil, God's word is clear that there is a line between good and evil: "Woe to those who call evil good, and good evil; who put darkness for light and light for darkness; who put bitter for sweet and sweet for bitter!" (Isaiah 5:20).

Death, both physical and spiritual, is the result of sin due to man's disobedience, and is the "enemy," according to Scripture (see Romans 5:12–17; 1 Corinthians 15:26). Spiritual death after physical death is eternal separation from life in God's presence. Death will be thrown into the lake of fire at the time of God's final judgment that will be an eternal punishment with no rest (Revelation 20:14).

"Do no harm" is the Wiccan creed. However, since Wiccans deny absolute good or evil, they have no standard by which to decide what harm is or if this creed has any authority behind it anyway. Thus, their notions of what constitutes harm are totally subjective. Wiccans believe that dark and light need each other in order to exist and that dark and light will always balance each other out.

Witches may claim the Bible does not condemn Witchcraft, since they assert that the real interpretation of the Hebrew word for "witchcraft" should be understood as sorcery or divination. This is technically correct. However, the point is moot since the Bible strongly condemns the worship of gods or goddesses other than the biblical God, divination, and spell-casting, all of which are practiced or endorsed by most Wiccans (Deuteronomy 4:19, 12:1–4; Romans 1:22–23).

Wiccans may argue that sorcery is black magic used for evil, and that they practice white magic — magic for good. But the Bible makes no distinction between "good" or "bad" magic or magic versus sorcery. All occult magic has the same source and is abhorred by God.[77]

Witches and Wiccans may assert that the original religion was centered on the Goddess, and that Christianity, being a patriarchal religion,

---

77. Selected Scripture verses on divination, sorcery, and magic: Exodus 22:18; Leviticus 19:26, 31, 20:6, 27; Deuteronomy 18:10–12; 1 Samuel 15:23; 2 Kings 23:24; 1 Chronicles 10:13; Isaiah 2:6, 8:19–20, 47:13–14; Ezekiel 13:20–23; Daniel 2:27–28, 5:15–17; Acts 13:7–10, 16:16–18; Galatians 5:19–20; Revelation 22:15.

suppressed the Goddess religions like Witchcraft. As mentioned earlier, archaeological and historical research show that although many cultures worshiped Goddesses, the Goddesses were consorts or counterparts of male gods. Another point to make is that although God is Spirit, He makes it clear in His Word that He desires us to think of Him as Father when we come to Him through faith in Christ. Jesus called God His Father. Moreover, it is the Christian Scriptures that speak of women as equals to men as opposed to most other cultural and religious teachings or practices. In John chapter 4, Jesus talks to the Samaritan woman at the well, an astonishing thing for a Jewish man to do in that day and in that culture. Not only does Jesus talk to her, but He reveals Himself as the Messiah to her. Then she, an immoral woman of the village, is the one to take the news to the men. It was women who discovered and reported the empty tomb after the Resurrection of Jesus. Scriptural passages teach men to love their wives as their own body, and to love them as Christ loves the Church, which is pictured as His bride in Scripture (Ephesians 5: 25–33; Colossians 3:18–19). There is no biblical endorsement for male tyranny or abuse.

Witches may claim that theirs is an ancient religion which predates Christianity. However, Christ, being the Son of God and God the Son, is eternal, which means He has no beginning. It is Christ who predates all religions and God alone is worthy of worship from the beginning of time.[78]

Witches frequently do not know the true gospel; their opposition is to organized religion, which they arbitrarily see as an oppressive system of control and rules. It is true that religion is often just that. But biblical Christianity is a relationship with the living Christ, not a system of rules, rituals, or self-help.

Keep in mind that some Wiccans have had hurtful experiences in churches. All humanity falls short of the standard — which is a perfect, righteous God.[79] The standard is not man or other Christians. *God* is that ultimate standard. This is why Christ came, to live the perfect life and pay the penalty for our sins so that through faith, one is reconciled to God.[80]

Dialoguing with Wiccans

There is no formula for witnessing to someone in Wicca, especially since Wiccans are inclined to be individualistic. The Christian should first regard the

---

78. John 8:56–58; Colossians 1:15–17; 1 Peter 1:19–20; Revelation 1:17, 13:8.
79. Romans 3:23–24.
80. Romans 8:1–4; 2 Corinthians 5:18–20.

person as someone made in the image of God and not just a Wiccan, and pray for courage as well as love in sharing Christ. Always speak with grace: "Walk in wisdom toward those who are outside, redeeming the time. Let your speech always be with grace, seasoned with salt, that you may know how you ought to answer each one" (Colossians 4:5–6). Since occult views vary, begin by asking what his or her particular beliefs are; don't assume anything.

Ask the person what drew him or her into Wicca.

It is helpful as well to find out the person's spiritual background, and why they reject Christianity. Listen respectfully, and calmly correct any major wrong views about the gospel, which is of primary importance. Avoid rabbit trails and secondary issues.

Ask questions that will get the person to think specifically about their ideas. For example, if the person believes that good and evil are relative, ask for examples and how that works in real life. If the person regards God as an impersonal force, ask, "Why then do you think it is that we are all beings who seek personal relationships?"

Don't use terms the person may not understand such as *atonement, redemption, justification,* etc.; it's better to give examples of what these are and take care to explain them accurately.

Christians are to be prudent, vigilant, and discerning, but not afraid; therefore, have no fear in speaking to anyone involved in Witchcraft.[81]

Don't try to prove the Wiccan wrong at every point; instead, seek to discuss the nature of God and Jesus, especially Jesus' power over nature, demons, and illness, as narrated in the Gospels.

Don't hesitate to stand on the truths of Scripture, such as Jesus being the only way to God, but do this with gentleness and love.[82] Unbelievers tend to not respect people who waver on their beliefs.

Let the person see Jesus' love in you. The person may be suffering the scary or damaging effects of occult practice but most likely will not share this information in an initial conversation.

A mini-gospel that could be presented would be: "Jesus is the Son of God who came to earth as man to live a perfect life in complete obedience to God, because none of us can do that. We are born with a desire to do our will, not God's will, and we do things every day that are opposed to God.

---

81. 1 John 4:4; 2 Timothy 1:7.
82. 1 Peter 3:15.

This is called sin, and it leads eventually to dissatisfaction and despair. The ultimate penalty for sin is death, eternal separation from God. But since Jesus lived the perfect life, He was able to pay for the penalty of sins when He died on the Cross. He bodily rose the third day, conquering death, which is an enemy. By believing in who Jesus is and that there is nothing you can do to pay for your own opposition to the one true God, you are forgiven of all your sins and have eternal life."

An Encouraging Word

Jesus is the Light, and those who believe in Him become "sons of Light" and are to walk "as children of Light."[83] Treating Wiccans with kindness and respect is a way to show them this Light that indwells us through the Holy Spirit. Witnessing to someone in Wicca or Witchcraft not only reveals Christ's love and truth to that person, but permits the Christian to experience His amazing love and power as well.

Summary of Wiccan Beliefs

Doctrine	Teachings of Wicca
God	Deny the existence of a sovereign, supreme god. Beliefs vary, but many look to goddesses and spirits associated with aspects of nature; many worship the Earth as Mother Nature and goddesses that emanate from the Mother Goddess; some believe the Goddess has a consort, the Lady and the Lord; others are atheistic or view the "gods" as psychological aspects of the material world.
Authority/Revelation	There is no standard work of Wiccan beliefs and practices, but the *Book of Shadows* and other modern writings guide many. Various modern authors have developed specific sects that are often blended together, despite their contradictory elements. Experience is more valuable than absolute truth.
Man	Mankind is born basically good, but is subject to becoming out of balance with self or nature through harm or wrongs done to them.

---

83. John 12:36; Ephesians 5:8.

Sin	"Do no harm" is the Wiccan creed of ethics. Nature is the model and standard for life's principles. Good and evil are determined by intentions.
Salvation	One must learn lessons to be a better person, but the need for salvation is foreign to Wicca. The afterlife is often viewed as a peaceful place or a place of preparation for reincarnation.
Creation	Views vary, with some embracing general evolutionary views while others accept various pagan mythologies; the biblical account is generally rejected.

Chapter 11

Druidism

Bob Gilespie

"Druids Recognized as a Religion in the UK"

Druids have been worshipping the sun and earth for thousands of years in Europe, but now worshippers can say they're practicing an officially recognized religion.

The ancient pagan tradition, best known for gatherings at Stonehenge every summer solstice, has been formally classed as a religion under charity law for the first time in Britain. That means Druids can receive exemptions from taxes on donations, and now have the same status as such mainstream religions as the Church of England.

Phil Ryder, the chairman of the 350-member Druid Network, said "It will go a long way to make Druidry a lot more accessible."[1]

While Druidry may seem to be an obscure religion, there are up to 50,000 practicing Druids worldwide. Over a half a million people regard themselves as pagan, and many would consider themselves inspired by Druidism.

---

1. "Druids Recognized as Religion in the UK," CBS News, October 2, 2010, http://www.cbsnews.com/news/druids-recognized-as-religion-in-the-uk.

Druids participate in a ceremony at Stonehenge

Ancient Druids

History of Ancient Druids

Druidism was the ancient religious faith found in Gaul and later England and Ireland as the Romans pushed northward. The term "Druid" derives from an old Welsh term for oak, implying that they are the people who know the wisdom of the trees.

The Druid religion is most commonly associated with the Celts, a European cultural group first evident in the seventh or eighth century B.C. who eventually occupied much of northern Europe. The Celts arrived in Ireland by the second or third century B.C., and possibly earlier, displacing an earlier people who were already on the islands. The Gauls, Britons, and Irish were all Celtic people. The Romans never occupied Ireland, nor did the Anglo-Saxons who invaded Britain after the Romans withdrew in the fifth century, so Celtic culture survived more strongly in Ireland than elsewhere.

There is disagreement about whether or not the Druids actually built Stonehenge. It is not clear exactly when the Druids came to Britain, but it is likely that they arrived after Stonehenge was built.

Although the Celts had a written language, it was rarely used or what had been written was destroyed or lost. Their religious and philosophical beliefs were preserved in an oral tradition — and much of that has likely been altered, lost, or embellished. We have no writings from the Druids, and what we know about them is through secondary sources. Many modern authors have colored our understanding of the Druids with claims that have no legitimate historical basis. Little of their early history remains, and most of our legitimate information about the Druids comes from Greek and Roman writers.

According to Julius Caesar, who is the principal source of information about the Druids, the Druids took charge of public and private sacrifices, and many young men went to them for instruction. They judged all public and private quarrels and decreed penalties. If anyone disobeyed their decree, he was barred from sacrifice, which was considered the gravest of punishments. Once a year the Druids assembled at a sacred place in the territory of the Carnutes, believed to be the center of all Gaul. All legal disputes were submitted there to the judgment of the Druids.[2]

The early Christian missionary St. Patrick is credited for bringing Christianity to Ireland in the fourth century A.D. As the Christian religion spread into Northern Europe and the British Isles, the Druid influence began to fade and eventually all but disappeared.

Beliefs of Ancient Druids

Within ancient Druidism, there were three groups with different functions:

- The Bards were "the keepers of tradition, of the memory of the tribe — they were the custodians of the

---

2. Encyclopedia Britannica Online, s.v. "Druid," accessed February 9, 2016, http://www.britannica.com/topic/Druid.

sacredness of the Word." In Ireland, they trained for 12 years learning grammar, hundreds of stories, poems, philosophy, etc.

- The Ovates worked with the processes of death and regeneration. They were the native healers of the Celts. They specialized in divination, conversing with the ancestors, and prophesying the future.

- The Druids formed the professional class in Celtic society. They performed the functions of modern-day priests, teachers, ambassadors, astronomers, genealogists, philosophers, musicians, theologians, scientists, poets, and judges. They underwent lengthy training; some sources say as much as 20 years. Druids led public rituals, which were normally held within fenced groves of sacred trees. In their role as priests, "they acted not as mediators between God and man, but as directors of ritual, as shamans guiding and containing the rites."[3]

The Druids believed that the dead were transported to the Otherworld by the god Bile (also Bel, Belenus).[4] Life supposedly continued in the Otherworld much as it had before death. The ancient Druids believed that the soul was immortal. After the person died in the Otherworld, their soul reincarnated and lived again in another living entity — either in a plant or the body of a human or other animal. After a person had learned enough at this level, they moved on after death to a higher realm, which has its own Otherworld. This continued until the individual reached the highest realm, the "Source."[5]

St. Patrick's confrontation with Druidism of fifth century Ireland can give us much insight into that culture, and is especially instructional to Christians today who are dealing with modern Druidism or other neopagan religions. After having been enslaved by Irish Druids, Patrick escaped to return home to England. There he studied Christianity and eventually returned to Ireland as a missionary to the very tribes that had enslaved him.

---

3. "Celtic Druidism: Beliefs, Practices & Celebrations," Religious Tolerance, accessed February 9, 2016, http://www.religioustolerance.org/druid2.htm.

4. Bel or Belus has often been denoted as a variant name of biblical Nimrod by historians and ancient researchers.

5. "Celtic Druidism: Beliefs, Practices & Celebrations," Religious Tolerance, accessed February 10, 2016, http://www.religioustolerance.org/druid2.htm.

St. Patrick understood that to engage Celtic Druidic culture was indeed a spiritual battle. Missionaries in similar tribal cultures will attest to that spiritual warfare. Patrick is credited with using a song or chant as he went out to minister. This song acknowledged the spiritual battle he faced and pointed the Druids to trusting in Christ as their salvation rather than their man-made traditions.

Many people have attempted to connect some of the various aspects of modern celebrations like Halloween and various seasonal festivals to the Druids. However, no records of these celebrations exists and we are left with only third-hand accounts to substantiate such claims. One thing that we can be sure of is the co-opting of certain pagan festivals by the Roman Catholic Church. The pagan celebration of the dead that occurred at the end of October was absorbed into the Roman Catholic feast of All Saints' Day, preceded by All Hallows' Evening — from which the modern name "Halloween" is derived. How much of the specific traditions we currently associate with Halloween is rooted in Druid practice is speculative. Regardless of their origins, many of these practices are unbiblical and we should guard ourselves against engaging in them.[6]

Culture of Ancient Druids

Ancient Druids acted as shamans who, through various rituals, consulted their ancestors who dwelt in the spirit world. The modern-day equivalent to these ancient Druids would be the witch doctors found in tribal animism. Modern Druids freely admit that their beliefs are animistic in nature.

"Druidry is essentially an animistic tradition."[7]

"For many people, myself included, Druidry and Animism go hand in hand."[8]

Because of the similarity between the Druids of the past and current animism, much can be learned about the ancient Celtic culture by looking at the animistic tribes that exist today. Encyclopedia Britannica describes

6. Bodie Hodge, "Halloween History and the Bible," Answers in Genesis, October 29, 2013, https://answersingenesis.org/holidays/halloween-history-and-the-bible.

7. "Are All Druids Animistic?" Druid Network, accessed February 10, 2016, https://druid-network.org/what-is-druidry/beliefs-and-definitions/faq/druids-animistic.

8. "Druidry, Animism, and the Meaning of Life," Witches and Pagans, accessed February 10, 2016, http://www.witchesandpagans.com/sagewoman-blogs/druid-heart/druidry-animism-and-the-meaning-of-life.html.

animism as a "belief in innumerable spiritual beings concerned with human affairs and capable of helping or harming human interests."[9] Many secular historians assume that animism dominated the world in "pre-historic" times, and that all religions evolved from it.

These historians are coming from an evolutionary perspective. We know from the history found in Genesis that Noah and his family were monotheistic. They worshiped the One and true Creator. After the Flood, people began to reject the truth and disobey God again. We are not sure what false religions and beliefs arose before the dispersion at the Tower of Babel, but with the dispersion people took their false beliefs with them throughout the world.

The true accounts of creation, the Fall, and the Flood were passed down from Noah and his family; however, these accounts were distorted over time. This is why we find creation and flood legends all over the world. All have been changed and perverted over time, but most retain the seeds of truth as recorded for us in Scripture. One such example is the Druid obsession with

special knowledge. Ever since Eve desired special knowledge and ate of the tree of knowledge of good and evil, people have desired the same thing. The Druids even associated this knowledge with a tree; this may be why the sacred oak trees became important in their beliefs.

Satan often provides a counterfeit to the truth. One of these false beliefs involved the idea that ancestors in spirit form could influence daily life. Those who took the role of connecting with these spirits became powerful shaman figures of the Ovate or Druid class in their society. This ancestor worship spread throughout the world as people groups migrated. Today it is found in tribal cultures all over the world.

Symbols of trees are used as amulets, and sacred trees are often used in Druid rituals.

Modern Druids

History of Modern Druids

Modern interest in Druidism can be traced to John Aubrey (1676–1697), who delved into the classical texts about Druids and suggested that the

---

9. Encyclopedia Britannica, s.v. "Animism," http://www.britannica.com/topic/animism.

Druids had worshiped at the old stone monuments in Wiltshire. His work began the modern association between Druidism and Stonehenge. Modern Druidism emerged into public notice in the next century when, in 1717, deist writer John Toland (1670–1722) was elected the chief of the first modern Druid order.

Building on Aubrey's work, the physician William Stukeley (1687–1765) did extensive observations in Wiltshire and brought the monumental structures to public attention. He published a book about Stonehenge in 1740. There is dispute about how involved each of these men were in actual orders, but the Enlightenment attitudes and acceptance of "free-thinkers" freed many to explore these ancient religions. It was out of this social framework that the neo-pagan resurgence occurred and modern Druidry emerged.[10]

Interest in Druidism as the traditional pre-Christian religion of the British Isles led to the formation of several Druid organizations throughout the 18th century. The most important was the Ancient Order of Druids founded in London in 1781. In the 19th century, the Druid movement spread across Europe and through the British Empire, though these groups remained small. Druidism only began to grow on the coattails of the larger neo-pagan movement. One of the most important Druid groups to emerge in England was the Order of Bards, Ovates and Druids founded in 1964.

In America, a new and separate Druid tradition was initiated in 1963 by students at Carleton College in Northfield, Minnesota, as part of a protest of compulsory chapel attendance at the church-related school. In order to gain permission not to attend chapel, the students fashioned a separate religion based upon their reading of books on ancient religion. Once the rules on compulsory chapel attendance were dropped, the students discovered that they liked what they had created. Thus was born the Reformed Druids of North America that spread through the neo-pagan subculture. In Berkeley, California, the movement found a new leader in the person of Isaac Bonewits, who emerged as the most visible spokesperson of Druidism in North America. In 1983 he left the loosely organized Reformed Druid coalition to found the Ár nDraíocht Féin (ADF), the largest Druid group in North America. It has in turn given birth to additional groups. But just to clarify, beliefs of modern Druid groups are not the same as the beliefs of the ancient Druids.

---

10. Ronald Hutton, *Blood and Mistletoe: The History of the Druids in Britain* (New Haven, CT: Yale Univ. Press, 2009), p. 125–134.

Beliefs of Modern Druidism

Although modern Druids attempt to draw their beliefs and teaching from the ancient Celts, they also incorporate ideas from modern psychology and the Human Potential and New Age movements. Membership is open to followers of any religion.

The Order of Bards, Ovates and Druids express their beliefs as follows (condensed):

> One of the most striking characteristics of Druidism is the degree to which it is free of dogma and any fixed set of beliefs or practices. There is no "sacred text" or the equivalent of a bible in Druidism and there is no universally agreed set of beliefs amongst Druids. Despite this, there are a number of ideas and beliefs that most Druids hold in common, and that help to define the nature of Druidism today.
>
> Since Druidry is a spiritual path — a religion to some, a way of life to others — Druids share a belief in the fundamentally spiritual nature of life. Some will favor a particular way of understanding the source of this spiritual nature, and may feel themselves to be animists, pantheists, polytheists, or even monotheists. Others will avoid choosing any one conception of Deity, believing that by its very nature this is unknowable by the mind.
>
> Although Druids love Nature, and draw inspiration and spiritual nourishment from it, they also believe that the world we see is not the only one that exists. A cornerstone of Druid belief is in the existence of the Otherworld — a realm or realms which exist beyond the reach of the physical senses, but which are nevertheless real. This Otherworld is seen as the place we travel to when we die, but we can also visit it during our lifetime in dreams, in meditation, under hypnosis, or in "journeying," during a trance.
>
> Most Druids adopt the belief of their ancient forebears that the soul undergoes a process of successive reincarnations — which continues until the individual reaches the highest realm, the "*Source.*" One Druid is quoted as saying, "All things are created from the Source, including the Gods. We are just sparks from its flame."

A clue as to the purpose behind the process of successive rebirths can be found if we look at the goals of the Druid. Druids seek above all the cultivation of wisdom, creativity and love. A number of lives on earth, rather than just one, gives us the opportunity to fully develop these qualities within us.

Woven into much of Druid thinking and all of its practice is the idea or belief that we are all connected in a universe that is essentially benign. Related to the idea that we are all connected in one great web of life is the belief held by most Druids that whatever we do in the world creates an effect which will ultimately also affect us.[11]

Within these claims, there are many arbitrary and self-contradictory claims. For example, the claim that they have no dogma and then go on to tell you what you believe if you are a part of Druidism is obviously self-refuting. The notion that there are many different ways to view Druidism shows the arbitrary nature of such a worldview. If there is no truth within the system, what value can it have and what hope can it offer? It can only offer self-fulfilling promise based on your own arbitrary opinions about the world.

Modern Druids in the Culture

In recent days, paganism, including Druidism, has seen a tremendous revival with a deliberate attempt to inject paganism into the mainstream culture. The founder of the ADF, Isaac Bonewits, has for his motto "paganize mainstream religion by mainstreaming paganism."[12]

This new paganism, sometimes called neo-paganism, traces its heritage back to native religious traditions of Europe and tribal traditions from North America. Many neo-pagan groups identify with Celtic (Druidic), Egyptian, Native American, Norse, or Roman traditions.

Ancestor spirits, a Mother Goddess, magic, witchcraft, sacred trees, and the like, are being incorporated into the mainstream through the media. The *Harry Potter* franchise is one such example. The *Lord of the Rings* movies brought magic, wizards, and a host of neo-pagan ideas. While these movies present a good over evil motif, one can see a not-so-subtle introduction of

---

11. "Druid Beliefs," Druidry.org, accessed February 10,2016, http://www.druidry.org/druid-way/druid-beliefs.

12. "Thirty Druid Groups," Reformed Druids of North America, accessed February 10, 2016, http://www.rdna.info/drulinks.html.

pagan practices into the mainstream culture. One is hard-pressed to find a Disney movie without pagan ideas mixed in. Children's cartoons are ripe with magic spells, ancestral spirit guides, and Mother Earth. There are countless video games that are full of pagan ideas. Children may even be exposed to paganism at school with the introduction of Eastern forms of meditation, talk of Mother Nature, and spirit guides. We can't leave out the influence of the *Star Wars* movies with the concept of the "Force," which is paganism dressed up in science fiction.

All of this has one intended goal, to mainstream paganism — starting with the children. As the older generation dies off, the younger generation will replace Christianity with a kinder, earth-friendly, and more "open-minded" belief. Of course, we must ask by what standard would they be kinder and on what basis would they hold such beliefs? After all, Christianity protects human life whereas the basis for pagan ideas like the Druids do not hold that life is special in any way, contrary to their assertions. They may promise the liberation from "outdated" Christian morality that holds us back, but it is all a cruel trick of Satan.

> While they promise them liberty, they themselves are the servants of corruption: for of whom a person is overcome, by him also he is brought into bondage (2 Peter 2:19; NKJV).

> There is a way which seemeth right unto a man, but the end thereof are the ways of death (Proverbs 14:12; KJV).

Satan's ultimate goal is to eliminate the truth from our culture and usher in the lies that will ultimately bring the very image bearers of God on earth into slavery. Without the truth found in the Bible and redemption in Christ, mankind is destined to the same fate as Satan himself, enslaved to outer darkness in eternal death.

Protecting Our Children from Neo-paganism

Children from Christian homes are prime targets of Satan and the influence of paganism. Neil Anderson and Steve Russo wrote a book on this topic called *The Seduction of Our Children*. They did a survey in Christian schools and found:

- 45% said they have experienced a "presence" seen or heard in their room that scared them

- 59% said they've harbored bad thoughts about God

- 69% reported hearing voices in their head

- 89% said they did not like themselves

As parents, we must help our children to bring "every thought captive to the obedience of Christ" (2 Corinthians 10:5) as we constantly point them to the salvation and renewal that comes only through repentance and faith in Jesus Christ.

Some of the first lies of Satan's influence on our children is that they are no good. They are just sinners so they might as well act that way. They don't know who they really are. All people are image bearers of our Creator.

While it is true that we are sinners, in Christ we become saints. The first step is to point your child to saving knowledge of Christ, and we must start while they are young. Second, we must immerse our children in the truth of who they are (or can be) in Christ. Pray as Paul did that your children's eyes may be opened, "that ye may know what is the hope of his calling, and what the riches of the glory of his inheritance in the saints, and what is the exceeding greatness of his power to us-ward who believe" (Ephesians 1:18–19; KJV).

While St Patrick was battling the Druids, his eyes were opened to the spiritual battle that he was in. We are in a spiritual battle as well, and we might want to pray the same type of spiritual affirmations over ourselves and our children that St Patrick did.

Satan is good at informing children how bad they are, so we must remind them of who they really are (or can be) in Christ.

- John 1:2 — I am God's child.

- Ephesians 1:1 — I am a saint.

- Ephesians 1:5 — I have been adopted as God's child.

- Ephesians 2:6 — I am seated with Christ in heavenly places.

- Ephesians 2:18 — I have access to God through the Spirit.

- Colossians 2:10 — I am complete in Christ.

- 1 Corinthians 3:16 — I am God's temple.

Reaching Neo-pagans for Christ

When engaging a Druid, or any neo-pagan for that matter, it is important to acknowledge, as did St. Patrick, that this is a spiritual battle with a demonic delusion and blindness to the truth. While they may pride themselves on claims of being tolerant and open-minded to all religions, being confronted with the truth from God's Word will often elicit an emotional response. The god of this world will not want them to hear the truth. A one-time confrontation with someone steeped in these beliefs will usually not bring about their conversion. Being a witness of the gospel is more of a conversation than a one-time presentation.

It is important to break out of our comfort zone and develop friendships with unbelievers — a relationship where the conversation can be picked up again at a later time, a relationship where one can feel safe and not threatened. Our actions will often say more than what we say in words. Our actions can go a long way in demonstrating the love that God has for them. Matthew 16:18 informs us that the gates of hell will not prevail again the rock of the gospel, so we can be confident in our witness (see also Daniel 2:35).

It can be beneficial to start with areas of agreement. Druids are correct in their assessment that there is more to life than this physical word. They also have a respect for life, love, and the improvement of self and all mankind. They also understand that our actions have consequences in the future.

Where does this commonality originate? Romans 1 tells us that all have an inborn sense of a Creator, and that the natural world screams of the Creator God. While Druids may be accepting of evolution, it is clear to them that there is some kind of spiritual, non-physical designer. Also inherent in the mind of all people is a sense of right and wrong and a desire to improve this world (Romans 2:15). From a purely materialistic, evolutionary perspective, there should be no need or compulsion for justice and improving the world if survival of the fittest is all there is, yet the neo-pagan are open about and embrace these ideas. Pointing out these similarities is a good non-confrontational way to start a conversation.

Some conversations could lead to pointing out why these ideas are predicated on Scripture to be true. Basic concepts like truth, love, right, and wrong are based on God and His Word, and the Druid has borrowed these concepts whether they realize it or not.

The difference between the Druid and the Christian is that the Druid has beliefs that are purely arbitrary. There is no source of authority that they can go back to; they claim that their beliefs are right purely because *they* say they are right. One might ask them how they can know for sure that they are right in what they believe.

If they are quick, they will probably return the question back to you, and your answer should be, "I am glad you asked." For here is the great difference — we have the truth directly from our Creator who revealed it to us. And since we are made in His image, we can know this. This truth is communicated to us in the context of the true history of the universe. The Word of God is what it says it is because the ultimate authority on all things (God) can only reveal Himself as the final authority. Thus, our beliefs are not arbitrary but are the only absolute truth directly from God.

But within the neo-pagan or Druid system of belief there is no absolute authority, that even the universe obeys. Who dictates what is right and wrong?

This is a great time to show the inconsistency of believing that all beliefs are true. The word "truth" itself implies that there is something called non-truth. Druids are accepting of any spiritual path, except the one that says Christ is the only way. So how can truth and not-truth both be acceptable? The fact is that they cannot. Thus, the neo-pagan belief is inconsistent right from the very start of their religious basis.

Here is also where logical arguments for the authority of Scripture come in. Starting with Genesis and just reading the truth is a powerful antidote to Satan's lies. At this point, they may be open to hearing good arguments against various forms of evolution, and how the Bible is consistent from beginning to end.

The main goal is to clearly explain the basic difference between Christianity and all other religions. All other religions seek a path to an alleged god, gods, or state of being, while Christianity is the only one where the Creator Himself has sought out a path to restore mankind back to Himself. Other religions often endeavor to do things to be united back with "*a creator*" (or the universe, etc.), while Christianity is just the opposite.

Our Creator has provided a way through Jesus Christ whereby we can receive grace. We can be brought back into fellowship with our Creator through nothing that we do but as a free gift. Finding oneness with our Creator is the heartfelt desire of all people, whether they know it or not.

Proclaimed from Genesis to Revelation, God's plan to restore man back to fellowship through Jesus Christ through repentance and faith is the key to reaching the neo-pagan for Christ. Jesus is God Himself, who took on human flesh, so He could die in our place and take our punishment. If we place out trust in Him, we are restored back to fellowship with our Creator.

Summary of Druid Beliefs

Doctrine	Teachings of Druidism
God	Deny the God of the Bible. Believe in a spirit world. Druids hold to a variety of beliefs about gods varying from a great "force" to various ancestor and nature spirits. Most would be polytheistic.
Authority/ Revelation	Reject the Bible as true. Do not look to any writing as divine or authoritative. Man is seen as the absolute authority. They pride themselves in accepting people and ideas of all beliefs.
Man	Various views exist. There is no concept of an innate sin nature. All men are born worthy of respect as part of the cosmos. Man is seen as a higher life form, but not entirely unique.
Sin	No absolute standard of sin exists. Sin is relative to the virtues of honor, loyalty, hospitality, honesty, justice, and courage to benefit all. Some hold a view similar to the law of karma.
Salvation	Various views exist. Through the process of reincarnation and acquiring special knowledge, individuals learn to be united with the ultimate "source" to live in an eternal state of unity or bliss.
Creation	Various views exist within modern Druidism. No known ancient creation myths exist. Many would acknowledge evolutionary ideas as consistent with their beliefs.

Chapter 12

Animism (Spiritism)

Mark Vowels

Do you have any superstitions? Have you heard that breaking a mirror causes bad luck or that walking under a ladder brings misfortune? What about the idea that seeing a black cat at night portends something bad might happen? Perhaps you know someone who says things like, "Knock on wood" or "Throw a penny over your shoulder." All of these ideas stem from the idea that somehow doing, or not doing, certain things affects the outcome of our future. When I was a child my schoolmates would say, "If you step on a crack it will break your mother's back!" As I walked to school each day I would carefully avoid stepping on cracks in the sidewalk for fear that the taunt might just be true.

In our culture, which places a high value on science and reason as a means of discovering what is true, most people grow out of their childhood fears and superstitions. We come to understand reasonable explanations for the mysterious happenings that we or others have experienced. We recognize that most superstitious beliefs come from incidents which took place at some point in time for which people had no explanation, therefore they assumed that something they had done, or not done, caused the problem and from that time took measures to avoid a similar experience in the future. Over time, those problem-avoiding measures, like not stepping on a crack or knocking on wood when wishing for something good to happen, become part of the culture and are continued out of habit. We see these concepts as mere fantasies or delusions.

What if you lived in a culture in which every aspect of life was governed by the thought that doing, or failing to do, prescribed behaviors would affect your future? Inevitably, you would develop a constant sense of fear that you might bring harm or misfortune upon yourself and your family. This is what it is like to live among people who are animists. Their entire lives are governed by fear. A typical Western view of superstitious practices holds that it is just bad luck or fate that produces negative consequences when the superstitions are violated. Animists, on the other hand, believe that spirit beings are directly responsible for everything that happens, both good and bad. So the only reasonable approach to this perceived reality is to do everything necessary to keep those spirit beings happy as much as possible.

All people everywhere have some sense that there is a spiritual dimension to life beyond the world they can see and touch. An innate sense of spiritual forces that in some way influence the destiny of one's life and fortunes is part of every person's perception. The world's various religions seek to provide some explanation for that basic sense that there is more to the world around us than simply what we can observe. Animism embraces the intuition that there are unseen spiritual forces at work around us that somehow affect what happens in life by attributing supernatural forces to all aspects of the natural world.

Definition of Animism

Animism takes its name from the concept that the physical world is inhabited, or *animated*, by spirits. Rocks, trees, rivers, lakes, mountains, valleys, and so forth, as well as animals, possess spirits that control all that takes place in a particular region. In order to procure favorable experiences in life, animists seek to interact with the spirits by either satisfying them or manipulating them. All religious practices in animism, which are often seen as primitive superstition by outsiders, are actually highly developed responses to the fear that animists have of offending the spirits, or rituals which are intended to in some way control the spirits.

Distribution of Animism

Animism is in many ways the default religion of the human soul. It has been described by some in the past as primal religion. Much of what the Old

Testament describes as paganism in ancient times was essentially animistic practice. Unlike most of the world's organized religious systems, animism has no sacred text or unified history, yet it is found literally throughout history and throughout the world. Any society or culture whose religious practice involves interaction with spirit beings is a manifestation of animism. This would include what is often referred to as indigenous religion, or the religions of indigenous peoples; that is to say, the religious practice of any people who are the original natives to a region. Most native African, North American, South American, Australian, Arctic, Asian, and even ancient European religion is either overtly animist or intertwined with animist beliefs and practices. In other words, the original religions of people in every part of the world are animistic.

The Bible's View of Animism

Why is this so? Are people simply incurably superstitious, or are there genuine spiritual beings who interact with human populations? The Bible clearly indicates that Satan and the demonic beings that assist him are at work in the world and seek to influence human activity. From the time when Adam and Eve were tempted by Satan in the Garden of Eden, actual spiritual beings have sought to manipulate human behavior. Likewise, from ancient times, humans have sought to manipulate the spirits. A prominent example from the Bible is the story of Elijah's interaction with the priests of Baal. In a contest to see whether Baal or Jehovah was the true God, Elijah challenged his opponents to call down fire from heaven. After all, Baal, it was supposed, was the god of lightning. According to 1 Kings 18:28, the servants of Baal "cried aloud and cut themselves after their custom with swords and lances, until the blood gushed out upon them" (ESV). Yet no fire fell on their altar. It is interesting that the Bible treats such examples of idolatry as worship of actual demonic beings rather than mere superstitious behavior.

Moses wrote about the idolatry of the Hebrews during their time in Egypt, saying, "They sacrificed unto demons, not to God; to gods whom they knew not, to new gods that came newly up, whom your fathers feared not" (Deuteronomy 32:17; KJV). Referring to the idolatrous practices of the people of Israel as they adopted the religious ways of the people of Canaan, the Psalmist wrote, "They served their idols: which were a snare unto them. Yea, they sacrificed their sons and their daughters unto devils, and shed innocent blood, even the blood of their sons and of their daughters, whom they sacrificed unto the idols of Canaan; and the land was polluted with blood" (Psalm 106:36–38; KJV).

Consider the attitude of the Syrians in 1 Kings 20:23, "And the servants of the king of Syria said unto him, Their gods are gods of the hills; therefore they were stronger than we; but let us fight against them in the plain, and surely we shall be stronger than they." As we will see further, this is a proto-typical animist response, assuming that various spirits control certain regions. They reasoned that Israel's God was no more powerful than their gods; He just happened to be powerful in the hills. In the New Testament, idol worship continued to be in practice among the Gentile people of the time.

The Apostle Paul gives his assessment of what took place in idol worship by saying in 1 Corinthians 10:20, "But I say, that the things which the Gentiles sacrifice, they sacrifice to devils, and not to God." In both Testaments, Scripture makes it clear that the earth is inhabited by deceptive evil spirits who in some way are organized for the purpose of opposing God's plan for humanity.[1] So the Bible's perspective on animistic practices is that they represent interaction between real demonic forces and people who are ignorant of God's way of salvation.

Beliefs and Practices of Animism

Because the actual practice of animism is closely tied to the specific experiences of the people among whom it is found, variations in animistic expressions abound. While there are similarities between the forms of worship of different animists, each expression of the religion will in some ways be unique. As already mentioned, there is no binding sacred text, no universalizing creed, no single creation myth, nor any unifying method of worship. The two things that all animists have in common is fear of the unseen spirits in their region and their attempt to coexist successfully with these spirit beings.

One of the questions that must inevitably be answered in animist societies is where did the spirits originate? Many believe that they are created beings that have varying degrees of power based on some kind of hierarchical relationship. In fact, this is similar to what the Bible teaches about evil spirits. Others believe that they are part of the earth itself and are manifestations of their view that nature is a living entity. The great majority of animists believe that at least some of the spirits are their deceased ancestors.

---

1. See Daniel 10:13 and Ephesians 6:12.

Good and Evil

Animists believe that there are both good and bad spirits, and that both types can be beneficial if properly engaged. Good spirits bring good things to the individual or to the community, such as good harvest, good health, fertility, or wealth. In order to encourage good spirits to serve their desires, animists make offerings of food or animals, or in some cases even of human beings. Each spirit is also believed to have a retinue of actions that either please or displease it, so believers are careful to say the right words, wear the right clothes, and perform the right rituals. These activities are sometimes referred to as *taboos*, meaning actions that must be properly performed (or not performed) in order to placate the spirits. This may include *talismans* or *amulets,* articles made to be worn or carried on one's body, which have some spiritual significance, in order to please good spirits or repel bad spirits.

Bad spirits can be either mischievous or outright sinister. They can play dirty tricks to entertain themselves or they can bring disease or disaster or even kill people. Part of the worldview of all animists is that *everything* that happens is the result of interplay with the spirits. Nothing occurs without a spiritual cause. The key to successful living is to prevent the spirits from doing harm and cajole them to do good. If someone becomes ill, it is not because a virus has infected his body; it is because a spirit has afflicted him. If someone has a good crop, it is not because he planted well and carefully nurtured his plants; it is because he has found favor with the appropriate spirit. Therefore, it is essential that an animist knows what the spirits like or do not like so that he or she can effectively satisfy them.

Interacting with the Spirits

Since there is no sacred text in animism to reveal what pleases the spirits, some sort of religious specialist must develop the ability to communicate with the spirits and discover their preferences. In all examples of animist religion it is thought that there are certain practitioners who can mediate between people and the spirits. These spirit mediums are called by different names in different cultures. Some are called *shamans* or *medicine men*. Others are called *witches* or *witch doctors*. Some are called *sorcerers* or *wizards*. In many situations, there will be different types of spirit mediums with different roles and powers. Some only interact with the evil spirits and some only with the good. Some use *magic* or *sorcery* to help, and some use it to damage.

If, for example, a wife wanted to ensure that her husband would love her and remain faithful to her, she might go to a witch who could provide some potion that would make the wife more attractive to her husband or make her husband become more devoted to her. The formulations of such concoctions are secrets known to the practitioner that may have been passed down for many generations or revealed by some spirit. In either case, the origin of such knowledge is supposed to have been derived from the spirit world. If a child dies, it is assumed that someone has either broken taboo or that a curse had been placed on the child. A shaman or sorcerer would determine which was the actual cause. Perhaps someone would need to be ritually punished for breaking taboo and may be disfigured or exiled from the community. If the shaman determines that the ill fortune was a result of someone placing a curse on the unfortunate sufferer, then he will practice some form of *divination* (using some ritual to discern a spiritual reality) in order to figure out who is responsible. Forms of divination may include reading the entrails of a slaughtered animal, seeing patterns in shells or sticks cast on the ground, using special cards (like tarot cards) in random sequence, or any other technique intended to reveal hidden spiritual realities. He may then, in return for some fee, place a curse back on the culprit. All of this sounds like fantasy to our Western minds, but this is just a small glimpse into the everyday life of those in an animist culture.

Variations of Animism

Today, animism is most directly associated with tribal people who live in relative isolation from modern society. For this reason it was once often supposed that if a group of animists was exposed to modern technology and scientific understanding, they would naturally abandon their religious practices as mere superstitions. This expectation, however, fails to take into account the fact that people who practice animism are not merely superstitious. They really do interact with spiritual beings (demons) and remain fearful, in spite of modern scientific advances, of offending them. That is not to say that all of their fears are valid and that none of their practices are simply superstitious. It is, rather, a recognition that at the root of their belief system are genuine experiences of supernatural interaction with the spirit world for good or for ill. This underlying characteristic of animism makes it a pervasive religious influence even where other religions have ostensibly superseded it.

For example, throughout most of the Muslim world, people adopt the external customs and doctrines of Islam while continuing to actively practice animism. Likewise, most Buddhists in the world do not practice pure Buddhism; instead, they mix Buddhist teaching with animistic practices. Even Christianity can be ostensibly practiced on the surface while people continue to use the rituals and taboos of animism to interact with the spirit world. These blended religious forms are known as "folk" religions, such as Folk Islam, Folk Buddhism, Folk Judaism, or Folk Christianity. As a general rule, adherents of folk religions look to the doctrinally pure form of the religion (Islam, Buddhism, Judaism, or Christianity) for existential reality, or big-picture thinking. These religions address the major issues of what is real and why we exist. They offer explanations about what happens after death. For the problems of everyday living involving relationships and wellness and personal success, folk religionists look to the spirits and shamans while continuing the practices of animism. When we take into account the number of people in other religions who also practice animism on some level, we see that, in actuality, billions of people around the world are animists.

Authority of Animism

There is no central founder of animism. Its roots go back to earliest times, making it the world's most ancient false religion. There are no universal writings or sacred texts that are common to animist peoples. In fact, because animism is most often associated with tribal peoples, many of whom have no written language, what is thought to be true is passed down orally.[2] For this reason, animism is sometimes labeled "oral religion." What then is the basis for authority among any group of animists? It is their tradition passed down from generation to generation. The multitude of taboos and customs, rituals and observances necessary to maintain balance with nature and the spirits inhabiting it are taught through stories and legends which become the core of that people's *worldview* or understanding of what is real.

Certain locations or landmarks are held to be sacred or, conversely, taboo. There may be a sacred tree or stone where important religious events are celebrated. Certain places may be avoided in order to not break taboo and consequently bring misfortune. How are these things known? They were found to be so through experiences that took place at some point in the people's

---

2. Some animists are literate and may have their own locally written materials. These usually take the form of magic books of secret formulas or spells. See Acts 19:19.

history and have ever since been marked as special. These beliefs guide the life cycle of animist peoples. All animists have some types of ceremonies to ensure proper interaction with the spirit world during important life events such as birth and death, puberty and marriage, planting and harvest, and so forth, but animism is non-institutional. Authority for daily spiritual direction rests with whatever person is most in tune with the spirit world, such as a shaman or witch. This person is able to enter the spirit world through a trance or by means of being inhabited by a spirit and can therefore know hidden mysteries which guide the decisions of an individual or the entire group.

Understandably, the leader (shaman, witch doctor, medicine man, etc.) frequently abuses this authority for personal gain in terms of wealth or power. While claiming to manipulate the spirits, the shaman may in fact be manipulating the tribe. This is certainly a common characteristic of sinful humans in any religion or society, but it is a mistake to assume that this is all that is taking place within the practice of animism. Though much of what is seen as supernatural in animism is surely attributable to the trickery of devious leaders, the practice of animism has continued through all these centuries, in spite of modernity, because there is real interplay between humans and the spirit world.[3]

Creation Beliefs of Animism

Interestingly, most animist systems hold to a belief in one supreme deity who is the creator of all that is. Variations exist about how or why this great being made the world and man to inhabit it, but some commonality exists regarding the character of the high god. Animism's view of God could generally be described as *deistic*. That is, God is indeed all-powerful, but He is also uninterested. At some time in the past He made the world and set things in order, but then something happened to offend Him and cause Him to depart. Though He still exists, He no longer interacts directly with humans, but allows lesser deities, or spirits, to do so. Animists generally perceive the high god to be angry and unreachable by humanity. There are a host of explanations for why the creator is angry, but most are simply fabulous tales of him being mistreated in some way.

---

3. A good example of this in the Bible is found in Acts 19:13–16. Apparently, the sons of Sceva were fraudulently taking advantage of the Ephesian people's fear of spirits. Yet in an attempt to use the name of Jesus as some sort of magic word, they discovered to their regret that a real evil spirit was at work.

For example, one African myth relates that God came to visit a family while the wife was preparing dinner. Because she was late in her preparations, she was working rapidly to pound her corn. In her haste she poked God in the eye and He became angry and left, never to return to interact with humans again.[4] The universal presence of such legends among animists allows for their universal denial of personal responsibility for being alienated from the Creator. In all animist creation myths, the creator left man and not vice versa. Therefore, man is not guilty of rebellion against God but still suffers the consequences.

The spirits that remain active in the world generally fit into several categories in animist thought. There are good spirits, which are lesser gods and perhaps related to the high god in some way. There are evil spirits, which are the enemies of both the high god and his associated lesser gods (good spirits) as well as humans. Finally, there are ancestral spirits, which can be either good or bad, depending on how they are treated.

While animists generally do not introduce evolutionary ideas into their creation accounts, they misunderstand the nature of God. The idea that He is offended with humanity is in fact correct, but it is not because He is capricious. Rather, He rejects man's sinful rebellion against Him. He has not abandoned man but has, in fact, sent His only Son in order to repair the relationship with man by atoning for our sin and accounting us as righteous. He has not, as animists suppose, relegated human affairs to lesser spirits, but is directly responsible for the good things that are evident in nature.[5] The Apostle Paul explained this to the animist thinkers at Lystra when he reasoned in Acts 14:17, "He did good, and gave us rain from heaven, and fruitful seasons, filling our hearts with food and gladness" (KJV). Part of Paul's message to these people was that God the Creator was actively involved in their daily lives whether they realized it or not.

Theological Concepts of Animists
Sin

Because animists generally dwell in corporate or tribal social environments, that is to say that they are more concerned with the group than

---

4. Philip M. Steyne, *Gods of Power: A Study in the Beliefs and Practices of Animists* (Columbia, SC: Impact International Foundation, 2011), p. 74.
5. The Bible clearly indicates that God often uses angelic beings to accomplish His work among people, such as the angels who rescued Lot, closed the lions' mouths to save Daniel, and freed Peter from prison.

the individual, concepts of evil are based upon what is deleterious to the group as a whole. Animists do not feel guilty because they have transgressed against God, but will sense shame if their actions are seen as harmful to the group. Acting in ways that bring the wrath of the spirits, such as breaking taboo or failing to perform prescribed rituals, is considered evil, and the group may move to punish the offender. Shame and fear are employed to motivate individuals to comply with social expectations. For the animist, iniquity is not a violation against God, but against one's social group. Right and wrong are not issues of personal morality, but of their practical effect on the group as a whole.

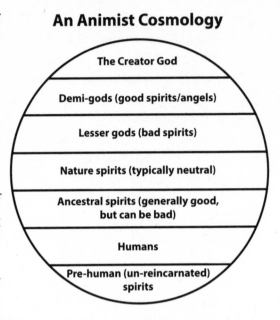

An Animist Cosmology

- The Creator God
- Demi-gods (good spirits/angels)
- Lesser gods (bad spirits)
- Nature spirits (typically neutral)
- Ancestral spirits (generally good, but can be bad)
- Humans
- Pre-human (un-reincarnated) spirits

Death

For the animist, death is part of the continuous cycle of nature. Everyone dies, but no one dies without some spiritual cause. Life can be shortened by living out of harmony with nature, by offending a spirit, or because an enemy has placed a curse. Animists believe that upon death, a person continues to live on in a different plane as a spirit. Eventually the spirit of the deceased will be forgotten from the living memory of the tribe and will then be reincarnated as a new baby among the same people. Animist society consists of the spirits of the yet unborn, the living, and the dead. They view each group as equally alive, and believe that they should continually interact with one another.

Salvation

Animists believe that death is simply the continuation of life, but in a different sphere, and that individuals continue as ancestral spirits until they are forgotten, and are eventually reborn as new persons. Therefore, there is little thought for salvation in the sense of eternal rescue. For the animist, the principal goal in life is to interact with the spirit world successfully so as to provide for tranquility and prosperity in the here and now. There is no single savior for the animist. He may look to a powerful spirit to vanquish other spirits, but the idea that God provides some ultimate means of conquering the power of the spirits and eliminating the need to manipulate them is unknown in animist thinking.

Communicating the Gospel to Animists

It is important to communicate with animists using concepts that are familiar to them and that speak to their central religious concerns (Colossians 4:2–6). Here is a sample of how one might present the truth of God's salvation through Christ to an animist:

> The Creator God made the original human parents and placed them in a perfect garden where all of their wants were satisfied. He forbade them to eat a fruit which would cause them to think and act independently of His loving kindness to them. An evil spirit, who was once one of the Creator's special and most powerful servants, but who had rebelled against Him, spoke lies to the first parents and deceived them into believing that God was not kind. They ate the forbidden fruit and immediately realized that they had acted in rebellion against God. Clearly, God was rightly offended by their hostile act. He had not abandoned them, but His cherished children had made themselves His enemies. This caused them to experience fear and shame for the first time. But the Creator God in perfect kindness came to search for them, even though they tried to hide themselves.
>
> He made a way for their rebellion to be forgiven and instituted a plan in which the sacrifice of an innocent animal could temporarily cover the stain of their shame and rebellion against Him. He gave them instructions for how they should live in compliance with His will for them. Most importantly, He promised that someday a man would be born who would be His own Son, one who would be both God and man, and this One would provide salvation once and for all for all people who believed on Him. He would give His life as the ultimate sacrifice for humanity's rebellion against the Creator God and completely remove all of

CONCEPTS ASSOCIATED WITH ANIMISM

Synonyms for Animism
Spirit Religion — so called because all animism by nature involves interaction with the spirit world
Oral Religion — so called because many animistic societies are pre-literate
Natural Religion — so called because animistic practice is highly holistic in its understanding of the relationship between humanity and nature
Primitive or Primal Religion — so called because many animistic peoples are pre-modern in their use of science and technology
Tribal Religion — so called because the majority of the world's animistic peoples live in tribal societies
Folk Religion — so called because animism is not a formal religion (no sacred writings or universal practices). Most formal religions have localized folk varieties (Folk Buddhism, Folk Islam, Folk Judaism, or Folk Christianity) which are highly dependent on interaction with spirit powers.

Elements of Power
Mana — a neutral force which is thought by some animists (mostly throughout Polynesia) to exist in nature, which can be harvested for use by humans
Witchcraft — the use of rituals, ceremonies, potions, or incantations to effect some result, usually harmful, which is beyond natural occurrence
Magic — any form of interaction with non-human powers. White magic involves using powers to bring benefit, while black magic involves using powers to bring harm. Specific types of magic include contagious magic, which uses something from a person's body (hair, nails, tooth, feces) to bring them harm or blessing, and imitative magic which uses a representation of a person to bring harm upon them (as in a voodoo doll).
Spirit Manipulation —direct interaction with a spirit being for the sake of garnering its favor for doing good or evil. This may involve sacrifice, offerings, deprivation, taking an oath, or allowing the spirit to use one's body for some purpose.
Taboo — a prohibition against saying certain words, going to certain places, performing certain acts, looking at certain things, etc. for the sake of not offending a spirit and thereby bringing misfortune upon oneself or one's community
Power Words — special words which are thought to have power in themselves to invoke either good or ill. These can include incantations, curses, or blessings pronounced to repel evil spirits.

Objects Associated with Power
Charms — any item, naturally occurring or specially created, which is thought to have power to ward off evil or draw good fortune
Talismans — a type of charm which has been prepared specifically for the purpose of providing good luck or protection from harm
Amulets — any form of wearable charm

Fetishes — an object specially prepared by a religious specialist (shaman, medicine man, etc.) that is thought to create a special relationship between the possessor and a particular spirit

Totems — physical representations of spirit beings, often associated with certain animals.

Sacred Objects or Places — items or places where a specific spirit or spirits is thought to abide and therefore to exercise special power. Examples could include things like sacred trees, rocks, streams, or hills.

Kinds of Non-Physical Beings

Creator God — animists have some concept of a single supreme being, but he is thought to be distant and unknowable.

Gods — powerful spirits which control the lives of animist peoples. Various explanations occur for the origin of these gods.

Ancestors — the spirits of the dead who are still remembered and are believed to continue to be dwelling among and interacting with the living. Ancestral spirits are generally considered helpful as long as they are respected.

Ghosts — the spirits of the dead who are no longer remembered and are therefore disconnected with the life of the animist society. They are angry as a result and are thought to be generally malicious.

Nature Spirits — less powerful spirits which inhabit all of nature. These are generally considered good and helpful.

Totemic Spirits — many animist peoples believe that they have a special relationship with the spirits of certain animals and therefore must interact with those animals in prescribed ways. These spirits are often represented through totems.

Religious Specialists*

Priest — any person who generally instructs animists in the proper functions of the religion

Medicine Man — name given in some animist societies to the person who attempts to use magic and spirit manipulation to bring healing and other benefits

Shaman — a general term for someone who has special spiritual knowledge through dreams or visions or by means of some connection with the spirit world

Witch — a person who has naturally occurring supernatural power, often inherited from a parent or grandparent. Witches can be male or female and are characterized by using their powers to bring harm.

Sorcerer — a person who has acquired supernatural power through ritual or study and uses that power to do harm for profit

Medium — a general term for anyone who has regular contact with the spirit world. Often a medium has a special connection with one particular spirit and experiences times of possession by that spirit.

* Note that while most organized animist societies feature each of these types of religious specialists, different expressions of animism use these terms interchangeably or not at all.

Means of Divination
Reading Signs — any method of discerning the otherwise unknowable by detecting random patterns understood only by the diviner. Examples include studying animal entrails, casting cowry shells, reading tarot cards, reading palms, reading tea leaves, etc.
Astrology — attempting to understand the future based on the movements of the stars
Interpreting Omens — recognizing certain occurrences (e.g., comets, eclipses, earthquakes) as portending the arrival of either good or bad fortune upon an individual or group
Ordeal — a test by which truth is revealed. Such tests usually involve afflicting a person physically or chemically and determining his or her guilt or innocence, suitability, or worthiness based on the reaction to the affliction.
Dreams/Visions — information revealed through the separation of the spirit from the body. Animists believe that the spirit is able to leave the body and return. Sometimes information that would otherwise be unknowable is discovered during this state of separation.
Spirit Possession — all forms of animism involve some kind of activity whereby the spirits take control over and communicate through particular human beings, generally spiritual practitioners such as the shamans.

the consequences of our rebellion, including our fear and shame. Salvation could be received by believing in this great promise.

Sadly, the great deceiving spirit, the enemy of God, continued to work to cause people everywhere to live in rebellion against their Creator. The deceiving spirit, Satan, has many other spirits who were also created by God to serve Him but who also chose to rebel and follow the deceiver. They inhabit the whole world and present themselves as friendly and helpful spirits, but they are not. Throughout the entire history of humanity they have made promises of power and success if people would serve and worship them. They have presented themselves as spirits of animals or of rivers or trees or mountains. When people serve them they sometimes give people power. But they continue to lie and say that the Creator God is unkind and unfair, just as Satan lied to our first parents. Worst of all, they say that there is no judgment for man's rebellion against the Creator. According to the deceiving spirits, people simply live and die and return again.

Fortunately, God, because He is actually so kind and good, has never stopped caring for humanity. He has always provided good by sending rain and harvests and by giving health and prosperity to many. He has also communicated to us through a special book, revealed to men who obeyed Him over many years. In His book, He explains that the One who was promised from the beginning, the One who would be both God and man, has come and did give His life as a sacrifice for our rebellion. He suffered a cruel death involving great pain by which He paid the cost of every evil deed and rebellious act ever committed. Then, He arose from the dead to prove that He had gained victory over all rebellion and death itself! When we stop believing the deceiving spirits and believe in the One who died to remove our shame and restore our honor with the Creator, God considers us as one of His own special children. Rather than being far removed and acting as one offended by us, He becomes our spiritual Father and we begin to know Him personally. When we die, He does not leave us here to wander about as an ancestral spirit, but takes us directly to live with Him in His home beyond the stars.

Only those who choose to believe these promises and turn away from serving any other spirits can experience the joy of becoming one of God's spiritual children. The spirits you have served will lie to you and tell you that they are more powerful than the One who was both God and man. But the truth, stated to us in God's book, is that when Jesus (the name of the God-man) paid for our rebellion and conquered death, He also conquered God's enemy, Satan, and all those spirits who followed him. In fact, by His victorious life, death, and Resurrection, Jesus gained all of the power of the universe. He alone can give us true harmony with the world we live in and with the Creator God to whom we are responsible. Those who follow Jesus are not victims of fate or of the spirit world; the lives of those who believe God's promises are controlled by God Himself and by the power of Jesus they live in victory over all of the spirits, even Satan.[6] If you will choose to follow the Creator God and His unique Son, the

---

6. It is important to communicate to animists the victory and power of Jesus over demon spirits. The New Testament often refers to this reality and the promise of genuine spiritual power to all believers. See, for example, John 12:31; Romans 8:31; Colossians 1:13; Hebrews 2:14; 1 John 3:8, 4:4.

God-man, you will join His side against all the other spirits in world who, in reality, are the enemies of God and all people.

Conclusion

We typically think of animism as something associated with pre-modern peoples — images of tribalists with scant clothing, led by shamans or witch doctors. Wild dances or animal sacrifices come to mind at the mention of the term animism. In reality, however, any form of interaction with the spirit world is a manifestation of animism. Witchcraft, the occult, fortune telling, communicating with the dead, and praying to those who are no longer living are all manifestations of animism on some level. In each case there is an attempt to obtain knowledge or manipulate circumstances through contact with the spirit world. Attempts to receive spiritual guidance from any source other than God and His Word are strictly forbidden for those who know Him.[7]

Animism is not an organized religion like many other religions. There are no sacred writings or historic founders featuring ordered systems and hierarchical structures, yet more than half of the people on planet earth practice some form of animism on a regular basis. Jesus conquered Satan and all of the fallen spirits who serve him by defeating sin and death at the Cross and through His physical Resurrection from the tomb. As followers of Christ, we must never fall for the lies of demonic spirits who would replace hope and grace with fear and promises of spiritual manipulation.

Satan wants us to believe that God only loves us when we are good or when we do things that please Him, but God loves us because He is good, not because of what we can do to gain His favor. He saves us, not because of what we have done, but because His Son paid the ultimate sacrifice for our rebellion against Him (Titus 2:11–14). We can never make God love or accept us more than He already does through Christ our Savior. That great deceiver, Satan, still tries to introduce animist concepts even into our relationship with our Creator. He wants us to believe that we can negotiate with God in order to receive good, or that we must do penance for our sin in order to restore God's favor. We must resist the devil's lies and wholly believe in God's love and forgiveness that was so fully demonstrated through Christ Jesus.

---

7. Deuteronomy 18:10–12; Isaiah 8:19–20.

Summary of Animistic Beliefs

Doctrine	Teachings of Animism
God	Acknowledge a supreme god, but generally have a deistic view. God is seen as distant and disconnected rather than personal. There are various views of lesser gods or spirits who interact with humans and nature.
Authority/Revelation	There are no authoritative texts, but each group has its own oral traditions that are passed down. Shamans or other leaders are seen as the authorities that can interact with the spirits.
Man	Man is a spirit that is part of nature and is reborn in cycles.
Sin	Sin is generally viewed as bringing harm to the tribe rather than an individual affront to a holy God. There is no concept of original sin.
Salvation	There are various views, but generally no view of a judgment in the afterlife.
Creation	Generally, a Creator God made the world but has abandoned it (deism). Generally deny evolutionary concepts or have no connection to them.

Chapter 13

Egypt's Ancient Religion

Dr. Elizabeth Mitchell and Troy Lacey

The ancient Egyptians were a very religious people. Hundreds of years after Homer sang epics about gods meddling in the Greek war with Troy, the Greek historian Herodotus of Halicarnassus (c. 484-425 B.C.) wrote of his visit to Egypt, then under Persian rule.

Herodotus recorded his observations and interviews for posterity. Though he himself came from a polytheistic people to whom the Apostle Paul later said, "Men of Athens, I perceive that in all things you are very religious" (Acts 17:22),[1] Herodotus wrote that Egyptians "are religious to excess, far beyond any other race of men."[2]

The pervasive influence of Egyptian religion on every facet of ancient life is evident in the artwork and inscriptions on its many monuments and artifacts and in papyrus documents that survived for millennia in the dry heat of northern Africa. Not only do the tombs of royalty and temples reveal the importance of religion, but the existence of many local village shrines and household shrines from the Middle Kingdom period onward affirm that religious interest was not reserved for the ruling classes.

Though then eclipsed by foreign powers, for much of its history Egypt had been a key power in the Mediterranean world. Herodotus deduced that

---

1. All Scripture in this chapter is from the New King James Version (NKJV) of the Bible.
2. Herodotus, *The History of Herodotus*, trans. George Rawlinson, vol. 2, section 37, Encyclopaedia Britannica, 1952.

ancient Egypt was the source of much in the classical Greek pantheon. He wrote, "Almost all the names of the gods came into Greece from Egypt."[3] Through its trade, might, and inherent appeal, ancient Egypt's religion influenced cultures near and far.

Egypt's pyramids and mummies are familiar testimonials to a culture seemingly devoted to death. Religious beliefs and practices reflect how people deal with the uncertainties of both death and life. For instance, the ancient Egyptians believed that proper preparation of a dead body, be it the body of a beloved family member or a revered ruler, was essential for the individual's eternal well-being.

Egypt's dry climate has preserved much evidence to help us piece together what ancient Egyptians generally believed about their origins and their eternal destinies. Their religion dictated how kings, priests, and people should interact with their gods in order to hold back chaos, ensuring a good life, a stable nation, and a secure future.

Unity of Religion and the State

Religious symbolism appears in Egypt's most ancient artifacts. Egypt's religion likely developed among those who settled it after the dispersion from Babel and therefore existed before its unification as a nation. Egypt's religion and government eventually became inseparable. Its king was seen as an incarnation of the god Horus, son of Osiris, and its economy, art, and architecture were devoted to the satisfaction and sustenance of the gods in order to preserve the natural order and protect the dead. A look at Cleopatra's Needle, now gracing the bank of the Thames in London, is a reminder of this theocratic union.

The obelisk was not commissioned by the famous Cleopatra VII but was named because it was moved to an Alexandrian temple that Cleopatra built to honor her Roman lover. The 68-foot obelisk had been constructed centuries earlier at the order of Pharaoh Thutmose III to mark sunset at Atum-Ra's temple in Heliopolis. As the supposed offspring of the sun god Ra and the vital link between Egypt and the gods, it was the pharaoh's duty to facilitate the daily life-giving cycle of the sun god, and he commissioned two obelisks for this purpose.

The companion to the obelisk on the Thames, taken from the eastern gate of the same temple, was built to mark Ra's daily rebirth or resurrection.

3. Ibid., vol. 2, section 50.

It now stands in New York City's Central Park. These obelisks, like the pyramids, also symbolized an element common to all Egyptian creation myths — the primeval mound from which the creator god Atum emerged to conquer chaos.

Battle with the God of Moses

Egypt's religious beliefs accumulated over time and were never codified in a holy book. They were, however, recorded in every facet of its culture. Certainly by the time of Moses and the Hebrews' Exodus, Egypt's system of gods was a force over which the Creator God, as the only true God, chose to show Himself powerful for the benefit of the Hebrews and the watching world.

When God announced the tenth plague to Moses, He explained, "against all the gods of Egypt I will execute judgment: I am the LORD" (Exodus 12:12). The Hebrews had long lived in Egypt exposed to Egypt's religion and, as God forged them into the nation through which He would reveal His Word (Romans 3:2) and eventually send the Savior into the world, they needed to be shown the power of the only true God. The Egyptian people themselves needed that lesson, and God told Moses:

> But Pharaoh will not heed you, so that I may lay My hand on Egypt and bring My armies and My people, the children of Israel, out of the land of Egypt by great judgments. And the Egyptians shall know that I am the LORD, when I stretch out My hand on Egypt and bring the children of Israel from among them (Exodus 7:4–5).

People of other pagan nations (such as Jericho, according to Rahab; see Joshua 2:8–10) also needed to see the proof of God's power over the false gods of this mighty nation. Pharaoh was considered the incarnation of the god Horus and the son of the sun god, Ra. If not divine during his time on earth (a status that varied over the centuries), he anticipated unification with the god Osiris after his death. Pharaoh represented Egypt to the gods. He therefore was not just a stubborn obstacle to Hebrew freedom but the point man for Egypt's "gods" in the battle that played out before Israel's departure.

Egypt's creation stories held that the gods emerged to create order out of chaos, and they themselves were part of that order. Keeping chaos at bay was one of the chief goals of Egypt's religion in general and therefore of pharaoh in particular. According to inscriptions recounting religious rituals, the pharaoh was pictured as Egypt's representative even as the priests ministered to the mythological beings they believed to be the authors and sustainers of all that was not chaos.

The office of pharaoh was identified with the god Horus. At death, if all rites were observed, the pharaoh was thought to become one with Horus' father, Osiris, the god of the underworld. Thus, the ten plagues preceding the Exodus under Moses dealt a series of blows to the status of many elements of nature that were personified as gods as well as to the quasi-divine pharaoh, son of the sun god, who was Egypt's intermediary with its pantheon.

It is difficult to be dogmatic about which plagues dealt blows to Egyptian perceptions of which specific gods. After all, Egypt honored around 1,500 gods, many manifested in nature. Two of the more obvious are the plague of frogs, in which the frog-headed fertility goddess Heket certainly lost face among her worshipers, and the plague on livestock, which took a shot at the sacred Apis bull and the bovine goddess Hathor.

Life and prosperity in ancient Egypt depended on certain cycles. For ancient Egyptians, the sun's daily renewal and the Nile River's annual flood were particularly important. Egyptians believed that properly cared for gods and goddesses would maintain these cycles on which their lives depended. Thus, the plague of darkness was a direct assault on the normally dependable sun god, Ra.

The Nile River also had divine status, and Hapy was the god of the all-important annual flood that imparted life-sustaining fertility to Egypt's soil. The first plague, turning water into blood, struck at the heart of Egypt's agricultural prosperity, the water that kept the dry desert's chaos from claiming Egypt's fertile lands. Ultimately, the ten plagues culminated in the death of the firstborn of Egypt, including the firstborn of Egypt's quasi-divine pharaoh.

Foreign Threat

As evident from Herodotus' testimony during his visit to a Persian-ruled Egypt, Egypt's religion weathered foreign rule, but not unscathed. Persia conquered Egypt in 532 B.C. and promptly slew the Apis bull and destroyed the statues of many gods. Cambyses, the Persian conqueror, even had the mummy of Pharaoh Ahmose II, who died in 526 B.C., taken from its tomb and cremated — thus destroying the essential nightly home on which the pharaoh's *ka* and *ba* depended for their eternal existence (see section below for an explanation of this concept).

Persian efforts to replace Egypt's religion with their own form of sun worship left a mark, even on some monuments. For instance, the sun's rays seem to have been added to some religious carvings, yet Egypt's ancient religion survived. Later, under the Ptolemaic rule that followed Alexander's Greek conquest of Egypt, Egypt's ancient religion, though mixed with elements of other religions and mysticism, continued to accord divine status to the Egyptian king.

Egypt's theocracy finally crumbled under the rule of Christianized Rome in the fourth century A.D. With the Renaissance, the modern world took an increased interest in all things ancient, especially things Egyptian. Egyptian symbolism and the enticing mysteries of the as-yet-then-indecipherable hieroglyphics intrigued many, including philosophers of the Enlightenment, theologians, mystics, secret societies, and revolutionaries.

Modern Interest in Egyptology

Things Egyptian became much more accessible to Europeans after Napoleon's conquest of Egypt and his subsequent defeat by the British at the 1801 Battle of Alexandria. Antiquities were popular and available. The cornerstone of Egyptology in the 19th century and beyond was the inscription on the Rosetta stone unearthed during Napoleon's brief rule. Its simple message recorded in three languages contained the key to deciphering Egyptian hieroglyphics. As Egyptology blossomed with the abundance of artifacts and the excitement of linguistic breakthroughs, some scholars hoped to discover the mysterious wisdom of a superior ancient philosophy, while others expected to find corroborating evidence for many historical accounts in the Bible's Old Testament.

Finding the footprints of a highly civilized, complex ancient culture in the monuments, artifacts, inscriptions, and documents they unearthed in Egypt, 19th-century scholars were puzzled to discover that evidently advanced people had worshiped gods represented as animals and animal-human hybrids. Mummified people was understandable to modern Western cultures with their own elaborate funeral rites, but what should the modern mind make of the many mummified crocodiles, cats, and bulls?

How could a highly civilized nation have arisen harnessed to a religion that seemed barbaric or even silly? And so began the quest to piece together the truth about what ancient Egyptians, from farmer to pharaoh, really believed about their origins, how they worshiped their gods, and what they thought would happen to them after they died.

Polytheism in an Advanced Civilization

Though ancient Egypt's religion is documented in surviving papyrus documents and artwork covering monuments, temples, and coffins, Egypt never developed a Bible-like book containing an official, authoritative version of their beliefs. Much of Egyptian mythology seems contradictory, but given the fragmentary nature of the evidence from which it has been recovered this isn't surprising.

Moreover, Egyptian gods and goddesses were believed to have co-existing multiple manifestations and characteristics. Thus, the sun god has more than one name, but the name changed according to the time of day. The rising sun was generally the scarab-headed Khepri, the midday sun Ra (or Re), and the setting sun Atum. And Aten was the name eventually applied to the radiant disk of the sun in the time of the Pharaoh Ahkenaten. Furthermore, every being also had a secret name reflecting his or her essence, and the goddess Isis once gained power over the sun god by tricking him into revealing his secret name to her. Thus, differing names were not seen as contradictory.

From the abundant yet fragmentary evidence, scholars have pieced together a reasonable understanding of the roughly 1,500 named gods the Egyptians revered and how they worshiped them. About some there is little more known than a name, but for many there is a great deal of information. Well-known are the mythological stories of Seth's murder of his brother Osiris — by tricking him into climbing into a box in which he was subsequently drowned — and of Osiris' ultimate resurrection as god of the underworld with the help of his wife, Isis, the posthumous conception and birth of their son Horus, and Horus' eventual revenge upon Seth.

In some ways, Egyptian myths resembled familiar Greco-Roman myths, though early Egyptologists had to wrestle with the philosophical nature of polytheism in addition to linguistic challenges and the cryptic preponderance of apparent animal worship in such an advanced culture.

Over the past couple of centuries there has been much debate about the nature of Egypt's religion. Some, perhaps spurred by the idea that only intellectually backward people would worship a pantheon of animal-like deities, theorized that Egypt's polytheism was a sublimated form of monotheism with multiple divine manifestations. (This view was even showcased in G.A. Henty's 19th-century historical novel *The Cat of Bubastes*.)

Some Egyptologists have suggested Egypt's ancient religion moved in a trajectory toward a "more civilized" monotheistic religion or recognition of some sort of omnipotent divinity. Each of these positions finds some support in various texts, but we should be cautious in trying to stretch those concepts to interpret the totality of Egypt's theology. In fact, during the New Kingdom, the pharaoh Akhenaten promoted a nearly monotheistic worship of Aten, often depicted as the radiant solar disk, to the exclusion of the rest of Egypt's menu of deities. After his death, Akhenaten's efforts were regarded as heretical and Egyptian worship returned to its firmly polytheistic form.

Animal Gods

Some of Egypt's gods, such as Nut, the goddess of the sky, were accorded human form. But of course, many were depicted as animals, animal hybrids, or animal-human hybrids. Though Egyptians took care to avoid offending sacred animals and revered zoologic manifestations of their deities, most scholars now believe that Egyptians did not think their gods necessarily looked like the animals in their divine menagerie. Rather, they believed their gods could manifest themselves as certain animals, often more than one.

Some gods were depicted alternately as a complete animal or an animal-human hybrid. For instance, Thoth, the god of writing and knowledge, who in one mythological story had healed the eye of Horus, could appear as a baboon, an ibis, or an ibis-headed man. Ra could be depicted by a falcon or by a human body with a falcon's head. The primary creator god Atum was depicted in fully human form wearing the crowns of Upper and Lower Egypt, as a man with the head of a ram, or in animal form as a serpent, a scarab beetle, a lion, a bull, a lizard, an ape, or a mongoose.[4]

The animal manifestation of a god sometimes provided a visual metaphor for some aspect of the god's character or behavior. The cat-headed goddess Bastet was generally a protector. In one depiction she is seen beheading

---

4. Richard H. Wilkinson, *The Complete Gods and Goddesses of Ancient Egypt* (London: Thames and Hudson, 2003), p. 100–101.

the serpent Apophis, promoter of chaos and enemy of Ra. She was seen as a protector of the dead and as a patroness of mothers, protecting women during pregnancy.

Litters of kittens were suitable gifts to commemorate the new year, perhaps in celebration of Bastet's protective role during the "demon days" that marked the end of each year. Sekhmet, Egypt's most prominent divine lioness, had a more mercurial nature. While Sekhmet could be a goddess of healing, she was also a goddess of plagues or war. Functioning as the all-seeing eye of Ra early in human history, Sekhmet is said to have wreaked havoc on mankind, nearly destroying the human race. Many mummified cats are preserved in cemeteries at Saqqara and Thebes. The cats appear to have died with broken necks at uniform ages, suggesting their mummies were not just remains of beloved pets, and reflecting the importance of feline manifestations in the Egyptian pantheon.[5]

In time, scholars came to understand that neither polytheism nor the worship of gods depicted as animals meant the ancient Egyptians were intellectually inferior. The unusual animal representations of deities in their various combinations carried symbolic meaning. For instance, Sobek was the croc-

Wall of relief of the Crocodile God Sobek in Egypt
(Shutterstock)

odile god and lord of the Nile. But in a statue found in the temple of Luxor in 1967 at a pit in which the sacred animals were likely kept, Sobek-Ra is depicted as a crocodile god with a solar disk on its head and the body of a man. Sobek-Ra's statue, because it has a man's body, is able to embrace a stylized statue of Amenhotep III, and Sobek-Ra is giving him an ankh. The *ankh*, a cross with a loop on the top, was a symbol for life. Scholars believe this statue indicates the sun god, the creator and sustainer of life, manifested himself merged with the crocodile god Sobek, which in turn passed the symbol of life

Ankh

---

5. John H. Taylor, *Death and the Afterlife in Ancient Egypt* (Chicago, IL: University of Chicago Press, 2001), p. 256.

to the pharaoh.[6] In other myths, Sobek shared his crocodile form with other gods, including Seth — the jealous, sneaky, power-hungry murderer of Osiris and enemy of Horus.[7]

Sophistication, Paganism, and the Gospel

Thus, Egyptologists today, having pieced together bits and pieces of information and studied the Egyptian religion though art, artifacts, inscriptions, and other written material, can now be confident that Egypt's polytheism, complete with all its animal forms, was highly abstract and sophisticated. It was, nevertheless, an utterly pagan substitute for the worship of the true God. As Romans 1 tells us of all such religions that reject the true Creator God, regardless of their level of sophistication or whether they are monotheistic or polytheistic:

> For the wrath of God is revealed from heaven against all ungodliness and unrighteousness of men, who suppress the truth in unrighteousness, because what may be known of God is manifest in them, for God has shown it to them. For since the creation of the world His invisible attributes are clearly seen, being understood by the things that are made, even His eternal power and Godhead, so that they are without excuse, because, although they knew God, they did not glorify Him as God, nor were thankful, but became futile in their thoughts, and their foolish hearts were darkened. Professing to be wise, they became fools, and changed the glory of the incorruptible God into an image made like corruptible man — and birds and four-footed animals and creeping things (Romans 1:18–23).

In his book *Eternity in Their Hearts*, missionary Don Richardson, also the author of *Peace Child*, notes that many pagan cultures with ancient roots harbor deep-rooted cultural beliefs that make it easy for them to understand biblical Christianity once it is presented to them. So it was with Egypt. For centuries, Egyptians believed their priest-like pharaoh was a son of their sun god, Ra, their intermediary with the gods, and a divine or semi-divine being identified with the god Horus. They believed that upon his death he would

---

6. Geraldine Pinch, *Egyptian Mythology: A Very Short Introduction* (Oxford: Oxford University Press, 2004), p. 53–54.
7. Ibid., p. 64.

become one with Osiris, his father and god of the underworld. As such, this "son of a god" and mediator would continue to influence the fate of those who died.

For anyone familiar with the biblical gospel of Jesus Christ, the parallels are impossible to miss. When Christianity was introduced in Egypt, many aspects of the true gospel had a familiar ring. Unfortunately the popularity of the Isis-Horus mother-child myth concerning Isis' care of her son Horus, miraculously conceived after the brutal murder of his father, Osiris, lent itself to counterfeits in the form of cultic associations. These mystery religions rivaled Christianity for centuries.

Nevertheless, the past had prepared the hearts of many to be forever changed by the knowledge and worship of the true Son of God, which came to Egypt early in Christianity's history. The hour had come when, like the Samaritans of whom Jesus said "you worship what you do not know" (John 4:22), many Egyptians would turn to "worship the Father in spirit and truth" (John 4:23), having learned that "there is one God and one Mediator between God and men, the Man Christ Jesus, who gave Himself a ransom for all, to be testified in due time" (1 Timothy 2:5–6).

By the end of the second century, Christianity had put down deep roots in the Nile Valley.[8] This long preceded its official acceptance as the religion of the Roman Empire. Yet in A.D. 452, after a century of Christianized Rome's domination and almost two centuries before seventh century Muslim forces overran Egypt, there is record of a group of Egyptians taking an Egyptian goddess (idol) south to visit "her" relatives in Nubia. The powerful and persistent influence of Egyptian religion on surrounding cultures is evident in the "mystery religions" that rivaled Christianity in the Greco-Roman world.

An Egyptian temple actively devoted to the worship of Isis and Osiris on the Nile island of Philae, built under Egypt's Ptolemaic rulers, co-existed with Christian worship until closed by order of the Byzantine emperor Justinian in the sixth century A.D. A cult based on the worship of Isis and Osiris acquired a widespread international following and long outlived the popularity of the Egyptian gods in Egypt itself.

Worldview, Mythology, and Eternal Concerns

There is great value in understanding the worldview of others past and present, though today you will not likely encounter worshipers of Ra and Isis

---

8. Wilkinson, *The Complete Gods and Goddesses of Ancient Egypt*, p. 242.

Temple of Isis from Philae at Agilikia Island
(Wikimedia, Ivan Marcialis)

in your evangelistic efforts to win your neighbors to Jesus Christ. Egyptian mythology reveals what these intelligent people valued and how they thought. For instance, their concern with the preservation of the body and elaborate provisions for the future of the dead reveals their concern about the afterlife. And their beliefs about judgment to be faced after death shows not only their concern with justice but also their appreciation that not just the letter of the law but also truth and the condition of the heart are important indicators of character and even eternal destiny.

The myths the Egyptians developed represent their attempt to explain their origins, understand their place in the world, justify their cultural norms and institutions, lend stability to their government, make sense of their sorrows, and to face death and the uncertainties of the afterlife. In short, Egypt's ancient religion dealt with the same questions that all humans face. In examining ancient Egypt's worldview, we see how, having rejected whatever knowledge of the true God the people retained from their Babel-based ancestors and from others like Abraham who crossed their path, they attempted to answer these timeless, universal human questions through the wisdom of men.

Egyptian mythology, with its rich imagery, despite its pagan roots, has, like classical Greco-Roman mythology, made a rich contribution to literature, even showing up in the writings of John Milton's *Paradise Lost* and in Mozart's opera *The Magic Flute*. Egyptian mythology lives on today in vivid fantasies built around the colorful and imaginative figures that populate Egyptian mythology — especially those in animal form.

The actual worship of these characters now being long past, such stories intrigue Christians and non-Christians alike. But we must remember that real people — people who built a complex, powerful, and influential civilization under the shadow of this pantheon — believed these gods and goddesses held the keys to their past, their present, the afterlife, and their national well-being. Therefore, they devoted their lives and their treasure to worshiping these gods in all their manifestations.

Given that God saw fit to have Moses record in Exodus His battle with the demonic forces personified as Egyptian gods, it is worthwhile for us to learn more about the beliefs of this mighty nation that so greatly influenced its neighbors. Some claim that the Genesis account of creation was influenced by Egyptian creation myths — though we would claim that any similarities to the corrupted versions in Egypt's mythos stem from a cultural awareness of the true history handed down by the descendants of Noah's family who eventually moved from Babel to Egypt.

Satan has been in the business of prompting people to create counterfeit religions that twist the truth of God into a lie and worship the creature instead of the Creator (Romans 1:25) for a very long time. In ancient Egyptian rituals for dealing with death and preparing for the afterlife, we see the earmarks of the same satanic lies that still abound in works-based religions that deny the grace of God available in Christ.

Egyptian Views of Creation

Nearly a dozen Egyptian creation stories distilled from archaeological evidence can be boiled down to three basic forms, based largely on documents and artifacts from three of ancient Egypt's religious centers. While on the surface they seem contradictory, it is best to consider them as complementary stories revealing various perspectives on origins, for there is no evidence that these stories competed with one another. (In a similar way, many people today erroneously think that the biblical accounts of creation recorded in Genesis chapters 1 and 2 are in conflict, when in reality they only focus on different aspects of the same event.)

Egyptians would have viewed these creation accounts — like many seemingly contradictory "versions" of the relationships between and actions of their gods — as simultaneously true, equally valid layers of the same reality. Furthermore, the creation stories all contain several common elements.

The primeval mound was one such common element. Ancient Egypt's religion at times seems like a personified metaphor based on the natural world in which many key elements are deified. Thus, it is quite possible that the primeval mound was a larger-than-life version of the mounds of land that appeared in the Nile River, the river without which life in Egypt could not exist.

These mounds of sand, silt, and clay called *geziras* are particularly prominent in the Nile Delta. Rising above the cultivated land, they were used in ancient times for settlements. In one story, when the mound rises up from the surrounding chaos, a bird lands on it and cackles so loudly that the silence is broken and life begins. In most Egyptian creation myths, a father of other gods somehow emerges from the mound and begins the work of creation, starting with the creation of many other gods.

From the "City of the Sun," Heliopolis, the original home of Cleopatra's Needle on the western gate of the Temple of Ra, comes one of the three creation myths. Heliopolis was a religious center devoted to the worship of the creator god Atum. Atum is often identified with the sun god Ra, though in some scenarios Atum is seen as the dying sunset that travels the underworld at night, and Ra is revered as the rising reborn sun.

In the Heliopolis mythos, in the beginning there was only the chaos of primeval water. Out of this water arose a mound from which the god Atum emerged. Standing on the mound, Atum sneezed out the air god, Shu, and spat out the moisture goddess, Tefnut. The offspring of these two were the sky goddess, Nut, and the earth god, Geb. The offspring of Nut and Geb were Osiris, Isis, Seth, and Nephthys, key players in Egypt's most memorable stories. These nine gods and goddesses, a group called the *Ennead*, were then responsible for different creative acts or attributes that built the world in which Egyptians played out their lives.

When a pharaoh — the offspring of Ra — died, he hoped to become one not only with Osiris but also with Atum, traveling the underworld each night to bring new life each morning (Pyramid Texts 147). Not just creator and one with the sun, Atum was also seen as the one who would someday un-create everything, returning the world to chaos and settling down to reign over it all as a serpent.[9]

From the fifth dynasty city of Hermopolis come texts describing a primeval egg in the waters of chaos. In this egg Atum, or Ra, the sun god, existed until he brought himself forth, initially as a lotus blossom, and stood on his mound. From there the sun god created four male-female pairs of gods — Nun and Naunet representing water, Heh and Hauhet representing infinity, Kek and Kaukey representing darkness, and Amun and Amaunet representing hiddenness. These eight divine elements then, of course, produced all the other gods and goddesses and the physical world they represent. Thus once again, to the life-sustaining sun, earth's nearest star, is ascribed the original creative power to produce all that makes our world habitable.

From the city of Memphis comes one of the best-preserved Egyptian creation myths. Recorded on the 25th dynasty Shabbat stone housed in the British Museum, the Memphite view of origins contains the oldest extrabiblical record of creation *ex nihilo* through the power of the spoken word. In the Memphis mythos, the god Ptah was the primeval water who formed himself into dry land — the primeval mound — and, embodying the male-female divine elements within himself, spoke into existence the familiar Egyptian pantheon, to whom he delegated further creative acts.

In all these Egyptian creation myths, the creation of the world was paramount. Although many of the Egyptian gods are depicted in animal forms, creation of man and the animals is something of an afterthought. In some versions, the creator god Ra sent his eye to search for his missing offspring, Shu and Tefnut. Returning, the eye — having become the lion goddess Sekhmet — is distressed that Ra has grown another eye and weeps. Those tears became humanity.[10]

For the most part, however, Egyptian mythology leaves the creation of each man to a lesser god, Khnum, who fashions people out of clay from the Nile River. By contrast, the Bible, God's eyewitness account of creation, in Genesis 1 and 2 explains that God spoke the physical world and all kinds of

---

9. In *Book of the Dead* 175, the god Atum makes this apocalyptic pronouncement to Osirus: "You shall be for millions of millions, a lifetime of millions. Then I shall destroy all that I have made. This land will return in to the Abyss, into the flood as in its former state. It is I who shall remain together with Osirus, having made my transformations into other snakes which mankind will not know, nor gods see."

10. Geraldine Pinch, *Egyptian Mythology: A Very Short Introduction* (Oxford: Oxford University Press, 2004), p. 60.

living things into existence in an orderly fashion. Then, having prepared the world, God created Adam and Eve and presented the world to them, placing it under man's dominion (Genesis 1:26, 28), giving Adam the responsibility of tending and keeping the Garden of Eden (Genesis 2:15).

Thus, in Egyptian mythology we see man as an afterthought at best and a product of divine distress at worst. By contrast, from the Bible we infer that man is the culmination of God's creative work (being the only creature made to bear God's image) and the designated recipient and steward of the created world. Furthermore, upon man's rebellion against God, humanity became the focus of the saving grace that God planned from the foundation of the world (1 Peter 1:20).

The late Dr. Henry M. Morris suggested that Satan believes that he was not created, but that "all of the angels as well as God Himself had just arisen from the primeval chaos . . . and that it was only an accident of the priority of time that placed him, with all of his wisdom and beauty, beneath God in the angelic hierarchy."[11] If that were the case, it would be natural for fallen man to carry forward mythologies in which a god came forth from nothingness. Satan desires to be worshiped as God, and we know that idols and false gods really are surrogates for demonic worship (Deuteronomy 32:17; 1 Corinthians 10:20). Sadly, many fall into this sort of trap — worshiping the creature, rather than the Creator.

These three creation myths share some common elements — a primeval watery chaos, a primeval mound of dry land, and the deification of many elements of nature. Because Egyptian mythology deifies only certain aspects of nature and not nature itself, it differs from truly pantheist religions. Nevertheless, ancient Egyptian religion is a vivid example of what the Apostle Paul describes as worship of "the creature rather than the Creator" (Romans 1:25).

In one of these ancient Egyptian myths we find the first mention, outside the Bible, of the idea that creation was accomplished through the power of the spoken word. Recall that Genesis prefaces each of God's creative acts with "And God said . . ." and in the New Testament John 1:1–3 identifies Jesus Christ as the *Logos,* the Word through whom creation was accomplished long before He came into the world as a man to die for and redeem mankind. The Apostle John, under God's inspiration, penned the New Testament verses describing the creative power of God's words long after the heyday of Egyptian

---

11. Henry M. Morris, *The Genesis Record* (Grand Rapids, MI: Baker Book House, 1976), p. 107–108.

religion, and Moses recorded the creation account preserved in Genesis at a time when Egyptian religion was already highly developed.

While we cannot be dogmatic about the path of ideas over the millennia, we know that the Egyptian people, like all people in the world, descended from Noah's family dispersed from the Tower of Babel. We can reasonably hypothesize that those people who came down to Egypt knew the true history of creation through this family heritage. Perhaps this creation-by-spoken-word — unusual in ancient mythology — is an element of the true origins history that survived in corrupted form to become part of the Memphite creation story.

The same may be said of many other elements in Egypt's creation myths, such as the raising up of dry land from an initial watery chaos, that bear some resemblance to the actual conditions prevailing at the time of creation as recorded in Genesis 1:9–10 under the inspiration of history's reliable eye-witness, the Creator God.

Egyptologists and other scholars have noted that the chaotic conditions prevailing early in the biblical creation week described in Genesis 1 are mirrored in Egypt's creation stories. This naturally has prompted some liberal theologians to speculate that Egypt's creation myths were source material for the Mosaic account. After all, Moses was educated in Egypt in pharaoh's household and would have known all about them.

Furthermore, the Hebrew people Moses led out of Egypt had been living under the influence of Egypt's gods for several generations at the time of the Exodus. Yet, according to the God-inspired Scripture, Jesus Christ clearly accepted Mosaic authorship of the Pentateuch under divine inspiration. Did Egyptian mythology influence the sacred text God inspired Moses to write? If so, God's true version of origins would have shown the ancient Hebrews what little truth was embodied in the corrupted Egyptian accounts. Stripping away Egyptian corruptions would have revealed, by contrast, "In the beginning God created the heavens and the earth."

God's truth about origins — then as now — refutes man's imaginative but baseless stories about the creation and the character of the Creator.

The creation account preserved in Genesis 1 and 2 and the history of man's rebellion against our holy omnipotent Creator in Genesis 3 is God's own eyewitness version of our history. In Egyptian creation stories, the first god (at best) exists in a primordial egg that emerges from chaos with the first dry land and proceeds to create other gods to help him out. Here we see an illogical construction, since the god who created the world must have been created by another god before that.

By contrast, the Bible reveals that the real Creator is one all-powerful, uncreated, eternally existent God. And while the Egyptian creator is part of the created order even as he commands it and fashions it from chaos, the biblical Creator transcends nature. The biblical Creator is above and outside His creation, though He is intimately involved with both the world and the people He created. In fact, God is so intimately involved that the Son took on flesh and became part of mankind to offer salvation through His life, death, and Resurrection.

While in some Egyptian myths the creator god creates by the power of the spoken word, even then the ancient Egyptian concept of a creator never separates the god from his creation. Like the modern "god" of evolution, the Egyptian god appears from chaos through natural processes and then puts the world in order. And though endowed with mythological divinity, the elements of nature — like those in evolutionary scenarios — create the rest of nature and eventually life itself from the natural elements.

Egypt's Gods and the One True God

Moses wrote in Deuteronomy 6:4, "Hear, O Israel: The LORD our God, the LORD is one!" The people to whom this was originally addressed had lived for four generations among the pantheon of Egypt. They were surely accustomed to hearing about a multiplicity of gods, regardless of what they believed. Children had grown up perhaps hearing the truth from their parents but nevertheless exposed to Egyptian mythology, not as fanciful stories but as the truth that ruled the government and day-to-day Egyptian life. In that context and for that audience, the boldness and the importance of this statement — *There is only one God!* — is apparent.

From Scripture we learn that God exists in three persons but He is one God. Furthermore, the biblical God does not create other gods or lesser gods as in the Egyptian myths. God created angels, but they are not gods. Hebrews 1:5–6 makes this clear:

> For to which of the angels did He ever say: "You are My Son, today I have begotten You"? And again: "I will be to Him a Father, and He shall be to Me a Son"?

But when He again brings the firstborn into the world, He says: "Let all the angels of God worship Him."

Unlike angels, Jesus Christ, the only begotten Son of God, though He entered our history and was born of a virgin in the flesh, actually co-existed with the Father from eternity past — He was not created. John 1:1–3 reveals for instance "In the beginning was the Word, and the Word was with God, and the Word was God. He was in the beginning with God. All things were made through Him, and without Him nothing was made that was made." Indeed, the Bible is clear that Jesus Christ is not only the author of our salvation but also the author of all creation. Colossians 1:15–17 informs us that Jesus "is the image of the invisible God, the firstborn over all creation. For by Him all things were created that are in heaven and that are on earth, visible and invisible, whether thrones or dominions or principalities or powers. All things were created through Him and for Him. And He is before all things, and in Him all things consist."

Egypt's Unholy Pantheon and the Holy God of the Bible

The Bible — starting in Genesis — reveals not only information about the origin of all things — the physical universe, life, man, male and female, marriage, sin, suffering, and death — but also reveals much about the character of God. We learn in the Bible that God is holy, just, merciful, gracious, loving, all-powerful, eternally pre-existent, all-knowing, and transcendent above His creation even as He interacts with it and with the people He created.

In contrast, in Egyptian mythology we meet multiple gods that are themselves created, flawed, capricious, and finite. They do not transcend creation but instead form parts of it. Though they spring into existence at the behest of the first god — himself a part of the creation to emerge from chaos — Egypt's gods require assistance from each other to create the elements of the physical world.

Far from holy, Egypt's gods engage in all manner of immorality, deceit, and cruelty to gain their ends. Sekhmet the lion goddess, and originally the eye of the creator Ra, for instance, went on a rampage to destroy humanity. Ra finally tricked the bloodthirsty goddess — actually a manifestation of the more benign Hathor — by getting her inebriated on blood mixed with beer in order to spare the rest.[12]

---

12. Pinch, *Egyptian Mythology: A Very Short Introduction*, p. 61.

Lust, promiscuity, murder, and complicated paternity issues are rampant among the members of the Egyptian pantheon. For instance, jealous of Isis, faithless Seth tricks and murders Isis' companion, his brother Osiris, dismembering Osiris's body parts in an attempt to ensure they cannot be reunited and reanimated. And just who exactly is Horus's father? Perhaps not even the gods know for sure — but after being posthumously conceived and raised by his mother Isis, Horus makes war to avenge his putative father's murder. As an aside, some skeptics try to say that the virgin birth is actually mimicking the story of Horus and Isis, but the details are often stretched or fabricated to make the two seem more similar than they are.

The goddess Isis poisons Ra, king of gods, and then tricks him into yielding up much of his power in exchange for a cure. Ra subsequently retires to the sky for a daily transit, his nightly underworld journey, and a glorious morning of rebirth. Interesting stories, to be sure. But the Egyptians created their larger-than-life gods in their own image — in humanity's sinful image. As such, their gods and the myths surrounding them reflect the capricious and cruel character of human beings, not the holy character of the biblical God.

Satan and Seth

Does Egypt's religion have an evil character corresponding to Satan? Some suggest Seth (Set) was essentially a Satan counterpart, but this is a poor analogy. Seth, one of the more disagreeable Egyptian gods, is one of the original group of gods in the Ennead. Following death, the person who fails his test with the feather of truth (see explanation below) would consider Seth his fearsome enemy, for the Seth animal would devour him. And while Seth is a god of violence and anger, a jealous murderer who killed his brother and went to war with his nephew, he also has constructive activity attributed to him. For instance, Seth rides the back of the sun god during his daily journey across the sky to combat the serpent of chaos, Apophis. And a winged Seth slays the serpent Apophis in artwork in the temple of Hibis.[13] Apophis, in contrast to Seth, is a uniformly reprehensible serpent deity that was not revered or worshiped.

While Egyptian mythology contained numerous serpent deities, most were not malevolent; Apophis was. In contrast, Amun and Osiris will supposedly one day be transformed into everlasting serpents to reign forever over an apocalyptic return of chaos. However, Egypt's pantheon provided

13. Wilkinson, *The Complete Gods and Goddesses of Ancient Egypt*, p. 199.

enough malevolent characters to go around, and trying to assign one to the role of Satan is an oversimplification. In any case, the numerous capricious actors in the Egyptian hit parade of gods provided ample explanation for the evil and suffering in the world.

A Most Religious People

Ordinary people would have had no access to the temple services and ceremonies by which the pharaoh and priests served the gods so that they would keep chaos far from Egyptian sands. Priests, even though they might hold ordinary jobs too, underwent rites of purification to even enter the inner regions where they bathed, dressed, and fed the statues representing Egypt's gods.

Nevertheless, evidence suggests that religion did not touch the personal lives of ordinary people. For one thing, ordinary people could make offerings of flowers, food, or votive statues in the outer courts of the temples. And during processions on festive occasions they could watch as priests carried the statues of the gods in sacred boats through the streets and put on mystery plays for the public.

Ancient Egyptians could seek advice from the gods through priestly oracles at the temples. They could even try to influence the gods by leaving offerings at "hearing ear" shrines built into the outside walls of many temples. Some picture a worshiper kneeling in prayer before a series of large ears.

Additionally, many local shrines were available where supplicants could leave offerings, beg healing, and touch sacred objects. People could leave statues of themselves there to beg for healing, interceding with the gods for them while they went about the business of living. Excavations have shown that the homes of ordinary people had places for household gods along with the images of dead family members.

This stela depicts a person in prayer appealing to the hearing ears of the gods. Artifacts like these are associated with the later centuries of ancient Egypt's history, during the New Kingdom.

Artifacts from the New Kingdom, later in ancient Egypt's history, reveal that some people were concerned with the problem of sin. "Penitential texts" recovered from excavations at Deir el-Medina include both brief and elaborate prayers. One of the best examples found there on the Stela of Nebre may be translated:

> Though the servant was disposed to do evil,
> The Lord is disposed to forgive.
> The Lord of Thebes spends not a whole day in anger,
> His wrath passes in a moment, none remains.
> His breath comes back to us in mercy,
> Amun returns upon his breeze. . . .[14]

Eventually, a personal relationship with the goddess Isis and the availability of salvation through her became a part of Egyptian religion accessible to those without royal blood or riches. The awareness of sin and concern about death reminds us that ancient Egyptians had the same concerns as modern people, even though they had rejected the God who could answer their needs.

Man and the Afterlife

Egyptian temples were devoted to the care and worship of the gods on whom the Egyptians depended to keep back the forces of chaos until the end of time. But with death, a person's fate became a more immediate concern. Unlike atheistic evolutionists, Egyptians did not assume that man was only an animal and that life ended forever at the grave.

What is man? Understanding the ancient Egyptian view of the afterlife requires knowledge of their answer to this question. While not much concerned with the origin of man, Egyptians were concerned with the essential elements of a person — his body, his name, and his shadow, his *ka* and his *ba*. Though scholars suspect that in early days the ancients believed only the pharaoh possessed all these elements, by later times the nobility and likely even common people were dignified by a nature worth preserving and protecting through ritual.

The Egyptians believed the physical body was inhabited by an invisible ka and ba that departed at death but were able to return to a properly preserved body. While the ka was more associated with attaining sustenance,

---

14. Wilkinson, *The Complete Gods and Goddesses of Ancient Egypt*, p. 51.

the invisible ba was more like a ghostly manifestation of the person, able to go to the world beyond and interact with the cosmos inhabited by the gods. Ongoing existence beyond the grave demanded a preserved body, one processed by rituals that often included various types of mummification. The body was not thought to physically move about or eat, but rather to provide a home to which the ka and ba would return from their excursions. Surrounding this preserved body would be instructions and amulets to assist the dead in facing judgment and in navigating the afterlife.

Like other ancient cultures that have left tombs filled with grave goods and evidence of companions to serve the departed in the life beyond, the ancient Egyptians' careful treatment of the dead and particular concern with the preservation of the body attest to their belief in an afterlife and some preoccupation with doing what they could to make the passage into death a safe one and the ongoing existence happy. Unlike some other ancient cultures, Egyptians were not in the habit of routinely slaughtering large numbers of people to serve the royal dead in the afterlife, at least not after the earliest years. From the Middle Kingdom onward the dead were instead supplied with statues called *shabti* — figurines of servants to take care of their needs in the beyond.

These shabti, housed at the British Museum, were once placed in ancient Egyptian tombs with the expectation that they would answer their master's call, not only serving his or her needs, but performing by proxy whatever labor might be required of the dead in an agricultural afterlife.

Monumental tombs of various sorts were built to house royals and nobles, so naturally there remains more evidence to reveal their expectations after death. The grave goods that accompanied such wealthy people included food, jewelry, furniture, and even boats. Artwork in the grave was supposed to have power to maintain the normalcy of life. Moreover, inscriptions containing spells, poems, and instructions for the dead person were carved on the walls of many tombs and on coffins. The oldest of these discovered thus far are the Pyramid Texts, about 800 inscriptions carved on the walls in nine Old Kingdom pyramids, some in language associated with pre-dynastic Egypt.

During the Old Kingdom, Egyptians may have believed that only pharaoh could have an afterlife, and these texts explain that he would undertake a journey fraught with peril, but if successful continue his existence as either the sun god or Osiris. Yet the discovery of ancient Egyptian bodies buried beneath desert sand, desiccated by natural processes and accompanied by grave goods, suggests that even common people had some expectation of life beyond the grave, regardless of whether that belief was reinforced by the official religion.

Later, Egyptians came to officially believe that the afterlife was also available to non-royal nobility. How far down the social scale this extended remains a matter of speculation. Men, and even women, could hope to become one with Osiris. Even later in Egypt's history, many people were therefore buried with little corn mummies made of grain, clay, and sand wrapped in bandages and decorated with pictures of Sokar, the falcon god of craftsmanship.

On the other hand, women — and even men — could hope to join with Hathor, the nurturing protective goddess of women and motherhood often depicted as a cow. This bovine deity — believed to give birth to the sun god each day and to travel with him — was naturally associated with rebirth and resurrection. It seemed only natural that Hathor might greet the dead as well as each day's dying sun with water to purify and refresh.[15]

The availability of the afterlife to the populace is attested to by over 1,000 "Coffin Texts," inscriptions and spells carved on coffins to provide instruction and protection to the deceased. By the time of the New Kingdom, many of these were collected as the *Book of the Dead*, also called "The Beginning of the Spells for Going Forth by Day," after the opening title.

---

15. Ibid., p. 143.

Though lengthy passages continued to be carved in tombs and on grave goods, personalized papyrus copies of the *Book of the Dead* inscribed with the name, genealogy, and occupation of the deceased were often buried with people. Amulets were also blessed with or even inscribed with spells from the *Book of the Dead* and buried with the body.

Importance of Preserving the Body

An Egyptian's afterlife was doomed to be disastrous if the body was not preserved. The elaborate ritualized process of mummification removed and preserved the vital organs in jars and essentially pickled, wrapped, and preserved the body itself, perhaps with a covering of sweet spices and a beautiful mask, in hope that the sleep of death would give way to a happy future existence. Egyptians would be particularly upset if the body of a loved one were not recovered. Thus, being devoured by a hungry crocodile or other beast was particularly distressing, even more than just the gruesome nature of such a death itself would warrant. And cremation was unheard of.

Many additional rites ensured the best chance for a safe trip into the afterlife. For instance, in the ceremony of the Opening of the Mouth, a priest would recite spells intended to revitalize the dead in the afterlife and enable a statue or image of the departed to act as the surrogate of the dead person.

Why would the dead need a body? Assuming the dead person passed through judgment successfully, the ba and ka could sail into eternal bliss on Ra's boat and then rise each day forever. The ba could look after the family left behind. Accordingly, Egyptians would write letters to a dead relative they believed had become a powerful *akh*. The ka could enjoy a variety of pleasant places and activities and commune with gods like Osiris, Hathor, Ra, or Thoth.

But the body needed a nametag of sorts, lest the ba and ka land in the wrong place. This was the purpose of the cartouche attached to each coffin. If the body was destroyed or the name obliterated, the ba and ka could not find their way back and would disappear forever. Though families were expected to pay mortuary cults to keep the dead supplied with food, just in case the generations eventually failed in their commitment, the images in the tombs were symbolically thought to assume the necessary roles.

So what did the ancient Egyptian — at least one wealthy enough to have a fully decked out tomb — expect after death? The cow goddess Hathor might welcome him or her to the underworld with water. Many Coffin Texts found on tombs throughout Egypt reveal the dangers people feared after death — hunger, thirst, aggressive serpents, fire, darkness, dismemberment by demons, wading upside-down through sewage, or having an uncooperative shabti.[16]

Coffin Texts empowered the deceased with the secret names of gods and demons, provided them with maps of the underworld so they could follow Ra's boat during its nightly transit toward the morning of resurrection, reminded the dead person to declare his heart to be pure, told him how to take on the role of a god and escape danger by reenacting his mighty acts, and gave him the words to spur a lazy shabti to obediently go work in the fields for his master.

After Death, Judgment

Worst in the gauntlet of dangers in death was judgment. Failure had dire and irrevocable consequences: to be devoured by Ammut, a ferocious goddess with the head of a crocodile, the front legs of a lion, and the back parts of a hippopotamus. The Egyptian concept of truth, justice, righteousness, and order was personified in the goddess Maat. Immoral and unrighteous behavior was considered a threat to order, so to enjoy the richness of the afterlife a person needed to be guiltless.

The jackal-headed god Anubis — who, myth held, had transformed Osiris into the first mummy — would escort the deceased to face a panel of 42 gods, presided over by Osiris.[17] The deceased greeted each and declared himself innocent of specific sins ranging from lying and theft to blasphemy and murder of a sacred bull.

Declaring innocence was only the first step in judgment. The heart had to be weighed on a balance against Maat's feather of truth. The heart, considered the seat of intelligence and preserved in place in the body, contained the record of a person's life and thus a memory of all guilt. Just as the Bible informs us that all are sinners (Romans 3:23), the Egyptians must have realized that they were not guiltless.

They feared their hearts would reveal the truth when weighed on Maat's scale. The *Book of the Dead,* a collection of spells to assist the deceased in his or her journey, was often buried with people and included a spell, activated

---

16. Pinch, *Egyptian Mythology: A Very Short Introduction,* p. 245.
17. Ibid., p. 206.

during the ceremony of Opening of the Mouth at the time of burial, commanding the heart to not reveal its owner's guilt.

Among the most important amulets placed with or even in a person's corpse was the heart scarab. The scarab beetle was associated with several gods, but none more important than Khepri, the scarab-headed man that represented the rising sun, reborn each morning after successfully negotiating the nightly journey through the underworld to bring "his" life-sustaining rays to the day.[18] Thus, the scarab was associated with resurrection. The heart scarab, an oval or heart-shaped scarab made of stone and inscribed with spells from chapter 30 of the *Book of the Dead*, was supposed to keep the dead person's heart from testifying against him or her when

This heart scarab, housed at the Brooklyn Museum, is inscribed with chapter 30 from the *Book of the Dead*. (Wikimedia)

facing judgment. Thus, while the judgment faced by the dead was concerned with weighing the works done in life to achieve justice, the condition of the heart was also relevant to the outcome of the scales of justice.

Osiris ruled the underworld and was generally the chief judge of the dead and much to be feared. He earned his place there after being murdered and dismembered by his brother Seth. Because Seth separated the pieces of the body in hopes they would not be recovered, the supremely heinous nature of the murder is apparent. In later times, Osiris' son, a hawk-headed Horus, is depicted as the judge holding two scepters, and possibly offering greater mercy than could be expected from Osiris.

Perhaps recognizing that no one is completely good, the Egyptian concept of innocence before judgment was, like that of so many people today, a relative thing — a matter of having done more good things than bad. Declaring himself or herself innocent before the 42 gods sitting in judgment, the dead person's heart was weighed by Anubis against the feather of Maat, the goddess of truth. Though other organs were ordinarily removed from the body and preserved in canopic jars, the heart was buried inside the body so that it would be available for this auspicious ceremony.

---

18. Wilkinson, *The Complete Gods and Goddesses of Ancient Egypt*, p. 231.

This illustration from a papyrus copy of the *Book of the Dead* depicts the jackal-headed Anubis weighing the heart of the deceased on the scale of Maat.
(Wikimedia)

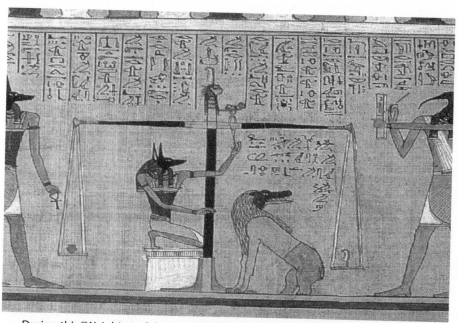

During this "Weighing of the Heart" ceremony, Ammut the devourer of the dead waits expectantly in case the deceased's heart is found wanting. Meanwhile, the ibis-headed scribe Thoth records the results.
(Wikimedia)

If the heart was heavy with evil outweighing the good, the person was declared a liar and the crocodile-headed demonic beast Ammut devoured his heart. With the neck, mane, torso, and forelegs of a lion or leopard, and the rear of a hippopotamus, Ammut was a composite of the most dangerous animals in Egypt. Pictured in the *Book of the Dead* chapter 125, waiting by the fateful scale, Ammut loomed as a fearsome danger that various spells — such as those inscribed on a heart scarab buried inside the chest — were expected to circumvent.

Egyptians properly equipped to face the dangers of death feared their own version of purgatory, but seemed to generally expect a good outcome, not so much through their own purity but through the spells that stacked the deck in their favor. If Ammut devoured a person's heart, he ceased to exist. Otherwise he could go on to various possible happy fates — joining with Osiris like the pharaoh, working on the crew of Ra's all-important ship as it sailed the underworld each night, traveling with Hathor in Ra's retinue, living in a mansion with Thoth the god of wisdom, or enjoying the rich fruits of his shabti's labors in the Field of Reeds. Some saw the eternal state of the justified as one of blissful sleep enlightened nightly by the passage of the sun god through the underworld.

Works, Grace, and the Good News

Sadly, without knowledge of God's grace available through faith in the God of the Bible, the ancient Egyptian's hope of escaping judgment and entering into a paradise was in vain. The Bible explains in the Book of Romans that even people who do not know the law of God from the Bible have knowledge of right and wrong. The Egyptian concept of the afterlife confirms this.

Like many people today, ancient Egyptians thought that if the good they did outweighed the bad, they would emerge unscathed from judgment and enjoy paradise. Yet God is holy and He is the true standard by which everyone in His creation is judged. God's Word makes clear that all people are sinners with a sinful nature, justly deserving condemnation.

No amount of good works can obliterate and nullify the evil a person does. Justice cannot be satisfied and sin paid for by burying it beneath an overwhelming number of good deeds. James 2:10 indicates that even one sin in a person's life is too much: "For whoever shall keep the whole law, and yet stumble in one point, he is guilty of all." Justice requires the price for sin be paid, and from the time Adam sinned, God began unveiling His plan to provide the payment for sin Himself. Salvation is therefore a matter of grace through faith in God's provision.

The ancient Egyptians also realized that true justice would consider not only the deeds a person had plainly done but also the hidden motives and secret sins. The Egyptians suspected that a divine being would be able to see the secrets of the heart. They thought that if the heart didn't condemn them, if the conscience were truly clear, the goddess that weighed the heart against a feather would pass them on toward paradise.

Yet God's Word indicates that — except for Jesus Christ, God's Son — every person born since Adam sinned has a sinful nature. We cannot through our own efforts purify ourselves, but the sinless Son of God offered Himself as a sacrifice for us so that we could be reconciled to God — so that we could truly become "the pure in heart" who "shall see God" (Matthew 5:8).

The ancient Egyptians were correct to expect judgment for their sins after death. Hebrews 9:27 says "it is appointed for men to die once, but after this the judgment." But they had unfortunately abandoned faith in the true Creator God known to their forebears descended from Noah's family. They put no trust in the God of Abraham, who had walked among them. Abraham was saved by faith; he believed God and His promises (Romans 4:2–5). Instead, the Egyptians put their trust in the false gods they invented and in their own abilities to meet the standards for good works that they themselves contrived. And like people who die today trusting in their own good works to save them, they stand condemned. Instead of fearing a false god like Ammut, they should have feared the true God of the Bible. It is a fearful thing to fall into the hands of the living God (Hebrews 10:31).

Summary of Ancient Egyptian Religious Beliefs

Doctrine	Teachings of Egyptian Mythology
God	Deny the biblical God. Various myths describe a supreme god and a pantheon of gods created by him or arising from the earth. Polytheistic in its reverence of many gods.
Authority/ Revelation	Various eras held to different sources of authority, but the *Book of the Dead* is a popular source describing the views of the afterlife.

Man	Various myths describe man as being created by different gods from tears, clay, and other sources. Man is not seen as particularly important within the world.
Sin	Sin is not clearly defined, but extends beyond actions to the intents of the heart.
Salvation	Upon death, the heart is weighed against the feather of truth in the presence of the gods. The dead use spells to conceal their guilt from the gods. If the heart weighs less than the feather, the person can pass to various places in the underworld. If not, it is devoured by a demonic beast. Simply, salvation is achieved if the good of your life outweighs the bad.
Creation	Various myths describe a supreme god creating the world and other gods from nothing, or the earth forming into various gods and man and creatures.

Chapter 14

Norse and Germanic Mythology

Dr. James J.S. Johnson

The Lord Jesus Christ endorsed Genesis truth while He walked the earth, including the origin of creation and the history of the worldwide Flood.[1] Inexcusably, however, the biblical account of creation is recklessly spurned by modern fans of Darwin's evolutionary model — sometimes even to the extreme of comparing ancient Norse mythology (i.e., the worship of Thor and Odin) to the Genesis record that the Lord Jesus endorsed.

For example, in one federal lawsuit (involving biblical creation–informed science education), the trial judge glibly said — in open court — that he could give justice to the case because he had already adjudicated controversies involving Thor worship and a marijuana cult, so adjudicating a case about biblical creation should be easy enough.[2]

Some might excuse the irreverence as attempted humor, but the result was not funny. How can such disrespect for God's truth be so outrageous?

Yet, evolutionary mythology is ubiquitous — it is "everywhere" — it is promoted by television, movies, cereal boxes, military leaders, closed-Bible

---

1. Ken Ham, "Did Jesus Say He Created in Six Literal Days?" chapter 20, *The New Answers Book*, 12-20-2007), posted at https://answersingenesis.org/days-of-creation/did-jesus-say-he-created-in-six-literal-days/ , citing John 5:45–47; Mark 10:6, 13:19; Luke 11:50–51, 13:14; etc.

2. *Institute for Creation for Research Graduate School v. Texas Higher Education Coordinating Board*, 2010 WL 2522529 (W.D. Tex.—Austin 2010) (erroneous naming of plaintiff in the original). Revealingly, the legal phrase "academic freedom" was never used anywhere within the federal judge's 39-page ruling.

pastors, and even in recipe books![3] Ironically, however (and perhaps not surprisingly), the underlying mythological beliefs and practices of ancient Norse and Germanic pagans are "reincarnated" in the evolutionary pantheism ("everything is god") of today's pagans.[4]

Where did the Norse and Germanic pagans go wrong?

There was never any legitimate excuse for these pagan mythologies. So why did they ever exist? Why were Norse and Germanic myths so popular in many lands for several centuries of time?

To really understand *why* ancient Scandinavians and Saxons held to these false religions, we must understand why false religion is so universally attractive to human sinners. *Why is false religion so popular, so attractive, anyway?*

How Do We Make Sense of Norse and Germanic Mythologies?

The introductory questions above presume that the pantheism of many modern-day evolutionists is comparable to the ancient polytheism of ancient Norse and Germanic pagans — but is it, really?[5]

If so, how does the comparison of those ancient and modern mythologies fit the modern world of evolution-dominated false religions?

---

3. James J.S. Johnson, "Hidden in Plain View: Evolution's Counterfeit History is 'Everywhere,' " *Acts & Facts*, 41(2):8–9 (February 2012), posted at http://www.icr.org/article/hidden-plain-view-evolutions-counterfeit/.

4. Edd Starr, "Can an Evolutionist Celebrate Earth Day?" Answers in Genesis, https://answersingenesis.org/theory-of-evolution/can-an-evolutionist-celebrate-earth-day/, saying: "Many of the people in this category would not consider themselves 'pantheists'; rather, they would simply consider themselves agnostics. However, individuals in this category believe that, regardless of evolution and the lack of a distinct god, nature is to be seen as inherently good, to be worshipped or honored, etc. Many common phrases associated with this type of environmentalism have a pagan origin — for example, 'Mother Earth' or 'Mother Nature,' the 'circle (or web) of life.' "

5. This study could have more precisely used the phrase "Scandinavian and Saxon mythologies" but the terms "Norse" and "Germanic" are more popularly understood as terms that fit this current chapter. Some writers prefer to combine those demographic categories under the term "Teutonic," so that term is sometimes used here, to avoid always saying "Norse and Germanic." Technically speaking, the term "Norse," when used as a linguistic label, refers to the Old Norse language that survives (to a large degree) today as the Icelandic language. But when used as an ethnic or cultural term, the word "Norse" often refers only to Western Scandinavians, at the expense of the Swedes and Swedish Finns. Here "Norse and Germanic" will refer to all of the Nordic peoples who spoke Old Norse, plus all of the continental European peoples who spoke a variant of German ("Saxon") during the Dark Ages, especially during the centuries known collectively as Europe's "Great Migration Period" (AKA the Völkerwanderung, the era when barbarian invaders broke up the Roman Empire, from just before A.D. 400 to 800) and the slightly overlapping "Viking Age" (from the late 700s to the century before or including the 1200s).

All of these questions require that we learn — at an overview level, at least — what the ancient Norse and Germanic mythologies were all about. Those false religions involved much more than comic-book stories about imaginary gods whose names appear on our calendars (e.g., Thursday from Thor's Day; Wednesday from Wodin's Day). The Norse and Germanic mythologies (sometimes labeled in combination as Teutonic mythologies) painted a confusing and magic-dominated hodgepodge of humans, gods, goddesses, giants, elves, and others, some of whom changed from one form into another.

> The old Norse religion . . . may be classified as an ethnic religion, meaning that it belongs to a specific people or group of people, in contrast to, for example, a religion like Christianity, which has become a universal or multi-ethnic religion. Traditional Scandinavian religion was polytheistic and comprised a large numbers of gods and goddesses, called *aesir* and *Vanir*, as well as many other groups: mythic giants . . . dwarves . . . female *norns* who sat in the center of the world and held power over the fate and fortune of individuals . . . valkyries . . . elves [who appeared to be] departed ancestors.[6]

To analyze the heartbeat of these false religions we need to review some relevant Scriptures, because *God's Word is always our starting point when we try to understand anything.*

Biblical insight #1: pagans prefer falsehoods over truth

> And this is the condemnation, that the light has come into the world, and men loved darkness rather than light, because their deeds were evil (John 3:19).[7]

These mythologies were accepted and promoted because unredeemed sinners prefer darkness over light, falsehoods over truth, and immoral priorities

---

6. Anne-Sofie Gräslund, "Religion, Art, and Runes," in *Vikings, The North Atlantic Saga* (Washington, DC: Smithsonian Books, 2000; edited by William W. Fitzhugh & Elisabeth I. Ward), p. 55. The Nordic mythology is perhaps best represented by the contents of Old Norse poetry fragments and the *Prose Edda*, which in aggregate describe "mythology, gods, and other supernatural beings," compiled by Snorri Surluson, the pre-eminent Icelandic/Nordic scholar of the A.D. 1200s, when the Viking Age closed near the end of the Dark Ages. (The Dark Ages finally broke with the "morning star" of the Protestant Reformation, John Wycliffe.)

7. All Scripture in this chapter is from the New King James Version (NKJV) of the Bible.

over moral values. People shy away from accepting the idea of God being holy and omniscient, knowing all of our faults, and disapproving all of our sins. People also like having "excuses" for their sinful thoughts and sinful actions — something a less-than-perfect deity can provide.

If a (mythical) god is selfish, it appears to excuse human selfishness. So, in order to deal with God's holiness, people imagine unholy substitutes for God, such as imaginary gods and goddesses who are selfish themselves.

Accordingly, if the gods practice fornication, that behavior appears to excuse the same sin when it is committed by humans. Likewise, if the goddesses tell lies in order to manipulate their personal agendas, that usage of deceit appears to excuse similar deceit by selfish humans.

Furthermore, if people dislike the Bible's report about our origins (which include the Bible's report on how our sin originated in Eden, how death originated, why husbands have primary responsibility for a marriage honoring God, etc.), people invent fables of their own liking, to explain the origins of things.

The root problem, here, is a refusal to accept truths about God Himself, compounded by a refusal to accept truths about how (and why) He made creation, and how He has been ruling it ever since.

In sum, the ancient pagans — such as those living during the Dark Ages, in lands speaking Germanic and Scandinavian languages — failed to accept God for who He really is, and His deeds, so they tried to imagine substitutes for God and His actions.

This can be analyzed as a series of three failures:

1. failure to give God due credit for *being the kind of divine Being He always is*

2. failure to give God due credit for *His past work of creating creation as He did*

3. failure to give God due credit for *His present work of ruling creation as He does*

The writings of the New Testament — especially Acts 17 and Romans 1 — help us to understand how these three errors ruined their worldview, leading them to adopt idolatrous mythologies. The overall result of these forms of paganism was a culturally accepted system of disgracefully wrong beliefs and tragically wrong behaviors.

Consider how plainly God has communicated Himself to His human creatures — God employs His creation to teach us how powerful He is, how knowledgeable He is, and how caringly and carefully He has designed and constructed and balanced His creation. Creation's components, both living and nonliving, prove to us that we are incapable of making the kind of creation we live in.

The real maker of all creation must be *more* powerful than we are, *more* knowledgeable than we are, *more* caring than we are, *more* careful than we are — He is immeasurably superior to us in all of these characteristics.

Obviously, therefore, we have no excuse for thinking that God is like us self-centered and finite-minded humans. If He were, which He is not, He could not have successfully made the creation we see all around us.

But what do unredeemed humans all too often do, when thinking about who deserves credit for creation?

Biblical insight #2: pagans replace God, in myths, by corrupt substitutes for God

For since the creation of the world His invisible attributes are clearly seen, being understood by the things that are made, even His eternal power and Godhead, so that they are without excuse, because, although they knew God, they did not glorify Him as God, nor were thankful, but became futile in their thoughts, and their foolish hearts were darkened. *Professing to be wise, they became fools, and changed the glory of the incorruptible God into an image made like corruptible man — and birds and four-footed animals and creeping things.* Therefore God also gave them up to uncleanness, in the lusts of their hearts, to dishonor their bodies among themselves, who exchanged the truth of God for the lie, and worshiped and served the creature rather than the Creator, who is blessed forever. Amen (Romans 1:20–25, emphasis added).

Notice that the Apostle Paul taught that humans who reject the evidence of God's creatorship "become fools" — they forfeited their earlier opportunities (with proper judgment) about issues of true versus false, right versus wrong, good versus bad, and worthy versus unworthy. Those who reject creation's witness of God's truth routinely receive a severe penalty, during this earthly lifetime: *ruined thinking*. The biblical name for this ruined thinking is a "reprobate mind" (Romans 1:28).

Only a truth-shunning (i.e., reprobate) mind can invent the kind of mythologies that the Norse and Germanic pagans invented — with beliefs in a pandemonium of imagined gods and goddesses (and other mythical beings), that *substitute for the real God* who created the heavens and the earth. Many of these imagined gods and goddesses are imagined as existing in images *made like corruptible man* (Romans 1:23) and behaving like sinful humanity (cheating, lying, stealing, coveting, etc.).

Sometimes reprobate thinking descends below attributing the traits of human sinners to deity — the notion of animals and nonliving substances are imagined as explanations for the existence of a god or goddess. This is the essence of a pantheistic religion with natural elements having god-like characteristics.

In the ancient Norse myths, the origin of some gods was deemed traceable to nonliving material components of creation, such as snow, or frost! In the best known collection of Nordic myths, the *Prose Edda*, Gangleri inquires about the origins of the world and of humanity. The reply is a fairy tale every bit as magical and pantheistic as the Mayas' *Popol Vuh* and Darwin's evolutionary story: storm waves hardened into a strange ice and the ice exuded icy rime that thawed and magically formed a giant:

> It [the thick ice and rime] thawed and dripped at the point where the icy rime and the warm winds met. There was a quickening in these flowing drops [of ice-melt water] and life sprang up [magically], taking its force from the power that sent the heat. The likeness of a [gigantic] man appeared and he was named Ymir. The frost giants called him Aurgelmir, and from him come the clans of the frost giants. . . . It is said that as he slept he took to sweating. Then, from under his left arm grew a male and female, while one of his legs got a son with the other. From here came the clans that are called the frost giants. The old frost giant, him we call Ymir.[8]

This pantheistic myth, therefore, begins its evolutionary tale with an inanimate physical substance, ice, somehow converting ("transforming") into a

---

8. Jesse L. Byock, *The Prose Edda: Norse Mythology* (London: Penguin Books, 2005), translating Snorri Sturluson's *Prose Edda* (12th–13th centuries), p. 13–15.

non-human life form, a frost-giant named Ymir. More rime-ice melted and dripped, magically forming a cow (named Audhumla) who produced four rivers from her udder.[9] From this cow's milk, Ymir is nourished. This magical cow, the *Prose Edda* creation myth continues, then proceeded to produce the gods that were imagined as the collective powers who produced and ruled the world thereafter.

How did this occur, according to Norse mythology?

The giant cow licked a salty ice-block, and out came a "whole man," Buri, who fathered Bor, who fathered Odin and others. Eventually, Odin and his brothers kill the frost-giant/ice-monster, Ymir, and transform his various body parts (flesh, bloody sweat, hair, eyelashes, and brains) into the earth, the sea, the air, the clouds, and the heavens.[10] Soon afterward, Odin and his brothers made a human man and woman from two tree logs they found on the seashore, magically providing the first "regular" humans with breath, life, intelligence, movement, shape, speech, hearing, and sight.[11]

Sound ridiculous and absurd? Of course it is.

Biblical insight #3: pagans worship inanimate stuff, rather than worship God

Yet the fairy tale described above is *no more nonsensical* than today's evolutionary big-bang-to-stardust-to-pondscum-to-humanity explanation of the origin of the universe and the life in it. All such nonsensical and insulting depictions of deity misrepresent God's dignity and glory, an obvious fact that Paul once proclaimed to ignorant-yet-arrogant Athenians:

> Then Paul stood in the midst of the Areopagus and said, "Men of Athens, I perceive that in all things you are very religious; for as I was passing through and considering the objects of your worship, I even found an altar with this inscription: TO THE UNKNOWN GOD.
>
> Therefore, the One whom you worship without knowing, Him I proclaim to you: God, who made the world and everything in it, since He is Lord of heaven and earth, does not dwell in temples made with hands. Nor is He worshiped with men's hands, as though He needed anything, since He gives to

---

9. Ibid., p. 15.
10. Ibid., p. 15–17.
11. Ibid., p. 18.

all life, breath, and all things. And He has made from one blood every nation of men to dwell on all the face of the earth, and has determined their preappointed times and the boundaries of their dwellings, so that they should seek the Lord, in the hope that they might grope for Him and find Him, though He is not far from each one of us; for in Him we live and move and have our being, as also some of your own poets have said, 'For we are also His offspring.' Therefore, since we are the offspring of God, we ought not to think that the Divine Nature is like gold or silver or stone, something shaped by art and man's devising" (Acts 17:22–29).

Yet we read of the Norse gods being represented by physical images — idols — inside temples made by human hands, and we later read of Christian Vikings, such as Olaf Tryggvason, who destroyed such physical idols.

A. Idolatrous belief in various gods and "goddesses" as substitute for the real God

In the ancient Norse/Germanic mythology's "pantheon(s)" there were various major and minor gods and "goddesses," a few of whom are listed below:[12]

1. *Odin/Wodin* (Old Norse: Óðinn; Old Saxon: Wôdan; Old High German: Wôtan) The presiding god of the heroic Aesir tribe of gods, the idolized ancients who migrated from Asia to a special place called Asgard (which Snorri identifies as Troy), a royal estate that included Valhalla, a hall of honored warriors killed in battle. Odin's name connotes "fury" or "frenzy"; he was imagined as the divine creator of other gods and of humans, as well as expert in wisdom, magic, poetry, illusion, deception, and prophecy, acquiring half of the warriors who die in battle. Wednesday is derived from ancient words meaning "Wodin's Day."

2. *Thor/Donar* (Old Norse: Þórr; Old High German: þonar; Saxon runic: ᚦᛟᚾᚨᚱ) The god of thunder and lightning, physical strength, and strong things like oak trees; Thor's name means

---

12. As in other ancient cultures, these gods could have been ancestors who lived unusually long lifespans after the Flood and viewed as demigods by their descendants whose lifespans were rapidly declining. Odin is present in several royal lineages in northern Europe.

"thunder"; Thursday is derived from ancient words meaning "Thor's day" (in German it is spelled "Donnerstag," i.e., "Donar's Day").

3. *Tyr/Teiws* (Old Norse: Týr; Gothic: Teiws; Old High German: Ziu; Old English: Tīw) The god of war, heroic glory, authority, law, and justice; Tuesday is derived from ancient words meaning "Teiws' Day" (Alemannic German "Zischtig," i.e., "Zîes' Day").

4. *Frey* (Old Norse: Freyr; Old English: Frea) The god of male fertility, sunshine, and fair weather, fruitfulness/agricultural fertility, and worldly prosperity; Frey's name means "lord" or "noble."

5. *Freya* (Old Norse: Freyja) The goddess of female fertility, female beauty, "love," sexuality, sorcery, and gold, and was imagined to select half of the warriors killed in battle, as well as women who died noble deaths. Freya's name means "lady" or "noblewoman." Friday is derived from ancient words meaning "Freya's Day."

6. *Loki* (also Loptr and Hveðrungr) A devilish god of evil, hatred, and deception, who is sometimes portrayed as a jötunn (frost-giant) and a bisexual shape-shifter. Loki's devilish nature is portrayed by his role in parenting Jörmungandr (the world-snake monster), Hel (queen of the dead doomed to an inglorious afterlife), Fenrir (a wetland-dwelling wolf-monster), and Sleipnir (an eight-legged horse).

7. *Balder/Baldur* (Old Norse: Baldr; Old High German: Baldere; Old Saxon: Baldag) The god of daylight, brightness, and purity, as well as light-like shining brilliance, bravery, and boldness. Balder was imagined as a son of Odin and a brother of Thor.

8. *Hel* (Gothic: Halja) The goddess of deadly plagues, graves, and ignoble deaths, was imagined as owning and operating the misty underworld "hall" of the dead who died of diseases

or old age, as opposed to dying noble deaths (such as in battle, in order to belong to Odin or Freyja). Hel's name is the root for the Anglo-Saxon word "Hell" (a short form of Helheim, meaning "Hel's home") as a label for the abode of those who die ignobly. Ancient pagans believed that Helheim was a huge underground hole beneath one of the three roots of Yggdrasil (the world tree).

In addition, the Norse myths imagined the existence and activities of other supernatural beings (i.e., non-humans with magical powers), such as frost-giants, fire-giants, trolls, valkyries, fates, etc.

Notice also that the reprobate-minded unbelievers — in their rebellious imaginations — insultingly transform the proper recipient of worship (God) into a collection of objects of worship that do not deserve our worship, such as animals and humans and other components of creation (Romans 1:23). By doing this, God was replaced in the minds of such idolaters by God-substitutes.

There are two idolatries here, where God is cheated out of glory and the credit due Him, namely (1) falsely attributing credit to someone or something other than God, for *creating* various components of creation; and (2) falsely attributing glory and credit to someone or something other than God, for *ruling* various components of creation. A few representative examples follow.

B. Idolatrous attribution of God's powers to someone/something other than God

In the Teutonic pantheon, various gods and goddesses are given credit for both *creating* and for *ruling* various components of creation. This is idolatry because it steals credit from God who alone *created* and *rules* all of creation.

> As in other polytheistic religions, the Viking gods [supposedly] ruled over different aspects of human life. The most important were Odin, Thor, and Frey.[13]

Also, various giants or gods were accredited, by the Norse and Germanic pagans, as creating and forming the world and all of its life forms. One

---

13. John Haywood, "Pagan Religion and Burial Customs," in *The Penguin Historical Atlas of the Vikings* (London: Penguin Books, 1995), p. 26. See also Gwyn Jones, *A History of the Vikings*, revised edition (Oxford: Oxford University Press, 1984), p. 73–74, 333–345.

example of such polytheistic idolatry is the Norse worship of Odin, known as Wodin by the Saxons:

> Odin was a rather sinister deity who, with his brothers, had created the human race and gave man the knowledge of poetry and of writing in runes [alphabetic letters]. Odin was the god of wisdom, power, war, and poetry: he was a sorcerer and could deprive men of their wits and exercise his power of life and death in wildly unpredictable ways. Odin's attributes made him the god of kings, chieftains, warriors and poets: both the Danish royal family and the Earls of Hlaðir claimed descent from him.[14]

Notice that Odin worship gave Odin credit for wisdom and knowledge, as well as its divine impartation to humans.[15] This blasphemously steals credit due the true and living God. Likewise, only the real God has power over life and death.[16] But, as the New Testament teaches us, only God has the power to deprive men of their reason by giving them over to a "reprobate mind"[17] and a "strong delusion"[18] as punishments for blasphemous imaginations.

Another example of such idolatry is the worship given to Thor, known as Donar by the Saxons:

> The most popular god among the peasantry was Thor, the god of physical strength, thunder and lightning, wind, rain, good weather and crops. Using his mighty hammer Mjöllnir, Thor defended the world against the destructive power of the giants [such as the ice-giants and the fire-giants]. Unlike Odin, Thor was straightforward, reliable god [sic], but he was none too bright and the myths concerning his deeds often highlight in a humorous way the limitations of brute strength. Pendants fashioned in the sign of the hammer were often worn by Thor's devotees.[19]

---

14. Haywood, *The Penguin Historical Atlas of the Vikings*, p. 26.
15. See James 1:5–6, 3:17; see also 1 Corinthians 1:19–31, especially verses 20–21.
16. See Psalm 68:20, 102:18, 139:13–16; Matthew 10:29–31.
17. See Romans 1:28.
18. See 2 Thessalonians 2:11–12.
19. Haywood, *The Penguin Historical Atlas of the Vikings*, p. 26.

Yet only God controls the weather. All of the world's winds,[20] rain,[21] hail,[22] thunder,[23] and lightning bolts[24] are His, and His only, to command. Thor is an imaginary counterfeit and a miserably unholy one. But the ancient pagans preferred an unholy counterfeit because unholy gods do not condemn unholy sinners for unholy behaviors.

A third example of such idolatry is the worship given to Frey (Freyr), which overlapped with the idolatrous worship of his sister Freya (Freyja):

> Freyr was the god of [material] wealth, health and fertility: he was portrayed [in a vulgar anatomical depiction]. Offerings were made to Freyr at weddings. The Swedish Yngling dynasty traced its ancestry to a union between Freyr and Gerd, a giant woman [i.e., a monstrous ogress]. Freyr had a sister [Freyja], who gave luck in love [as pagans defined "love"] and represented sensuality. Freyja was the leader of the *disir*, a race of female demigods who presided over fertility in nature and in humans.[25]

But what accounts for fertility in crops or in livestock or in human families? The pagans in Scandinavia and in Saxland (the ancient name applied to all European lands where the ancient German language dominated) gave credit to the vulgar Frey and Freyja, but that was profane idolatry. The Scriptures teach that God alone enabled His creatures to "be fruitful, and multiply" so that His earth could be filled with humans, plants, and animals.[26]

The Scandinavian polytheism did not attempt to portray gods who were inherently holy. Rather, like other heathen polytheists (such as the ancient Babylonians, Egyptians, Greeks, and Romans), they were as corrupt as sinful humans, and Loki even more so — Loki was somewhat like (though not completely like) the Satan of Scripture.

---

20. See Genesis 8:1; Psalm 107:25, 135:7, 147:18, 148:8; Jonah 4:8; Matthew 8:26–27; Mark 4:37–41; Luke 8:23–25.
21. See Genesis 2:5–6, 7:4, 7:12, 8:2; Deuteronomy 11:14; Isaiah 55:10; Jeremiah 10:13, 14:22, 51:16; Amos 4:7; Matthew 5:45; Acts 14:17; James 5:17.
22. See Exodus 9:18–29; Joshua 10:11; 2 Samuel 22:15; Job 38:22; Psalm 78:47–48, 148:8; Isaiah 30:30; Haggai 2:17; Revelation 8:7, 11:19, 16:21.
23. See Exodus 9:23–34; 1 Samuel 2:10, 7:10, 12:17–18; 2 Samuel 22:14; Job 28:26, 38:25, 37:4–5; Psalm 18:13, 29:3, 77:18, 104:7; Revelation 4:5.
24. See Job 37:3, 38:35; Psalm 18:14, 77:18, 97:4, 135:7, 144:6; Jeremiah 10:13, 51:16.
25. Quoting John Haywood, *The Penguin Historical Atlas of the Vikings*, p. 26. See also Jones, *A History of the Vikings*, p. 330.
26. See Genesis 1:20–22, 1:28, 8:16–17, 9:7; Psalm 102:18, 127:3–5, 128:3.

> The god Loki was a cunning, witty mischief-maker [i.e., worker of wickedness], whose schemes were always getting the gods and himself into trouble. Though he was not an unambiguously evil figure like Satan, Loki was capable of great wickedness and treachery, and the Vikings believed that this scheming would lead in the end to [the doom of] Ragnarök.[27]

In the ancient Teutonic mythologies pantheism blurred with polytheism. Inanimate glaciers were imagined as ice-monsters, jötunn (also known as rime-giants and frost-giants). The fire from a volcano was imagined as a fire-monster (e.g., Surtr).

In other words, inanimate components of nature — such as volcanoes and glaciers and huge granite rocks — were believed to have spirits associated with their physical substance, and sometimes were believed to have shape-changing ("transformative") powers to resemble humanoid giants (i.e., ogres or trolls). Rocks and glaciers were deemed to have powers to think and to act, so all of the physical creation was imagined to have selective powers.

Theologically speaking, this generalized animism is *pantheism blurred with and into polytheism*, an inane idolatry that worships elements of creation rather than the Creator.

Ironically, the pagan Norsemen and Saxons were ancestors to many who would evangelize the world, by boat, in partial fulfillment of Noah's blessing to their common ancestor, Japheth.[28] This providential pivot in world history is illustrated in the Viking-to-Christianity conversions that led to Nordic and Anglo-Saxon nations sending Christian missionaries all over the world, following the Apostle Paul's Macedonian call.

> From the westernmost shore of Asia [e.g., including Jerusalem and Antioch], Christianity had turned at once to the opposite one in Europe [beginning with Paul's missionary journeys to Macedonia and other parts of Europe]. The wide soil of the

---

27. Haywood, *The Penguin Historical Atlas of the Vikings*, p. 26.

28. See Genesis 9:27 with 10:2–5. Linguistically speaking, it appears that the Scandinavians and Saxons are two closely related offshoots of one subset of Japheth's descendants, the people descended from Ashkenaz. Since the original dispersion of people groups was caused by linguistic division (Genesis 11:1–9), that makes demographic sense. Notice how the consonants in the ethnic terms "Scandians" and "Saxons" resemble those in the ethnic term "Ashkenaz."

continent which had given it birth could not supply it long with nourishment; neither did it strike deep root in the north of Africa [despite Philip's evangelism of the Ethiopian eunuch]. Europe became, and remained, its proper dwelling-place and home. It is worthy of notice, that the direction in which the new faith worked its way, from South [Europe] to North [Europe], is contrary to the current of migration which was then driving the nations from the East and North to the West and South. As spiritual light penetrated from one quarter, life itself was to be reinvigorated from the other. . . . Slowly, step by step, Heathendom gave way to Christendom. Five hundred years after Christ, but few nations of Europe believed in him; after a thousand years the majority did. . . .[29]

As experienced mariners,[30] many of Japheth's descendants connected lands and peoples by seagoing travel and transactions. Even the distant shores of Iceland would receive the Christian religion.

The summer Christianity was made law in Iceland, one thousand years had passed from the Incarnation of our Lord Jesus Christ. That summer, King Olafr disappeared from the Long Serpent [longboat] by Svoldr in the south [Baltic Sea] on the fourth [day] before the ides [i.e., 15th day] of September. He [i.e., King Olaf] had been king in Norway for five years.[31]

In time, even distant Iceland would embrace the Lutheran Reformation. (The details of that history exceed our current study.)

How Were Norse/Germanic Mythology Religions Practiced?

Unlike the Holy Bible, the Scandinavian/Saxon pagans had no authoritative book of theology, much less any sacred book that provided a logically

---

29. Jacob Grimm, *Deutsche Mythologie*, volume 1, translated from the 4th edition, as *Teutonic Mythology* by James Steven Stallybrass (Mineola, NY: Dover Publications, 2004), p. 1.

30. Notice that the Scandinavian Vikings (who sailed oceans and the Baltic Sea habitually), as well as the coastal Saxons, easily fit the coastal mariner lifestyle indicated by Genesis 10:5. In Old Norse a saltwater inlet was called a "vik" (e.g., Reykjavik = "smoky bay"), so even the word "Viking" indicates a people who were famous for their coastal activities.

31. Siân Grønlie, *The Book of the Icelanders: The Story of the Conversion* (London: University College London & Viking Society for Northern Research, 2006), translating Ari Þorgilsson's Íslendingabók Kristni Saga (early 12th century A.D.), p. 50.

consistent systematic theology of big-picture truth.[32] Rather, the beliefs of the Teutonic pagans are recognized in bits and pieces, as they are illustrated in the surviving poems, sagas, and other writings that show what the ancient pagans thought and taught.

> Unlike Christianity, Scandinavian paganism [and the same was true for Germanic paganism] did not have a systematic theology and lacked absolute concepts of good and evil or of the afterlife. Religion was a matter of correct performance and observance of sacrifices, rituals and festivals, rather than personal spirituality. There was no full-time priesthood [or full-time clergy]; it was usually the king or local chieftains who had the responsibility for ensuring that festivals were observed.
>
> A cycle of cosmogonical myths told of the creation of the world and of its ultimate destruction at Ragnarök]. Vikings believed that all things were subject to fate, including the gods who would perish at Ragnarök, the final cataclysm that would destroy the world.[33]

However, just because the Teutonic myths were not organized in written forms for many centuries, does not detract from the fact that these heathen beliefs steered the behaviors of those who held those beliefs.

Biblical insight #4: believing pagan myths routinely produced pagan behaviors.

> For as he thinks in his heart, so is he (Proverbs 23:7).

In the Norse and Germanic myths, the gods and goddesses were imagined as killing and stealing whenever doing so was deemed a prudent deed, similar to modern "situational ethics" immorality.

Unsurprisingly, the Vikings copied the immorality of their gods and goddesses, and practiced a "might-makes-right" approach to social behavior. Slaves and peasants were offered as human sacrifices because the lives of humans were not valued as precious people made in God's own image.[34] Kidnapping the weak was deemed a valiant display of manly power,

32. Jones, *A History of the Vikings*, p. 73–74, 330, 333–345.
33. John Haywood, *The Penguin Historical Atlas of the Vikings*, p. 26.
34. Genesis 1:26–28.

so Vikings and Saxon warriors routinely killed, raped, plundered, and enslaved victims — anywhere in Europe where they raided or conquered. Ancestors were worshiped, as were imaginary gods (often depicted by physical idols "dwelling" in temples), and even the forces of nature (such as thunderstorms) were venerated as if divine manifestations of the pagan pantheons.

Because the inherited sin from Adam was not believed, and many sins were even praised as meritorious accomplishments of selfish "winners," there was no concept of redemptive salvation in the Norse and Germanic mythologies. Living a "noble" life should qualify one for an afterlife of fighting and drunkenness in Valhalla (or in Freyja's many-seated hall), but those who died "weakly" — such as by disease or accidental injury — were "doomed" to a dark and humble afterlife in Helheim (Hel's underworld).

Ironically, the Norse belief in giants appears to be a corruption of pre-Flood memories — an oral tradition that recalled how super-powerful giants (*nephelim*) raged violently against ordinary humans.[35] In fact, the ancient Anglo-Saxon epic Beowulf appears to include some memories of the world-wide Flood as a divine punishment of such giants.[36]

Should We Reach Out to Norse and Germanic Pagans Today?

This may seem like an obsolete question, because the ethnic Scandinavians and Germanic tribes no longer adhere to the mythologies they endorsed during the Dark Ages. But is that really the case?

There has been a resurgence of various forms of pagan mythology in the 19th and 20th centuries, including the worship of Thor, Odin, and other gods, known as Asatru, Germanic neo-paganism, or Heathenry. While there are a relatively small number of followers of various sects primarily in Europe, North America, and Australia, you may find yourself talking to one of these practitioners on a plane or park bench. Their religious convictions are often blended with other practices, but they will commonly perform rites at certain times of the year while wearing traditional dress and guided by priests and priestesses. During a blót, sacrifices of various forms are offered along with feasting and alcoholic drink. Some adherents will

---

35. It is also reasonable to think that these references could refer to the post-Flood giants mentioned in the Bible, including the descendants of Anak (Deuteronomy 9:2).
36. Bill Cooper, *After the Flood* (Chichester, West Sussex, England: New Wine Press, 1995), p. 146–147.

place idols around shrines in homes and wear various pendants — often of Thor's hammer, Mjölnir. Some holidays include Yule (winter solstice) and Merry Moon (May Day).[37]

These groups have no authoritative sources upon which to base their religious practices or their moral code. As such, many of their practices are blended with traditions from various pagan beliefs. Their moral code often focuses on loyalty, hard work, courage, and integrity. While these are noble ideas, they have no source of truth to look to and no honorable models of these behaviors in their gods and goddesses.

While sacrifices to the various gods and spirits are seen to gain their favor, there is ultimately no solid notion of sin or salvation within this religious view. This makes sense when we consider the character of their gods and heroes. As Christians, we need to help these people see the futility in worshiping gods that were invented in the minds of men — an invented god is no god at all. We must help them to see that there can only be one true God who is the Creator and ruler over all who would claim to be gods (Isaiah 41:23–24). We need to point them to the perfect life, sacrificial death on the Cross, and death-defeating Resurrection of Jesus Christ, which called them to repent of their fundamental sin of rejecting the true Creator-God — by trusting in His amazing solution for sin, the Lord Jesus Christ — thereby rejecting the idolatrous worship of the pantheon including Odin and Thor.

And there is another similar group to consider. Although the myth-makers in northern Europe (and in other lands dominated by what we call Western Civilization) rarely speak of Ymir, Audhumla, Odin, Thor, Freyr, Freyja, Hel, valkyries, and frost-giants, that doesn't mean that another group of modern pagans has escaped similar myths that blend pantheism with polytheistic animisms. Anyone who says that natural elements like fire and ice and rain and stone can create and "select" and "favor" some animals over others, or some humans over others, is not that far from the magical myths of the ancient Teutons.

How were Teutonic myths defeated in the hearts and minds of medieval pagans such as Leif Eiriksson and Olaf Tryggvason? By the gospel of Christ, of course, and one soul at a time. It's the same with today's educationally

---

37. "Asatru: Norse Heathenism," *Religious Tolerance*, accessed September 30, 2015, http://www.religioustolerance.org/asatru.htm.

evolutionized pagans, who nowadays embrace the "Big Bang-to-stardust-to-pondscum-to-humanity" cosmogony as an explanation for the origin of the universe and the life in it.

Are we ashamed of the Lord's gospel? Shame on us if we are. For God has chosen to empower the message of the gospel for reaching the souls of men and women, boys and girls, regardless of the false system of beliefs they embrace. And the proper foundation for the gospel message summarized in John 3:16 is the book of beginnings — Genesis.

Summary of Germanic and Norse Mythology Beliefs

Doctrine	Norse Mythology
God	A pantheistic and polytheistic collection of various beings and gods who have no absolute power or authority and are in conflict with one another. The gods include Odin, Thor, Frey, Freyr, and others.
Authority/Revelation	There are no authoritative sources apart from the collection of myths and sagas in the *Prose Edda*.
Man	Odin and his brothers made a human man and woman from two tree logs they found on the seashore.
Sin	There is no clear idea of sin apart from loose moral codes based on honor and integrity.
Salvation	There is no consistent view on the afterlife, but many believe that one will enter other realms after death based on the worth of one's life and the manner of death. Some also believe in reincarnation or the continuation of various aspects of the soul.
Creation	The world was formed by the gods from the remains of an ice-giant they killed. This ice-giant and a cow had been formed from thawing ice in a gap between the fire and ice realms. Many different realms where different beings exist are connected to different parts of the world tree, Yggdrasil.

Chapter 15

Syncretism in Latin American Religions

Joe Owen

Before I was a Christian, I remember how I was convinced that part of critical thinking was to disassociate myself from what I heard as a child with respects to a biblical understanding of the world. I learned to watch documentaries on other cultures and see their beliefs from a relativistic point of view. At least that is what the narrator of these clips pushed on the viewer.

Although we see the depths of human depravity in these cultures as a result of the effects of Genesis 3, we are told by *our* depraved culture that what we observe is only natural, and any objection to cultural differences is a result of closed-mindedness.

Latin American Culture and Background

Being that North America is a neighbor to the Latin American countries, many of us have been conditioned to look at the paganism there as a cute aspect of our vacation destination. We are expected to celebrate the cultural diversity without acknowledging the utter hopelessness experienced in paganism.

The first book in Spanish that I read was *Las Leyendas Mexicanas (Mexican Legends)* when I was in my second year of Spanish in high school. I was enamored by the legends like the creation of the "new sun and moon" by a meeting of the gods in Teotihuacán (about 25 miles north of modern-day Mexico City) and the history of the pyramids.

What I did not even care to understand then is what many admirers of such legends fail to understand — where such a worldview came from and how it is still prevalent today. Although the legends are considered by most to be just that — legends — the underlying worldview has *not* suffered the same fate. These beliefs remain active throughout Latin America today. There are many ways in which this belief system, which is a direct contradiction to Scripture, manifests itself, but we will extract the three most basic tenets and the three ways that they affect people's worldviews in Latin America today.

Pre-colonial Latin America consisted of three major people groups (Aztecs, Mayas, and Incas) and many minor offshoots. These groups were polytheistic, animistic, and involved in ancestor worship, although the practice of each differed throughout the regions.[1] There was a dualistic system of dark and light similar to Manichaeism (an old Persian mixture of religions), including a constant need to appease their pantheon of gods.

On some of the ziggurats (step pyramids) used in their religious practice they conducted countless human sacrifices to satisfy their gods. There are many interesting documentaries that you can watch to learn about this fascinating, yet disturbing, history. Nonetheless, you will have a difficult time finding much written on how this worldview has not only survived colonization, but has flourished under diverse religious garb.

The three major ways that these beliefs have survived (in order of least to most subtle) are outright witchcraft, syncretism with Roman Catholicism, and syncretism with Evangelicalism. Syncretism, "the combination of different forms of belief or practice,"[2] is often not as obvious as one might think and can get a little complicated. There are different degrees of syncretism and they will be discussed below.

Syncretism in the Latter Apostolic and New Testament Age

The error of syncretism is not a new challenge to the proclamation of the pure gospel message. The Apostle John was already dealing with what seems like the inception of what would later be known as the heresy of Gnosticism. According to Gnosticism (from the Greek *gnosis* — knowledge), the

---

1. For example, the Mayans left artifacts that "reveal gods and goddesses, creators of rain and winds . . .": John Lynch, *New Worlds, A Religious History of Latin America* (New Haven, CT: Yale University Press, 2012), p. 7.
2. Merriam Webster Online, s.v. "Syncretism," accessed January 4, 2016, http://www.merriam-webster.com/dictionary/syncretism.

universe is a dualistic system where all matter or flesh is inherently evil and the spiritual is inherently good.

In this worldview, a person can move up the deification ladder by gaining secret knowledge. Gnosticism not only served as a denial of the biblical deity of Christ, but also found itself in a crucial quandary: if all flesh is inherently evil, then how could Jesus have been born as a human and not be evil?

This is where someone has to pay the bill. You can't have both contradictory doctrines — either the dualistic system was wrong or Jesus couldn't have come in flesh, but only in an illusory body. And that is why these groups denied the physical body of Jesus, in order to not have to discard their foundational belief of dualism.

What is most interesting, though, is the Apostle John's response. His intolerance of this religious system would be considered quite closed-minded in our days. Here, though, we can come to an understanding that truth is exclusive in nature and that unity or social peace does not take precedence over biblical conviction. In other words, truth is not up for a vote.

> And every spirit that does not confess that Jesus Christ has come in the flesh is not of God. And this is the spirit of the Antichrist, which you have heard was coming, and is now already in the world (1 John 4:3).[3]

> For many deceivers have gone out into the world who do not confess Jesus Christ as coming in the flesh. This is a deceiver and an antichrist (2 John 1:7).

The Apostle John had already made it clear with this assertion:

> And the Word became flesh and dwelt among us, and we beheld His glory, the glory as of the only begotten of the Father, full of grace and truth (John 1:14).

With this in mind, we deal with false religions with a grace-filled proclamation of the truth without compromising on either of the two — just as Jesus is full of grace and truth.

Witchcraft — Brujería

Latin America has many *curanderos* (healers) who will perform ritual healings for the right price, as well as *brujos* (witches) who practice either "white

3. Scripture in this chapter is from the New King James Version (NKJV) of the Bible.

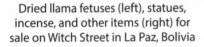

Dried llama fetuses (left), statues, incense, and other items (right) for sale on Witch Street in La Paz, Bolivia

magic" or "black magic." In places such as Bolivia, the Aymara people sell sacrifice kits and llama fetuses used to appease gods for various reasons. I personally witnessed an Aymara woman burning a sacrifice kit on a curb in La Paz, Bolivia, hoping to bring protection to drivers experiencing a high accident rate in that area. One of my most interesting travel experiences has been a trip to see where these kits sell for a bargain price on *La Calle de las Brujas* (the Witch Street).

Where in the world would somebody come up with a basis for this idea? Although there are some written sacred texts in these regions, like the *Book of Chilam Balam*, most people will never see a copy in their lifetime. This worldview is passed from generation to generation, and the belief that "the world of the spirit and the flesh were closely merged."[4] In an animistic belief, humans have the power to direct much of the spirit world, and certain humans have more power than others.[5]

Animism remains the belief that all things material have a spirit. Special ceremonies were the way in which humans could move or even control the interaction between the spiritual and physical. The sobering fact about such a mythical mindset is that it continues as a prevalent belief throughout Latin America. Of course, this view is purely arbitrary and based solely in man's explanation of the world around him without revelation from God.

4. Lynch, *New Worlds, A Religious History of Latin America*, p. 7.
5. See chapter 12 in this volume for a full description of Animism.

Additionally, the refutations given in the witchcraft chapter in this volume also apply here as well.[6]

What Does the Bible Say?

These people groups mentioned are not the only ones dabbling in witchcraft. We know from Scripture that God took the Hebrews from slavery in Egypt to settle in Canaan, and that He took them the long way.

> Every commandment which I command you today you must be careful to observe, that you may live and multiply, and go in and possess the land of which the LORD swore to your fathers. And you shall remember that the LORD your God led you all the way these forty years in the wilderness, to humble you and test you, to know what was in your heart, whether you would keep His commandments or not. So He humbled you, allowed you to hunger, and fed you with manna which you did not know nor did your fathers know, that He might make you know that man shall not live by bread alone; but man lives by every word that proceeds from the mouth of the LORD (Deuteronomy 8:1–3).

Although provoked by the people's disobedience, one of the reasons why God made a 40-year journey out of a 250-mile stretch was to set apart a nation for Himself that would depend wholly on God and submit to His Word for direction. This preparation would be crucial, as they were to settle in a land surrounded by many different pagan religions and practices, in which sorcery and witchcraft were included. God gave this nation a stern warning:

> When you come into the land which the LORD your God is giving you, you shall not learn to follow the abominations of those nations. There shall not be found among you anyone who makes his son or his daughter pass through the fire, or one who practices witchcraft, or a soothsayer, or one who interprets omens, or a sorcerer, or one who conjures spells, or a medium, or a spiritist, or one who calls up the dead. For all who do these things are an abomination to the LORD, and because of these

---

6. See chapter 10 in this volume for a full description of Witchcraft.

abominations the LORD your God drives them out from before you (Deuteronomy 18:9–12).

The question of why it is an abomination for mankind to seek out the spirit world and communicate to help manage how daily circumstances are played out in the physical realm is important. The answer can be found back in the created order. In Genesis 1 and 2, we see that God created mankind and walked with them in the garden. We see a relationship in creation that mankind enjoyed that had no extra-human involvement as man was created in God's image and likeness, apart from all other life. This relationship was severed by man's disobedience in Genesis 3, but God's eternal plan to provide and appeasement to satisfy His own just wrath against sin was given in Genesis 3:15:

> And I will put enmity between you and the woman, and between your seed and her Seed; He shall bruise your head, and you shall bruise His heel.

A non-mortal blow (to the heel) would be given to the Seed of the woman, as He would deal a mortal blow (to the head) to the serpent. God would provide a way to reconcile Himself to mankind in the Seed, Jesus Christ. There is, though, an entire spiritual realm. The Bible is clear that man was originally given dominion over the earth (Genesis 1:26–28) but had essentially forfeited that dominion to Satan, the serpent, along with one-third of heaven's angels, which were cast down along with Satan in the great rebellion.[7]

The Bible also reveals that there is much interaction between the spiritual realm and the physical realm. For instance, Satan fought the archangel Michael over the physical body of Moses (Jude 1:9), and followers of Christ are in battle against "principalities, against powers, against the rulers of the darkness of this age, against spiritual hosts of wickedness in the heavenly places" (Ephesians 6:12).

This is all to say that although it is an abomination for humans to communicate and make use of spirits, it doesn't mean the extreme opposite in denying their existence. Naturalism is not the answer to this evil, but would simply be an "out of sight, out of mind" way of ignoring such a great reality. The answer is the gospel of Jesus Christ and a total repentance of any interaction with spiritual mediums. You need to understand that we have

---

7. Isaiah 14:12; Luke 10:18; Revelation 9:1, 12:3–9; Hebrews 12:22.

a perfect mediator, Jesus Christ, the great High Priest. He is the promised Seed who reconciles repentant believers to God by grace through faith in His all-sufficient substitutionary sacrifice on the Cross and His subsequent Resurrection from the dead on the third day.[8]

Syncretism: Roman Catholicism, Witchcraft, and Ancestral Worship

When Hernán Cortés reached Mexico, he brought with him a Roman Catholic tradition and power structure. Major Aztec temples (such as the Templo Mayor in Tenochtitlan, or today's Mexico City) were destroyed or covered and a physical cathedral erected in their place. Many idolatrous customs of the indigenous people groups were banned by force, replaced with a Roman Catholic tradition.

The Templo Mayor, the historic center of Mexico City, where many pre-colonial human sacrifices took place.
(Shutterstock, Javarman)

This conquest may look like the vanquishing of a pagan, murderous religious society, but the truth is that there is one irreplaceable word that is missing: gospel. To better understand how this happened, we need to skip back about a thousand years before

Metropolitan Cathedral, Mexico City, next to the Templo Mayor
(Shutterstock, Nfoto)

Roman Catholicism reached the New World. By the fifth century A.D., the bishop of Rome, Leo I, had gained much political power due to the fact that the other major bishops (in Jerusalem, Antioch, Alexandria, etc.) were part

---

8. 1 Timothy 2:5; Hebrews 4:14–16, 9:11–12, 10:10–14; 2 Corinthians 5:18; 1 Corinthians 15:3–4.

of the Eastern church. The Roman Emperor was in Constantinople in the east, and there was a consolidation of church and state that resulted in the Holy Roman Empire. The bishop of Rome took on the title "Pope."[9] By the 15th century, the Roman Catholic "church" had dominated Europe with its political power. So when the Catholic Spaniards reached the shores of the New World, a focus on individual regeneration through the gospel had long since been lost, having been replaced by an imperial attitude.

Instead of hearing of the "new creation" experience of a hopeless sinner being reborn into the Last Adam, Jesus Christ, wherein he learns to have a renewed mind, a large society was forced into submission under the standards of the Roman Catholic empire. The natural consequence was a syncretism that is found throughout Latin America to this day.

The best way to understand how this syncretic system works is to give practical examples of how it is carried out in day-to-day life.

Witchcraft

In Mexico, many believe in what is called *el ojo* (the eye). In instances when a baby cries or gets a fever, it is believed that an adult stared too long at the baby and passed on a bad energy or spirit to the baby. The remedy is to use an egg, a special branch, oil, etc., and chant. Added to this spell is the recitation of the Lord's Prayer, Ave Maria, a Rosary, etc. As spell casting is concerned, there is a false belief in a white, good magic and a black, bad magic. If someone would like to cast a spell for good luck, fortune, or love, that spell can be considered white magic and in accordance with a good, Catholic lifestyle by the majority of the Latin American society. Also, on Witch Street in La Paz, Bolivia, Roman Catholic saints stand among the pagan sorcery items and trinkets for sale.

Seen in this picture from a storefront on Witch Street, La Paz, Bolivia, is Saint Expeditus, a Christian martyr from the late second century. The writing on this incense package states, "For redemption, hope and to attract money." The fact that this saint is used in a superstitious way to "expedite" things does not come

9. Gregory was the first "official" pope in A.D. 590.

from Inca syncretism, though. These superstitions are found throughout Roman Catholicism, making it clear that syncretism started many centuries before reaching the shores of the New World and added to the folk religions.[10] And as far as witchcraft goes, these are only a small sampling of its saturation and how it plays a major role in Latin American societies.

Ancestor Worship

The indigenous ancestral worship found a compromise with the Roman Catholic Church (RCC) in exchanging ancestral "worship" for the "veneration" of RCC saints. For even the moderately observant tourist, the fact that Mexico has a peculiar endearment for their saints becomes obvious very quickly. The roadways have temples in curves and mountainsides with different saints for protection. Markets are full of trinkets for different saints in promise of different favors or relief. Streets are closed for processions as flowers are laid down for the carrying of large statues of saints for various festivals. But, again, it is worth mentioning that this "veneration" of dead saints past is practiced around the world. This unbiblical practice was brought to Latin America and simply incorporated into the folk religions — praying to ancestors was replaced with praying to saints.

Another example of an instance where compromise appears via syncretism is in All Saints Day. *Día de los Muertos* (Day of the Dead) is celebrated on All Saints Day every November 1.[11] This is mostly a Mexican celebration involving a parade to the cemetery to visit dead ancestors. This ceremonial celebration predates the colonization period, but has really only changed dates to comply with the RCC's tradition.[12] In Mexico

Typical Day of the Dead cemetery vigil

10. Example: http://catholicherald.com/stories/A-patron-saint-for-procrastinators,18693, accessed January 4, 2016.
11. Bodie Hodge, Halloween History and the Bible, Answers in Genesis, October 29, 2013, https://answersingenesis.org/holidays/halloween-history-and-the-bible/.
12. Some sources state that the Día de Muertos was originally celebrated in the beginning of the summer before the Spanish rule.

City, the deceased children are visited on November 1 and the deceased adults on November 2. The families cook the loved one's favorite dish, taking it to the cemetery in hopes that their spirit will visit to dine once again. In some villages, the bones of the deceased are dug up and washed.

This unhealthy interest in death has brought on a new "saint" for Latin America — *La Santísima Muerte* (Saint Death). This brand of "venerating" or worshiping a personification of death comes out of a great admiration and respect for death's power. Saint Death is found on trinkets, shirts, hats, and even full statues of what many in the Western world would consider to be the Grim Reaper as seen in the picture. According to a leading popular webpage that gives specific prayers to Saint Death, this is the beginning and end of the structure of a prayer:

> Lord, before Your Divine Presence God Almighty,
> Father, Son and Holy Spirit,
> I ask for your permission to invoke the Holy Death.
> My White daughter.

And then it ends with:

> (Pray three "Our Fathers")[13]

What does the Bible say?

Interestingly, the Bible doesn't allow for communication with any spiritual being except God, whether saint or death itself. The Bible speaks of death as an enemy that was brought into the world through sin and will one day be defeated forever. Jesus Christ defeated death through His work on the Cross (1 Corinthians 15:24–28; Colossians 2:13–15; Revelation 20:11–15). To offer prayers to the enemy of Christ while invoking His name is a strange fire to offer at the altars to Saint Death.

The prophet Habakkuk, after his inquiry on why God allows evil, and after God's response, continues to exhort, then, those who speak to idols:

> What profit is the image, that its maker should carve it,
> The molded image, a teacher of lies,
> That the maker of its mold should trust in it,
> To make mute idols?

---

13. "Very Powerful" Prayer of Protection, La Santa Muerte, http://www.santamuerte.org/oraciones/3745-plegaria-de-proteccion.html, accessed January 4, 2016.

Statues including the Grim Reaper

An altar of *Santísima Muerte*, Saint Death

> Woe to him who says to wood, "Awake!"
> To silent stone, "Arise! It shall teach!"
> Behold, it is overlaid with gold and silver,
> Yet in it there is no breath at all.
> But the Lord is in His holy temple.
> Let all the earth keep silence before Him (Habakkuk 2:18–20).

In the case of any idol, whether saint or death, just because one recites a prayer asking God to give permission to speak with this person doesn't mean that God grants the permission. On the contrary, the Bible teaches the opposite. When King Saul wanted to beg the dead prophet Samuel for help, he didn't go to God asking for permission because he knew it was against God's will. He foolishly went to a medium (witch) to get an audience with the dead. In doing that he broke God's law. The only mediator (not medium) that we have to communicate to a Spirit is Jesus Christ — granting us an audience with the Father (1 Timothy 2:5).

Animism

As previously mentioned, the foundation of these mystical, superstitious, and pagan beliefs in Latin America, as well as in some other parts of the world, is animism. Instead of a sovereign God who directs the affairs in the material and spiritual realms, animism is taking a stab at achieving human sovereignty. If a human can pronounce a spell or mix just the right elements in a potion of eggs and oil he can manipulate the spiritual world, which in itself coordinates the affairs of the physical world.

In this system there is recognition of a world where things are not as they should be, but there is no hope. There is no great systematic storyline of a holy, just, and loving God who is working out His will to usher in the

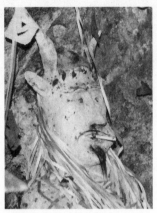

consummation of His plans for an eternity of a pure, perfect, and reconciled relationship with humans. There is no notion of being redeemed through Christ as He redeems everything that is in heaven and earth (Colossians 1). There is just each man on his own, working things out to the best of his abilities for his own personal benefit. In this sad system, you can beseech the spirit of the wind for tranquility, sacrifice and chant to *Pachamama* (Mother Earth) for a good harvest, and bring offerings to *El Tío* (the Uncle, god of the underworld) for safety in the mines, but there is no guarantee for any of it.

El Tío, the Uncle, in the mines of Potosí, Bolivia

Animistic attitudes, with only a small degree of discernment, can be seen in their most common manifestation — superstition. In superstition, fate is considered easily controlled by certain words or actions. For example, in Latin America (at least in most parts, especially with the least amount of European immigration), sarcasm is not taken well. A sarcastic statement is thought to be dangerous. By declaring something sarcastic, the spirit world is not privy to your real intentions but will react according to what was said.

That said, the manner in which animism has found itself into a syncretic system is more disturbing and, in a more subtle way and unbeknownst to multitudes, has invaded what many might consider evangelicalism. This most subtle syncretism is probably the largest problem facing the Latin American church at this time.

There has been a type of spin-off of Montanism (an early Christian heresy)[14] from the second century that has resurfaced in churches throughout

---

14. New Prophecy heresy from the middle of the second century wherein much attention was given to an imminent Second Advent that would take place in Phrygia, in that certain people receive new prophecy that was very sporadic and nonsensical, even speaking in the first person, "I am neither angel nor ambassador, but I God and Father, who am come." Epiphanius, *Heresies*, 48.11; Stevenson, 107. http://earlychurch.org.uk/article_montanism.html, accessed January 4, 2016.

the globe. The exceptional challenge that this brings to Latin America is that it closes the gap by reconciling an experiential religious anomaly and animism, and therefore has exploded in the last few decades.

This is known to most as Prosperity Theology or Prosperity Gospel and has taken over whole communities throughout Latin America. Every Sunday, many "templos" are filled to the brim with thousands upon thousands of devoted followers. Thankfully, a growing number of Christians are concerned about this syncretism

Cash Luna, Guatemalan prosperity leader, one of Latin America's most well-known prosperity animists

and are working to usher in a biblical gospel message alongside the barrage of confusing messages.

> The evangelical movement in Bolivia began over a hundred years ago in rural areas. But the country actually banned evangelical churches from cities until 1945 due to its bad reputation for mysticism and animism (influenced by Andean culture). Decades later, the church remains weak, characterized by captivating faith and prosperity teachings that replace reliance on God's word with a confidence in leaders referred to as apostles and prophets.[15]

There are a number of movements that have "Apostles" as the directors who speak as if from the Lord, or at least convince many to believe so. They will make such statements as, "Don't get lost among so much knowledge of the Word: Believe! That is what is important!"[16] And, "What are the 7 things that you desire in 2016? I declare 21 days of miracles over your life as you begin this New Year in prayer, fasting and offerings!"[17]

15. Patti Richter, "Bolstering Biblical Ministry in Bolivia," The Gospel Coalition, http://www.thegospelcoalition.org/article/bolstering-biblical-ministry-in-bolivia, accessed January 4, 2016.

16. Cash Luna, http://restablecidos.com/wp-content/uploads/2015/03/cash-luna-no-te-sumerjas-tanto-conocimiento-palabra-solo-cree.png, accessed January 4, 2016.

17. https://www.facebook.com/apostolgmaldonado/?fref=ts, accessed January 4, 2016.

What these false teachers figured out was how to play off of an animistic culture's superstition and "declare" how they can thus move the spirit world and circumstances of their life. Playing off of the misunderstanding about the relationship between laypeople and clergy, the average person is not "spiritual" enough to make much of a demand, so mediums are put in place and the syncretism is made clear by the title of "Apostle."

A sad truth is that in many cases these "Apostles" cannot be confronted in even the most biblical of ways without an all-out excommunication of the soul who dared to make such a challenge. According to many of their followers, they have the authority to make certain declarations that, in all practicality, carry the weight of Scripture within the community they control.

They are modern-day mediums for fortune and good luck and sadly claim the title *Evangelical*. In many of these cases, somewhere down the line many people adopted the title "evangelical" but never believed that Jesus is sufficient. This group has fallen into dualism again, and a demoted Jesus merely ends up being a superhero in the background on our side with our local Apostle fighting against the powers of darkness in the universe to take back what has been stolen — our health, wealth, and happiness.

What Does the Bible Say?

No matter what the culture or people group, we all spread out over the face of the earth from Babel until now with our own versions of man-made religions that all stem back to what was trying to be accomplished there — man making his own way to his idea of a god, deciding his own purpose and what was most important in life. This is humanism in its broadest sense.

Most people recognize the fact that we are spiritual beings, and not just material (except for the staunch naturalists and materialists). Most try to reach out for contact with the spiritual world they are certain exists. This venture, unassisted by the Word of God and carried out by an unregenerate person, is already doomed to failure. It is easy to say that the gospel is the answer, but as we have noted in this chapter, many people try to add a false version of the gospel to their animistic worldview, and thus miss out on the true, saving message of salvation in Jesus Christ alone.

The answer to this false religion is a biblically based message of hope through Jesus without the leeches of syncretistic falsehood that suck the lifeblood from the gospel, keeping so many from hearing the unadulterated Word of the living God.

But we have renounced the hidden things of shame, not walking in craftiness nor handling the word of God deceitfully, but by manifestation of the truth commending ourselves to every man's conscience in the sight of God. But even if our gospel is veiled, it is veiled to those who are perishing, whose minds the god of this age has blinded, who do not believe, lest the light of the gospel of the glory of Christ, who is the image of God, should shine on them (2 Corinthians 4:2–4).

So if they who are lost die in their disbelief, let it only be due to their blindness, not accompanied by our deceit.

If anyone teaches otherwise and does not consent to wholesome words, even the words of our Lord Jesus Christ, and to the doctrine which accords with godliness, he is proud, knowing nothing, but is obsessed with disputes and arguments over words, from which come envy, strife, reviling, evil suspicions, useless wranglings of men of corrupt minds and destitute of the truth, who suppose that godliness is a means of gain. From such withdraw yourself (1 Timothy 6:3–5).

Because the true gospel is:

For I delivered to you first of all that which I also received: that Christ died for our sins according to the Scriptures, and that He was buried, and that He rose again the third day according to the Scriptures (1 Corinthians 15:3–4).

Chapter 16

Greek Mythology

*Don Landis and the Ancient Man Team
at Jackson Hole Bible College*

Come hither, tell of Zeus your father and chant his praise. Through him mortal men are famed or un-famed, sung or unsung alike, as great Zeus wills. For easily he makes strong, and easily he brings the strong man low; easily he humbles the proud and raises the obscure, and easily he straightens the crooked and blasts the proud — Zeus who thunders aloft and has his dwelling most high.[1]

What we now refer to as "Greek mythology" began as unreliable, convoluted oral tradition passed down from generation to generation. In fact, there is no single document or text that outlines and describes the complete Greek system of beliefs. Instead, there are various pieces of written literature, poems, and stories that describe and elaborate on the origins, purposes, and characteristics of these alleged gods and man's purpose.

According to the myths, it appears that the ancient Greeks had a religious system similar to the majority of the pagan religions of their day (950–250 B.C.). Various deities governed the natural forces of the world. The gods and goddesses of Greek mythology controlled everything from the sky and

1. Hesiod, *Works and Days*, translated by Hugh G. Evelyn-White, http://www.sacred-texts.com/cla/hesiod/works.htm, accessed February 20, 2015.

sea to vegetation, earthquakes, and marriage. They were powerful but quarrelsome and seemed to lack self-control and wisdom.

Like all pagan religions, the beliefs of the ancient Greek culture stood in direct contrast to the truth of God's Word. The Greeks resolutely dismissed the existence of the one true God and history as outlined in Scripture. Their religion was sourced in their own authority. Remember that long before the Greeks started making up stories about gods like Zeus, Prometheus, and Aphrodite, mankind had decided to reject the truth and forge their own way.

The origin of all post-Flood pagan religions was the Tower of Babel, when mankind came together in an effort to usurp God's authority and proclaim their own. Even after being scattered across the planet, their defiance against God didn't die but rather blossomed into paganism of various forms — all sourced in the original rebellion.[2]

Greek mythology is perhaps one of the most famous and well-known ancient mythological religions. It had a profound impact on the ancient world because it was spread so widely by the conquest of Alexander the Great, and later broadly adopted by the Romans (they merely changed the names of the gods). By studying Greek beliefs about origins, God, man, morality, and the afterlife, we will gain insight into the minds of the ancient people and even learn about our own pagan tendencies.

Although not in written form for years, it is clear that the average Greek had a general knowledge and understanding of the gods and goddesses. When early authors like Homer (whom scholars date around the eighth or ninth century B.C.) wrote literature about the gods, they did not describe much about their character or origins. This knowledge was assumed to be already well-known. It wasn't until around 700 B.C. when the poet Hesiod wrote *Theogony* that the origins and nature of the Greek pantheon (all the gods and goddesses of their religion) were officially described. Other authors, playwrights, and poets elaborated on the myths, expanding the narratives individually. In the first century B.C. the Roman historian Gaius Julius Hyginus compiled all this mythological literature into a structure.

The Origin of All Things

The first Greek creation story was written around 700 B.C. by Hesiod (quite late in comparison to other origin myths). According to Hesiod, though

2. Don Landis, ed., *The Secrets of Ancient Man: Revelations from the Ruins*. 1st ed. (Green Forest, AR: Master Books, 2015).

there are variations of the story among other writers, the universe started out as Chaos (the primeval void) and out of Chaos came Erebus (darkness) and Nyx (night). It wasn't until the coming of Eros (love) that Erebus and Nyx bore light (Aether) and Hemera (day). After the coming of light, the great domains, Gaia (earth), Ouranos (sky), Pontos (sea), Tartarus (underworld), and other primordial beings personifying everything from sleep to fate, were born from the union of these beings. The Titans, Olympians, monsters, and minor gods were born from these primordial beings. In *Theogeny*, Hesiod focused on the emergence and lineage of the gods and monsters, all connected in a large convoluted family tree. He also described many fantastic tales about the wars and struggles between the gods, Titans, and monsters.

Primordial Gods	Titans	Olympians	Heroes	Monsters
The first deities who created the universe and produced the next generation of gods, the Titans	Sometimes known as the elder gods, the children of Earth (Gaia) and Sky (Ouranos)	Twelve gods who ruled from Mount Olympus after the overthrow of the Titans	Individuals who achieved semi-divinity or were specifically recognized for their greatness	Monsters and other mythical creatures feature prominently in many Greek tales
Gaia Ouranos Eros Tartarus Chaos Pontos Ourea Aether Hemera Nyx	Rhea Cronos Helios Phoebe Theia Hyperion Perses Prometheus Epimetheus Atlas Mnemosyne Tethys Themis Oceanus Coeus	Zeus Poseidon Hera Artemis Athena Dionysius Demeter Ares Apollo Hermes Hephaestus Aphrodite Sometimes included: Hestia Hades	Heracles Achilles Callisto Theban Helen Theseus Odysseus Perseus Orpheus	Pegasus (winged horse) Centaurs (part man part horse) Sphinx (part woman and part lion) Cyclops (one-eyed giant) Unicorns Gorgons Minotaurs Satyrs Dragons

Because the ancient Greek religion does not have any one specific and comprehensive text to reference, charts like the one above are likely to differ from one another depending on the sources used to obtain the information. The chart above is simply a helpful reference for common classification of some of the mythical Greek characters.

Atlas was a Titan who was supposedly punished by Zeus and forced to hold up the earth.
(Wikimedia Commons, Biatch)

Prometheus delivers fire to mankind, previously in darkness.
(Wikimedia Commons, Heinrich Füger)

The Origin of Mankind

According to the Greek myths, there was a long time in history when only the immortal gods existed. It was not until after the war between the Olympians and the Titans (in which the younger Olympian gods defeated the elder Titans) that humans and animals appeared on the earth. Zeus, the new Olympian king of the gods, rewarded two of the Titans who had joined their side (Epimetheus and Prometheus) with the creation of animals and humans. Epimetheus made all of the different animals, giving them gifts of speed, strength, wings, fur, and other strong attributes. This left Prometheus without any gifts, so he made man out of clay and then Athena (goddess of wisdom) breathed life into his clay forms. Prometheus created them in the image of the gods, standing upright with the same countenance. He also stole some skills from Hephaestus (god of craftsmanship) and Athena to bless his new favorites. In an effort to help them, he gave them control over fire. The first humans were all male and lived in harmony with the gods.[3]

3. *The Prometheus of Aeschylus* (Cambridge, MA: Harvard University Press, 1888), p. 343, https://books.google.com/books?id=YkygMobybKUC.

However, Zeus (god of storms) was angry that man had been given fire, forming a rift between men and the gods. According to the myths, in his anger he punished them with the gift of womankind.[4]

The first woman was called Pandora. Zeus had Hephaestus create her, and she was given gifts of beauty and guile. In Hesiod's tale *Works and Days,* the gods created her and gifted her out of spite to cause suffering to mankind. The gods created her with "cruel longing and cares that weary the limbs" and a "shameless mind and deceitful nature." She was "bedecked with all manners of finery" and yet filled with "lies and crafty words." She was given as "a plague to men."[5]

Artist's impression of Pandora attempting to close the box she opened out of curiosity as the evils she has released taunt her while they escape.
(Wikimedia commons, F.S. Church)

Hesiod claims that before women appeared, men lived "free from ills and hard toil and heavy sickness." But Pandora brought a jar with her (commonly referred to as Pandora's Box). Though warned never to open it, she could not resist the temptation. Upon opening the jar she released every kind of evil upon mankind including toil and death. And yet the one thing that didn't escape was Hope. It remained in the jar, closed under the lid.[6]

Judgment

Because of the evil unleashed and the resulting chaos as man was given over to corruption, Zeus and the other gods punished them by sending a flood to wipe out all mankind. Only a noble man named Deucalion and his wife Pyrrha (daughter of Pandora) were spared because Prometheus warned them of the coming disaster. They built a boat and floated for nine days before landing on Mt. Parnassus. Upon landing they were told to throw stones behind them; each stone thrown by Deucalion turned into a man, and each stone thrown by Pyrrha turned into a woman. They then sired their own

4. Stephanie Lynn Budin, *The Ancient Greeks: An Introduction* (New York: Oxford University Press, 2009), p. 244.
5. Hesiod, *Works and Days.*
6. Ibid.

children from whom all Greeks are descended. (The stones populated the other areas of the world.)[7]

Drawing Comparisons

Without delving any further into the convoluted details of Greek mythology, the basics of this pagan religion are already clear and lie far outside of biblical truths.

Gods and Goddesses

As seen in the tale of the origin of the universe and the creation of mankind, the Greek gods are nothing in comparison to the one true God. Though some of the gods, Zeus in particular, seem to mirror many of the characteristics of the God of the Bible, they were certainly not all-powerful or all-knowing, and they often got tricked by others, even mortal men. They show themselves to be petty, quarrelsome, unjust, and cruel. They were violent, jealous, prone to anger and deceit, and often shown to be limited in their abilities and strength. The Greeks replaced the incomparable, omniscient, omnipotent God, in whose image they were made, with a myriad of weak, unreliable gods and goddesses created in their own image.

The ancient Greeks considered the gods morally perfect. (Hesiod claimed that "true judgment is of Zeus and is perfect.")[8] However, even cursory readings of Greek mythology prove that idea to be completely untrue from a biblical perspective.

Yet to the Greeks, the most defining attribute of a god was not goodness or omniscience or perfection, but *power*. And usually that power defined a god as a specific kind of force or action (Aphrodite was the force of love, Zeus was the god of the storm, etc.).[9] Perhaps this explains why the gods were often attacking each other and seemingly capricious. They were defined and directed by their power, they did not command or control it.

The Nature of Man

According to the origins story, mankind was originally and internally good; it was not until Pandora released evil into the world that mankind started to

---

7. John H. Haaren and Addison B. Poland, *Famous Men of Greece* (New York: American Book Company, 1904), p. 20–24, https://books.google.com/books?id=OLsBAAAAYAAJ.

8. Hesiod, *Works and Days*.

9. *God and Men in Greek Religion*, http://faculty.gvsu.edu/websterm/gods&men.htm., accessed February 19, 2015.

do wrong. Even then, the evil of mankind is attributed to the evil spirits that had been released around them, not to man's internal evil nature.

In fact, according to Hesiod's *Works and Days*, women in general are the source of evil and trials. In contrast to God's Word, women were apparently sent as a punishment to mankind, not created as a helpmate and fellow image-bearer. Pandora is called a "beautiful evil" in *Theogony*, a "deadly race and tribe of women who live amongst mortal men to their great trouble, no helpmeets in hateful poverty, but only in wealth." They were "an evil to mortal man, with a nature to do evil."[10]

In this perversion of biblical truth we can see traces of Adam and Eve's history and the effects of the curse visible between the lines. This mythology reflects Satan's lies as a distortion of what really happened.

Morality

From their literature it is clear that the Greeks believed in some sort of moral code and that it was somewhat governed by the gods. Hesiod teaches that Zeus gave man "right," in contrast to the animals who knew nothing of right and wrong. According to *Works and Days*, doing right would lead to prosperity. But those men who lied and "hurt Justice" and sinned "beyond repair" would be left to obscurity.[11] Moreover, "badness can be got easily and in shoals: the road to her is smooth, and she lives very near us. But between us and Goodness the gods have placed the sweat of our brows: long and steep is the path that leads to her, and it is rough at the first; but when a man has reached the top, then is she easy to reach, though before that she was hard."[12]

This passage from *Works and Days* describes how Zeus continued to create many generations of men that always fell into evil. The author bemoans his life among the evil of his generation, and his description of those evils is intriguingly similar to biblical passages:

> Thereafter, would that I were not among the men of the fifth generation, but either had died before or been born afterwards. For now truly is a race of iron, and men never rest from labour and sorrow by day, and from perishing by night; and the gods shall lay sore trouble upon them. . . . The father will not agree

---

10. Hesiod, *The Theogony of Hesiod*.
11. Hesiod, *Works and Days*.
12. Ibid.

with his children, nor the children with their father, nor guest with his host, nor comrade with comrade; nor will brother be dear to brother as aforetime. Men will dishonour their parents as they grow quickly old, and will carp at them, chiding them with bitter words, hard-hearted they, not knowing the fear of the gods. They will not repay their aged parents the cost their nurture, for might shall be their right: and one man will sack another's city. There will be no favour for the man who keeps his oath or for the just or for the good; but rather men will praise the evil-doer and his violent dealing. Strength will be right and reverence will cease to be; and the wicked will hurt the worthy man, speaking false words against him, and will swear an oath upon them. Envy, foul-mouthed, delighting in evil, with scowling face, will go along with wretched men one and all.[13]

Many of these are biblically based ideals (similar to verses such as those found in Proverbs and Ecclesiastes). How is it that the Greeks seemingly borrowed from the Bible in their pagan mythology? They definitely had no intention of aligning themselves to the teachings of God, and yet the author ached for justice and righteousness, for honesty, love, and kindness. Is it any surprise that these good attributes were missing from their society when the gods and goddesses they worshiped were constantly manifesting evil tendencies?

As the Psalmist rightly notes, "those who make [idols] are like them; so is everyone who trusts in them" (Psalm 135:18; KJV).

Life after Death

The ancient Greeks believed that death occurred when the breath left the body. They believed in a soul-like, ghost-like entity called a *psyche* that left the body upon death to enter an afterlife. They believed that the next life would be spent in the underworld, which was ruled by the god Hades. It appears from the literature that the afterlife was a depressing reality to the Greeks — a weary and tedious place (as described by Achilles in Homer's *Odyssey*).

And yet an alternate condition is also described in later Greek literature with three areas of the underworld offering a more hopeful, positive outlook.

---

13. Ibid.

The first area was Tartarus (also known as the pit), which was split into two different sections. The first and lowest section was the prison of the gods; monsters and other powerful beings were placed in this area.[14]

The second section of Tartarus was imagined by fifth-century Greek poets like Homer and Hesiod who repurposed the pit to include the most despised sinners. It was the lowest area where humans could be sent and was the place where the worst of the worst went to endure eternal torment.[15]

The middle area, the Fields of Asphodel, was where the vast majority of people went. These had done nothing particularly evil so as to deserve the punishment of the lower realm but had also

Hades was the god over the underworld, pictured here with the three-headed dog, Cerberus.
(Wikimedia Commons)

not done anything particularly good in order to deserve Elysium. Here they would experience neither joy nor torment; instead it was listless, dull, and forgetful.

The highest area was Elysium, the goal of all people. In Elysium there was endless celebration. It was reserved for those who did good works to earn their way in. Only the greatest heroes and most honorable humans would achieve Elysium.

Even later, another shift occurred in the Greek ideology about death as many came to believe in a form of reincarnation. If a person died and went to the Fields of Asphodel, they could choose to live again for a chance to receive the reward of Elysium. They would not remember who they were; they would be different people (though they started out as animals, Herodotus made the statement that it took three thousand years to return to human form), allowing them a chance to receive the greater reward. Clearly influenced by Eastern and/or Egyptian ideas, the Greeks believed if you

---

14. These aspects are described in various sections of Homer's *Iliad* and other writings.
15. Sarah A. Scull, *Greek Mythology Systematized* (Philadelphia, PA: Porter & Coates, 1880), p. 99–104, https://books.google.com/books?id=Lm0ZAAAAYAAJ.

lived enough good lives, you would eventually end up in Elysium.[16] These ever-changing ideas about the afterlife are evidence of the truly arbitrary nature of their beliefs, having no grounding in a legitimate authority.

The Purpose of Life

For the Greeks, the purpose of life was twofold — to worship and please the gods and to achieve honor and glory for themselves to gain entrance to Elysium. Since pleasing the gods was the primary way to reach Elysium, these purposes were closely tied together.

Man was created to be subject to the gods and to please them with sacrifices and other forms of worship. However, the true reason a Greek would strive to live a life of honor, and the reason they wanted to perform great deeds and to become well known, was simply because they desired Elysium. Therefore, just like every other man-made religion in the world, the Greeks relied on their own works to be saved from punishment.

They were constantly working to appease the fickle gods, both for blessings in this life and in order to achieve happiness after death. It was a tedious way of living, involving various sacrifices, rituals, and careful maneuvering in order to avoid upsetting the deities.

While Elysium was the goal of most men (one only achieved by great heroes such as Achilles, Odysseus, Helen, Menelaus, Perseus, Theseus, etc.), the very greatest of heroes were granted an even greater reward — godhood. This was the ultimate gift granted to a select few, including the great heroes such as Heracles and Dionysus (the only one to become an Olympian). Most men could not hope to achieve such standing, but it is interesting to see how they still believed it was possible.[17]

Once again we see the ancient goal of Babel reflected in Greek religion — mankind desiring the domain and authority of God, trying to make a "name" for himself.

Judeo-Christian Beliefs in Greek Mythology

To be clear, it should be noted that Greek mythology did not *intentionally* borrow anything from God's revealed religion (that would eventually reach its fullest expression in Christianity). Like all man-made religions, Greek

---

16. Budin, *The Ancient Greeks: An Introduction*, p. 301.
17. The explanations of deifications, known as apotheosis, are found in later writers like Cicero and Pausanias.

mythology has its origins at the Tower of Babel. At Babel, Satan influenced mankind to start a one-world religion and government that was anti-God. However, it is important to remember that Satan cannot create, he can only pervert. Therefore, he set up a *counterfeit kingdom* and a *counterfeit religion*. Aspects of this counterfeiting can be seen in all of the false religions in the world. They all take a portion of truth and then twist it so it is almost unrecognizable. These truths were known by the people at Babel and carried with them as they traveled around the globe, being distorted in various ways over time.

Creation

The creation story of Hesiod's *Theogony* is a clear distortion of biblical truth. Now this may seem like a strange claim as the mythology of the Greeks seems to be far different than the truth of God's Word. However, look at the first two things that came into being from the Chaos — darkness and light. While it may seem inconsequential, it is something taken directly from true history as recorded in the Bible. Also the claim that at the beginning of creation Chaos was simply a great void is another distortion of the creation account in the Book of Genesis (Genesis 1:2). Other aspects of their creation story, such as the forming of man from the clay, even the creation of animals and man around the same time and man being created before woman has a kernel of biblical truth.

Sacrificial System

Another aspect the Greeks borrowed from the Judeo-Christian worldview is the sacrificial system. This religious practice was borrowed by every single ancient culture — they all had some form of a sacrificial system created to appease whatever gods they served. In the Bible, this system was initiated right after the Fall of Adam and Eve when God killed two animals and made clothes out of them. This first sacrifice was developed further in the account of Cain and Abel. Throughout the Old Testament, sacrifice as a covering for sin is practiced by Job, Abraham, and others. It is codified for the Israelites under Moses, but finds its perfect fulfillment in Jesus Christ and His death on the Cross. Because of His amazing sacrifice to take away the sins of those who believe in Him, there is no longer any need to maintain the old sacrificial system described in the Old Testament. The Greeks sacrificed to appease their gods as well, yet they had no promise or assurance of salvation from a coming Messiah. In reality, their sacrifices were piteously ineffective, proving the disastrous results of perverting God's system.

The Appearance of Evil

The next similarity is the entrance of evil (sin) into the world. According to the Greeks, the first woman, Pandora, was given a jar that she was not allowed to open. Her curiosity of what might be in the jar proved to be too strong and she opened it, releasing evil into the world. This story is a twisted version of the account of the Fall of Adam and Eve in Genesis chapter three. Eve, the first woman, was tempted by Satan to eat from the one tree that was forbidden by God. Satan tempted Eve by appealing to her curiosity and pride.

The Flood

Another piece of the biblical account taken by Greek mythology is the story of Deucalion and the flood. Just as in the biblical account, a flood is sent by the gods to punish the wickedness of mankind. Again, the Greeks skew the history — only Deucalion and his wife are spared and the flood only lasts for nine days. However, the concept was clearly taken from the true account of Noah and the Flood sent by God as described in the Bible. There are many religions from ancient times that twist the account of the Flood; they are merely distorted versions of the actual event that remains in their cultural memory from Babel.

The Afterlife

The last primary element that seems to have similarities to the Judeo-Christian worldview, is the organization of the underworld. In the Old Testament, the temporary holding place of those who died is set up in a fairly similar way. Recall that Tartarus in Greek mythology was a prison for supernatural beings including the gods. In the Bible, Peter uses the same word to name the holding place for the angels who sinned (2 Peter 2:4). Furthermore, when studying the Old Testament and the Jewish understanding of Sheol, it appears as if the Jews believed in a multi-level place with an area of rest and waiting (Psalm 86:13) but also a lower part of fire and torment (Deuteronomy 32:22). In Psalm 16:10 and 45:15 David indicated that he would not stay in Sheol, but somehow be redeemed.

The Foolishness of Greek Mythology

The inconsistencies and arbitrariness of Greek mythology make it a truly sad religion to follow, especially in light of the similarities to biblical truths. The basic lack of any clarity and definitive teaching make it seem hopeless and unfulfilling. Imagine trying to serve and please the dozens of gods and immortal creatures of the ancient Greeks. All of them were so different — by pleasing one you might upset another. The gods were constantly turning on each other, so how would you know who was currently more powerful and who to side with?

Moreover, there was no authority to rest upon — it seems like any deep thinker or writer could simply use their imagination and expand on the existing myths with details that suited their own purposes. The Greek religion was an ever-changing story that, though fascinating and exciting to read about, seems to leave the follower/believer in a state of confusion and anxiety. There is no security and, like the story of Pandora's jar, no real hope of redemption.

It seems like much of their literature was written to critique, analyze, and make sense of the world around them. Yet the literary works were inconsistent and constantly evolving because their authors lacked the authority and knowledge to correctly explain reality. The angst, bitterness, struggle, and conflict outlined in the epics and poems portrays the state of the human souls living according to this system of flawed paganism, always striving but never finding rest.

As Romans 1:21–23 proclaims:

> Because, although they knew God, they did not glorify Him as God, nor were thankful, but became futile in their thoughts, and their foolish hearts were darkened. Professing to be wise, they became fools, and changed the glory of the incorruptible God into an image made like corruptible man — and birds and four-footed animals and creeping things.

There is no better way to describe the elaborate and confusing tangle of Greek mythology than "futile thinking." They rejected God and were forced to worship a mere distortion based on their own fallible, sinful imagination.

Salvation from the Snare of Greek Paganism

You may wonder why this chapter has found its way into a book on world cults and religions when it is obviously a dead mythology that no one believes anymore. Or so you may think.

Many today worship the god of reason with the proclamation of "I think, therefore I am."
("The Thinker" by Rodin, Wikimedia)

In reality, our culture is not so different from that of the ancient Greeks — and neither are our beliefs. People may not sacrifice to Zeus or Poseidon or erect temples to Athena or Artemis anymore, but we have made gods of the same powers and forces around us. Remember that it was the force or power that defined the Greek gods and goddesses. Those powers and forces still govern our lives today and demand our worship — if we let them.

Who can say that Dionysus, the god of wine, is not alive and well today, worshiped and sacrificed to by millions?

What about Athena, the goddess of reason? Have many not bowed down to her, denying the God of the supernatural and worshiping science, logic, and human intellect?

Aphrodite was the goddess of love, desire, and beauty. Who can deny that humanity still worships sex, is overpowered by lust, and constantly seeks to worship beauty?

What about Ares, the god of war, or Apollo, the god of youth and healing? How many put their hope in these false gods?

It is evident that many people in our culture still worship the same powers that the Greeks revered. In truth, we all struggle with them in some sense.

> For we do not wrestle against flesh and blood, but against principalities, against powers, against the rulers of the darkness of this age, against spiritual hosts of wickedness in the heavenly places (Ephesians 6:12; NKJV).

But there is good news! Unlike the Greek's false religion, there is true hope! Christians know the one true God who conquered all powers and all authorities. He alone is the truth, undistorted and pure. He is not arbitrary or capricious. He remains the same forever, and He loves us! He created us male and female in His own image with a purpose — to glorify, love, and enjoy Him forever. This is only possible by His mercy and grace, shown by the ultimate act of love: sending His Son to die on the Cross in our place. And He has given us assurance of this by sealing us with His Holy Spirit.

This good and gracious God commands us to love Him first and to have no other gods or idols before Him (Exodus 20:3–6). His Son, Jesus Christ, deserves all glory and praise.

Is He the one and only pursuit in your life? Or have you bought into the ways of this world, the ways of the ancient Greeks, the ways of Babel? Heed the Apostle Paul's warnings and flee from idolatry (1 Corinthians 10:14)!

> And we know that the Son of God has come and has given us an understanding, that we may know Him who is true; and we are in Him who is true, in His Son Jesus Christ. This is the true God and eternal life. Little children, keep yourselves from idols. Amen (1 John 5:20–21).

Summary of Greek Mythological Beliefs

Doctrine	Teachings of Greek Mythology
God	Deny the God of the Bible. Hold to a pantheon of gods beginning with the primordial gods and proceeding to many lesser gods including the Titans, Olympians, and others. The various gods personify different aspects of the universe.
Authority/ Revelation	Oral traditions that were eventually recorded in various epics and poems that changed over time
Man	Men were created by the gods from clay as morally good beings that were influenced to evil and corruption through the influence of evil spirits and gods. Women were created later.
Sin	Sin is poorly defined and often associated with offending various gods.
Salvation	The pursuit of a moral life and achieving greatness through pleasing the gods could earn one a spot in various levels of the afterlife. A few were able to achieve godhood through extreme valor and pleasing the gods.
Creation	The primordial god Chaos gave rise to the physical creation and other aspects of the universe. Gaia is the goddess that represents the earth, with other equal and lesser gods creating the various aspects of reality.

Chapter 17

Stoicism (with Notes on Epicureanism)

Dr. Greg Hall with Troy Lacey

Beware lest anyone cheat you through philosophy and empty deceit, according to the tradition of men, according to the basic principles of the world, and not according to Christ (Colossians 2:8).[1]

I (Dr. Hall) work where ideas are highly valued. Higher education is a marketplace of ideas. Ideas operating in this marketplace have changed the world. The great advances in technology, scientific discovery, or medicine that have come from institutions of higher education have blessed the human race in unimaginable ways. God has blessed mankind, and we see an important aspect of the Imago Dei (being created in God's image) when we consider the great power and results of human reason applied to solving problems we face.

But I have found when it comes to engaging the deepest and most profound issues of human existence and purpose such as why we are here, how we got here, where we are all going, why the world is in such a mess and the potential solution, that not all ideas are equally valid. It is not that mankind has not thought about these questions or postulated answers. It is, however, that when their answers are not based upon Scripture they become futile

---

1. Scripture in this chapter is from the New King James Version (NKJV) of the Bible.

speculation that darkens the mind, and the result is a captivity of the mind that ends in deceit. It is the mind full of the ideas of men instead of the mind devoted to Christ.

The Bible is a book devoted to presenting the truth of the Creator, God. God is the source of this book and it's tantamount to reading the "Owners Manual." It teaches us the truth about origins, about purpose in life while living in this world, and about the coming consummation of all things. The Bible gives answers to the questions our Creator knew would perplex the human mind. God created mankind with an insatiable appetite for understanding. We have a deep-seated need to contemplate the profound questions of life. Our problem is that we are looking for comprehension, understanding, and knowledge in all the wrong places. I say again, not all ideas are equally valid.

Paul and the Stoics

In chapter 17 of the Book of Acts, the apologist and Apostle Paul was sent to confront the prevailing philosophers of the day with the truth of God's Word. He knew God's Word alone gives understanding to the inquiring mind. God's Word is what Francis Schaeffer called, "true truth." It is here in Acts 17 at the Areopagus that Paul faced off with the Stoic and Epicurean philosophers, giving us not just an understanding of the humanistic philosophical mind, but the exact way to confront it and offer the truth of God as the remedy for false ideology. This is the great legacy of Acts 17.

The Areopagus was located in Athens, Greece, and it seems to have looked a lot like the universities of our culture. The "intelligentsia" of the day spent their time doing nothing more than hearing and promoting the latest "ideas." The Areopagus has traditionally been understood to be a place near the Acropolis, but it may actually be a reference to an advisory council in Athens that dealt with ethical, cultural, and religious matters, and the supervision of education.[2]

Paul was apparently quite familiar with both the Stoics and the Epicureans, and this assisted him in framing his conversation with them. When you consider Paul's message in Acts 17, how he formulated his argument, and what he wanted these philosophers to know about truth, it becomes apparent he was quite well versed in Greek philosophy. In fact, as we shall

---

2. Robert L. Thomas, *New American Standard Updated Edition Exhaustive Concordance of the Bible* (La Habra, CA: The Lockman Foundation, 1994) p. 4770.

see later, Paul utilized the same divide and conquer strategy between the Stoics and Epicureans as he had when getting the Pharisees to side with him over the Sadducees (Acts 23:6–9).

Founding Beliefs

According to John Drane in *Introducing the New Testament,* Stoicism was based on philosophical speculation about the nature of the world and its people. The philosophy was founded by Zeno in Greece during third century B.C. and developed by later thinkers including Marcus Aurelius, Seneca, and Epictetus. At its heart, matter was considered the ultimate reality. To the Stoic, God was an abstract of human thinking sometimes referred to as Fate. But God is also the source of humanity's soul through the primordial essence of fire (logos), which was given to the primordial couple and passed on to their offspring through procreation. The Stoic's god was ill-defined, generally based in pantheism with God as the Creator and essence of everything in the universe.

Morality was determined by human reasoning and generally consisted of avoiding passions and aligning one's actions with the natural course of things. Wisdom, justice, temperance, and courage were the four principle virtues viewed as honorable. For Stoics, "salvation" was found in self-sufficiency and alignment with the cause and course of the cosmos. They sought self-mastery over themselves so as to be "one with nature." Stoics had no future hope or expectation of rewards or judgment beyond the grave.[3] It is a philosophy of hopelessness. Based in the pure arbitrary opinions of each individual, there is no ultimate source of truth or determining what is right or wrong. We can see these same ideas present in various forms of Humanism today.

Shared Beliefs

Paul also recognized a few commonalities and used them as a wedge to gain a foothold for the gospel, and to openly denigrate the Epicurean position. For example, Stoics did believe in some form of divine creation, which the Epicureans denied. The Stoics also believed that there was something beyond the strictly material. The Stoics also believed that animals and mankind were not just created, but that this creation involved a purpose and design in

---

3. "Stoicism," Internet Encyclopedia of Philosophy, http://www.iep.utm.edu/stoicism.

body parts and functions.[4] The Epicureans were truly the complete evolutionists, believing that everything came about through random chance and was purposeless, but only mimicked design because of the massive amounts of variation in nature.[5]

In fact, early in Paul's gospel defense on Mars Hill, he quickly uses the creative works of God to gain a foothold with the Stoics in the crowd. "God, who made the world and everything in it, since He is Lord of heaven and earth . . ." (Acts 17:24). The Stoics would have immediately thought to themselves that this foreigner aligned more with their philosophy than with the Epicureans. Paul further gains the attention of the Stoics toward the end of his speech with his declaration of man's moral responsibilities toward God and also the partial quotation from two Greek poets (Acts 17:27–30). The poets Paul quotes are Aratus and Cleanthes; the first was revered among the Stoics, and the second was the Stoic "patriarch" who studied under Stoicism's founder, Zeno.

However, Paul was also aware of the many differences between Stoicism and Christianity. His closing words were intended to show that both Stoics and Epicureans needed to turn from their sin and embrace the risen Savior, Jesus Christ. His rather pointed phrasing about living in ignorance and needing to repent in order to avoid judgment (Acts 17:30–31) would have been regarded as shocking or offensive to many in the audience. Paul would have known that the more learned Stoics thought that they were self-sufficient and morally righteous, and the Cross of Christ would have indeed been regarded as "foolishness" to them. Dr. David Naugle in his paper "Stoic and Christian Conceptions of Happiness" attributes this predisposition to intellectual elitism on the part of Stoic sages:

> Stoicism aggrandizes the individual who through practice and self-discipline is able to make the whole life harmonious by bestowing upon him the title of "Sage." The Stoic sage is completely self-sufficient and happy because of his virtue. For the "virtuoso," the conduct of life presents no problem. His life consists in a regular and effortless flow in harmony with human rational and ultimate metaphysical nature all of which constitutes

---

4. David Sedley, *Creationism and Its Critics in Antiquity* (Oakland, CA: University of California Press, 2009), p. 206–208, 214–216.

5. Ibid., p. 150–155.

genuine virtue. The Stoic sage has advanced to a point where a life of courage and wisdom, justice and temperance comes easily and naturally, without struggle and without repining.[6]

So, how amazing it is that as Paul confronted the vain, deceitful philosophy of the Stoics he first began his presentation of the truth by proclaiming the God who is Creator of everything that exists, something the Stoics would have mentally assented to, at least in principle. It is Paul employing the use of creation evangelism.[7] Paul did what we should do — any apologetic approach to philosophers of any pagan ideology must begin with establishing the truth on origins. Paul begins by getting the attention of the philosophers.

> Then Paul stood in the midst of the Areopagus and said, "Men of Athens, I perceive that in all things you are very religious; for as I was passing through and considering the objects of your worship, I even found an altar with this inscription: TO THE UNKNOWN GOD. Therefore, the One whom you worship without knowing, Him I proclaim to you" (Acts 17:22–23).

Once he has captured their attention, he launches his defense of Scripture and the God of the Bible with these inspired words:

> God, who made the world and everything in it, since He is Lord of heaven and earth, does not dwell in temples made with hands. Nor is He worshiped with men's hands, as though He needed anything, since He gives to all life, breath, and all things (Acts 17:24–25).

To clearly proclaim the truth of God beginning with the claims of Genesis 1:1 is the way to contend with any pagan philosophy. The late Francis Schaeffer said if he had an hour to talk to someone about the gospel, he would spend the first 55 minutes establishing the truth of creation and the last 5 minutes explaining the gospel of Christ. The reason is, he knew what the Apostle Paul knew — you cannot understand the gospel and our need for a Savior without first establishing faith in the true account of the God

---

6. http://www3.dbu.edu/naugle/pdf/stoic_christian_views.pdf, extended quote taken from p. 15.

7. For more on creation evangelism please see Ken Ham, *Why Won't They Listen?* (Green Forest, AR: Master Books, 2002).

who created *ex nihilo* (out of nothing) and to whom we will give an account of our lives.

A Modern Echo

The late Dr. Henry Morris, a scientist and well-known refuter of evolutionary philosophies, in his book *The Genesis Record*, put it like this:

> It is quite impossible, therefore, for one to reject the historicity and divine authority of the Book of Genesis without undermining, and in effect, repudiating, the authority of the entire Bible. If the first Adam is only an allegory, then by all logic, so is the second Adam. If man did not really fall into sin from his state of created innocency, there is no reason for him to need a Savior. If all things can be accounted for by natural processes of evolution, there is no reason to look forward to a future supernatural consummation of all things. If Genesis is not true, then neither is the testimonies of those prophets and apostles who believed it was true. Jesus Christ Himself becomes a false witness, either a deceiver or one who was deceived, and His testimony concerning His own omniscience and omnipotence becomes blasphemy. Faith in the gospel of Christ for one's eternal salvation is an empty mockery.[8]

All worldly philosophies have the same goal: produce ideas that will give mankind so-called "answers" to the great metaphysical questions of all time. Where did we come from? What is our purpose? Where are we going? Is there any meaning to life? Is there life beyond the grave? But the worldly philosophies do not generally allow for God to enter the equation, and if the concept of God is allowed in the conversation, it is an anemic, powerless deity, the exact opposite of the God of Scripture. It is an "unknown god" as Paul described in Acts 17:23.

Again, quoting from Dr. Henry Morris:

> Actually all such false philosophies are merely different ways of expressing the same unbelief. Each one proposes that there is no personal, transcendent God; that ultimate reality is to be found in the eternal cosmos itself; and that the development

---

8. Henry M. Morris, *The Genesis Record* (Grand Rapids, MI: Baker Book House, 1976), p. 22.

of the universe into its present form is contingent solely on the innate properties of its own components. In essence, each of the above philosophies embraces all the others. Dualism, for example, is a summary form of polytheism, which is the popular expression of pantheism, which presupposes materialism, which functions in terms of evolutionism, which finds its consummation in humanism which culminates in atheism.

The entire system could well be called the system of atheistic evolutionary humanism. Other philosophical ideas could also be incorporated into the same monstrous structure: naturalism, uniformitarianism, deism, agnosticism, monism, determinism, pragmatism, and others. All are arrayed in opposition to the great truth — marvelously simple, and understandable to a child, yet inexhaustibly profound — that "in the beginning, God created the heaven and the earth."

It is remarkable that, when there have been so many antitheistic philosophies (ancient and modern) affecting untold millions of people, the book of God makes no attempt to prove that God exists. The opening verse of Genesis simply takes this fact for granted, as though it were so obvious that only a fool could say "there is no God" (Psalm 14:1).[9]

So Paul, under the direction of the Holy Spirit, confronts the pagan ideology and worldly philosophy of the Stoics with a clear and simple, yet profound, proclamation of the Creator, God. He reminds them of "the God who made the world, and everything in it." He knew that the philosophy promoted by these ancient philosophers and their forebears all end in the same direction: the supposed explanation of the origin of life without reference to the Creator God of the Bible. While the Stoics believed in a creator and rejected random chance as the originator of the universe, they had in mind a notion of a vague and impersonal intelligent designer.

The Role of Chance

By contrast, the Epicureans totally embraced "chance" as the agent responsible for all matter. This is the very fabric of the philosophical naturalism being presented to a generation of students today, and naturalism is not

---

9. Ibid., p. 38.

based on scientific inquiry — it qualifies only as a false religion. You must have great faith in fallible man's ideas about the origin and nature of the world and universe around us to buy into naturalism. Naturalism is religion, and evolution is its dogma.

Students who have been told evolution is scientific fact may find it hard to comprehend that it is more a philosophical position than a scientific one. Even evolutionary scientists will admit evolution is a fundamental tenet of the ideology of humanism, a secular religion — a full-fledged alternative to Christianity. This was true of evolution in the beginning, and it is true of it still today.[10]

This is why Dr. Henry Morris says that today's secular scientist must believe in evolution in spite of all the evidence, not because of it. And speaking of deception, note the following remarkable statement that Dr. Morris comments on:

> We take the side of science in spite of the patent absurdity of some of its construct. . . . in spite of the tolerance of the scientific community for unsubstantiated commitment to materialism. . . . we are forced by our a priori adherence to material causes to create an apparatus of investigation and set of concepts that produce material explanations, no matter how counterintuitive, no matter how mystifying to the uninitiated. Moreover, that materialism is absolute, for we cannot allow a Divine Foot in the door.[11]

[Morris] The author of this frank statement is Richard Lewontin of Harvard. Since evolution is not a laboratory science, there is no way to test its validity, so all sorts of just so stories are contrived to adorn the textbooks. But that doesn't make them true! An evolutionist reviewing a recent book by another (but more critical) evolutionist, says:

> We cannot identify ancestors or "missing links," and we cannot devise testable theories to explain how particular episodes of evolution came about. Gee is

---

10. Michael Ruse, "Saving Darwinsim from the Darwinians," *National Post* (May 13, 2000), p. B3.
11. Richard Lewontin, review of *The Demon-Haunted World*, by Carl Sagan, New York Review of Books, January 9, 1997.

adamant that all the popular stories about how the first amphibians conquered the dry land, how the birds developed wings and feathers for flying, how the dinosaurs went extinct, and how humans evolved from apes are just products of our imagination, driven by prejudices and preconceptions.[12]

[Morris] A fascinatingly honest admission by a physicist indicates the passionate commitment of establishment scientists to naturalism. Speaking of the trust students naturally place in their highly educated college professors, he says:

> And I use that trust to effectively brainwash them. . . . Our teaching methods are primarily those of propaganda. We appeal — without demonstration — to evidence that supports our position. We only introduce arguments and evidence that supports the currently accepted theories and omit or gloss over any evidence to the contrary.[13]

[Morris] Creationist students in scientific courses taught by evolutionist professors can testify to the frustrating reality of that statement. Evolution is, indeed, the pseudoscientific basis of religious atheism, as Ruse pointed out. Will Provine at Cornell University is another scientist who frankly acknowledges this.

> As the creationists claim, belief in modern evolution makes atheists of people. One can have a religious view that is compatible with evolution only if the religious view is indistinguishable from atheism.[14]

[Morris] Once again, we emphasize that evolution is not science, evolutionists' tirades notwithstanding. It is a philosophical worldview, nothing more.[15]

12. Peter J. Bowler, review of *In Search of Deep Time* by Henry Gee (New York: Free Press, 1999), *American Scientist*, vol. 88, March/April 2000, p. 169
13. Mark Singham, "Teaching and Propaganda," *Physics Today*, vol. 53, June 2000, p. 54.
14. Will Provine, "No Free Will," in *Catching Up With the Vision*, ed. By Margaret W. Rossiter (Chicago, IL: University of Chicago Press, 1999), p. S123.
15 Henry M. Morris, The Scientific Case Against Evolution, www.icr.org/resources.

Together, the humanistic philosophy and the evolutionary science, so far, seem to have won the day in the classroom, having declared evolutionary storytelling to be true, in spite of the growing evidence against it. The reason the interaction of the Apostle Paul with the Stoic philosophers in Acts 17 at the Areopagus is so significant in our times is it shows how philosophy and ideology drive the marketplace of ideas and how worldly philosophy mitigates against the Word of God. In a very real sense the issue of our day, the origins debate, is ultimately driven by the philosophers masquerading as scientists.

Answers in Genesis has shown for a long time, and in highly academic fashion, that the science behind evolutionary claims is very suspect to say the least and, in reality, based on falsehood. Many world-class scientists believe today that the evolutionary model is massively implausible, if not entirely false. So how does it persist? The answer can be seen in this Acts 17 passage, and it is why understanding the prevailing philosophies of the day is so important. We need to understand the Stoics and every philosophical system since and argue against them just like Paul did at Mars Hill (Areopagus).

In the origins debate today, philosophy rules, not science. This may surprise you. Naturalism is the religion of the age, and evolution is its dogma. It is the philosophy of naturalism most at stake in the battle, not the science that is used to promote evolution or creationism. The science of creationism clearly wins the day. Evolution persists because naturalism demands it persist! Naturalism demands the origin of everything must be explained without reference to a Creator.

And so, under the anointing of the Holy Spirit, the Apostle begins his apologetic masterpiece in Acts 17:22–23.

> Then Paul stood in the midst of the Areopagus and said, "Men of Athens, I perceive that in all things you are very religious; for as I was passing through and considering the objects of your worship, I even found an altar with this inscription: TO THE UNKNOWN GOD. Therefore, the One whom you worship without knowing, Him I proclaim to you.

This is where evangelism should begin today and why apologetics is such an important discipline: we begin with the Creator and His creation. This fact must be presented in all its clarity and power before the gospel will ever be understood. It should be obvious that the foundation of the gospel must be present so that he gospel will make sense. The gospel is only understood in terms of God being both Creator and Redeemer.

> In the beginning, God created the heavens and the earth (Genesis 1:1).

It was the starting point in ministry to the Stoics at Mars Hill and to every philosopher since. It is so crucial to see the apologetic argument unfold as Paul confronts the pagan philosophy of the Stoics and Epicureans because it is the divinely inspired thought that still reaches the pagan philosophies and philosophers of our day. They may no longer be called Stoics, but their "offspring" has as its purpose to replace the truth of the Creator and His creation with the false explanation of moral self-sufficiency, naturalism, or any number of other vain philosophies.

Paul teaches them of "the God who made the world and everything in it" (Acts 17:24).

He made from one man (Adam) every nation of mankind to live on all the face of the earth (yes, Adam and Eve *are* the sole progenitors of the human race). He further determined periods and boundaries, with the intent of mankind seeking God (verse 27). God is close to us, Paul teaches, "In Him we live and move and have our being" (verse 28). Paul quotes one of the Stoic poets, Aratus, from his poem, "Phainomena," when he says, " 'For we are also His offspring.' Therefore, since we are the offspring of God, we ought not to think that the Divine Nature is like gold or silver or stone, something shaped by art and man's devising. Truly, these times of ignorance God overlooked, but now commands all men everywhere to repent, because He has appointed a day on which He will judge the world in righteousness by the Man whom He has ordained. He has given assurance of this to all by raising Him from the dead" (verses 28–31).

So there it is — the perfect, God-given argument for pagan philosophy of any kind. God is Creator, ruler, judge, and redeemer. This is an argument with no further debate. It is settled by the God with sovereign power to create everything out of nothing (*ex nihilo*) by His spoken Word, alone!

The Response to Paul

The result of this apologetic presentation is what can be expected in our evil, sinful, and broken world: "And when they heard of the resurrection of the dead, some mocked, while others said, 'We will hear you again on this matter.' So Paul departed from among them. However, some men joined him and believed . . ." (verses 32–34).

To the Stoics who professed to shun creature comforts in favor of what they termed virtuous acts (but was really self-righteousness), the only "good" they could conceive of was devotion to Stoic principles. So when confronted with Christ's death, burial, and Resurrection for their sins, they were confounded.

For example, Christians think of Christ's sacrifice in terms of John 15:13 — "Greater love has no one than this, than to lay down one's life for his friends." This was antithetical to Stoic thinking, as Charles Taylor notes that "the Stoic sage is willing to give up some 'preferred' thing, e.g., health, freedom, or life, because he sees it genuinely as without value since only the whole order of events which, as it happens, includes its negation or loss, is of value. . . . The [John 15:13] sentence would lose its point in reference to someone who renounced life from a sense of detachment; it presupposes he is giving up something."[16] Therefore, the Stoics couldn't reconcile Christ's death as meaningful to them.

Personally, I find that students coming to the university from state schools have obviously been fully inculcated with the beliefs of evolution as a worldview. I have also found there is great confusion about the very term "evolution," especially in its biological sense. Many students do not understand the meaning of evolution in the scientific sense, and especially in its implication in the areas of cosmology, geology, and biology. Some students believe evolution simply means "change." Creationists believe in change, and by this simplistic definition could be called evolutionists! So clearly this simplistic view is unacceptable.

Some believe the term *evolution* is equivalent to the concept of "natural selection," or "survival of the fittest," but they have merely confused evolution with these ideas that are part of the supposed evolutionary process. I find many students surprised that evolution in the naturalistic scientific community ultimately means that at a time in the primeval past, inanimate (nonliving) material through the mechanism of random chance and natural laws become animate (living) matter (chemical evolution). This

---

16. David Naugle, "Stoic and Christian Conceptions of Hapiness," http://www3.dbu.edu/naugle/pdf/stoic_christian_views.pdf, extended quote taken from p. 29.

living matter somehow obtained the ability to reproduce itself through the passing of information (whether RNA or DNA), and a single cell became the common ancestor of all living things (biological evolution). This unobservable and unrepeatable belief requires great faith to believe — it is far from the scientific method and actually a dogma of the philosophy of naturalism.

Many students also attribute the concept of evolution to Charles Darwin's writings in *On the Origin of Species*. They are sometimes surprised to learn evolutionary ideas, as a proposed alternative to biblical creationism, precedes Darwin by many generations — including the Epicureans that Paul also confronted in Acts 17.

This is why the presentation of Paul at the Areopagus is so significant. The concept of evolution as a proposed explanation of origins goes back into antiquity, even prior to the Stoic and Epicurean philosophers addressed by the Apostle. True philosophy is always Christ-centered (Colossians 2:8–10). Vain or worldly philosophy is always an attempt to explain origins, or any other of the profound issues of life, without reference or commitment to God — particularly the God of Genesis, the God of Scripture.

The Stoics and Epicureans of Acts 17 represent a long line of philosophers before them, and a longer line since, who offer humankind an alternative to biblical creation and instead try to explain origins in terms of impersonal design or "chance" evolution. In truth, of the science behind evolution and the philosophy behind the science, neither one are compatible with the biblical truth.

For a full treatment of the history of the idea of evolution, see Dr. Henry Morris' book *The Long War Against God*. Of special note is the chapter entitled "The Conflict of the Ages." You will see that evolution is an idea as old as man himself. It certainly did not originate with Charles Darwin. Dr. Morris writes:

> All these ancient atheistic philosophers, as well as the ancient pantheistic philosophers (Pythagoras, Plato, Aristotle, etc.) were highly intelligent men and made many great contributions to science, mathematics and general learning. Nevertheless, all rejected the true God of creation and promoted one or another evolutionist system of cosmogony and primeval life history. The evolutionary philosophy that completely dominates the modern

Western world has now been traced back all the way to ancient Greek philosophy, beginning about 2,500 years ago.[17]

I think, too, that beyond the ancient Greek or pre-Socratic philosophers, evolutionary concepts can be traced back to early descendants of Noah listed in Genesis 10 and 11. That argument, however, is beyond the scope of this chapter. The point again is clear — evolution is a very ancient idea possibly going back to early people after the Flood.

At this, it is crucial students see the point. Evolution, to quote one author, "is a theory in crisis."[18] It is based on extrapolation of certain changes and taught as a "fact" of science to unsuspecting multitudes of students. Though scientific evidence is used to support the evolutionary interpretation of our origins, this view is at the very least "massively implausible." It persists among those who adhere to the philosophy of naturalism because of a prior commitment to the philosophy and with a clear goal — to get God out of the picture.

This is why today the creation/evolution debate is predominantly a philosophical debate, not a scientific one. This is a point worthy of repeating.

To make this abundantly clear, consider this quote from the book, *Total Truth*:

> A few more examples drive the point home. During the Ohio controversy, one of the drafters of the controversial state guidelines wrote a letter to *Physics Today*, insisting that, in order to be considered at all, "the first criterion is that any scientific theory *must be naturalistic*."[19] In other words, unless a theory is naturalistic, it will be ruled out before any consideration of its merits. The editor in chief of *Scientific American* then entered the fray, stating that "a central tenet of modern science is methodological

---

17. Henry Morris, *The Long War Against God* (Green Forest, AR: New Leaf Publishing, 2000), p. 218.

18. Michael Denton even titled his book *Evolution: A Theory in Crisis* in 1985 as a result of his research on evolution.

19. Mano Singham, a physicist at Case Western Reserve University, writing in *Physics Today*, June 2002, emphasis added. To buttress his argument, he quoted paleontologist George Gaylord Simpson, who wrote, "The progress of knowledge rigidly requires that no non-physical postulate ever be admitted in connection with the study of physical phenomena . . . the researcher who is seeking explanations must seek physical explanations only" in *Tempo and Mode in Evolution* (New York: Columbia University Press, 1944), p. 76.

naturalism — it seeks to explain the universe purely in terms of observed or testable natural mechanisms."[20] But who says we have to accept naturalism as a "central tenet" of science? As one professor I know retorted, "Who made up that rule? I don't remember voting on it."

In other words, why should we acquiesce in letting philosophical naturalists prescribe the definition of science itself? The only reason for restricting science to methodological naturalism is if we assume from the outset that philosophical naturalism is true — that nature is a closed system of cause and effect. But if it is not true, then restricting science to naturalistic theories is not a good strategy for getting at the truth.[21]

Today, a naturalistic definition of science is taught as unquestioned dogma throughout the public [state-run] education system, even to young students who lack the background to challenge it. Read this quotation from a typical high school textbook: "Many people believe that a supernatural force or deity created life. That explanation is not within the scope of science."[22] Notice that the book does not say creation has been proven false or discredited by facts, but only that it falls outside a certain definition of science. It has been ruled out by definition.

Another high school textbook says, "By attributing the diversity of life to natural causes rather than to supernatural creation, Darwin gave biology a sound scientific basis."[23] Note how the text equates "sound" science with philosophical naturalism.

Clearly, philosophy has gained primacy over the facts.[24]

---

20. John Rennie, "15 Answers to Creationist Nonsense," *Scientific American*, June 17, 2002.
21. See Del Ratzsch, *The Battle of Beginnings: Why Neither Side Is Winning the Creation-Evolution Debate* (Downers Grove, IL: InterVarsity Press, 1996), p. 167. For a more recent and more academic, discussion of philosophical issues, see Del Ratzsch, *Nature, Design, and Science: The Status of Design in Natural Science* (New York: SUNY Press, 2001).
22. *BSCS Biology: A Molecular Approach*, 8th ed., Jon Greenberg, revision editor (Everyday Learning Corporation, 2001), p. 446.
23. Neil A. Campbell, Jane B. Reece, and Lawrence G. Mitchell, *Biology*, 5th ed. (Reading, MA: Addison Wesley, 1999), p. 426. A helpful analysis of textbooks can be found in Norris Anderson's "Education or Indoctrination 2001," at http://www.alabamaeagle.org/education_or_indoctrination_2001.htm.
24. Nancy Pearcey, *Total Truth* (Wheaton, IL: Crossway Books, 2005) p. 169.

Responding in a Modern Marketplace of Ideas

In this current environment, students are asked to discriminate among the various ideas of the marketplace, distinguishing between truth and falsehood. It is possible for us, with careful study, using the minds with which we were created and especially under the instruction of the Holy Spirit, to determine what is true. In fact, Scripture promises the Holy Spirit will "guide [us] into all truth" (John 16:13).

But we must see, it is all about the "starting point," and what we believe is foundational to our epistemological approach. Epistemology is the study of knowledge, the study of how we know what we say we know.

Consider this: in the creation/evolution debate, all scientists are looking at the same information and data — everyone has the same evidence. How is it that they reach such different conclusions? The answer is in the philosophy that undergirds their investigation. As we have seen, if that philosophy is naturalism you will reach naturalistic conclusions and exclude any supernatural explanations. If that foundation is the Word of God you will view all the data through that lens. We need to be honest and acknowledge that our starting points will influence our conclusions.

Paul knew the debate of origins or any other concept of significance was going to have a "starting point" issue for the philosophers at the Areopagus. So he stood firmly upon the Word of God. And if you are a believer you should too. There is absolutely no reason to deviate from the message of Scripture. It is God's revelation to us. And I, for one, will stand on God's revelation any day rather than the ideas of human philosophy.

I have heard scientists say, "Well, science has proven the Bible is false." That is manifestly not true. Scientists have not proven anything about Scripture untrue, nor could they, since God's Word is always true. I've heard others say, "Well, the Bible is not a textbook on science." That may be true, but as the Word of God, it has given us the truth on every subject it speaks of, including scientific topics. But I would go further — because the Bible is true, science is possible. The truths about God and nature in the Bible provide the necessary framework for observable and repeatable science to be possible.[25] This foundational element was missing from the philosophy of the Stoics and Epicureans, and it is missing from the naturalists of the modern era.

---

25. Jason Lisle, *The Ultimate Proof of Creation* (Green Forest, AR: Master Books, 2009).

The issue at stake in the creation/evolution debate and in the interaction with Paul and the Stoics is this: to whom will you look as the source of truth, God or man? The matter of truth seeking must be of paramount importance to the source of truth, God himself. In Romans 1:18 we read:

> For the wrath of God is revealed from heaven against all ungodliness and unrighteousness of men, who suppress the truth in unrighteousness.

To suppress truth is obviously egregious to God. To pursue truth, the student finds a clear plain path in the Word of God. The very character and nature of His invisible attributes, His eternal power, and divine nature are clearly perceived, *since the creation of the world,* in the things that have been made. We are without excuse if we suppress the truth that is evident in nature and even more clearly expressed in the Bible. God's Word is clear and understandable, though admittedly deep and mysterious in areas. But He has made the main thing the plain thing (Romans 1:18–20).

We can know Him, honor Him, and turn from futile thinking, like the hopeless ideas of the Stoics, on these eternal matters. Our foolish hearts need no longer be darkened.

Summary of Stoic Beliefs

Doctrine	Teachings of Stoicism
God	Deny the Creator God of the Bible, but have a vague deistic view of a god as Nature or Fate. As the entire universe is considered all that exists and expresses itself in living things, Stoicism can be seen as a form of pantheism.
Authority/Revelation	Through reasoning in accord with Nature, man can determine what is true and virtuous apart from any direct revelation from Fate. Deny religious writings as authoritative, but recognize they may contain truths in accord with Fate.
Man	The souls of men and animals are emanations of the active Fate (Logos) of the universe. The goal of man is to avoid suffering by living in accord with Reason and Nature.
Sin	Sin is equivalent to acting contrary to nature and reason (vice), bringing misfortune and unhappiness on an individual. Wisdom, justice, temperance, and courage are the four principle virtues. If these are present in the soul, the soul is good.

Salvation	The soul may return to its union with the universal Fate, as it is not a distinct entity. There is no concept of punishment or rewards in an afterlife.
Creation	The universe is eternal and composed of passive matter generated by active Fate. The Fate (a fiery ether) directs the passive matter as it wills.

Chapter 18

Shinto

Michiko Mizumura

An article in *Asahi Shinbun* in December 2014 reveals this intriguing news: "A Tokyo project will avoid building over 'cursed' grave associated with samurai's head." The large 1.43-billion-dollar project involves construction of two skyscrapers which house offices, a hotel, and multipurpose concert halls in central Tokyo. Yet they avoid removing the small grave of a 10th century samurai because they fear a curse. We live in the 21st century, and this antiquated, superstitious thinking may cause many of us to wonder! But many Japanese still feel uneasy about upsetting spirits of the dead that had become gods. This reflects the Shinto way of thinking.

Another modern news topic concerns Japanese politicians making visits to Yasukuni shrine, which was built to commemorate the war dead. Because the shrine is Shinto, the war dead (even war criminals) become gods, and about 2,460,000 gods are enshrined there. Many cabinet members, including the prime minister, visit Yasukuni to pay their respects to the spirits of the dead as gods. This has led to a controversial issue in foreign diplomacy — most likely concern over enshrining war criminals and violating the principle of separation of church and state. Yet most Japanese are lenient about it because of Shinto culture.

The Japanese people of today are still deeply affected by Shinto, both in their culture and thinking. This is one of the reasons it's difficult for them to accept monotheistic religions such as Christianity. Looking closely at Shinto can give us a better understanding of the underlying fundamental beliefs that shape the thinking of the Japanese people. In this chapter we'll examine what Shinto is.

What Is Shinto? Brief Overview

Shinto is an indigenous religion originating with the Japanese. It is only practiced within Japanese communities, and it provides the backbone of Japanese culture and national identity.

The annual statistics of the religious population, taken by the Japanese Agency for Cultural Affairs in 2011, show that there are over 100 million Japanese people adhering to Shinto (51.2%), 85 million to Buddhism (43.0%), 1.9 million to Christianity (1.0%), and 9.5 million in other religions (4.8%).

It is important to note that the total number of the religious population exceeds the actual population of Japan, which is about 130 million. Some people identify with multiple groups, and the history of Japanese religions is responsible for this phenomenon. This will be further explained later.

Shinto Definition of "God"

Shinto is written in two Kanji (Chinese characters), 神道, namely, 神 which is "god(s)" and 道 which is "way." So it can literally mean "god's way" or "gods' way" (in Japanese, there are no explicit singular or plural forms, so it is determined by context).

In Shinto, a god is not like the God of the Bible who is the omnipotent Creator of the world. Shinto gods are basically spirits that are everywhere in nature and also in men — hence the assumption of many gods. Exactly how many? One may wonder. The phrase *Yaoyorozu* (meaning 8,000,000) is used to express the innumerable gods in Japan.

Shinto originally began as a form of animism. The early Japanese feared the natural forces and believed those forces came from the power of the spirits living in various natural entities, such as forests, rocks, oceans, etc. The habitats of the spirits, considered sacred, were called *Yorishiro*, but Yorishiro themselves were not the subjects of worship. In Shinto, therefore, the subjects of worship are not creatures or visible idols but spirits that are believed to have supernatural power. Both benevolent and malevolent spirits are called *kami* in singular or *kami gami* in plural, meaning "gods."

As Shinto developed, not only spirits living in nature but also ancestors' spirits were enshrined as gods. After death, ancestors' spirits were believed to become guardian gods, watching over and protecting their living descendants. Furthermore, some distinguished persons became enshrined for various reasons. Michizane Sugawara, a famous scholar and aristocrat of the ninth century who is now viewed as a god of academics, was originally thought to have become an *onryo*, a cursing spirit, because he was falsely charged with treason and died a regrettable death. Tenman Shrine was originally built to placate his spirit to avoid his *tatari* (curse). Another famous enshrined person is Ieyasu Tokugawa, the primary shogun who established the Tokugawa administration. He was enshrined in Nikko Toshogu Shrine to authenticate and authorize the supremacy of the Tokugawa family to rule over the nation during the Edo period.

Shinto Beliefs

Shinto does not have scriptures such as the Torah of Judaism or the Bible of Christianity. Instead, its adherents rely on the folklore and ancient histories that are kept in *Kojiki* (meaning "old matters") and *Nihon Shoki* (Japan chronicles), which give some background accounts to Shinto beliefs. In those books are written the accounts of how the gods created various physical entities including the islands of Japan. They also explain how gods and men once lived, even marrying each other. Those gods are now viewed as guardian angels, thus they are respected. *Kojiki* and *Nihon Shoki* also record that Japan's emperors are the direct descendants of the famous Amaterasu, the goddess of the sun — with special care being taken to explain how emperors are fully sanctioned to rule over Japan. This leads to worshiping the emperor as a living god — seen recently in the days of World War II.

Because Shinto gods are related to the nation's folklore and legends, some people view Shinto merely as tradition and culture — not as a religion. Shinto deals mostly with this life, and issues such as personal salvation or life after death are not discussed.

Shinto Practices

There are over 80,000 Shinto shrines in Japan. Some distinguished shrines, such as Yasukuni, Ise Jingu, and Izumo Taisha gather many visitors from all over Japan, but most shrines are visited locally, as they enshrine gods of the area or *Uji-gami* (guardian gods of clans living in the area).

Shinto does not require one to affiliate with it by denying other religions, so it welcomes anyone who visits Shinto shrines to pay respects to gods whenever the individual wishes. This explains why many Japanese can identify with Shinto and other religions at the same time. When visiting shrines, the following is the common protocol:

1. Bow at the *Tori-i* gate before entering the shrine precinct.

2. Wash hands and mouth (there is usually a water fountain at the entrance of the shrine precinct).

3. Move forward to *Haiden*, the hall of worship building, located in front of *Honden*, the main sanctuary building where gods reside.

4. Make offerings at the offertory box.

5. Ring the large bell by pulling the attached rope to call the gods' attention.

6. Make a specific worshiping action, such as "bow twice, handclap twice, and bow once." Usually prayers are made after the handclapping.

Quintessentially, the Japanese people visit shrines on New Year's Day to pray for safety, good health, and prosperity in the coming year. This tradition is called *Hatsumoude* (meaning the first visit of the year). People also visit shrines for traditional festivals or seasonal events, as each shrine holds annual *Matsuri* (meaning festival or ritual ceremony).

At different life stages, typical Japanese follow specific Shinto traditions. When a baby is born and reaches the age of one month, parents usually take the infant to a local shrine to give thanks and pray for good health for their little

Main Gate at Ise Grand Shrine in Ise, Mie, Japan
(Kanchi1979, Creative Commons)

one. The same is done for children turning three, five, and seven years old. When students take entrance exams for schools, they go to the shrine of gods of academics to ask for success and to buy good luck charms. Some young couples choose to get married at a shrine, as there are gods of good marriage, and they also go to a shrine devoted to the gods of childbearing when they wish to conceive, praying also for a safe delivery. As life advances, some families opt for funerals in Shinto style, though most of them are done according to Buddhist rites because of traditions added to the culture during the Edo period.

Shinto and Politics

Shinto has always been present on the political scene of Japan. In ancient times, a shaman or shamaness was the leader who enshrined and performed rituals to please gods. He or she also practiced divination to discern the will of the gods so that people knew such things as when to sow seeds. In the early days of Japan, shamans held high positions not only in rituals but also in politics. Later, the imperial family, viewed as the descendants of gods of Japan, became responsible for performing rituals and governing the country. Japanese political structure emerged from the integration of Shinto rituals and government (similar to a theocracy), and this was kept until the end of World War II. The remnants of such customs can be seen even today.

History of Japan and Shinto

In this section, let us examine more closely how Shinto was shaped throughout Japanese history.

Early Form of Shinto

Where did the first people of Japan originate? It is believed that during the Ice Age[1] Japan was connected to the Asian continent by land, enabling various people to migrate across the Asian continent to the far eastern end of it after spreading out from Babel. This area later became the islands of Japan as the sea level rose. But even after the islands were disjoined from the continent, people were able to make the trek by sea, as recorded in ancient texts. Nothing definite can be said as to exactly which ethnic tribes reached

---

1. Mike Oard, "Where Does the Ice Age fit?" *New Answers Book 1*, ed. Ken Ham (Green Forest, AR: Master Books, 2006), p. 207–220.

Japan. In all likelihood, it was not a single tribe but multiple tribes bringing different cultures.[2]

With distinct seasons and with abundant natural resources such as the ocean, rivers, and forests, the Japanese islands provided a perfect environment for fostering in its residents a sense of awe toward nature. Climate and topography were both instrumental in nurturing animistic beliefs and provided a background for developing folklore, especially the mythological stories of spirit gods living with and interacting with men.

When rice cropping was brought to Japan in the third century B.C., people started to settle down into villages, forming units in an agricultural society. It is most likely that at that time the prototype of Shinto was formed. People tried to placate perceived spirits by worshiping them as gods and making sacrificial offerings to them — even going so far as to offer up the lives of women and children (according to lore). This was done in order to secure the villagers' lives and crops from natural disasters. Festivals were held according to the farming calendar, and shamans exercised paramount roles in practicing divinations and instructing people in the will of the gods. This early form of Shinto, therefore, consisted of animism and shamanism.

Rise of Yamato Dynasty (the Imperial Family)

Several ancient Chinese records (*Records of Three Kingdoms* and *Book of the Later Han*) explain that there was a countrywide war in Japan in the second century A.D., a conflict lasting over 70 years. The war finally ended when they placed Himiko as their common ruler. Himiko was a female shaman and the queen of Yamataikoku; she lived from late second century to mid-third century A.D.

Himiko was also mentioned in another record as having sent her delegates to China, where she was recognized as ruler of Wa, the name given to Japan at that time. Himiko was given a special golden seal by the Chinese emperor around 238 A.D., confirming that she had great power in Japan in her day. It is not exactly known where Himiko's kingdom Yamataikoku was, but it is said that Yamataikoku ("Yamatai kingdom") could be related to the Yamato dynasty — the only dynasty that ever existed in Japan, becoming the imperial family that includes the present emperor of the nation.

By the fourth century, Yamato kings reigned as the rulers of Japan. Both governing and performing rituals were important duties of the ruler.

---

2. For more on some of the possible tribes please see Bodie Hodge, *Tower of Babel* (Green Forest, AR: Master Books, 2013), p. 166–167.

They made sure to perform ceremonies for Amatsukami, gods who live in the heavens and created the land of Japan, and Kunitsukami, gods who reside on the earth and protect the land of Japan. The Yamato dynasty also enshrined Amaterasu, the goddess of the sun who is viewed as their ancestor, in Ise Jingu Shrine, the most prestigious Shinto shrine in Japan.

Emperor Tenmu ordered the compilation of national chronicles in the late seventh century. The writing of *Kojiki* was completed in 712 and *Nihon Shoki* in 720. These two texts are the foundational sources upon which Shinto beliefs are based. Both of these texts cover stories of the creation of Japan as well as the genealogies of Yamato kings. Folklores about stories of the gods are much like Greek mythologies, since gods of Japan are very much like humans, emotional and imperfect, getting married, and having children. The genealogies inform us that Yamato kings were descendants of Ninigi, the grandson of Amaterasu. It is important to note that one of the reasons these two texts were written was to authenticate the Yamato kings as the authorized rulers of Japan by tracing back their bloodline to the gods of Japan, especially to Amaterasu.

By the beginning of the eighth century the Yamato dynasty achieved centralized power and established a new governmental structure called the *Ritsuryo* system, similar to the one in China. In this new structure, a specific religious bureau was installed wherein the government could carry out Shinto rituals. The rituals, *Matsuri*, defined under Ritsuryo system, are listed in Table 1. The religious bureau became superintendent of all the shrines in the country. The shrines were ranked, and 22 shrines related to the imperial family or to the dominant clans were chosen to be operated at public expense. An interesting fact is that this system evaluated and put rankings on gods, just as it did on human officers. In Shinto, gods became ranked according to their abilities and titles.

Ritsuryo system was in operation for about three centuries. By the end of the tenth century, it became difficult for the government to keep centralization of power, and a new system was installed. For religious matters, the spread of Buddhism changed the position of Shinto in the culture.

Introduction of Buddhism

The introduction of Buddhism had an enormous impact on Shinto.

In the mid-sixth century, Buddhism was officially brought into Japan from Baekje (one of three kingdoms of Korea at that time). Seong, the king

Table 1: List of Matsuri under the Ritsuryo system

Time	Name of the Rituals (Matsuri)	Religious Practice
February	Pray for the Year Matsuri 祈年祭（としごいのまつり）	To pray to Amatsukami and Kunitsukami for abundant harvest year
March	Flower Appeasing Matsuri 鎮花祭（はなしずめのまつり）	To pray for plague or diseases to depart from the country, at Oomiwa Shrine and Sai Shrine
April & September	God Clothing Matsuri 神衣祭（かんみそのまつり）	To offer clothes to Amaterasu at Ise Jingu Shrine
April	Three Branch Matsuri 三枝祭（さいぐさのまつり）	To decorate Sake (rice wine) barrel with lilies at Isagawa Shrine
April & July	Large Sacred Matsuri 大忌祭（おおいみのまつり）	To pray for good rain and harvest for rice crops at Hirose Shrine
April & July	Wind God Matsuri 風神祭（かぜのかみのまつり）	To pray for rice fields to be protected from bad storms or floods at Tatsuta Shrine.
June & December	Monthly Matsuri 月次祭（つきなみのまつり）	To pray for the welfare of the imperial family at Ise Jingu Shrine (it used to be done every month)
June & December	Feasting God Matsuri 道饗祭（みちあえのまつり）	Make a feast for evil spirits so that they don't come into the town

June & December	Fire Appeasing Matsuri 鎮火祭（ひしずめのまつり）	To pray for safe fire
September	God's Meal Matsuri 神嘗祭（かんにえのまつり）	To offer the first fruit of the year to Amaterasu at Ise Jingu Shrine
November	Partaking God's Meal Matsuri 相嘗祭（あいにえのまつり）	To offer the first fruit to gods and partake of it together
November	New Meal Matsuri 新嘗祭（にいなめのまつり） 大嘗祭（おおにえのまつり）	To celebrate the harvest, the emperor offers the new meal to gods, and he partakes too
November	Soul Appeasing Matsuri 鎮魂祭（たましずめのまつり）	To pray for peace of the emperor's soul
June & December	Purification Ceremony 大祓（おおはらえ）	To remove the impurity accumulated over the 6 months, done on the last day of June and December.
As needed	Special New Meal Matsuri 践祚大嘗祭	The first New Meal Matsuri since the emperor's enthronement

of Baekje, presented Buddha statues and scriptures to Kinmei, the emperor of Japan. Unsure of what to do, Kinmei consulted his court advisors. Some said to accept Buddhism, as it was already accepted in countries such as

China and Korea, while others said to refuse it, for Japan had its own gods, and accepting a new god like Buddha might upset the nation's original gods. Therefore, from the onset, Buddhism was not accepted well in Japan. To make a definitive contrast with Buddhism, Japan's indigenous religion began to be called Shinto.

But it was not long before Buddhism began to be accepted in Japan. The famous Prince Shotoku, who was regent to Queen Suiko in late sixth century, adopted and promoted Buddhism. Buddhist temples and statues began to be crafted at public expense. But Prince Shotoku was wise enough not to deny Shinto worship, issuing a law ordering people to continue worshiping Amatsukami and Kunitsukami. He was politically savvy enough to respect both the new and the old to avoid religious conflicts.

The Buddhism brought into Japan was Mahayana Buddhism with influences from other religions such as Confucianism, Taoism, and even Christianity.[3] Compared to this Buddhist admixture, Shinto is a simple ritualistic religion with few doctrines. Shinto deals with present happiness and not with personal salvation or afterlife. Folklore and traditions, on which Shinto is established, do not offer ethics or discipline to improve one's character. On the other hand, Buddhism has doctrines of enlightenment and commandments to follow. Sacred texts of Buddha can be studied by erudite scholars, and mysterious disciplines can be performed by practitioners. Buddhism offered what Shinto could not. Consequently, Buddhism attained the higher position in Japanese religious circles.

Syncretization of Shinto and Buddhism

As Buddhism became widely accepted in Japan, there followed a phenomenon called *Shin Butsu Shugo*, which means syncretization of Shinto with Buddhism.

This syncretization can be seen in the following phenomena:

- Shinto gods were accepted as the guardian gods of Buddhist temples, and Shinto shrines were built on the grounds of Buddhist temples.

- Temples were also built on the grounds of Shinto shrines to help Shinto gods to become Buddha, since Shinto gods were

---

3. See chapter 19 in this volume for a full description of Buddhism, chapter 20 for Confucianism, and chapter 3 for Taoism.

acknowledged as lower.than Buddha and therefore needed to attain nirvana in the manner of humans.

• Certain Shinto priests became Buddhist monks hoping to attain their own personal "salvation" or enlightenment.

Further advancing the amalgamation of Shinto and Buddhism, the concept of *Honji Suijyaku* was developed. Shinto gods who supposedly created Japan and had been protecting the nation came to be viewed as the Buddha's personification. In this, worshiping Shinto gods was understood to be worshiping Buddha. In some cases, Buddhist monks even performed Shinto rituals. This strange mixture of Shinto and Buddhism was present in Japan for a long time, from the 10th century until the end of the Edo period in the mid-19th century when a new government ordered the separation of Shinto and Buddhism.

Uji-gami Beliefs at Local Shrines

Buddhism also affected Shinto's Uji-gami beliefs that were seen among common people at local shrines.

In Shinto the places of worship were at Yorishiro, the sacred dwelling places of gods such as woods, rocks, mountains, and other monumental natural objects. In the early days there were simple altars at Yorishiro, but later, larger buildings were constructed on premises as shrines.

In these local shrines each clan (Uji) or village enshrined its own guardian gods of their ancestor (Uji-gami) or of their village (Ubusuna-gami). Seasonal festivals were held at shrines to please these gods, and participation in various events at the local shrine was mandated in order to be part of the village community. This simple, traditional Shinto belief among common people was called Uji-gami belief, and it dealt with the interest of the entire village, not with personal interests or wishes.

When Buddhism, which deals with personal faith and "salvation," came along and began to spread among the common people, it profoundly affected and modified Shinto practices. It became acceptable to pray about personal matters at shrines.

Also, the efficacy of each god was defined so that people would visit shrines whose gods seemed to answer their specific prayers. Shrines began to recruit gods with certain efficacies from other shrines. By a process called *bunshi*, a god's spirit could be split to live in a new shrine as well as in the original shrine. In this way, popular gods were invited into many shrines and shared by more people. By way of example, the Inari god, originally living in Fushimi Inari Shrine, had the purported power to bring agricultural harvest and business success. This was a popular god, and his spirit was split into as many as 32,000 bunshi shrines that still exist today. This is an example of the arbitrary way Shinto gods are viewed.

Corruption of Buddhism and Re-evaluation of Shinto

During the 16th century Samurai wars, Catholic missionaries such as Francisco Xavier arrived and evangelized Japan. Amazingly, many Japanese received the good news of salvation through Christ, and as many as 1,000,000 people, including samurai lords and common people, converted to Christianity. But by the end of the century, Christianity was banned by Hideyoshi Toyotomi, the top Samurai who had become the ruler of the country. Severe persecution against Christians started. Shogun Ieyasu Tokugawa overturned Toyotomi and ended the long age of Samurai wars by establishing the Tokugawa Administration as the unified governing power in the Edo period (1603–1868). But the Tokugawa Administration also enforced anti-Christian policy.

As part of its thrust against Christianity, the Tokugawa Administration utilized the Buddhist temples as monitoring offices to ensure that people did not practice Christianity. They initiated a system called "Temple Binding" (*Tera-uke*), which mandated that every person had to belong to a Buddhist temple. Without a registration document from the temple, a person could not do any business, could not travel to other towns, and could not get married or conduct funeral services. This system led to corruption and secularization of many Buddhist temples and monks because they all too easily procured for themselves much capital and labor from the indigenous populace bound for the temple. The oppressed people were unhappy, but they had no choice.

Over the span of 250 years in the Edo period, peace was maintained within Japan enabling art and literature to flourish. Scholars again studied *Kojiki* and *Nihon Shoki* and were reawakened to the significance of these Japanese classics. They established a new field of study called *Kokugaku*, meaning "national studies." *Kojiki* and *Nihon Shoki* provided not merely information on the early history of the nation but also the reminder that the original Shinto was the vital religion and true identity of Japan. The inevitable conclusion was that the Japanese people should go back to original Shinto. This brought about the rejection of Buddhism-influenced Shinto as secular and the removal of Buddhist influences to restore the nation's original religion.

This movement to restore Shinto by the Kokugaku scholars provided the philosophical base for the revolutionists who overturned the Tokugawa Administration, ending the Edo period. The new Meiji government elevated the emperor, believed to be the true descendant of Japan's gods, as the ruler of the country, established a policy of "Separation of Shinto and Buddhism," and tried to restart the Shinto rituals at the national level as in the Ritsuryo system of the eighth century. Thus began the National Shinto system, under which all Japanese citizens were viewed as servants or children of the emperor, a living god.

Emperor Meiji ordered construction of the predecessor of the Yasukuni Shrine in Tokyo to enshrine the war dead from the civil battles that occurred during the transition from Edo to Meiji. Since then, Yasukuni enshrines all Japanese who die in any war for the country.

View of Divine Nation and "Kamikaze" in War Times

In Shinto, there is always the concept of Japan being the gods' country or "divine nation," protected by its guardian gods. This concept emerges whenever Japan engages in battle with foreign countries.

The mention of a "divine nation" first appears in *Nihon Shoki* with respect to an incident as early as the third century. When Empress Jingu sent troops to rule over three kingdoms of Korea, one of the kings surrendered without a fight, saying, "They are divine troops from a divine nation, sent by a holy king of the East; therefore we are better off not to resist." This quote of a Korean king may not be authentic, as it was probably written to glorify the emperors of Japan, yet it verifies that there was already the concept of Japan as a divine nation from the early days.

Another incident worth mentioning is that of a Mongolian invasion in the late 13th century. The Mongol Empire, which extended its power over China and Korea, tried to approach Japan twice. However, with the help of strong *Kamikaze*, which translated means "divine wind," Japan was able to chase off the outnumbering Mongolian troops from the coastline both times. At this point in history, the myth developed that Japan could not be invaded because the guardian gods of Shinto protected its islands.

When the samurai age ended and the modern nation started in the mid-19th century, the National Shinto provided the image of the new Japan as being the divine nation since antiquity. Eager to catch up with technologies and military powers of Western countries, the Meiji government utilized Shinto to unite Japanese citizens by ordering them to pay respects to the guardian gods of Japan and their descendants, namely the emperor and the imperial family.

After winning the wars with China in 1895 and with Russia in 1905, Japan was recognized internationally and became confident enough to enlarge its territories over Asian countries to create "Greater East Asia Co-Prosperity Sphere." The Shinto view enabled Japanese military officers to rationalize it as Japan, the divine nation, being given the authority to free and protect Asian countries from control by Western nations.

In 1910, Japan annexed Korea. In 1932, Japan assisted in establishing the independent Manchukuo nation from China. Believing that America was trying to stunt Japan's advancement, Japan eventually entered the war with America by attacking Pearl Harbor in 1941. When the war situation worsened, the Japanese government put enormous emphasis upon the idea of the divine nation under the emperor, the living god, to prevent any resistance from its citizens. This emphasis also served to motivate soldiers that it was an honor to die for the living god. Thus were born the famous Kamikaze (divine wind) pilots, who gave their lives in suicide attacks on American war ships. Even ordinary citizens were commanded not to surrender but to die for the nation and the emperor. Tragic suicidal death took its greatest toll in victims among the citizens of the Okinawa Islands, with many women and children included.

Post WWII Shinto

When World War II drew to a close, the Allied Powers sent General Douglas MacArthur and his team to occupy and restructure Japan. They spared the lives of the emperor and the imperial family since they were merely used by the government and the military, but they made the emperor declare himself to be an ordinary man and not a god. Today the emperor of Japan is a figurehead and cannot be engaged in political issues. However, he still performs the Shinto rituals as the head of the country, according to traditions of the imperial courts. Even the head of the Cabinet (i.e., the prime minister), the head of the Congress, and the head of the Supreme Court attend some of the major rituals performed by the emperor. It is not discussed openly in public, but there still exists the problem of separation of religion (Shinto) and government in Japan.

The National Shinto was disassembled right after the war, and all Shinto shrines became private religious corporations according to the new constitutional policy of the separation of religion and government. Yasukuni Shrine also became a private corporation, though it still embodies the notion of a national reposing monument. As mentioned in the story at the beginning of this article, the problem of politicians visiting Yasukuni exists because now it is a private Shinto shrine.

For most Japanese people, the long history of religious syncretization deeply affects their religious positions. Shinto and Buddhism — both cultivated in Japan for many centuries — are regarded as a tradition and culture. Affiliations with Shinto shrines or Buddhist temples are just the remains of the Uji-gami community or Temple Binding system from the previous eras. A person can be counted in both Shinto and Buddhist populations, but it does not mean that the person has an active personal faith in these religions. Therefore, when asked about his or her faith, many Japanese would find that question difficult to answer.

Comparison between Shinto and Christianity

It is easily recognized that Shinto is quite different from Christianity. The following summarizes the views of Shinto and Christianity with respect to some fundamental doctrines.

Table 2: Comparison of Shinto and Christianity

	Shinto	Christianity
View on God	Polytheism (Innumerable gods)	Monotheism (Triune God)
Character of God	Not omnipotent Gods can die Good and bad	Omnipotent God lives forever Good all the time

Sacred Text	None *Kojiki* and *Nihon Shoki* are used as the source for Shinto mythology	The Bible
Target	Japanese only	All mankind
Human nature at birth	Neither good nor bad	All men inherit the original sin committed by Adam
Sin	Can be cleansed by a ritual called *Misogi*, washing with water	Cleansed by animal sacrifice in Old Testament pointing to Jesus' final atoning blood in the New Testament
Salvation	Not discussed	Through faith in Jesus Christ
Life after death	Existence of the underworld where all the dead go is mentioned.	The saved go to heaven, and the unsaved go to hell.
Judgment	Not discussed	All mankind must face God in judgment
Moral Value	Not explicitly stated General respect toward nature and life is suggested	Laws and commandments in Old and New Testaments
Believer's priority	Man-centered worship of gods in order to receive safety, success, health, and prosperity	God-centered worship because of love toward God

Unlike Christianity, Shinto does not claim to be the only truth nor the only way to heaven. Therefore, arbitrariness and inconsistencies inherent in Shinto are not considered to be of great significance.

- Shinto mythology is not to be taken literally; even Shinto priests would say it's a folk tale.

- Shinto gods act like humans — imperfect and quite emotional. They demand being enshrined and respected by making people fear a curse.

- Many Shinto practices are merely customs and traditions for the Japanese, but most Japanese don't know how such practices originated and why they do what they do.

- Shinto is superficial. Sin and uncleanness are easily relieved by performing some outward rituals, without any inward repentance. Success and prosperity are ensured by purchasing *ofuda* (paper with a god's name on it) or *omamori* (good luck charms) at shrines.

For people accustomed to monotheism, Shinto probably appears to be naïve or unsophisticated, yet this religion is what has been fostered in Japan for nearly two millennia. Most Japanese would not care how illogical or inconsistent Shinto is; they respect it out of a deeply ingrained sense of tradition and ethnic identity.

Further Discussion

Early Christian Influences on Shinto

From the basic facts (as shown in the chart above) and histories, Shinto looks quite different from Christianity. Interestingly, though, influences from Christianity are still evident. This is due to the unofficial but probable historical accounts detailing how early Christians from the school of Assyrian Churches of the East had come to Japan between the second and seventh centuries with teachings from the Bible, which then became syncretized with Shinto mythology and practices.

According to "official" history, Christianity was first brought to Japan in 1549 by a Jesuit missionary, Francisco Xavier, from Europe. Although many believers came to faith during this time, under the fierce persecution in the Edo Period from the 17th to mid-19th century, only a few survived. In 1873, the Meiji government once again permitted the practice of Christianity, making way for the arrival of Protestant missionaries from the United States and Europe. In both cases, these missionaries had come from the Western countries. Thus, in the minds of many Japanese today, Christianity is still viewed as Western religion, and this view continues to serve as a chief alienating factor.

In studying the "unofficial" historical accounts (preceding 1549), researchers have found that missionaries could have arrived from Eastern countries as early as the second to third centuries with the emigration of a group of Christians of the clan of Hata (秦) from the ancient country of Yutsuki in central Asia. There is little information on Yutsuki, but the country is believed to be a small Christian nation evangelized by missionaries from Assyrian Churches of the East.

Shinsen Shoujiroku, compiled in A.D. 816, records that the prince of Yutsuki and his people arrived in Japan and became naturalized either in the 8th year of Emperor Chuai (A.D. 199) or in the 14th year of Emperor Oujin (A.D. 283). The clan of Hata had a reputation for excelling in the production of silk. If the clan of Hata brought not only the advanced technologies and skills available in Assyria and Persia but also the biblical cultures and teachings that had spread to those nations, then some traces should be seen mixed in and syncretized with the original culture of Japan. Vestiges of Christianity should be detected in the account of mankind's origins and in various objects and rituals of Shinto.

First, let us look at the origins account in Shinto and see if there are some influences of the Bible present.

Origins Account in Shinto

As mentioned previously, Shinto's mythology is recorded in two ancient texts, *Kojiki* and *Nihon Shoki*, compiled in the early 8th century. The following is a summary of the relevant origins stories of Shinto.

- The beginning of the heaven and the earth

    * *Kojiki* describes that in the beginning, when the heaven and the earth were separated, there were three gods, Amenominakanushi (天之御中主神, the central master in heaven), Takamimusuhi (高御産巣日神, high creator god), and Kamumusuhi (神産巣日神, divine creator god) in *Takamanohara*, the heaven.

    * When the earth was without a form, "like oil in water and floated like jellyfish," two gods sprang up like reeds.

    * Then the names of two gods and five pairs of gods are listed and are known as seven generations of gods, *Kamiyonanayo*. The last pair on the list are Izanagi (man deity) and Izanami (woman deity), who would create the islands of Japan.

- Creation of islands of Japan by Izanagi and Izanami

  * Other heavenly gods ordered Izanagi and Izanami to make something firm out of the formless earth. The two gods stood on the bridge between heaven and earth, and pierced a halberd-like long spike into the earth and stirred it. When they took the spike out, salty water dripped and crystalized into a small island. The two gods went down to the island, mated, and produced the islands that compose Japan.

- Izanagi and Izanami bearing various gods, death of Izanami

  * After bearing the Japanese islands, Izanagi and Izanami bore the many gods who reside in nature (ocean, river, mountains, etc.), in housing, and in many other objects. Finally Izanami bore a god of fire, but she was burnt by the fire and died. When she died, she went to the underworld, a place like hades.

  * Saddened at losing his wife, Izanagi visited Izanami in the underworld, but her body was already decomposing. Izanagi grew terrified and ran away. Upset by his escape, Izanami cursed the living world to kill 1,000 people a day. But Izanagi blessed the world by bringing 1,500 births a day to counteract it.

- Purification bathing of Izanagi and the birth of three noble gods

  * Coming back from the underworld, Izanagi performed purification bathing, called *misogi*, in the ocean. Out of his clothing, gods were born, and through his bathing, more gods were born. Finally, as Izanagi washed his eyes and nose, three noble gods were born: Amaterasu (goddess of the sun, in charge of the heavens), Tsukuyomi (god of the moon, in charge of the night), and Susano-o (god of the storm, in charge of oceans).

- Amaterasu's hideaway in a cave

  * Susano-o was a rough god, causing much harm in both the heavens and on the earth. This disturbed Amaterasu greatly, and she decided to hide away in a cave and shut the door. Darkness filled heaven and earth, and evil prevailed. The gods in heaven conferred with one another and decided to throw a

big noisy party in front of the cave to interest her. Eventually she got curious and opened the door slightly. A powerful god pulled her out of the cave, thus returning light to the world.

- Ninigi as the ruler of Japan

  * Ookuninushi, the descendant of Susano-o, rose up as the first ruler of Japan since its creation. Watching it from above, Amaterasu decided her son should be the ruler instead. So she sent several messengers to Ookuninushi, and eventually he agreed to hand over the position without much ado. Ninigi, the grandson of Amaterasu, descended from heaven along with some attendant gods and three sacred treasures to assume the throne. Ninigi became the first heavenly approved ruler of Japan.

  * The great-grandson of Ninigi, Iwarebiko, known as Emperor Jinmu, was the first emperor of Japan. Thus, the present imperial family is viewed as the direct descendant of Ninigi and Amaterasu.

It is logical to acknowledge these accounts as nothing but myth, yet mythological stories may contain traces or evidences of real incidents or of borrowed stories from other folklore or religions. Some researchers say that the concept of "the beginning of the heaven and the earth" is not originally in Shinto mythology and is most likely included because of early Christians introducing the Genesis account. It is also possible that a clan of people brought this history to Japan with them after the scattering at the Tower of Babel. It merely became corrupted and mythologized as history proceeded. Consider that the first three gods that were present from the beginning of creation seem also to have their origins in the triune God of the Bible.

Early Eastern missionaries could easily account for other corruptions or even information emanating from Solomon's day where people came from around the world to hear Solomon's wisdom. For example, the story of Amaterasu's hideaway in a cave could be related to Joshua's long day in Joshua, chapter 10, in the Bible. If the sun stood still in the middle of the sky for a day in Israel, allowing Joshua's troops to overtake the Amorites, a night would have fallen for the same amount of time in Japan, which is on the other side of the globe. It must have been frightening in Japan not to see the sun rise for a whole day, and this may have led to the folklore that the sun goddess had hidden away in a cave.

Similarities in Objects and Rituals

There are some objects and rituals that bear resemblance to Christianity. This resemblance cannot be used as conclusive proof of the Bible's influence on Japan's indigenous religion, but the observations are fascinating and might encourage one to do further research.

Mikoshi vs. the Ark of Covenant

Mikoshi is a temporal housing for gods, used during ceremonies or festivals to move gods from one place to another. It is a gold-covered wooden box supported by two wooden carrying bars. An ornate golden phoenix stands on top of the housing.

Mikoshi
(By 663highland, Wikipedia Creative Commons)

The general appearance of Mikoshi resembles the ark of the covenant in the Bible. The golden phoenix, a fictional bird with its wings spread out on top of the box, reminds us of cherubim with their outspread wings on top of the ark. Both are carried on poles by men in a similar way.

Shrine Structure vs. Tabernacle/Temple Structure

In early Shinto there was no shrine structure. Yorishiro alone or simple altars in front of it were the places of worship. However, by the fourth century, shrine buildings were constructed. The layout of a shrine precinct is similar to that of the biblical tabernacle or temple with the holy of holies.

Tori-i vs. Passover Gate

At the entrance to the shrine area, or precinct, there is a gate called Tori-i, which is composed of two columns and a beam across the top. The purpose of the gate is to separate the secular world and the sacred place. Today unpainted Tori-i are quite common, but many are painted red, bringing to mind the doors of the Israelites' homes on the day of Passover, where the blood of the lamb was applied to the top and sides of the doorframes.

A tori-i at the entrance of Yasaka Shrine in Kyoto
(I, KENPEI, Wikimedia Commons)

Purification Rituals: Misogi and Harae

Shinto holds to the concept of ritual uncleanness, brought upon one's person when touching dead bodies, etc. Shinto values purification before facing gods; therefore, there are cleansing rituals known as *misogi* and *harae*.

Misogi is ritual bathing. A person goes into water to wash off the ritual uncleanness and sins — similar to Jewish customs.

Harae is a ritual whereby a Shinto priest shakes *onusa*, a wooden staff with a bundle of zigzag-shaped white papers, over an unclean person or thing. The uncleanness is taken away from the person or thing and gets attached to the onusa or a doll used for the purpose. This could be related to the custom of Azazel, the scapegoat of Israel, upon which the nation's sins were placed, as well as the ritual cleansings performed by Israelite priests.

Assyrian Churches of the East and Keikyo, the Luminous Religion

It is worth mentioning that Christianity is not just a Western religion but should also be considered an Eastern religion. Acknowledging the work of the churches of the East is imperative because Japanese people would note the geographical proximity and would be more open to Christianity if its history in the East would be emphasized to a greater degree.

Assyrian Churches of the East, which had headquarters in Edessa (Urfa in modern Turkey), exerted great influence in the evangelization of Asian countries such as Persia, India, and China. Thomas, one of the 12 disciples of Jesus, was known to have gone to Assyria to build churches before going farther eastward to Persia and India. Also, there were Assyrian witnesses at Pentecost in Acts 2, who in all likelihood went home with the good news of salvation through Christ and probably helped establish churches with Thomas.

The Assyrian Church is also known as the Nestorian Church. It was rejected as heretical by the Roman Catholic Church in 431 because Nestorius denied Catholicism's veneration of Mary as the "Mother of God." From the biblical point of view, of course, Nestorius' teaching was not heresy. But the unfortunate labeling of the Nestorian Church as heretical resulted in Western Christian schools' lack of appreciation for the great work and history of Assyrian Churches.

Assyrian missionaries officially visited the Chinese emperor in A.D. 635. They were called the "Luminous Religion" (*Keikyo,* 景教 in Japanese) and were allowed to publicly teach the Bible. They built Keikyo temples in Chang'an, the capital of China at that time.

When the famous Japanese monks Kuukai and Saicho visited Chang'an to study Buddhism in the seventh century, they probably encountered Keikyo missionaries and learned some biblical concepts. They probably did not distinguish between Buddhist and Christian ideas, thus bringing back to Japan a conglomeration of Buddhism, Keikyo, and other religions and philosophies. This is probably why Buddhism in Japan is somewhat different from the Buddhism in other countries. And of course this mixture also affects Shinto.

Assyrian missionaries probably reached Japan well before the 16th-century time frame of Francisco Xavier, though this is not recorded officially. It's possible that the history was rewritten to hide Christian influences, or the teachings were simply taken as a style of Buddhism and all got syncretized. It would be interesting and eye opening if researchers studied this matter further.

Analysis of the Japanese Mindset

It is important to know that Shinto still exerts a profound effect on the unique worldview that runs deep within the hearts and minds of the Japanese populace. To sum up, there are three main characteristics found in the typical Japanese mindset influenced by Shinto:

- *Superstitious:* Today's Japanese people are fond of horoscopes and other fortune telling means in their daily lives. They buy good luck charms (*omamori*) from shrines. Some even like to visit "power spots" where they hope to get healings and energies from spirits or gods. Japanese people like to "feel" rather than "think logically" in spiritual matters.

- *Tolerant:* Throughout the ages, Shinto was able to accept Buddhism and other ideas, and it allowed syncretization to maintain the co-existence of various religions within the nation. Therefore, the Japanese are good at tolerating and respecting assorted religions and views. It is difficult for the Japanese to sympathize with religious conflicts that involve violence, such as that which occurs in the Middle East.

- *Very little interest in an afterlife:* Shinto deals with this life. People go to shrines to pray for safety and prosperity in the here and now. The general picture of life after death is that every dead person becomes a spirit and then watches over the living in the air or from the sky (heaven). There is no concept of judgment, so no ultimate motivation for living a moral life pleasing to God.

To ponder the mindset of the 21st-century Japanese is truly a fascinating, compelling study in contrasts. As mentioned in the opening paragraph of this chapter, builders of a 1.4 billion dollar skyscraper project in modern Tokyo avoid moving one small samurai grave because they are afraid a curse may fall on their new buildings. This kind of news and stories are not uncommon in today's modern Japanese societies, as it has deep roots in a centuries-old thinking process that has been fostered through Shinto, Japan's indigenous religion. Therefore, it is especially meaningful and helpful for Christians who are evangelizing the Japanese to know and understand this background.

Good News for the Japanese

The Japanese people are, in a sense, quite devout — seen in the fact that they are capable of respecting not only Shinto gods and Buddha but also other gods that are highly valued. Sadly, the one eternal God is not known by most Japanese. This eternal One is the only absolute and omnipotent God, the Creator of the world.

Because this Creator God is completely different in power and authority from other gods, the word "God" with upper case "G" is used to distinguish

Him, in English, from the many other so-called "gods" with lower case "g" who are not absolute and omnipotent.

> In the beginning God created the heavens and the earth (Genesis 1:1).[4]

The Bible testifies that this God alone created the physical universe. Therefore, He is more powerful than the universe itself. God created the earth as the perfect environment for mankind and for all His creatures as well — the birds of the air, the fish in the sea, and the animals on the ground. When mankind sinned against God, God's Curse fell upon the earth. This God who created our earth with such intricacy and beauty is without a doubt the Almighty One of incomparable intellect, possessing the highest, ultimate artistic sense.

Today, however, we are taught the religious ideas of evolution (which is now being syncretized into Japanese culture as well). Especially in Japan, school textbooks and television proclaim that everything came into existence through the natural process of evolution and that it is proven by "science." Most Japanese think "science" is the way to the truth and would be surprised that there are people who "still" believe in the biblical creation view. They consider the Bible's description of there being one God who created everything an old-fashioned religious myth. Also, the biblical creation idea is seen as coming from Western cultures, thus the Japanese do not generally respect it or feel responsible to study it.

Most Japanese are not exposed to learning that evolution is not supported by "observable science" and is merely an idea that actually contradicts many observations and laws of nature. They have no opportunity to learn that "observable science" better supports the biblical creation view. When properly confronted with scientific facts supporting creation by the Intelligent Designer, people can start to see how illogical and unreasonable it is for evolution to bring this intricate world into existence.[5] If evolution is not the truth, then considering the Creator God and the biblical account should be taken more seriously by everyone — including the Japanese.

According to the Bible, God created the entire universe. He created the earth and filled it with plants and animals and then, finally, created the

---

4. Scripture in this chapter is from the New American Standard Bible (NASB).
5. The entire discussion of creation and evolution can be studied through the website and publications of Answers in Genesis (answersingenesis.org), so it is not discussed here.

first man and woman with special care. All men and women, regardless of their ethnic or religious identities, are the descendants of the first man and woman God created — Japanese included.

Not only is there one true Creator of all races, but the Creator is also the Savior of the world. Shinto does not explain the afterlife or what happens to a person after death, but that does not spare a person from the ultimate judgment. The Creator God, who loves His creatures deeply, made a sacrifice and prepared a way for any person to be saved, if he or she repents and places faith in Him.

The Bible tells us mankind was created in God's image; thus, they have a moral will. But the first man and woman freely chose not to obey God but to do their own thing. This sin unleashed upon mankind unspeakable suffering and death — death not only of the body but also of spiritual separation from the Creator Himself. This sinful state also includes the certainty of facing God in the final judgment and eternal punishment in the afterlife.

> For the wages of sin is death, but the free gift of God is eternal life in Christ Jesus our Lord (Romans 6:23).

The Bible proclaims that Jesus Christ is the Creator God: "For by Him all things were created. . . . He is before all things, and in Him all things hold together" (Colossians 1:16–17). As the King of the universe, He has infinite power and authority. Yet, in His infinite love, He humbled Himself and became a man to provide a way to save people from eternal suffering. Jesus took the sins of mankind upon Himself, endured suffering and death on the Cross, and endured from the wrath of God the Father on behalf of His people. His death paid the penalty for their sin. Jesus was resurrected from the dead with a glorified body on the third day and now sits enthroned in heaven. The good news is that anyone who turns from their sin and trusts Jesus as his personal Savior can have his own sins forgiven as a free gift from God. Along with this forgiveness comes wonderful, beautiful eternal life.

I sincerely wish for these Japanese to come to know their true identity and accept their true Creator and Savior. They would be free from fearing curses of Shinto gods or spirits. They would truly be "children of God" and be a member of the true divine nation, the eternal kingdom of God, mentioned in the Bible. How much better to live for the true God than for whimsical Shinto gods!

As maintained throughout this chapter, Shinto is mythology deeply entwined with Japanese national history and ethnic identity. For those who wish to share the gospel with the Japanese, it is important to understand how their mindset is influenced by these Shinto roots and approach them carefully. Logic would demand that the sincere Japanese seeker of truth would serve himself best by turning to the One who knows him best, his omnipotent Creator and Savior, Jesus Christ. May the Japanese people open up their hearts to know the One who said, "I am the way, and the truth, and the life" (John 14:6).

Summary of Shinto Beliefs

Doctrine	Teachings of Shinto
God	Deny the God of the Bible, but worship many local gods and ancestors
Authority/ Revelation	*Kojiki* and *Nihon Shoki* are used as the source for Shinto mythology
Man	Men are neither good nor bad
Sin	Sin can be cleansed by a ritual called *Misogi*, a washing with water
Salvation	Existence of the underworld where all the dead go is mentioned, but there is no concept of judgment
Creation	Several gods were involved in the creation of the earth and the land

Dedication

This chapter is dedicated to my daughter, Rieko. May she find the Savior Lord in her life even while she grows up in the Shinto culture of Japan.

Acknowledgments

My beloved husband, Souta, who always stands beside me, encourages me, and honors the Lord. Mrs. Pat Kovacs, my dear sister and mentor in the Lord, who took much time to read and check my English thoroughly.

Chapter 19

Buddhism

Dr. *Thane Hutcherson Ury*

Some say if you compare the Sermon on the Mount, Buddha's *Dhammapada*, Lao-tzu's Tao-te-ching, Confucius' *Analects*, the Bhagavad *Gita*, the Proverbs of Solomon, and the *Dialogues* of Plato, you will find it: a real, profound, and strong agreement. Yes, but this is ethics, not religion. . . . Ethics may be the first step in religion but it is not the last. As C.S. Lewis says, "The road to the Promised Land runs past Mount Sinai." — Peter Kreeft[1]

About six centuries before Jesus walked the earth, a young Hindu prince is said to have escaped the trappings of materialism and found the path to enlightenment. Now known as the Buddha — *the enlightened one* — he left behind a formula to help others trace the same nirvanic path. These teachings have been distilled in the belief system known as Buddhism, a humanistic and essentially monistic religion.[2] As one of history's oldest surviving global religions,[3] it is one of today's fastest growing faiths, and currently boasts almost

---

1. Peter Kreeft, "The Uniqueness of Christianity," http://www.peterkreeft.com/topics-more/christianity-uniqueness.htm.
2. Some Buddhistic strains have animistic, deistic, and/or polytheistic elements.
3. Unlike other religions, Buddhism has no deity, resembling more of an ethical school. But in the centuries following Gautama Buddha's death, various devotees have revered him as a godlike figure.

half a billion adherents worldwide. This makes it one of the largest blocks of people groups unreached with the gospel.

In countries like Thailand, Tibet, Bhutan, Cambodia, Laos, Myanmar, and Sri Lanka, over 60 percent of the populace could be described as "folk Buddhists." Thailand is 95 percent Buddhist, with Myanmar and Cambodia about 90 percent. But Buddhism is not just for the Far East anymore, as the United States has become a prime mission field for Buddhism, gradually achieving mainstream acceptance. "Probably the most attractive of all the non-Christian religions to the Western mind,"[4] notes J.N.D. Anderson, America now has two million homegrown Buddhists. Though it took millennia for Buddhism to be established in Asia, it has taken deep root in Western countries in a fraction of that time — perhaps due to compatibility with the naturalistic evolutionary worldview that now permeates the Western World.

Historical Overview

If Gautama Buddha or his earliest disciples ever wrote down his teachings, such has perished, meaning no one has been able to claim with high confidence exactly what he taught. In fact, written records about Siddhartha don't appear until at least four hundred years after his death. Before this we have only scattered Sanskrit accounts and oral tradition. Thus a pale of historical uncertainty has resulted, with Buddhist scholars even conceding that falsehoods have leached into most biographical accounts about the Buddha, not to mention outlandish embellishments. For example, one account says that within seconds of birth, he stood, walked, and scanned in all directions before nobly claiming that he was the foremost being in the world, and that this would be his last rebirth. During his quest for enlightenment he is said to have survived on one grain of rice daily for a few years. The last two years before his "awakening," he completely abstained from food or water.[5]

---

4. J.N.D. Anderson, *Christianity & Comparative Religion* (Downers Grove, IL: InterVarsity Press, 1970), p. 46.

5. When it comes to the *Bibliographical Test*, the Buddhist "Pali Canon" fails miserably. Since we do not have the original manuscripts of any ancient religion, how confident can we be that what we read today is the same as the original writing? Thankfully, scholars have developed ways to assess this very issue. The gold standard in this regard has been to combine the *External Test, Internal Test,* and *Bibliographical Test*. Since copyist errors, copyists' redactions, or embellishments have crept into the copying process over so many centuries, the Bibliographical Test centers on assessing the transmissional fidelity of extant copies. The test focuses particularly on two factors: the number of manuscripts we now have, and the estimated time gap between when the originals were first written and the date when the oldest existing copy was penned. The layperson is generally unaware that (1) these tests

Roughly 2,500 years ago in Kapilavastu at the foothills of the Himalayas, a young aristocrat named Siddhartha Gautama was born in the lap of luxury. His father carefully insulated his heir from the real world beyond the palace walls, and allegedly gave him three palaces and 40,000 dancing girls.[6] However, Siddhartha inadvertently caught glimpses here and there beyond the royal walls. The following sights in particular gripped Gautama's heart: 1) a crippled man, 2) a leper, 3) a rotting corpse, and 4) a pious ascetic. These later came to be known as the *Four Passing Sights*, which so moved him that he renounced his life of comfort and luxury to pursue enlightenment. This *Great Renunciation*, as Buddhists call it, included Gautama abandoning his wife and child, for "distractions"[7] such as these would impede his quest to untie the Gordian knot of pain, sickness, old age, and death. The driving motivation of Buddhism's founder was to pinpoint the origin of pain and suffering and to propose a solution.[8]

As with many Hindus (the culture and worldview he was born into), Gautama found the standard Indian theodicy[9] for pain and death to be dreadful and deeply unsatisfying. Legend has it that six or seven years after his *Great Renunciation*, his long search paid off. Tranquilly seated in the lotus position under a fig tree (later commemorated as the Bodhi tree[10]), Gautama meditated for a long time.[11] Freed from distractions, he persevered, he was

are in the background of everything they read and take for granted in ancient history, and (2) based on these tests alone, the Christian Scriptures' credibility is empirically demonstrated to be eons ahead of all the scriptures of the world. The comparison is really not even remotely close.

6. Some embellish the opulence of Gautama's life so as to magnify the gravamen of his renunciation.

7. Siddhartha's son was named *Rahula*, meaning "hindrance" or "chain." In the Dhammapada, part of the Buddhist canon, we find this teaching: "Those who love nothing and hate nothing, have no fetters."

8. Sadly, he never encountered the theodicy of Genesis 3, which answers the question of the origin of death and suffering, and points to the need for a Savior who conquers both.

9. Theodicy describes the general understanding of how a good god — usually the biblical God who is all-loving and all-powerful — and evil can exist at the same time. Hinduism denies the actual reality of evil; it is illusion (*maya*). Karmic debt must be paid for our injustices performed in previous lives. Any Buddhist or Mother Theresa–like compassion disrupts the karmic cycle and brings bad karma. Hinduism and Buddhism both agree that we are in a cycle of misery, but disagree on the "entrance and exit ramps" of life's carousel of suffering.

10. Note the similarity of the words *bodhi* and *Buddha*. The first means enlightenment (or wisdom), and the second means enlightened or awakened one.

11. Some sources add that at this time Māra, the demon of sensual desire, threw all his minions and tactics at Gautama. Buddha was tempted to enter nirvana immediately, so the story goes, so he couldn't tell others the way to enlightenment. But Brahma, the Hindu creator god, came and told him to continue on (become a bodhisattva) for the sake of others.

able to recall his previous lives and learn the cycles of birth, death, and rebirth. The rubrics of Buddhist dharma were then revealed to him, and he attained ultimate bliss,[12] becoming the enlightened one — hereafter simply *the* Buddha.

In the wake of attaining *nirvana*, the Buddha began traveling itinerantly with five companions, sharing with them the insights learned under the tree of wisdom. His first teaching was the *Sermon at Benares*, which included *The Four Noble Truths* and *The Eightfold Path*. These two groups of dharma, if followed while navigating *The Middle Way*, will guide imperfect aspirants to escape from the cycle of reincarnation and attain enlightenment.[13] The Buddha did retain some of his former Hinduism, but added nuance to reincarnation and a few other precepts. In fact, he simply hoped to be a force of reform within Hinduism.

An Answer to Suffering: Buddha's Main Quest

Ever since the *Four Passing Sights*, Gautama's *Great Renunciation* was fueled by a hunger to find an answer for the pain and suffering in life. When it came to solving the problem of evil, the Buddha took a very different path from Hinduism. The latter saw evil as *maya* (illusion), while the Buddha taught evil is not only real, but that it can be overcome by methodically removing desire — the source of all suffering.[14] Eliminate this craving and you eliminate suffering. Such gives birth to the stereotypical view Westerners have of monks seated yoga-like and seeking complete detachment from the world. Through discipline and patient determination all passions can be "blown out."

For the last 45 years of his life, the Buddha pointed encumbered seekers toward the way of liberation from the cycle of birth and death. The timing

---

12. As legend has it, at the exact moment of bliss, the moon lit up the heavens, the earth shook, and lotus blossoms rained down from the heavens.

13. Before discovering *The Middle Way* of meditation that paved the path to enlightenment, the Buddha had experienced the extreme opposites of princely abundance and extreme self-mortification, both of which hinder spiritual growth. Thus, striving for a middle ground between too much worldliness (self-indulgence) or too much of asceticism has become a non-negotiable commitment for bona fide Buddhists ever since.

14. The Scriptures tell us that the evil desires and sin nature that permeates us all can be attributed to the Edenic fall. James 1:13–15 clearly teaches that our desire brings forth sin, and sin brings about death, which is the punishment for sin. This explains why Jesus had to suffer and die in our place to make salvation possible. He substituted Himself for us. The Buddhist recognizes that suffering and death is real, but they have no basis for why it exists and how it has been conquered by God. The only way to remove this sin-nature desire is through Christ, not meditation.

In a monastery in NW China, one monk among many trying to follow the precepts of the Buddha.
(Photo: Thane Ury)

could not have been better, as his method came in a period when there was a huge discontent with the drudgery and vagaries of Hinduism. The Buddha's teachings seemed logical, elegant, and appealing — especially with the suffering class — and so his views progressively gained traction. For the next few centuries Buddhism spread widely in East Asia, across China, and over to Japan and Korea. The desire for some viable, but god-free, answer to the problem of pain and suffering, partially explains why many moderns adopt the Buddhist path.

For all the superficial similarities some may propose between classical expressions of both Buddhism and Christianity, when it comes to theodicy any notion of a concord implodes immediately. For most of the time prior to the advent of Charles Lyell's uniformitarianism, traditional Christianity applied a normative reading to the opening chapters of Genesis; i.e., tending toward accepting the creation and Flood narratives at face value. This meant that Christianity's dominant theodicy for its first 18 centuries was that it was the original disobedience of a historical Adam and Eve that ushered in both moral and natural evils. When our *imago dei*, was fractured, perfect communion with God was lost, and all sufferings and relational dysfunctionalities flowed from this breach. E.L. Mascall succinctly explains:

> It was until recent years almost universally held that all the evils, both moral and physical, which afflict this earth are in some way or another derived from the first act by which a bodily creature endowed with reason deliberately set itself against what it knew to be the will of God.[15]

---

15. E.L. Mascall, *Christian Theology and Natural Science: Some Questions and Their Relations* (New York: Ronald Press Company, 1956), p. 32. See also Thane Ury, "Luther, Calvin, and Wesley on the Genesis of Natural Evil: Recovering Lost Rubrics for Defending a Very Good Creation," in *Coming to Grips with Genesis: Biblical Authority and the Age of the Earth,* Terry Mortenson and Thane Ury, eds. (Green Forest, AR: Master Books, 2008), p. 399–423.

It is perhaps not surprising that evolutionary thinking finds greater unity with Buddhism in particular and Eastern thought in general, but exploring this is beyond the scope of this present chapter.

Present-day Buddhism

> Entering Zen is like stepping through Alice's looking glass. One finds oneself in a topsy-turvy wonderland where everything seems quite mad — charmingly mad for the most part, but mad all the same. It is a world of bewildering dialogues, obscure conundrums, stunning paradoxes, flagrant contradictions, and abrupt non sequiturs, all carried off in the most urbane, cheerful, and innocent style imaginable. — Huston Smith[16]

Through two and a half shaky millennia, Buddha's philosophy has not only survived but it has flourished.[17] And although it is the majority or state religion in a dozen countries, it has remained anything but monochromatic in the 21st century. Variant forms and sects abound, with at least 238 distinct ethnolinguistic Buddhist people groups.[18] Theravada (or Hinayana) and Mahayana are the two major sects of Buddhism and are actually quite different from one another.

Theravada Buddhism

Theravada (The Teaching of the Elders), about 38 percent of all Buddhists, has remained the school truest to original Buddhism, and is more conservative. It tends to be more dominant in China, Japan, Korea, Mongolia, Taiwan, and Tibet. It is also called Southern Buddhism and holds that only monks can reach nirvana. This school is deeply monastic, seeing meditation as the main key to "salvation" and quite inwardly focused.

Mahayana Buddhism

Mahayana (The Greater Vehicle) is more popular at 56 percent, and more liberal than Theravada, and dominates in Cambodia, Laos, Myanmar, Sri Lanka, Singapore, and Thailand. It is also called Northern Buddhism, and contends that even the laity can reach enlightenment. Meditation is vital

---

16. Huston Smith, *The Religions of Man* (New York: Harper & Row, 1958), p. 140.
17. Buddhism has survived episodic setbacks, including a resurgence of Hinduism in India, rivalries with Confucianism and Taoism, a backlash in the Tang Dynasty, plus Hun and Islamic invasions.
18. Paul Hattaway, *Peoples of the Buddhist World* (Carlisle, UK: Piquant, 2004), p. xx.

for this school, but puts more emphasis on selflessness and altruism (i.e., helping others in order to help yourself) to attain salvation (in their belief system); and thus is more outwardly focused than Theravada Buddhism. Additionally, about 700 years after Buddha died, this school had a tendency to see him as a divine. They also have many tantric and occult-like practices.

Other Buddhist Sects

The *Vajrayana* school (The Diamond Vehicle, aka Lamaism or Tantra) is a third, much smaller group at 6 percent, and prevalent in Tibet. It would hardly bear mention were it not for its most famous representative, the exiled Dalai Lama. But all factions of Buddhism can be traced back to this triad of the Mahayana, Theravada, and Vajrayana schools. While each has distinctive dogma, all embrace what we will call "mere Buddhism."

Other variants bear brief mention. *Zen Buddhism* is a spinoff of Mahayana Buddhism, concentrated in Japan. Generally, Zen is a non-doctrinaire road to transcendence, is extremely esoteric, and believes enlightenment is attained by chanting rote phrases, names, or texts. It is not preoccupied with logic and is the most philosophical school. Zen is characterized by an emphasis on detachment from one's desires, seeking to attain extinction (*parinirvana*), with the distinct nuance of experiencing *satori* (the sudden awareness of one's absolute Buddha nature, accompanied by inner joy and harmony).

Pure Land Buddhism (aka Amidism) splintered off of the Mahayana school as well. Pure Landers regard the personality Amitabha Buddha as a savior through whose merits one can achieve nirvana. Pure Land targets the layperson. Engaging in something as simple as a mechanistic chanting of "Praise to Amitabha Buddha" (the *nembutsu*) can clear the way to be reborn in the paradise called Pure Land. This is a mythical place "created" by Amitabha where pursuing enlightenment takes less effort.

Last, *Nichiren Buddhists* are very mystical and stress that they represent true Buddhism. This school is enticing because of its emphasis on material-ism, basically being an Eastern expression of prosperity theology — a view thoroughly at odds with the Buddha. Devotees follow scriptures like *The Lotus Sutra* and teach that by chanting before the *Gohonzon* (a scroll or box with the names of key religious figures in the *Lotus Sutra*), one can bring his life into balance, achieving health and wealth. This sect is also unique in that it seeks to refute other schools and proselytize.

The above distinctions in the Buddhist family tree are crucial for apologists hoping to penetrate hearts from each offshoot. But with so many schisms — and the blurring within each — classification will remain exceedingly difficult.[19] Try to imagine, for example, being invited to chart the common Christian ground of a Pentecostal in the Appalachians, with those of a Filipino Roman Catholic, or a Nigerian Seventh-day Adventist. Since an equally wide swath exists with Gautama's heritors today, we must join leading missiologists and think more in terms of *Buddhisms* on a vast spectrum. Our evangelistic tack with a saffron-robed Buddhist in Qinghai will be quite different than with the Buddhist in the pew in Ulaanbaatar. Zen Buddhism in Japan and Vajrayana Buddhism in Tibet "feel" similar, but look very different. And a Nepali villager may never have been taught Buddha's *Four Noble Truths*, but if you showed them to her she'd likely say she shares such convictions.

East Is East, and West Is West, and Never the Twain Shall Meet?

Contra Kipling's poem, through Buddhism the twain have met indeed. And in America it is the list of high-profile converts that has given it some major street cred.[20] Sports personalities like Tiger Woods, David Beckham, and Phil Jackson (former NBA coach) have turned their hearts East, as have Jerry Brown (governor of California) and luminaries like the late Steve Jobs and Rosa Parks. While not a convert, Bill Clinton has adopted a vegan diet and hired a Buddhist monk to tutor him on proper meditation technique. And the Dalai Lama, the figurehead of an oppressed people group, is treated like a rock star in America, having been invited to the White House, the UN, and wining and dining with the cultural elite.

Los Angeles has been called the most diverse Buddhist city in the world. Complementing this is a list of Hollywood elites who have embraced Buddhist principles, including Richard Gere,[21] Keanu Reeves,

19. See Christmas Humphreys, *Buddhism: An Introduction and Guide* (London: Penguin Books, 1951), p. 71–73, for a proposed platform of 14 tenets that every Buddhist can embrace.
20. Buddhism first established a beachhead in America via Chinese railroad laborers. By the end of the 19th century, hundreds of "joss houses" had sprung up on the West coast.
21. On the heels of 9/11, Gere was booed off stage at a memorial. Why? For asking for a moment of silence . . . for the terrorists! He was also interviewed by ABC Radio, where he counseled Americans to respond with "the medicine of love and compassion." While it's natural for Americans to identify all those murdered and the massive suffering in the wake of the attacks, Gere asked us to also have compassion for "the terrorists who are creating such horrible future lives for themselves because of the negativity of this karma," http://

Tina Turner, and Harrison Ford.[22] Iconic director George Lucas was very transparent that his agenda for the Star Wars series was to introduce Buddhism to the West.[23] The *Force* symbolizes the impersonal energy of Eastern mysticism.[24]

Authors like Thomas Merton, D.Z. Suzuki, Alan Watts, and popular movies like *Seven Years in Tibet, The Little Buddha,* and *What's Love Got to Do with It?* have all contributed to the romanticizing, allure, and mainstreaming of Buddhist-type thinking. Even TV, movies, and music have

been adopting subtle Buddhist elements, like the TV series *Lost* (think Dharma initiative), *Point Break* (with Bodhi — a lead character) and the band Nirvana.

Buddhism's Allure

A full assessment of the Buddhistic worldview's popularity is beyond the scope of this chapter, but a few suggestions for its appeal can be posited. Becoming disillusioned with one's own religious background, Western culture in general, or the rat race of American society have all contributed to hearts turning East.

In all of God's image bearers is a longing soul, like this woman searching for truth at a Buddhist temple. (Photo: Thane Ury)

abcnews.go.com/Entertainment/story?id=101959&page=1. We address karma below, but consider the worldview between Gere's ears. Those in the Twin Towers were not victims, but somehow deserving of their fate, and any suffering in the aftermath of 9/11 was a rebalance for past offenses. Further, the efforts of the Red Cross and Salvation Army, and any relief effort is to be frowned upon, for such bucks against the law of karma. And the sword cuts both ways, for those who escaped the tragedy must somehow be morally upright.

22. Others in Hollywood tied to Buddhism include Orlando Bloom, Oliver Stone, Angelina Jolie, Brad Pitt, Jennifer Lopez, and Leonardo DiCaprio. Raised a Buddhist, Uma (meaning *Great Middle Way*) Thurman holds herself more Buddhist than not. Her father was the first Westerner ever to be an ordained Tibetan Buddhist monk.

23. Buddhist scholar Alexander Berzin notes that prior to making *Star Wars*, Lucas visited a Tibetan monk named Tsenzhab Serkong Rinpoche, who in fact became the basis for the diminutive Grand Jedi Master known as Yoda. In a 2002 interview with *Time*, Lucas was asked if he held a religion, and responded: "I was raised Methodist. Now let's say I'm spiritual. It's Marin County. We're all Buddhists up here." See, John Baxter, *George Lucas: A Biography* (London: Harper Collins, 1999), p. 165, passim. It is known that Joseph Campbell and Carlos Castaneda also deeply influenced Lucas' thinking.

24. Others claim the series also contains subtle hues of Hinduism, Taoism, and/or Zoroastrianism. In an interview with Bill Moyers, Lucas noted that he included mythical elements from multiple cultures and religions, but it is clear that Buddhism is the core philosophy in the universe of *Star Wars*.

Buddhism's rubrics of tolerance, wisdom, compassion, lovingkindness, nonviolence, and personal transformation have also no doubt enticed spiritually awakened and hungry souls. With so many varieties to choose from, Buddhism has enough flavors to accommodate the palates of any individual, even the raging atheist. Consider further that in our sensate world of chaos, materialism, and the erotic, Buddhism's combo of inner tranquility, enlightenment, and easy-believism are an irresistible escape hatch. Our society has also accepted meditation and yoga as great stress relievers, with little regard that these have become gateway disciplines to a deeper exploration of Gautama's path.[25]

Others are no doubt uncritically enamored by the idea of reincarnation, conditioned perhaps by countless wholesome portrayals in modern films.[26] At a superficial level, some may think reincarnations gives them endless chances to get things right. Hollywood, academia, the media, and the social elites all too often give Buddhism a free pass from critical assessment simply because they love its non-judgmental, non-theistic, and non-violent emphases. In addition to appearing hyper-tolerant, Buddhism offers a guilt-free ethical framework with no external god to whom we are accountable. Such is not too far from the flaccid convictions of liberal Christianity — a view paying lip service to a wrath-free deity, whose ecumenical arc has no room for sin, a Christ on a Cross, the exclusive truth claims of a risen Savior, or any suggestion of a final and lasting judgment.[27]

Does Buddhism Have Its Own Scripture?

Islam has the Qur'an, Christianity has the Bible, but Buddhism has no absolute canonical authority binding on all its splinter groups. That being stated, a key textual authority providing some uniformity for most Buddhists is found in the *Pali Canon* — a collection of writings 11 times larger than the Christian Scriptures! The *Pali Canon* is divided into three parts — each called *pitaka* or "basket" — and thus has come to be known as the Tripitaka.

---

25. Esther Baker, an ex-Buddhist nun, provides a fuller list as to why Buddhism may be so attractive to Westerners in her *Buddhism in the Light of Christ* (Eugene, OR: Resource Publications, 2014), p. 3–4.

26. Films like *Avalon High, Brother Bear, Fluke, Cloud Atlas*, and *Birth* contain reincarnation themes.

27. H. Richard Niebuhr famously conveyed such sentiment in his work *The Kingdom of God in America* (New York: Harper & Row, 1937) p. 193.

Tripitaka, or Pali Canon		
Vinaya Pitaka:	Sutra Pitaka:	Abhidhamma Pitaka:
(Basket of Order)	(Basket of Discourses)	(Basket of Higher Teachings)
Code of monastic discipline for the community of monks	Conventional teachings believed to have come straight from Gautama Buddha or his closest followers	Texts in which the Sutta teachings are arranged to help in the study of the nature of mind and matter

Opinions vary within Buddhism regarding the authority of these writings.

Some claim the whole Pali Canon is binding. Others contend that no "basket" can relay rationally warranted beliefs, so the Buddhist canon carries no binding authority. Additional thinkers hold that the enlightened Gautama provided reliable knowledge through his lectures, but no Buddhist texts are authoritative.[28]

While there is no god in Buddhism, the thoughts and teachings of the Buddha (written centuries after his death) are generally taken as an underlying authority to guide Buddhists. But really, at base, a traditional Buddhist takes *himself* as an authority, as he must work out his own salvation. The Buddhist *ordo salutis* is very self-oriented.[29] Regardless, the authorities listed here are *man*. Man is ultimately seen as the absolute authority on Buddhist teachings. This is actually arbitrary, creating a system that allows all things to be true while nothing is true — a state that cannot logically sustain its own weight.

Last, while Buddha's image is often worshiped by some of his followers around the globe, he never considered himself a god or even a revelation from a god. He never even intended to start a new religion, but originally hoped to be a force for reform within Hinduism.

Two major misconceptions linger in the West. The first is that Buddha is the name of a god. But Buddha is just a title that means "enlightened/awakened one" or "teacher." Anyone who has grasped the nature of ultimate

---

28. Other writings looked to as authoritative in the Buddhist world include the *Abhidaharma* (philosophical discourse of Buddhist teaching), the *Vinaya* (monastic regulations), and the *Mahavastu, Milindapanha, Saddharma Pundarika,* and *Prajnaparamita Sutras.*

29. In a famous excerpt from the Tripitaka, the Buddha tells a young monk, Ananda, that monks are to be their own lamps and take refuge in nothing outside of themselves.

Many in the West wrongly associate the portly statues of Budai (left) with the founder of Buddhism (right).
(Photo on left: Creative Commons; photo on right: Umanee Thonrat, Shutterstock)

reality or has been enlightened is a Buddha, and thus, in Buddhism, there are many Buddhas. The second erroneous view is thinking that the corpulent, laughing figurine popular in many Chinese restaurants is the Gautama Buddha of history. But this is actually Budai, a tenth-century quirky Chinese Zen monk, who carried a stick with a bag on it. The Buddha fasted regularly and walked thousands of miles, so a chubby Buddha statue is about as plausible as a chubby Jesus.

Foundations and Beliefs

There are several common beliefs that all Buddhists embrace. Front and center are the "Three Jewels" in which all Buddhists find refuge, reassurance, and dignity. They are the *Buddha* (the yellow jewel), the *teachings* (the blue jewel, or *dharma*), and the monastic order (the red jewel, or *sangha*). One can hear these three gems in the following popular mantra that Buddhist monks chant through the day:

> *Buddham Saranam Gachchami* [I take shelter in Buddha]
> *Dhammam Saranam Gachchami* [I take shelter in dharma]
> *Samgham Saranam Gachchami* [I take shelter in community with monks]

Then we have The Four Noble Truths, which essentially retraces Gautama Buddha's own road toward enlightenment. They are as follows:

1) *Dukkha*, or suffering, is inescapable plight of existence
2) *Samudaya* (or craving) causes dukkha, and grates against all reality
3) *Nirodha* (cease) is the key to overcoming dukkha
4) *Marga*, cessation of suffering comes by following The Eightfold Path

This *Eightfold Path* is key to the cessation of suffering and is congruent with one's move toward enlightenment. The eight steps are:

Training in Wisdom (*Prajan*)	**Right views** — believe The Four Noble Truths, rejecting all false views
	Right intention — improper thoughts must be purged
Training in Morality (*Shila*)	**Right speech** — truthful, clear, non-harmful communication
	Right action — live non-exploitatively and properly toward others
	Right livelihood — live simply
Training in Concentration (*Samadhi*)	**Right effort** — work toward detachment from the world
	Right mind — understand the nature of oneself and reality
	Right meditation — dispel all distractions, total focus on enlightenment

One cannot help but ask who defines "right." If it is just a man, like a monk, Buddha, or anyone else, why presume that they have all knowledge to know the true nature of reality? To know absolute right, one must have absolute knowledge, which no man has. The only one in a position of knowing absolute right (and absolute wrong) is an all-knowing God, not a man. Yet Buddhism has no all-knowing God nor a revelation to man. When men merely have the opinion that something is right or wrong, then it is merely an opinion, a form of arbitrariness.

Several Buddhist tenets are familiar, at least in name, to non-Buddhists in the West. These include karma, reincarnation, the transmigration of the soul, nirvana, and dependent organization.

- Good or bad *karma* dictates everything. Depending on the virtue or depravity of one's actions in prior lives, such determines how one will be manifested in the next life. You literally will sow what you reap. What we are now is a direct effect of actions from a previous incarnation, which in turn are based on the previous lives *ad infinitum*. While Hindus held that one can't break free from this cycle, Buddha iconoclastically claimed not only that one could break free, but also that this escape was available to all castes.

- In the Buddhist view, *reincarnation* normally refers to the endless cycle of birth, life, death, rebirth, and redeath that all must experience on their journey toward enlightenment. The Buddha denied that individual souls come back in other forms, so Buddhism typically rejects the theory of a transmigrating permanent soul.[30]

- *Transmigration of the soul* refers to the passage of the soul from one body to the next in successive incarnations. In Buddhism one doesn't die, but just keeps coming back again and again until enlightenment is achieved. The Mahayana sect embraces the concept of an individual soul, so rebirth is also seen as transmigration. In contrast, however, the Theravada school rejects the idea of the transmigration of the soul (i.e., self, person, or enduring mind) from a prior life.[31]

- *Nirvana* has different nuances among Buddhists, but there is agreement that at nirvana the fires of greed, hatred, ignorance, delusion, and attachment are snuffed out. For some, nirvana denotes a state of absolute bliss, while for others it is the ultimate

30. Recalling how many varying schools of Buddhism there are, we can expect that there will not be uniformity in how terms are understood across "denominational lines." Some sidestep the issue, by claiming differences between reincarnation and transmigration are mere semantics, and thus the terms can be used interchangeably. While that practice is generally acceptable, we must try here to capture some of the subtle differences. Metempsychosis and palingenesis are other terms used with varying nuances in discussing different schools of thought on "rebirth."

31. A few other suggested differences between reincarnation and transmigration deserve mention. Some see reincarnation as rebirth in human form, whereas transmigration refers to a rebirth into a non-human form. Many reincarnationalists (mostly in the West) resist the idea that a human soul can be "rehoused" in anything other than a human being; but transmigrationalists (so we're told) believe that a human can be re-embodied as a wombat, fruit bat, or meerkat. Some say that reincarnation refers to each instance of being reborn, whereas transmigration refers to the whole process. As we can see, there's no boilerplate for either of these categories in today's Buddhism.

liberation where the soul — like a candle's flame — is completely extinguished.[32]

- *Dependent Organization* is the Buddhist metaphysical idea that all things arise together as an interdependent whole. Given our ever-changing, impermanent, essenceless cosmos, this arbitrary "law" accounts for the order and consistency we "observe."[33]

View on Origins

As noted above under the umbrella of Buddhism, while the Theravada, Mahayana, and Vajrayana strands share common ground, they also have doctrinal convictions that totally clash with each other. This holds true for a Buddhist perspective on origins, which is anything but lock step. Yet even allowing for variations, a few precepts remain uniform across their spectrum. Since Buddhism holds that there is no god, no schools can accommodate a supreme creator.

Given Gautama Buddha's opposition to key features of India's Brahmanism, its not surprising that he never was even remotely concerned with accounting for the order in our world[34] or any notion of a first cause. For us to be concerned with the origins of the cosmos (or other "unconjecturables") is a distraction, as Buddha attempted to demonstrate in his famous parable of the poisoned arrow. Picture a man, he asks, shot with a poison arrow. He could alleviate his suffering by simply removing the arrow. But would it not be odd if the wounded refused to have the arrow removed until a number of queries were answered first, questions like the archer's identity, details of the bowperson's family tree, and plotting the arrow's trajectory, aerodynamic integrity, color, weight, composite material, and whether this was volitional or accidental (a hunter's arrow intended for small game?), etc. Buddha's point was that just as suffering would not be alleviated in the least by such conjectures, neither will cosmological contemplations do anything to address our current sufferings. Since the Buddha's main goal was

---

32. The root meaning of the word *nirvana* literally means "to blow out," as in a candle being extinguished.
33. We clearly hear echoes of Heraclitus here, the pre-Socratic who — about the same time as the Buddha — invoked the *ad hoc* doctrine of *logos* as an "ordering principle" for a reality that he also claimed was impermanent and in continual flux.
34. In the *Pali Aggañña Sutta*, Buddha parodies Brahmin views, instead of offering a model of origins.

the elimination of suffering (pulling out the poison arrow), speculations on the origins of the cosmos are relegated to the dustbin of uselessness.[35]

> Some people prefer to call Buddhism a way of life and thought. In Asia, "Buddhism" is often [seen] as an alien term, because to them it merely refers to reality. Because the Buddha wouldn't deal with certain questions basic to metaphysics, there are reasons why his path isn't considered a philosophy. Likewise, because he never resolved questions about God or gods or an afterlife, his teachings aren't precisely a religion. And since it teaches that self is an illusory construct, it can be tricky to categorize it exactly as a psychology. — Gary Gach[36]

Since the Buddha is not known to have ever speculated on human origins, it is warranted to infer that he didn't see such as basic to proper spirituality. This is not surprising because his opinion was that most theological issues were unedifying and unworthy of reflection. Paradoxically enough, for one whose majority platform was built on illusion, it is ironic that the idea of discussing origins involved too much metaphysical speculation for the Buddha.

Thus, on the Buddhist view there is no other option except to believe the universe arose through random and impersonal natural laws. Further, the Buddhist quest to raise cosmic consciousness has even been called *spiritual evolution*, a mantle the New Age movement has been all too happy to pick up.

We generally find crude evolution-like (Chain of Being) underpinnings in all major Asian worldviews. This is true of Confucianism, Taoism, and

---

35. This is clearly a gratuitous and false analogy, for in the real world if a homicidal archer shot arrows one's way, only an irrational person would behave in the manner implied by the parable; i.e., focus on the arrow only. In the real world, one would instinctively and quickly try to determine from whom and which direction the arrow came, to immediately seek cover, and avoid further piercing. Every sane person would agree that tending to the wound is paramount. In failing to consider that a Hindu just might be able to limp and chew gum at the same time, Buddha commits the either–or fallacy (false dichotomy) by omitting a third option: namely, one could, in triage fashion, address the arrow while *also* deducing as much evidence as possible to avoid being a target for follow-up woundings. In the real world, Buddha ultimately succumbed to the arrow's wound — an effect of sin — and regrettably never learned the true genesis of the arrow of suffering and death.

36. Gary Gach, *The Complete Idiot's Guide to Understanding Buddhism* (New York: Penguin Group, 2002), p. 16.

Hinduism. But the Buddhistic cosmogony is unlike other major non-Christian religions in that it has no creation myth.[37] Wayne House distills the Buddhist creational view as follows.

> Buddhism does not refer to the creation of the universe. Instead it refers to everything in the universe as "reality," with all phenomena of the world originating interdependently. Reality is characterized by impermanence,[38] insofar as everything eventually perishes. Reality is understood in terms of processes and relations rather than entities or substances. Human experience is analyzed in five aggregates (*skandhas*). Form (*rupa*) denotes material existence. The other four refer to psychological processes: sensations (*vedana*) perceptions (*samjna*), mental constructs (*samskara*), and consciousness (*vijnana*). The causal conditions for such human experience are found in a 12-membered chain of dependent organization (*pratitya-samatpada*). The links in the chain are ignorance, karmic predisposition, consciousness, name-form, the senses, contact, craving, grasping, becoming, birth, old age, and death.[39]

A Buddhist believes the cosmos is fragmentary and impermanent, and that in a sense, *he* continually creates and recreates his world through karma. We can clearly see that the Buddhist idea of origins is multi-layered, not prone to falsification, and thus has precious little to bring to the empirical table in the contemporary discussion on origins.

View of the Afterlife

All Buddhists believe if they follow the *Eightfold Path* they can achieve liberation from the hamster-wheel of birth, death, and reincarnation. The great yearning is release from this world of maya (illusion), detachment from craving, and that perfect state bliss (nirvana), where pain and suffering are no more (cf. Revelation 21:4). Nirvana is the final state of nothingness for Buddhists. They don't hold to any type or heaven or believe in any type of eternity whatsoever. In other words, their goal is a form of final death with vain hopes that there is nothing beyond this death.

---

37. Some Buddhists allude vaguely to a "creative cloud" with waters initiating a "water cycle."
38. Buddhism's dogma of impermanence is so pervasive that nothing has a permanent essence.
39. Wayne House, *Charts of World Religions* (Grand Rapids, MI: Zondervan, 2006), chart 67.

The idea of hell is also foreign for most of Buddhism, but is allowed for in certain strains of their worldview. I grew up in Asia, and vividly remember as a boy seeing murals on the wall of a Buddhist temple — grotesque frescos of the horrors that awaited some Buddhists.[40] Like Dante's *Inferno*, the images stuck to the canvas of my mind for years, and I've seen similar gruesome vignettes in my nearly 40 trips to China. Those depictions capture the fate for truly

Beijing hell mural
(Photo: Thane Ury)

wicked souls. The silver lining for these Buddhists is that there's a purgatory-like limit to this purging, meaning one will eventually be "freed" to return to the cycle of birth, death, and reincarnation on the path toward nirvana.

Consider the psychological effect of such fatalistic indoctrination. If one's whole existence is determined and the benefits of our current actions are not realized until some successive stage, hopelessness seems assured. Something of this despair can perhaps be seen empirically. Buddhist-dominant countries tend to have very high suicide rates. In fact, J. Warner Wallace has noted that the "the top twenty most suicidal countries are almost all countries with strong Buddhist or Communist (atheist) histories."[41] In Buddhist countries,

40. Buddhism's view on the afterlife is multifaceted, with differing models of hell arising in splinter groups. One view arose in the T'ang dynasty, suggesting hell had 18 levels, each one lasting twice as long as the previous, and each being 20 times more excruciating. Another suggestion arose that there are 12,800 hells beneath us, and 84,000 miscellaneous hells on the cosmic periphery. Assorted Buddhist writings describe these abysses in gruesome detail. Punishments in some hells include being perpetually skewered, dismembered, disemboweled, fried in cauldrons of boiling oil, mauled and ripped to shreds by predatory animals, boiling liquids forced down one's throat, and perpetually forced through a meat grinder with dogs waiting on the receiving end to consume sinners. These ghastly punishments never bring death, and are repeated until one is returned to the reincarnation cycle. These barbaric stations are theoretically tailored to match a person's deeds. Thus, those in occupations as butchers, fishermen, or exterminators would be treated likewise, and so it's not surprising that seeing such graphic murals was enough to terrify many into changing their profession.

41. J. Warner Wallace, "22 Important Questions for the Buddhitic Worldview," Cold-Case Christianity, September 11, 2014, http://coldcasechristianity.com/2014/22-important-questions-for-the-buddhistic-worldview.

the suicide rate is about 18 in 100,000 annually. In Thailand there is a suicide every two hours, and in China there is a suicide every two minutes.

> How many people have provoked this question — not "Who are you?" . . . but "What are you?" . . . Only two: Jesus and Buddha. — Huston Smith and Philip Nova[42]

Buddhist Perspectives on Christ

While every biblically grounded Christian holds to the divinity of Jesus, Buddhists of any variety deny that Jesus was divine. They do not deny, however, that he is a pivotal person in history. Interestingly, since Buddhists believe the Buddha had a miraculous birth, they have few quibbles with Jesus' miraculous birth. They deeply admire his social teachings and particularly his selfless work on behalf on others, but a deity he was not. Instead, he is to be revered as a *bodhisattva*, who allegedly postponed nirvana for the sake of others.[43] Terry Muck even points out that high-level Buddhists show far greater respect for the historical Jesus than liberal exegetes of the Jesus Seminar."[44] But even if the honor these Buddhist leaders accord Jesus as a great teacher seems genuine, fans of C.S. Lewis will wonder how these doyens might respond to the *trilemma*. Lewis wrote:

> I am trying here to prevent anyone saying the really foolish thing that people often say about Him: I'm ready to accept Jesus as a great moral teacher, but I don't accept his claim to be God. That is the one thing we must not say. A man who was merely a man and said the sort of things Jesus said would not be a great moral teacher. He would either be a lunatic — on the level with the man who says he is a poached egg — or else he would be the Devil of Hell. You must make your choice. Either this man was, and is, the Son of God, or else a madman or something worse. You can shut him up for a fool, you can spit at him and kill him

---

42. Huston Smith and Philip Novak, *Buddhism: A Concise Introduction* (New York: HarperOne, 2003) p. 21.

43. In Buddhism, a *bodhisattva* is one who postpones enlightenment to help others attain nirvana. While Buddhism is atheistic, some schools express devotion to various "deities," which often are merely bodhisattvas — somewhat reminiscent of the canonization of saints seen in Roman Catholicism. Besides Gautama, Buddhism recognizes at least 27 other bodhisattvas.

44. Terry C. Muck, "Jesus Through Buddhist Eyes," Books and Culture, accessed February 2, 2016, http://www.booksandculture.com/articles/1999/marapr/9b2046.html.

as a demon or you can fall at his feet and call him Lord and God, but let us not come with any patronizing nonsense about his being a great human teacher. He has not left that open to us. He did not intend to.[45]

Similarities between Buddhism and Christianity

When it comes to dovetailing Christian theism and Buddhism, there has been no shortage of thinkers like Thomas Merton (Trappist monk) and Thich Nhat Hanh (Buddhist monk)[46] — who are among many who have become apologists for such syncretism. And at first glance, superficial parallels between Buddhism and Christianity are abundant. For example, Buddha taught that "self" is the most deceitful of delusions, and Christianity seems to find agreement in Paul's writings,[47] but such agreement is superficial, for *self* is referred to in very different ways. Buddhists have no concept of the sin nature to which Paul is pointing.

Another obvious similarity is the prospect of ultimate peace promised by both religions. But again, the Buddhist brand of peace is unlike Christianity because it is "works-based," where one attains peace through mere meditation. Christianity, on the contrary, contends that real peace only comes through being made new creations in accepting Jesus, the Prince of Peace, as Savior.

Many suggest that Jesus and the Buddha wore comparable halos, and few would disagree that the similarity between their lives is indeed interesting. Consider that each was a monastic leader who . . .

- didn't seek personal power
- taught through parables
- didn't leave any personal writings behind[48]
- established an all-encompassing way of life
- condemned prevailing religious and social norms of the day

---

45. C.S. Lewis, *Mere Christianity* (London: Collins, 1952), p. 54–56.
46. Thich Nhat Hanh, *Living Buddha, Living Christ* (New York: G.P. Putnam's, 1995). Hanh asserts, "When you are a truly happy Christian, you are also a Buddhist. And vice versa."; *Jesus and Buddha: The Parallel Sayings*, ed. Marcus Borg (Berkley, CA: Ulysses Press, 1997); and Paul F. Knitter, *Without Buddha I Could Not Be a Christian* (Croydon, UK: Oneworld Publications, 2013).
47. Cf. Romans 6:11; 2 Corinthians 5:17; Galatians 2:20, 5:24. See also Luke 9:23–24 and John 12:24.
48. Although we have no words written by His own hand, we must acknowledge His words recorded in the Bible, which is Jesus' Word.

- experienced huge opposition from local authorities
- stressed living simple, righteous, and compassionate lives
- condoned strong moral conduct (e.g., prohibitions against killing, stealing, sexual misconduct,[49] lying, and a litany of abuses)
- taught that materialism interferes with spiritual growth
- urged adherents to strive toward perfection
- encouraged community and altruism in his followers
- emphasized a love and respect for all people

Yet, as interesting as these parallels are, the fundamental and irreconcilable contrasts between the two faith systems are quite stark, as highlighted in the following table.

No additional antidote is needed to vanquish futile attempts by creative inclusivists who propose a compatibility between the Buddhist and Christian traditions. The core teachings are hopelessly irreconcilable, and yet the "politically correct tractor beam" of modern pluralism and "forced neutrality" is relentless. Many in the Christian church have gone along for fear of being labeled Buddhaphobic, or similar epithets.

In fact, the motivation behind the production of the volume you are now holding will be judged by many as bigoted and intolerant. It is not because of material presented here (which is written in an honest fashion), but because of intolerant and bigoted positions of those projecting their intolerant and bigoted position toward Christianity. But such is the risk of lovingly and thoroughly assessing the truth claims and congruity of Christianity's contemporary rivals to which we are called (2 Corinthians 10:4–5; 1 Peter 3:15, etc.). The perspicuity of John 14:6 does not cease to exist just because it is ignored — Jesus is *the* way, *the* truth, and *the* life. Ecumenical bartering to dissolve the sharp distinctions listed above can only be done at the high price of abandoning true truth. Additionally, to trivialize the vast chasm between the teachings of the Buddha and those of Jesus is to do a great injustice to the intent of both men. Any promise of a pluralistic potluck reveals a substantial ignorance of both systems as classically understood and of the milieus in which they were birthed.

For most of Asia the rhythm has hardened into a recurrence.

---

49. Almost every country with a Buddhist tradition has made pornography illegal.

| Some Incongruities between Buddhism and Christianity ||
Buddhism	Christianity
No personal God exists (atheistic)	A personal God exists (theistic)
No creational model	God is the creator of all that is
There may be a moral law, but not absolute	There is absolute moral law because God is the absolute law-giver
The fundamental problem is suffering	The fundamental problem is sin, which is responsible for suffering and finally death
"Sin" is ignorance of reality's true nature	Sin is rebellion against God
"Redemption" comes from within	Redemption only comes through Christ
Key moment happened *under* a tree	Key moment happened *on* a tree
Buddhist teachings do not depend on Buddha	There is no Christianity without Christ
Buddha died and was cremated	Jesus died and rose incorruptible
Personhood hinders liberation	Personhood is central*
The ultimate goal is nirvana	The ultimate goal is a personal relationship and reconciliation with God
Completely subjective	Grounded in objective reality
An inward focus prevented development of science	A love and study of creation gave rise to science
Followers should resist critical analysis	Followers are instructed to test all things (1 Thessalonians 5:21–22)
Piety is inwardly focused	True piety looks beyond self
We die perhaps tens of thousands of times	We die just once (Hebrews 9:27)
Merit accrues over thousands of lives	Salvation by faith through God's grace alone
Ultimate reality is *sunyata* (emptiness)	Ultimate reality is fullness in Christ

Cyclical view of life and history	Linear (telic) view of life and history
Followers must empty themselves of desire	Followers can overcome unholy desires; Jesus fulfills our desire
Buddha: "Be ye lamps unto yourselves"	Jesus: "I am the light of the world"
The soul does not exist	The soul does exist
There is no afterlife	There is an afterlife

* So much could be added here. For example, Buddhism sees enduring personhood as an illusion, with nirvana annihilating personhood. But for Christians, we are image bearers of a three-person God, so personhood is essential to Trinitarian thought, and our person endures beyond the grave — being made in the image of an eternal God. The individual (person) is often underemphasized or completely ignored in most Asian traditions. When personhood is ignored, a preoccupation with caste, family, or society rushes to fill the vacuum.

It is no longer merely a rather topsy-turvy sort of world; it is a wheel. . . . [Asia has] been caught up in a sort of cosmic rotation, of which the hollow hub is really nothing. In that sense the worst part of existence is that it may just as well go on like that forever.
— G.K. Chesterton[50]

Arbitrariness and Inconsistencies within Buddhism

Buddhism resembles more of a mystical construct than a tightly formed philosophy with a healthy respect for logic and empirical data. Gautama Buddha himself saw theological reflection as mere speculation, unedifying, and not conducive to attaining spiritual liberation. It is nothing short of painful irony that his view itself would be hard to exceed in its metaphysically conjectural scope.

Christianity of course is also a faith. But it is a faith that is said to rest on historical events. In fact, given the centrality of the Christ's Resurrection, it can truly be said that the Christian faith stands or falls on a single historical

---

50. G.K. Chesterton, *The Everlasting Man* (New York: Dodd, Mead & Co., 1925), http://www.areading.net/The_Everlasting_Man/40.html.

event that is claimed to have taken place in space and time (1 Corinthians 15:12–19). In strong contrast, traditional Buddhists place little to no emphasis on objective data. Ultimate reality is indescribable, indefinable, unknowable, deep things that can only be met with "noble silence."

> "If one cannot empirically know the minds of other people, then pursuing knowledge of other minds is inconsistent with the Buddha's doctrine regarding the kind of knowledge necessary to end suffering. . . . Is not compassion then inconsistent with the kind of knowing that leads one to be able to end one's suffering?" A head monk answered, "If someone truly understands the Buddha's teaching, they will see that compassion is meaningless." Collender comments, "If metaphysical claims are that which we cannot possibly verify, then the Buddha cannot verify . . . that there are any individuals beyond himself. This makes the Buddha's epistemology an enemy of compassion." — Michael Collender[51]

Those who give credence to things like the law of non-contradiction may find encounters with Buddhists quite frustrating. Reasoned arguments and logic will not typically fall on fertile soil, as *Tripitaka* faithful Buddhists seem relegated to mere subjectivism and experientialism at every turn.

But picture a monk looking both ways before crossing a busy Bangkok street to beg for alms; the incongruity of how his meta-rational convictions fits with (1) avoiding being run over, and (2) dependence on others, is perhaps not even realized much less explained. To the average Westerner such irreconcilable contradictions seem pervasive throughout Buddhist dharma. Non-Buddhists, for example, might note the following conundrums:

- Since souls are impermanent — i.e., there is no real self — how can Buddhism refer to nirvana as *achieved* or *experienced*?

- When Buddhism teaches reincarnation, but also denies that souls exist, what then is reincarnated? With no self to be reborn, how can cycles of rebirth occur?

- If all things are impermanent, does not that very conviction implode?[52]

---

51. Michael Collender, sharing his experience during a visit to Wat Thai, a Theravada monastery in the Los Angeles area. *To End All Suffering* (Eugene, OR: Wipf & Stock Publishers, 2014), p. 190.

52. This is an example of *self-referential incoherence*, or a self-defeating assertion. Famous ex-

- Karma entails that past acts and future incidents are inseparably linked together (i.e., we truly reap in this life what we've sown in a previous one). But how can this be if nothing is permanent?

- The Buddhist's whole worldview is predicated on overcoming suffering, but how can this be if (some of the same) Buddhists deny that suffering is real?

- Buddhism infers one has no personal significance. But then why do some Buddhists seem to live as if they *do* have some modicum of significance?

- How can Buddhism claim that suffering comes from the pursuit of private fulfillment, and then pursue (desire) a private fulfillment like nirvana?

- As part of our world of sensory illusion, how are ethical notions (like *good* and *evil* or cruelty and non-cruelty) even sustainable?[53] Specifically, what objective moral basis can Buddhism provide to distinguish between them?

- It is commendable that Buddhists live ethically. But by holding that ultimate reality is impersonal — with distinctions between good and evil being illusory — isn't such an ethic wholly arbitrary with no objective underpinning?[54]

- With no personal God, who/what decides whether an act deserves "good" or "bad" karma?

- How is it even known that the search for enlightenment is worthy?

---

amples are, "All things are relative!" and "There are no absolutes!" Each collapses under its own logic.

53. Buddhism's pessimistic view that life is suffering is logically inconsistent. L.T. Jeyachandran frames it this way: "Philosophically, one cannot define a negative entity such as suffering or evil except as the absence of corresponding, positive entities, namely pleasure and good. If everything were suffering, we would not know it to be suffering!"; L.T. Jeyachandran, *Beyond Opinion: Living the Faith We Defend*, ed. Ravi Zacharias (Nashville, TN: Thomas Nelson, 2007), p. 92–93.

54. Buddhists and New Agers, like secular humanists, all hold to moral values of course. But what ties them together is that neither can provide an objective, ontological rationale for such convictions; forced instead to subjectively embrace a moral framework by sheer fideistic fiat. If no personal God exists, a concept like *The Four Noble Truths* becomes problematic, for on what objective basis are we to determine what is *noble* and what is *truth*? The same applies to the eight *rights* in *The Eightfold Path*. Right by whose standard?

- If self-effort is imperative to curry good karma, how does this mesh with the aid of a bodhisattva?

The list could go on, but one last glaring fallacy bears mention. Buddhism advocates selflessness and liberation from craving. And yet the whole goal of *attaining nirvana* ironically appears to be the ultimate form of selfishness, since it is a completely self-centered experience. Johnson summarizes the contradiction clearly.

> The moral contradiction is precisely this: A person should want to get saved from desire or selfishness. But wanting to save oneself is just as selfish as any other act for selfish ends. If a person wants enlightenment, he still *wants*. And *wanting, desiring*, is the very fault which [sic] prevents enlightenment.[55]

Illogical thinking, of course, is not the exclusive domain of Buddhists, as such manifests itself at some level with all views opposing biblical truth. Nor is it implied that those who pride themselves in logic are automatically superior or logical, much less correct. But with Buddhism (and Taoism also) contradiction actually seems essential to the system, and thus is not only tolerable but even somewhat of a badge of honor. All this comes as no surprise; being the logical outcome of a worldview that teaches that reality is just an illusion. Since any "rules of reasoning," whatever they may be for each individual, are part of a reality that is illusory, then such rigid laws cannot exist, much less be codified in an ethereal worldview.

> Even among the Zen masters themselves there is a great deal of discrepancy, which is quite disconcerting. What one asserts another flatly denies or makes a sarcastic remark about it, so that the uninitiated are at a loss what to make out of all these everlasting and hopeless entanglements. — D.T. Suzuki[56]

Intra-faith dialogues with diehard Buddhists will have no shared appreciation of the logical and linear reasoning that Westerners take for granted. In fact, it will be extremely difficult to fathom why Buddhists themselves fail to see logical contradictions within their framework, their holy books,[57]

---

55. David Johnson, *A Reasoned Look at Asian Religions* (Minneapolis, MN: Bethany House, 1985), p. 130.
56. D.T. Suzuki, "The Koan," in Nancy Wilson Ross, *The World of Zen, an East-West Anthology* (New York: Vintage Books, 1964), p. 54.
57. See https://www.jashow.org/articles/apologetics-2/contradictory-teachings-in-zen-buddhism/.

their practice, or why the law of non-contradiction is not taken as a universal truism. Greg Bahnsen suggests that if someone denies the law of non-contradiction, you could just respond, "Oh, so you don't deny it." When they counter with, "No, I do deny it," then you can simply respond, "Yes, but if you deny it, then you also don't deny it." Since they have given up the law of non-contradiction, then they can't appeal to that law when you contradict their position. The force of Bahnsen's words is hard to escape.

Tips for Sharing the Gospel with Buddhists

Having been introduced to *mere Buddhism*, you can see that this religion is every bit as diverse as Christianity (this happens when a religion has been around for a long time), and as such, just about every assertion and assessment in this chapter could be endlessly qualified. The same holds true for strategies in sharing Christ with Buddhists. There is no cookie-cutter approach. What may have been fruitful for the T'ang dynasty Nestorians will prove sterile 1,300 years later in Marin County.

We all know how daunting it can be to share Christ with family and friends, but getting to Calvary with Buddhists can be even more overwhelming, especially when tacking on cultural and language barriers. Yet be encouraged, as God has helped many just like you to handle these hurdles. A powerful and proven mix involves three things: a little preparation, courageously stepping out in faith, and knowing that God is with you! You will learn, grow, and gain confidence with each encounter. Additionally, previous evangelism by others has plowed the way for you, just as you may be tilling the ground for others or watering what they planted (1 Corinthians 3:5–8). Centuries of prayer cover precedes you too.

Some have long ministered in the Buddhist world. When they share methods that have proved fruitful, and others that have flopped, we should listen. The following common sense suggestions can be adapted according to context.

- This is spiritual warfare, so start with prayer! The Holy Spirit has long tilled the soil in Buddhist hearts, and will continue to do so.

- The demonic is often in play. Do not tread flippantly onto the battlefield.

- Be pre-emptive (1 Peter 3:15). Research Buddhism. Truly understanding a Buddhist's faith is key and shows respect. Familiarity with things like *The Four Noble Truths*, *The Eightfold Path*, and *The Middle Way* is imperative. If you get pressed into a discussion, do not be afraid to ask questions about what the Buddhist believes so that you can properly discuss the issues.

- Similarly, have you delved into a personal study of theodicy (the existence of suffering, especially in the creation of an omnipotent and holy God)? Indications that you've reflected deeply on pain and suffering will send a positive signal. We must be as serious about our beliefs as Buddhists are about theirs.

- You must learn to distinguish original Buddhism from modern variants, in addition to determining which school of Buddhism your friend embraces. When in a discussion, do not be afraid to ask respectful probing questions.

- Buckle in for the long haul. There really are no shortcuts to the time it takes to earn trust and the right to speak truth to the Buddhist.

- Building relational bridges is essential. Do whatever it takes to understand their personal world, listen, and answer questions.

- Dialogical approach is best — listen very well. Residual aggressiveness or condescension must give way to gentleness and reverence (1 Peter 3:15). Being overly confrontational is a killer in general, but more so in an Asian context. Become familiar with and avoid tactics that cause one to "lose face."

- Speaking the truth *in love* is essential in witnessing to Buddhists, respectfully and patiently highlighting essential differences.

- Timing is crucial. Ask God when it's right to advance — and when it's best to pull back. Premature attempts to draw the net can be counter-effective if proper foundations aren't in place.

- Christians committed to their own spiritual disciplines have better rapport with Buddhists. But casual Christians who don't know their sources, or who don't pray, fast, etc., don't foster the same sense of credibility with Buddhists.

- Drawn-out diatribes of comparative religion have rarely worked. Aside from Christ, don't focus on the Buddha or other personalities. Concentrate on issues.

- Share Christ winsomely and patiently. Buddhists usually know little about Jesus, so while an overview of His uniqueness may take time, it is non-negotiable.

- Make no assumptions and patiently clarify key terms. Buddhists are rarely conversant with biblical concepts and terms Christians take for granted. Don't assume Buddhists understand sin, judgment, vicarious atonement, heaven, hell, or resurrection. This is doubly important because some, like the Dalai Lama, substitute terms like *compassion, peace,* and *harmony* with Tibetan words that have very different meanings.

- The concept of a relational God offering forgiveness to His image-bearers has deep appeal for Buddhists.

- The thinking Buddhist wants escape from the cycle of karma, suffering, and incessant striving for self-perfection. Sharing your personal narrative of how Christ freed you from similar bondage and what it's like to have a personal relationship with a living God will be quite powerful.

- Be prepared to explain the differences between *heaven* and *nirvana*.

- Engaging in too much comparative religion (i.e., highlighting common ground) can be a diversion. Focus on Jesus, Jesus, Jesus.

- As you would expect, nomenclature like "born again" or "regeneration" and the like can be problematic, being heard very differently by Buddhist ears. Such terms can't be avoided, of course, but exercise extreme wisdom in explaining the differences between regeneration and reincarnation. One source wisely suggests substitute terminology like "endless freedom from suffering, guilt, and sin," "new power for living a holy life," "promise of eternal good life without suffering," or the "gift of unlimited merit."[58]

- Make sure to give Buddhist friends a Bible, stating your willingness to answer questions. Suggest the Gospel of Mark as a starting point.

- As you began with prayer, likewise end with prayer. In the wake of each encounter, ask God to continue to work on the heart of each

58. North American Mission Board, http://www.4truth.net.

future ex-Buddhist.

Summary of Buddhist Beliefs

Doctrine	Teachings of Buddhism
God	Deny the existence of the biblical God. In its pure form, Buddhism is atheistic; however, some sects revere the Buddha as a godlike figure. Other sects are polytheistic, honoring various lesser gods. All deny Jesus was divine, but many would acknowledge His miraculous birth and see Him as an enlightened teacher.
Authority/Revelation	The authority of the *Tripitaka*, or *Pali Canon*, while variously revered among the sects, is at least acknowledged as a source of Buddhist teachings. Other assorted writings are used by rival sects. Ultimately, each individual is his own authority.
Man	All life forms and men are part of a cycle of life and death whose self is seeking to achieve nirvana. Individuals are born subject to the law of karma, not with a sinful nature, based on their performance in the previous life.
Sin	Sin is loosely defined as doing wrong and having desires that attach one to the world. All suffering is the result of wrong desires and holding wrong thoughts and intentions. Sin is seen as the ignorance of true reality.
Salvation	The individual is intent upon removing all desires and attachments to the world to remove any form of suffering. Following the Eightfold Path, each person can achieve the state of nirvana, having their existence extinguished and removed from the cycle of reincarnation and suffering.
Creation	Deny the existence of a supreme creator. Consider questions about origins a distraction from achieving enlightenment. May embrace evolutionary ideas as a part of the chain of being.

Chapter 20

Confucianism: A Humanistic Wisdom Tradition

Dr. Thane Hutcherson Ury

"Confucianism buried the Chinese . . . it became the curse on China!"[1]

Confucius (551–479 B.C.) has been referred to as China's first teacher; even as the Socrates of the East,[2] and an "unsceptred king, ruling over the Chinese intellectual world for over two thousand years."[3] Far from being a mere punch line or patron sage of fortune cookie wisdom, he is one of the most influential figures in world history. His moral school evolved to become the State-cult in imperial China. Confucius saw the need for ethical scaffolding at every societal tier, and felt precise moral education and the practice of virtues and rites could accomplish that.

---

1. Church leader to author, Sichuan province 8/11/2015.
2. Western philosophy has often been facilely likened as mere footnotes to Socrates, but in the East it is much less hyperbolic to say that all post-Confucian philosophy is a series of footnotes to his ideas.
3. Chen Jingpan, *Confucius as a Teacher: Philosophy of Confucius with Special Reference to Its Educational Implications* (Beijing: Foreign Languages Press, 1990), p. 11.

Historical Overview

Confucius

Five hundred years before Christ, the "wild union" of a 60-something general and a teen concubine, led to the birth of Kong Qiu,[4] born into a feudal state near present-day Qufu, Shandong province. While data on Confucius' early life is either skimpy or unreliable, there is a consensus that he was born into a good family, the youngest of 11 children. After the death of his father, the family fell on hard economic times, but he was still able to get a good education.[5] His early years were challenging. At age 19 he married, had a few children, and later divorced. As time went on, he found employment as a granary bookkeeper, clerk, cowherd, and "Minister of Crime,"[6] before he found his calling as a teacher.

Confucius was self-taught, never had a job of any clout, didn't seek fame, and never imagined he'd become a cultural hero. He did not pretend to be a prophet, promised no riches, power, or fame to his pupils, and none of his disciples ever became a famous leader. Still, he dedicated his life to the battle for the mind and soul of China, and ultimately changed the course of history with a philosophical influence that's lasted two and a half millennia. His ethics continue to impact the lives of well over 1.6 billion people.

Confucius' teachings were initially rejected, but finally and posthumously percolated through every echelon of Chinese society, and took center stage during China's gilded age. While the taxonomy of Confucianism is

---

4. The honorific title, K'ung Fu-tzu (Grand Master Kong) came later. In the 16th century, Jesuit missionaries Latinized this to "Confucius." Outside of China, the terms "Confucianism" and "Confucian" are common but are virtually unheard of referents in Mainland China.

5. Early data on Confucius's life has been notoriously spotty, most turning to Han dynasty historian Sima Qian, but recent scholarship has often found Qian unreliable, and thus we can be justifiably dismissive at times of what appear to be romanticized embellishments by a Confucian apologist. The process of demythologizing the apocryphal Confucius from the Confucius of history is ongoing.

6. For a sampling of the outrageous apocryphal hagiography that was glommed on Confucius's birth, see Lee Dian Rainey, *Confucius and Confucianism: The Essentials* (Malden, MA: Wiley-Blackwell, 2010), p. 12. Spoiler alert: it involves unicorns, dragons, celestial music, and vomiting out jade books.

resistant to easy classification, we here submit that it is that school founded on the premise that people can achieve moral perfection by self effort, frequent introspection, following rules of good conduct, and having a committed sense of duty toward family and society, which all lead to harmony. While there was some fine-tuning or minor straying in subsequent generations, Confucius' basic precepts wavered little, and his legacy and continued influence on the intellectual and social history of South East Asia are incalculable.

He eventually started a school to train leaders, and his reputation as a wise teacher grew. He was a true polymath,[7] and became known as a "one-man university." With an "at-home feel" and Socratic teaching style, he taught history, government, philosophy, and ethics. He also placed a high premium on music, poetry, and the arts in general. And while he shied away from what we would call "theological reflection," he did delve into divination.

Confucius lived during the Zhou dynasty, which had ruled in relative harmony for half a millennia. For a maze of reasons, this calm gave way to storm with a growing disregard for time-honored values. Destabilization rushed into the moral vacuum, and surrounding states became red in tooth and claw. Huston Smith offers the following graphic snapshot.

> Instead of nobly holding their prisoners for ransom, conquerors put them to death in mass executions. Soldiers were paid upon presenting the severed heads of their enemies. Whole populations unlucky enough to be captured were beheaded, including women, children, and the aged. We read of mass slaughters of 60,000, 80,000, 82,000, and even 400,000. There are accounts of the conquered being thrown into boiling caldrons and their relatives forced to drink the human soup.[8]

We could also add oppressive slave labor, crushing taxation, etc. to the mix to highlight the state of moral mayhem confronting Confucius. The collective Chinese mind had an excessively romanticized view of earlier dynasties; a supposed *Golden Age* characterized by harmony and order. But now that societal standards and respected traditions were hemorrhaging badly, a new social philosophy was needed. Confucius was not looking for his 15 minutes

---

7. A person with a wide-range of knowledge.
8. Huston Smith, *The Religions of Man* (New York: Harper and Row, 1965), p. 166.

of fame, but it was looking for him. And he became the architect of a plan that would eventually restore China back to more pastoral days.

Various dueling ideologies in the background added to the drama. The triumvirate of Buddhism, Confucianism, and Taoism — which would later collectively shape the majority worldview of the Chinese — were all gaining traction at this time in history.[9] Yet, in the immediate context, it was the legalist/realist view that was most resistant to Confucian reforms. According to this school, the lives of the citizenry had to be tightly regulated. And while mere overregulation would also be a hallmark of mature Confucianism, the legalists saw the best manner to secure domestic stability was via the "rule of law" — with laws, intimidation, and harsh punishment.

Confucius' sociopolitical model, in contrast, began with individual hearts. The idea was that if the relational mortar of benevolence, trust, and fidelity were refined at the family level, such would result in societal cohesion. The legalist/realist model has been accurately described as an attempt to legislate morality from the top down, whereas Confucius was attempting to reform culture by cultivating goodness from the bottom up.

> In the last 4,000 years, China has produced only one great thinker: Confucius. In the two-and-one-half millennia since his death, China's literati did little more than add footnotes to the theories propounded by Confucius and his disciples, rarely contributing any independent opinions, simply because the traditional culture did not permit it." — Guo Yidong, aka "Bo Yang"[10]

It sounds odd, but there are two reasons that Confucius was not technically the founder of Confucianism as we know it.[11] First, he said, "I have transmitted what was taught to me without making up anything of my own." He was merely a conduit of the paleo-orthodoxy from China's golden past; reviving for China and his disciples the "seminal expressions"[12] of Chinese civilization.

---

9. Few are aware that many philosophies arose concurrently during this pivotal era. At about the last known sighting of the ark of the covenant (586 B.C.), we have the advent of the pre-Socratics, the Upanishads being written, and the arrival of Zoroaster, Buddha, Lao Tzu, and Confucius.

10. https://www.thechinastory.org/yearbooks/yearbook-2013/forum-counting-and-corruption/the-ugly-chinaman/.

11. What we label Confucianism today was originally just called the "School of the Learned"; *ru*, referring to the word scholars. In the annals of Chinese history, the school was also called "the way of the gentleman" and "the forest of the learned."

12. Raymond Dawson, trans., *Confucius: the Analects* (Oxford: Oxford University Press, 1993).

Second, as will be shown below, most of Confucius' ideas and sayings were recollected and recorded by his followers long after his passing. So ripened Confucianism, then, has derivative and collaborative qualities — drawn from material *before* Confucius and basically reconstructed from second-hand accounts *after* Confucius. Having said this, the Confucian repository of materials written, edited, and compiled by Confucius and his followers were quite distinct.

Religion or Philosophy

According to Cantwell-Smith, the question "Is Confucianism a religion?" is one that the West has never been able to answer, and China never able to ask.[13] That may be true, yet the perennial question remains: Is Confucianism[14] a religion or merely a philosophy? Quick answer: Yes, as it seems to be a wisdom tradition with religious qualities. But the question's hidden value is that it forces us to more fully engage the subject. Namely, it forces us to parse and grasp the meanings of *religion* and *philosophy* — which are intricately interconnected. While Confucianism has been labeled a "moral code" or, more creatively, as a "wisdom tradition" — something akin to a cultural foundation[15] — we must look at why the wrangling over "religion or philosophy?" has taken place, and why the issue will probably never be settled.

Some Reasons Confucianism Is Considered a Philosophy

Those who deny that Confucianism is a religion, highlight the obvious demarcation that it has no deity. As such, this wisdom tradition downplays the supernatural, stressing ethical conduct instead. Yes, there are statues of Confucius all over Asia and countless Confucian temples, but these were not originally intended for worship but only as a display of deep reverence directed toward mortals.

---

13. Wilfred Cantwell Smith, *The Meaning and End of Religion* (Minneapolis, MN: Fortress Press, 1991), p. 69.
14. Here we will attempt to engage the root; i.e., *original* Confucianism. Further, with Confucianism sprouting in China — along with most Confucians, past and present, residing there — this chapter will tend toward assessing matters mostly through a Chinese filter. This will be somewhat artificial for scholars and followers of Confucius, but until the topics at hand can be fleshed out in a book-length treatment, such delimitations are needed.
15. The present government in China officially recognizes only five religions: Buddhism, Catholicism, Taoism, Protestantism, and Islam. While it is interesting that Chinese authorities perceive Catholicism and Protestantism as two different religions, the salient point here is that they do *not* categorize Confucianism as a religion, despite it being freely and widely practiced across China.

Confucius never claimed to be a prophet, or claimed divinity, though long after his passing he was venerated. Neither has a claim of divine inspiration ever been made for Confucian texts. There is no organized membership, and instead of a priesthood, we find only an official scholar class.

Classic Confucianism frowned on asceticism,[16] monasticism,[17] and ritual, practices *allowed* within but not *generated* by Confucian principles. Last, Confucianism is decidedly mute on origins or a theory of the afterlife. Additionally, there is no conversion process, no renunciation of another faith to become Confucian, and no moment of transformation, much less marking such with baptism or other ritual.

Another suggested point, often overlooked, is Confucianism's ability to be grafted into other religions, even allegedly exclusive ones. If Confucianism were a religion, this couldn't be done, or so the thinking goes. Those making this point contend in this way: just as Thomism pairs well with Christian convictions, or as some fancy themselves Christian Platonists, so too Christianity can embrace much of Confucianism.

In fact, Dr. Gregg Ten Elshof, philosophy professor and director of Biola University's Center for Christian Thought, sees no reason why there can't be "Confucian Christians."[18] Similar impulses can be found as far back as Matteo Ricci in the 16th century and in any number of more recent luminaries who suggest that Christianity need not replace other faith traditions,[19] but are ripe for a healthy comingling.

Clear-thinking Christians can recognize that there is much moral good in Confucianism, and assuming one is firmly grounded in Christian theology, there is nothing spiritually unhealthy about observing interesting parallels between Confucian convictions and Christian dogma. But what we are not obligated to do is let down our guard every time syncretists drag

---

16. Avoiding indulgence and self-discipline.
17. Renouncing worldly pursuits to follow spiritual pursuits.
18. Jonathan Merritt, "Confucius for Christians? Evangelical College Professor Learns from Unlikely Source," September 8, 2015, http://jonathanmerritt.religionnews.com/2015/09/08/confucius-for-christians-evangelical-college-professor-learns-from-unlikely-source. Reticent souls will want to hear from Ten Elshof how he decides which Confucian rubrics are compatible with Christianity, and which ones are not. Consider Confucius's assertion that "Absorption in the study of the supernatural is most harmful." Lionel Giles, *The Sayings of Confucius* (London: John Murray, 1917), p. 94.
19. William Hocking, Paul Tillich, et al. Even the magisterial sinologist, James Legge, felt that Confucianism is not antagonistic to Christianity in the way that Buddhism and Islam are.

their "electromagnetic crane" over Taoism, Buddhism, and Islam. Something always sticks.[20]

In exploring the Christian-friendly aspects that radiate from Confucianism, perhaps Ten Elshof is only highlighting such as indicators of the natural law that the Lord has lodged in the human conscience, or something equally nonthreatening (see below). If that's all, then we can live with that. But if left unchecked, let's envisage "Elshof 2.O" in the future; some colleague willing to push the envelope just a hair further. What might we brace ourselves for in this future scion?

- Perhaps 2.0 would agree that a *dual belonging of faith* is unacceptable for Christians, instead only affirming that dual citizenship of culture is unavoidable. Perhaps not.

- Perhaps 2.0 will preach the dangers of "Jesus *plus*" thinking. Perhaps not.

- Perhaps 2.0 knows that the suggestion that Christians can accommodate adjectives like "Confucian" will find little support in Scripture,[21] Church history, or the premier Christian apologists of our day. Perhaps not.

- Perhaps 2.0 could point us to references where Paul, Augustine, Luther, Calvin, Wesley, or similar icons would buy into exhortations that there should be "Confucian Christians." Perhaps not.

- Perhaps 2.0 would draw the line if his students began worshiping or offering sacrifices to ancestors in a local Confucian temple, or worked the *I Ching* into their devotions. Perhaps not.

- Perhaps 2.0 will specify how Christianity benefits from even the appearance of a philosophical liaison with a worldview that so many Chinese Christians consider a curse on China. Perhaps not.

---

20. Similarity in moral systems does not make them equal. Other systems that have truth are merely confirming Romans 2, which indicates that in each image-bearer is a God-given conscience (natural law) that reigns in our conduct.
21. See Paul's thoughts on this in 1 Corinthians 1:12–13, 10:18–22.

- Perhaps it will just appear that 2.0 is suggesting that Christianity is internally lacking in something that can only be supplemented (for some) by wrestling with the *Analects*. Perhaps not.

- Perhaps 2.0 will be even more open than his predecessor to "the rich tradition stretching back" to Buddha or Muhammad becoming "God's chosen instrument for affecting change for the better?" If not, perhaps he'll spell out why not.

When considering the supposed merits or pressures of hyphenating our faith, we would do well to remember the Chinese proverb, "A small hole not repaired, in time will become more difficult to mend."

While spirited in-house debates on inclusivism will continue in the West, an inclusive spirit comes "pre-installed" in most Asian religions. For example, Confucian temples often double as Buddhist and Taoist temples.[22] Ralph Covell also notes this interpenetration of Confucianism with adjacent religions, a comingling so pronounced that Chinese could worship in a Confucian facility one day and not think twice about burning joss sticks in a Buddhist temple the next. And as if that's not enough, priests in those very temples often can "not explain to visitors whether the temple was Daoist, Buddhist, or Confucianist."[23]

Two popular Chinese sayings are "Every Chinese wears a Confucian cap, a Taoist robe, and Buddhist sandals" and "Chinese are Confucians at work, Taoists at leisure, and Buddhists at death."

Some Reasons Confucianism Is Considered a Religion

On the other hand, some say that Confucianism bears some of the classic earmarks of religion, siding with Robert Bellah who labels it a "civil religion."[24] It has been variously referred to as a "diffused religion" and

22. Such pluralism, largely a hallmark of Asian culture, can be seen in the Hanging Temple of Hengshan. Hailed as one of the world's architectural wonders, this temple is dedicated to Confucianism, Taoism, and Buddhism. Any concern to keep clinically precise lines between the triumvirate may be a predictable, if not artificial, Western construct. Stated very broadly, Western ideas of religion are usually tethered to recognized canons, formal authority structure, distinct dogma, faiths named after founders, and membership rolls, etc. But in Eastern thought we find a much more nuanced allowance for the comingling of disparate beliefs. See Jordan Paper, *The Spirits are Drunk* (New York: SUNY Press, 1995), p. 7–8.

23. Ralph Covell, *Confucius, the Buddha, and Christ: A History of the Gospel in Chinese* (Eugene, OR: Wipf & Stock Publishers, 2004), p. 9.

24. Robert Bellah, *The Broken Covenant: American Civil Religion in a Time of Trial* (New York: Seabury Press, 1975).

"religious humanism." Michel Masson, a Jesuit scholar, has convincingly demonstrated that faith permeates the Confucianism paradigm.[25]

What are we to make of the claim that Confucius himself followed no deity and downplayed otherworldly matters? We could suggest that this was merely pragmatic or utilitarian, namely, to get folks focused on this world. Even if we grant some truth here, compelling arguments must be built on something more than interesting conjecture.

The same applies to those on the other side who point out that Confucius *did* favor practices which objective observers would immediately recognize as religious. The nuances in this debate cannot be teased out here, and the debate will never be settled, but we can at least highlight why some believe the label of *religion* is warranted.

For example, like its neighboring non-theistic constructs, Buddhism and Taoism, Confucianism also impacts every significant area in one's life. Moreover, Confucianism has seldom been mute about spiritual things, making a generous place at the table for what we might call *soft supernaturalism*. A prime example is the deified principle of *Tian* that brings order to the cosmos. In honoring the teachings from China's past, Confucius not only allowed for "the way to Tian," but in many ways his goals depended on such. Thus, we shouldn't be surprised when some detect, correctly or incorrectly, the faintest brushstrokes of the supernatural in mature Confucianism.

Confucius also saw rituals as essentially non-negotiable to the inner stability of the individual at the micro level — which in turn fortified families and society at the macro level. The man in the street was given wide berth in animistic rites. The thought was that they had a duty to honor spirits of departed ancestors. This intense reverence involved prayers and sacrifices. And of all the issues that early missionaries to China wrestled with, "ancestor worship" proved one of the most delicate and heated.

It is of no minor consequence that Confucius condoned the presenting of sacrifices to *Tian*,[26] that faceless force which governs our life from the

25. See Michel C. Masson's Philosophy and Tradition: The Interpretation of China's Philosophical Past: Fung Yu-lan, 1939–1949 (Taipei: Ricci Institute, 1985).

26. For Peter Berger this alone determines the answer of the "religion or philosophy debate," http://blogs.the-american-interest.com/2012/02/15/is-confucianism-a-religion/. Lit-Sen Chang, a former Confucian, concludes that Confucianism is not a religion. See his Asia's Religions: Christianity's Momentous Encounter with Paganism (Phillipsburg, NJ: P&R Publishing, 1999). It could also be the case that those who energetically push the "religion card," at least in China, do so because they feel an inferiority that their country does not have its own homegrown religion.

cosmos, and kept rulers accountable to the "mandate." He warned that "He who offends against Tian has no one to whom he can pray."[27] While not personally believing in a god(s), Confucius had the reformational zeal of a Martin Luther.

His ardent disciples also exhibited what is indistinguishable from what in any other context would be labeled "religious character." These followers attempted to wed the sacred and the profane, minus the God hypothesis. Confucians, in the wake of their founder, were decidedly worldly, allowing no spiritual distractions. Instead of focusing on the afterlife, they saw it better to focus on healing wounds on this side of eternity. Stephen Prothero summarizes the Confucian's concerns as "ethical rather than eschatological, practical rather than metaphysical."[28] And in forfeiting any possibility of a transcendent relationship, Confucians had to settle for a form of religiosity in its most sterile form — they wanted morality and a moral culture, without bothering to clarify how such could be done without reference to an absolute, transcendent, objective source of moral authority like a personal God.

We've seen that the question of whether Confucianism is a religion or a philosophy is thorny. The better part of valor might be to recognize this as a false dilemma. If so, when asked if Confucianism is a religion or a philosophy, we would be wise to don our Confucian caps and answer, "Yes!"

Does Confucianism Have Its Own Scriptures?

A few years before his death, Confucius undertook the task of collecting, editing, and adding commentary to key historical writings. The result was an anthology of the most pivotal works in Chinese history. Most people are unaware that the Shandong sage was determined to be unoriginal, that most of the key Confucian texts long predate him, or that he did not actually pen much of the teachings attributed to him.

It was only after Confucius' death that followers collated and redacted his thoughts, so we cannot be certain about any of the precise words attributed to him. And it must be noted that no scholar of any merit has ever suggested that the transmissional fidelity of key Confucian texts can hold a candle in comparison to the painstaking copyists' methods

---

27. Analects III: 13. Some translations have "sin" instead of "offends."
28. Stephen Prothero, *God is Not One: The Eight Rival Religions that Run the World and Why Their Differences Matter* (Victoria, Australia: Black Inc, 2010), p. 113.

and trustworthiness boasted by the Old and New Testament documents.[29] Still, it is generally, albeit arbitrarily, accepted by critical scholars that even though we may not have Confucius' exact words in most cases, we can be confident that we have the basic contours of his thoughts.

The following nine works constitute the Confucian canon and became the embodiment of moral law for the collective Chinese conscience. The works are the Five Classics and the Four Books —though some also refer to the Thirteen Classics.[30]

The Five Classics of Confucianism[31]

These works form the core of Confucianism teachings, represent the zenith of Chinese culture, and were developed *before* Confucius. Their centrality became clear when considering that for more than a thousand years anyone considering a career in civil service had to memorize all five works!

1. *I Ching* (*Book of Changes*): A work on yin/yang,[32] cosmology, divination, magic, etc. It attempts to chronicle the readings from *plastromancy* and *scapulimancy* (reading the cracks from heated tortoise shells and ox scapula). The book was considered so vital to Chinese tradition that Emperor Qin spared it from flames during his infamous purge. Confucius placed this work above the other eight, and toward the end of his life said he'd need 50 more years to grasp the *I Ching's* wisdom.

2. *The Classic of Poetry*: A compilation of 305 poems used widely by Confucius, dealing with customs concerning courtship, marriage, war, feasts, sacrifices, agriculture, etc.

3. *The Classic of History*: Includes history, ancient documents, and speeches. Importantly, Emperor Shun from the first recorded

---

29. See F.F. Bruce's timeless *The New Testament Documents: Are They Reliable?* (Downers Grove, IL: IVP, 1943), and Walter Kaiser's *The Old Testament Documents: Are They Reliable and Relevant?* (Downers Grove, IL: IVP, 2001).

30. The Thirteen Classics are the Five Classics and *The Analects* and *The Book of Mencius*. In addition, these texts include three commentaries on the *Spring and Autumn Annals* and five other texts, including the *Classic of Filial Piety*, and the work *Near to Correctness*.

31. A sixth work, *The Book of Music*, has not survived antiquity.

32. The yin and yang symbol is sometimes used to represent the balance found in Confucian ideals. China is philosophically dualistic in many ways, due in large part to the influence of the *I Ching*.

dynasty is said to have sacrificed to *Shang Di*.[33] It also contains reference to *The Mandate of Heaven*, by which every ruler (the *Son of Heaven*) was expected to abide.[34]

4. *The Book of Rites*: Book of ceremonial rituals and etiquette.[35]

5. *Spring and Autumn Annals*: A history of the Dukes of Lu, Confucius' native province.

The Four Books of Confucianism

1. *The Analects*[36] (or "edited conversations") of Confucius: A compilation of nearly 500 of Confucius' thoughts that reached its final form around the second century B.C.[37] The content is mostly on ethics and government. Elias Canetti sees *The Analects* as "the oldest complete intellectual and spiritual portrait of a man. It strikes one as a modern book."[38]

2. *The Great Learning*: Author unknown. A philosophy of the self-made man and the ideal leader.

3. *Doctrine of the Mean*: Written by Confucius' grandson, with the idea that the harmonious development of human nature, decorum, sincerity, and other virtuous conduct comes from following the middle way.

---

33. *Shang Ti* is a common variant spelling.
34. NB: In all of Confucius's known teachings, he personally refers to *Shang Di* only once.
35. As with most of the Confucian canon, this work in its present format is considered to have come after Confucius. Former Confucian, Lit-Sen Chang, notes that in his role as compiler of elements in the *Book of Rites*, Confucius "winnowed away some materials of high spiritual value" and could thus be likened to liberal or modernist theologians: Lit-Sen Chang, *Asia's Religions: Christianity's Momentous Encounter with Paganism* (Phillipsburg, NJ: P&R, 2000), p. 42.
36. Though surviving manuscripts of the *Analects* have variant readings and uncertainties that textual criticism may never solve, it remains the best source for understanding Confucius's thinking. Scholars like E. Bruce and A. Taeko Brooks in *The Original Analects* (New York: Columbia University Press, 2001) argue that only 16 of the *Analects* are actually from Confucius, and that the Confucius of history is much different than the sage presented in past and contemporary literature. See also Lionel M. Jensen, *Manufacturing Confucianism* (Durham, NC: Duke University Press, 1998).
37. Here is one of the most famous aphorisms: "Tzu-kung asked, 'Is there a single word which can be a guide to conduct throughout one's life?' The master said, 'It is perhaps [reciprocity]. Do not impose on others what you yourself do not desire.' "
38. Elias Canetti, *The Conscience of Words*, trans. Joachim Neugroschel (New York: Farrar, Straus & Giroux, 1984), p. 173.

4. *The Book of Mencius*: Written by Mencius, who helped to make Confucius' teachings a national philosophy in China, it includes treatises on good government and the essential goodness of humans.

Emperor Wu, of the Han dynasty, made mastery of the Confucian canon essential for those going into civil service. Such cushy positions used to be the birthright only of the noble class, but the long reach of Confucius shifted things more toward a meritocracy. The penetration continued such that eventually a cult of Confucius developed, where it became compulsory for all those in government to make sacrifices to Confucius. The Classics were later engraved on huge tablets, now preserved in Xi'an, Shaanxi province.[39]

Confucianism 101: Ten Fundamentals

With all the social and ideological unrest in the air in Confucius' day, a blueprint was needed to defuse the chaos and restore social harmony. His solution was as ingenious as it was foolhardy: simply cobble together a mosaic of the best of all possible moral rubrics from China's past: educate everyone about the duty and benefits of the new paradigm, and push the restart button. Space constraints allow us to list only ten of a whole cluster of fundamentals that Confucius pulled together, and/or which post-Confucius adherents deem derivative from his teachings.

Fundamental 1: Benevolence

Ren (also *jen*), for Confucius, was the keynote virtue of the "superior man." Ren is variously translated as righteousness, love, benevolence, empathy, and very often human-heartedness. Attributes like strength, guileless, and reserve come close. But ren was understood in Confucian circles as the loftiest trait — one of always thinking of others — a quality that the present writer calls "othercentricity." This spirit of altruism (*shu*) essentially says, "Judge others as you wish to judged." Confucius affirmed, "The good man is one who, wishing to establish his character, self-deprecatingly establishes the character of others, and, wishing to develop himself, develops others. To be able to use one's own needs as an example for the treatment of others is

---

39. If the reader is ever in Xi'an, it must be a priority to visit the Beilin Museum (Forest of Steles), housed in a former Confucian Temple. Here you will see key Confucian works etched in huge slabs of stone, and nearby the famous Nestorian tablet.

the way to practice ren." When a disciple asked Confucius how to practice ren, the simple answer was "Love people."

Classic Trinitarians, who appreciate the richness of what it means to be image-bearers of a triune God, will appreciate this facet of Confucianism. We were made as social beings, to live a life of ren with others if you will, in pure selfless love. So when Confucians practice this, it is merely an expression of having been stamped deeply with the divine image. We can appreciate the similarity, but must note a least one huge difference: Christians see sin as relationally destructive to the "five bonds," whereas for Confucianism education is the key to eradicate disharmony.

The idea of reciprocal faithfulness is another parallel between Confucianism and Christianity. This is seen clearly in Confucius' negative version of the golden rule. In the *Analects*, he asserts "What you do not want yourself, do not do to others," an idea later echoed in Matthew 7:12.

Confucius urged a return to a golden age when wise rulers were men of ren. Those times were golden because of ren, not vice versa. He insisted that everyone on the social spectrum — from emperor to rice farmer — was obligated to perform certain righteous duties (*yi*). If ren is the inner essence of goodness for the gentleman, yi serves as the external praxis by which the gentleman's character may be authenticated.

Fundamental 2: Etiquette

The concept of *li* (variously translated as etiquette, custom, propriety, or ritual action) is key to developing ren. Li is very complex and laced with nuances. Confucius felt a civilized life would be characterized by ritualizing an entire way of life. The cultural ground and grammar of a harmonious society is made up of individuals "within a framework of fixed convention" who intentionally own up to their ethical role. They must do this almost as performing a sacred rite. Our conduct should reflect goodwill in an appropriate, honorable, and virtuous way in *every* sphere and action.

These social norms are to be expressed in the relationships between (a) ruler and subject, (b) father and son, (c) husband and wife, (d) elder brother and younger brother, and (e) elder friend and younger friend.[40] A dual assumption is at play in these "five bonds." First, these five relations are

---

40. With the hindsight of history, the first "three bonds" have long been assessed as contributing to (not causing) despotism, patriarchalism, and chauvinism. See brief mention below of the stark contrast between early Confucian and early Christian attitudes toward women.

infused with something like the honor a son gives his father (filial piety). Second, with varying degrees, there are reciprocal obligations between both parties. Friendships outside the family are "ritually constrained."

Confucius stated, "Do not look in a way which is not li, do not listen in a way that is not li, do not speak in a way that is not li, do not move in a way that is not li" (*Analects* XII: 1). Li has to do with respecting all rites, social mores, ethical norms, conventions, and political protocol — from the minutia of social etiquette in marketplace greetings, to the elaborate ceremonies of the emperor and ancestor worship, all is tightly prescribed.[41] Morally binding social customs filter down to everything from what to wear, who bows first, to honoring the departing. Nothing is improvised. Ames and Rosemont capture the span of li, as having to do with:

> meaning-invested roles, relationships, and institutions which facilitate communication, and which foster a sense of community. The compass is broad: all formal conduct, from table manners to patterns of greeting and leave-taking, to graduations, weddings and funerals, from gestures of deference to ancestral sacrifices — all of these, and more, are *li*. They are a social grammar that provides each member with a defined place and status within the family, community, and polity.[42]

Essentially, as we have inherited *li*, so too are we to pass on this hermeneutical repository of social grammar to the next generation. To cultivate these is to cultivate harmony. But for Christians, constraining outward human action says nothing about reining in a carnal heart. For those who claim that Confucianism is only a philosophy, they must admit this pervasive ritualizing of all of life does emit the persona of a religion.

---

41. For an example of the meticulous scripting in Confucianism, consider the manner of grief and mourning that a filial son must follow in the wake of his father's passing: "When mourning, a filial son weeps without wailing; he performs funeral rites without attention to personal adornment; he speaks without rhetorical flourish; he feels uncomfortable in fine clothing; he feels no joy on hearing music; he does not relish good food. . . . After three days he breaks his fast. . . . The period of mourning is not allowed to exceed three years. . . . The body shrouded, is lowered into the encased coffin. . . . Beating the breast and jumping up and down, the mourners bid the last sad farewell. The body is laid to rest in the burial place selected by divination." Quoted in Kenneth Kramer, *The Sacred Art of Dying: How the World Religions Understand Death* (Mahwah, NJ: Paulist Press, 1988), p. 88–89.

42. Roger T. Ames and Henry Rosemont, Jr., trans., *The Analects of Confucius: A Philosophical Translation* (New York: Ballantine Books, 1998), p. 51.

Early Chinese characters were basically pictograms, and often made from combining radicals/words to form a new word. In its traditional form, the character yì offers a staggering example of this. Yi is a composite of two words/characters; the upper portion 羊 [lamb] and the lower portion 我 [me] are fused together into a single word, yì, which means "righteous." Non-theists have yet to offer a convincing explanation for this character's origin. In other words, at least six centuries before Christ, what would have been the basis for ancient Chinese to pictify righteousness as "a lamb over me"? Biblically, righteousness comes when we put ourselves under the blood of the Lamb, so it is fascinating to find this character embedded in the content of the I Ching! The author took these photos in Xi'an, at the Forest of Steles. Yi can be seen carved in stone, on both the I-Ching (left) and on a rice paper rubbing of the Nestorian Stele (right).

Fundamental 3: Ideal Man

Junzi means the "ideal man." While Confucius had faith in humanity's innate goodness, he also believed it was best for us to follow an example. Thus, our great need is for a superlative model for society to emulate — what Confucians call a junzi (contrasted with *xiao ren*, meaning "small man" or "commoner"). The word *junzi* is ideally rendered as "superior man" or "gentleman," but previously meant "son of a ruler."

The junzi exhibits the qualities of yi, ren (see below), and *de* (moral force) in all they do. The junzi combines not just the qualities of a gentleman, but also a saint and scholar. The junzi is calm and at ease, while the small man is nervous and uncomfortable. The junzi is a moral guide for the rest of society. He is the model partner in any relationship, the perfect gentleman, who displays honesty, confidence, generosity, humility, and openness. In Confucianism, everyone should strive to be a junzi.

Fundamental 4: Moral Righteousness

Yi, most often rendered as righteousness, is central to Confucianism. The idea is that of "moral sense" and refers to that ethical penchant to do what is right according to one's virtue. This also has to do with discerning what is right according to the situation. Yi is probably second only to jen of all the Confucian virtues. They are companion virtues logically, for how could we radiate "humaneness" toward others without yi? Yi is also closely tied to ritualism, which gives outsiders the distinct impression that Confucianism is a religion. Before Confucius, yi was focused more on things like ritualized ancestor worship. But Confucius widened and applied yi to every area of life.

Fundamental 5: Middle Way

The *Doctrine of the Mean* is to Confucians what the *Tao Te Ching* is to Taoists, and the *Diamond Sutra* is to Buddhists. Aristotle and the Buddha also had their versions of the middle way. Many essential teachings for Confucians are elaborated here, and with an entire book in their canon dedicated to the *mean*, it should be clear just how essential this idea is. Consider the range of translations given for the title: *The Doctrine of the Mean* has been variously translated by some scholars as *Constant Mean, Middle Way, Unwobbling Pivot*, and even *Focusing the Familiar*.

The common denominator is to pursue proper conduct between the ways of two extremes. The essence of the mean is to never act excessively, and as such, the mean is so all-encompassing that it represents every venue in life, particularly equilibrium, honesty, moderation, objectivity, rectitude, sincerity, propriety, truthfulness, and dispensing with prejudice. The objective of the mean is to pursue, reach, and preserve a state of perfect balance in all of life.

Fundamental 6: Right Names

The *Rectification of Names* is a key idea in Confucianism. If chosen to govern a state, Confucius said he would first rectify the names. This meant calling things what they truly are, with the other side of the coin being that things should actually correspond to what they are called. For Confucius, subjects must behave in a manner fitting to their social position as subjects. Sons must behave like sons, fathers like fathers, rulers like rulers, ministers like ministers, and so on. Society must know (1) what each term means, (2) the social roles denoted by these, and (3) act consistent with one's role. Failing to do so is sure to initiate the ripples of disharmony throughout every stratum of society. Harmony comes when a person's behavior corresponds to his name. To reduce the rectification of names to mere observance, manners, and ritual — as so many do — is to trivialize Confucian thought.

Fundamental 7: Knowing Ming

> If my principles are to prevail in the world, it is *Ming*. If they
> are to fall to the ground, is also *Ming*.[43]

> He who does not know *Ming* cannot be a superior man.[44]

Knowing *Ming*. Ming has been translated as fate, destiny, decree, mandate, forces of the heavens, or Will of Heaven. According to Yu-lan Feng, for Confucius, knowing Ming referred to "the Decree of Heaven or Will of Heaven" which "was conceived of as a purposeful force."[45] For some, this means that while there are other things we can affect, most things in our lives are beyond our control. We are to do all we can, of course, but beyond that we must calmly accept most outcomes as inevitable. This is what most Confucians mean when teaching of "knowing Ming."

Others flesh this out differently, asserting that "knowing Ming" allows one to act virtuously with complete disregard for personal gain. One should do what one ought to do simply because it is the right thing to do. So a Ming-knowing ruler will behave virtuously no matter what the potential fall-out might be for himself. And since acting morally always benefits the self-less altruist, at least in Confucius' mind, our moral choices should never be deterred by possible negative consequences. The ideal Confucian, then, acts nobly with no thought of self, and accepting the results as his Ming (fate).

Fundamental 8: Tian

Every key component in Confucianism is disputed to some degree but few more vigorously than the idea of *Tian*, and the debate won't be settled here. Some see Tian as the Zeus in the pantheon of Chinese mythology. Others reduce Tian to something akin to the pre-Socratic notion of *logos*, an impersonal dynamism which is the ordering principle of all reality, and not too unlike Buddhism's *Dependent Organization*.

Show the character Tian (天) to contemporary Chinese and the first thing they'll think of is sky. But in ante-Confucian times Tian signified the Heavenly Emperor who ruled over everything. The idea was far from monochromatic, and could accommodate notions of fate, impersonal nature, and deity.

---

43. Confucius, *Analects* XIV: 38.
44. *Analects* XX: 2.
45. Yu-lan Fung, edited by Derk Bodde, *A Short History of Chinese Philosophy* (New York, NY: Free Press, 1948), p. 45.

A.C. Graham notes that Confucius himself seems conflicted about Tian. Sometimes he seems "convinced that he enjoys the personal protection and sanction of Tian," while at other times "he seems caught in the throes of existential despair, wondering if he has lost his divine backer at last."[46]

Deeply embedded in China's past are six tacit ideas of Tian: (1) Tian is anthropomorphic, (2) Tian's "will" is unpredictable, (3) Tian is absolutely sovereign, (4) Tian is in some degree dependent on mere mortals, (5) Tian is always associated with moral goodness, which, (6) gives moral authority to the emperor, who was seen as the "Son of Heaven" with a mandate derived from *Tian*.[47] In all of these we can hear echoes of the truth about God, likely maintained in the culture from the time of Babel.

Nothing from Confucius suggests that he would challenge these assumptions. He said, "He who offends against Heaven (Tian) has no one to whom he can pray." To be sure, his use of Tian is not to be taken as a pure synonym for God (*Shang Di*[48]), which can be somewhat confusing since the two terms were widely interchangeable at times. Could it be that earlier Chinese were more concerned with plumbing Tian's relationship with man than with philosophical abstractions? If Tian were personal, then of course prayer, worship, and obedience would be approached very differently.

But if Tian is merely an impersonal, ordering force, one is relegated to religion without relationship. It cannot be pursued here, but it is widely held that long before Confucius, China embraced a clear monotheistic view, but this conviction degraded over time.[49] Aside from all the yet-to-be-settled points above, there is no scholarly disagreement regarding the centrality that Tian

---

46. A.C. Graham, *Disputers of the Tao: Philosophical Argument in Ancient China* (La Salle, IL: Open Court, 1989). The author's thoughts in this section are considerably indebted to Graham's insights.

47. The *Mandate* was conditional. Emperors were to "rule by virtue," but if it were determined they ruled non-virtuously (evidenced by disharmony or natural disaster, etc.), the mandate was nullified.

48. In the early-Shang dynasty, *Shang Di* literally meant 'Heavenly ruler' or Supreme Being. With the Zhou era, the term Tian gradually displaced the term Shang Di, though there was an element of interchangeability between the two. *Shang Di* was more personal, while Tian captured more of a flavor of abstraction for the Almighty. See G. Wright Doyle's insightful assessment of this very point at http://www.globalchinacenter.org/analysis/articles/names-for-god-shang-di.php.

49. On China's alleged primordial monotheism, see John Ross, *The Original Religion of China* (Edinburgh: Oliphant, Anderson & Ferrier, 1909), p. 18–25; James Legge, "A Letter to Professor Max Müller," *The Chinese Recorder and Missionary Journal*, XII (1881): 35–53; Matteo Ricci, *The True Meaning of the Lord of Heaven*, trans. Douglas Lancashire and Peter Hu Kuo-chen, ed. Edward Malatesta (St. Louis, MO: Institute of Jesuit Sources, 1985).

played in Confucianism — not to mention other Chinese -isms like Taoism and Moism. For all of these, Tian was the source of moral law in the cosmos.

Fundamental 9: Filial Piety

Far prior to Confucius, filial piety was deeply rooted in feudal China as the bedrock of ethical conduct, social harmony, and sociopolitical stability. Confucius elevated filial piety as the moral gold standard, which in turn was the foundation for ren. So filial piety undergirds Confucian ethics. It can be summarized as follows: the respect, devotion, loyalty, duty, and/or obedience owed by younger members of a family toward elders and ancestors — and more particularly, the loyalty of a son toward his father. For Confucius, reverence for parents was the linchpin virtue for all other social relations. Without filial piety, no other virtues are possible.

> Few of those who are filial sons and respectful brothers will show disrespect to superiors, and there has never been a man who is respectful to superiors and yet creates disorder. A superior man is devoted to the fundamental. When the root is firmly established, the moral law will grow. Filial piety and brotherly respect are the root of humanity.[50]

Fundamental 10: Wen

Wen, in essence, is an appreciation of art and a direct antithesis to "brutishness." Far beyond mere appreciation, though, disciples of the Confucian way are to be conversant in each skill. The arts are not just inspiring but become a cultural vehicle for moral education. Confucius spread his views using arts, ritual, drama, and song. He and his disciples sang and played instruments together, and learning the "Odes" was mandatory. Confucius personally mastered archery, calligraphy, charioteering, and mathematics, and listed calligraphy, poetry, painting, and music as the prime arts. Tian is peppered with creativity, order, and patterns, and mankind is to reciprocate; not just in the visual arts, but even in ritual patterns.

View of Origins

As with Buddhism and Taoism, Confucius and his followers barely thought of origins. Some of this is due to Confucianism being "long on practice and short on the theory . . . [with] an almost pathological horror

---

50. *Analects* I: 2.

of abstractions."[51] But truth be told, it is rare to find *any* early Asian thinker deeply reflecting on ultimate origins, and Confucius is no exception. In Confucianism, since the universe was seen as self-generated, self-contained, and self-maintained, there is no need for a creator. There was a consensus with the scholar class that family, marriage, and government — the key rubrics of social order — were but echoes of the structure of the cosmos. And most notably, the office of emperor was deeply ingrained in the celestial order.

Zhu Xi, an important 12h century Neo-Confucian, and subsequent thinkers, made primitive stabs at cosmological reflection, but given the era, they can't be faulted for only going so far. China was forced to borrow ideas from Indian and Islamic astronomies until the telescope was finally introduced in the 17th century. With longtime disregard for ultimate origins, the dye was cast whereby Confucians never let a Creator's foot in the door. The situation hasn't changed with current "naturalism, materialism, or agnosticism," whereby the living and Almighty God is expelled and has "no relation with the lives of the Chinese people, though they are not aware of this serious fact!"[52]

View of the Afterlife

Though Confucius was very meticulous on how ancestors were to be venerated after their passing, he did not delve into the hereafter. This, as cited above, is one of the main reasons Confucianism is received more as a philosophy than of a religion.

His focus was on the here and now and has nothing to offer on the soteriological (salvation) or eschatological (final and afterlife events) plateaus which are so important in Christianity. Confucianism offers no hope beyond the grave. When asked about death, Confucius famously replied by saying, "If we don't know about life, how can we know about death?" But such answers only serve to underscore the stereotype that Confucian apologists often sound profoundly sagacious, when in fact they regularly only traffic in non-answers or mere platitudes.

Two Key Proponents of Confucianism

Such a melee of intellectual activity arose between 551 and 233 B.C. that the era became known as the *Period of the One Hundred Schools*. Tucked in the

---

51. Diane Morgan, *The Best Guide to Eastern Philosophy & Religion* (New York: Renaissance Books, 2001), p. 178.

52. Lit-Sen Chang, *Asia's Religions: Christianity's Momentous Encounter with Paganism* (Phillipsburg, NJ: P&R Publishing, 1999), p. 51.

middle we have the Warring States Period (401–256 B.C.), that bloodstained era when the Zhou Dynasty was split between eight states. In this epoch, two thinkers arose who expanded Confucius' scope — Mencius (372–289 B.C.) and Xunzi (310–220 B.C.).

These two remain the most well-known early interpreters of Confucian thought. Mencius became known at the "Second Sage," being the most influential Confucian after the "Supreme Sage," Confucius. Areas of concord between them are not hard to find, but we must highlight perhaps the most significant point of disagreement. Many centuries before Pelagianism[53] hit the West, Mencius in the East was already stressing the inherent goodness of human nature, and that we are corrupted only by external factors. This was a key plan in Confucian thought. For nearly two thousand years, the first sentence a Chinese child was taught to read was the Confucian maxim, "Human beings are by nature good."[54] Of course, such could not be more contrary to Scripture (Genesis 8:21; Jeremiah 17:9).

Xunzi, however, did later contend that we are born with an evil nature. On the surface, this reminds us of Pauline dogma (Romans 3:10)., but the similarity is only superficial in that, in Xunzi's view, the evil nature is nothing like the sin-cankered state man is in due to Eden's curse. Xunzi's "cure" for innate evil nature was education; quite different from biblical regeneration which comes only through Christ's atoning work on the Cross. Xunzi offers a Band-Aid, while Paul knows a heart transplant is needed.

Negative Reception

Confucianism's road to becoming *the* orthodox school of thought in China — supported by the majority of emperors for two thousand years — was anything but smooth. To "teach a new dog old tricks" of this magnitude — i.e., to salvage and reanimate the dead, antiquated ritualism of China's past — would require more than one lifetime, and Confucius never lived to see the Chinese utopia of his dreams.

While pursuing reform, Confucius survived near-starvation, endured banishment, and dealt with much rejection. Three rulers were so threatened by Confucius that they tried to have him assassinated. Toward the end of his

---

53. Pelagianism is a 5th century A.D. heresy denying that man inherited a sinful nature. Human nature being unmarred by original sin, thus can freely choose to be good without divine aid.
54. Huston Smith, *The Religions of Man* (New York: Harper and Row, 1965), p. 166.

life, Confucius considered himself a failure, and others agreed. Little could he or they have known the profound influence his ideology would eventually have on billions of Asians through time.

Subsequently, emperors — even up to the modern era — have tried to mold Confucius in their own image, and Confucianism has been bent to symbolize either the good or bad in Chinese history. Emperors and ministers in the Han Dynasty (206 B.C.–A.D. 220) co-opted Confucianism to legitimate their reign, shore up the kingdom, and of course control the populace. But any illusion of uniform respect is dispelled when considering the likes of Han Fei Tzu, a post-Confucian philosopher and apologist for the Legalist philosophy, who ridiculed Confucianism as a parasite. And Liu Bang — first emperor of the Han Dynasty — so despised Confucians that whenever he ran into them, he'd snatch their pointy caps and urinate in them. Under the reign of Emperor Qin, Confucian scholars were severely persecuted. Qin decreed a book burning, consigning many ancient texts to oblivion. Hundreds of Confucian scholars who resisted the edict were buried alive or slaughtered.

After falling out of favor for a season, Confucianism once again became the state ideology from 1392 to 1911. Both the Nationalists under Chiang Kai-shek and Mao's Communist Party (holding to humanistic and materialistic religions) rejected Confucianism. Mao depicted Confucianism as a relic of the imperial past, an ideology of reaction and repression. He vilified Confucius during the Cultural Revolution and compared him to an enemy general who had tried usurping Mao's rule. In an anti-feudalistic rage, Confucian temples and ancient writings were torched.

In contrast, Deng Xiaoping, the communist leader of China after Mao, saw Confucianism as a means for establishing national order and stability. China's current president, Xi Jinping, references the "brilliant insights" of Confucius quite often to back up his own views. He recently touted the Chinese Communist Party as a defender of ancient virtues epitomized by Confucius and his collected teachings, *The Analects*.

The Chinese government spends a great deal of money on the restoration of ancient Confucian temples, and places statues of Confucius in tourist areas. Across the board in Asia, a resurgence of Confucianism and Taoism is taking place. Clearly, Confucius' worry that he made little impact has proven to be inaccurate.

A Snapshot of Present-day Confucianism

While it would be a reckless generalization to say that all of East Asia is Confucian, it would not be an overstatement to claim that Confucian ripples are felt everywhere. Current data estimates there are a mere 6 million Confucians worldwide — a comparatively minor worldview. This number becomes even more modest when considering that 99.4 percent reside in Asia, and the numbers dip further if we count only those who strongly embrace the *entire* Confucian worldview.

However, the important thing here is that more than one-fifth of the world has been seriously conditioned (culturally if not subliminally) by Confucian precepts, and could be labeled "cultural Confucians." Add to this that the Chinese government has funded the establishment of nearly 500 Confucius Institutes worldwide,[55] and Christians have a worldview that needs to be reckoned with.

We cannot lump all Confucians together; like Buddhism, there are many different branches. In this chapter we are focusing for convenience on what we will coin as "mere Confucianism," fully aware any designation will fall short somewhere. The Confucian family tree has many branches, including:

- Neo-Confucianism
- Korean Confucianism
- Japanese Confucianism
- Singapore Confucianism
- Contemporary Neo-Confucianism
- Cultural-Nationalist Confucianism
- North American New Confucians

Confucianism's Allure Today

Quietly gazing over every Supreme Court decision in Washington, DC, Confucius joins an elite group of moralists like Hammurabi, Moses, and Solomon in a marble frieze at the U.S. Supreme Court. While Jews and

---

55. Over the last decade, Beijing has sponsored at least 70 Confucius Institutes in the United States. The Confucius Institute is a Chinese state-run venture which partners (mostly) with American schools to promote Mandarin language and foster cross-cultural collaborative initiatives. However, concerns about lack of transparency and curbing of academic freedom have led the University of Chicago, Penn State, and Stockholm University to shut down these institutes on their campuses. A spirited debate continues as to whether these institutes serve as a Trojan horse for political propaganda.

Christians might quibble over the merits of including some of the 18 lawgivers immortalized there (Muhammad?), there's no question that Confucius can be respected. Thomas Paine, one of the founding fathers of the United States, respected Confucius and Jesus as the two most influential moral teachers in history.

For a variety of reasons, Confucianism strikes a positive note with many. Whether this is due to its non-sectarian bent or the precise opposite, each heart has its reasons. Confucianism might also be seen by some as a "preservative" of Asian culture. We should also recall that Confucianism arose in response to chaotic times. It is not a huge news flash, therefore, that given the moral mayhem of our day we find some hoping for a revival of Confucianism,

Confucius immortalized in marble at the U.S. Supreme Court, Washington, DC

even recommending that it be added as a sixth official religion in China.

But what are we to do when mere respect gives way to something more? Consider the aforementioned Biola professor who sees no incongruity in the idea of "Confucian Christians." Is it such a stretch to envisage an impressionable student, perhaps disillusioned with institutional religion, finding some implied imprimatur (if not invitation) from Prof. Ten Elshof? The student — let's call him Blake — a missionary kid who grew up in Japan might quietly ponder and put in an email:

> Dr. Elshof . . . what a godsend. So cool!! How could he know when he spoke in class today that it's been ages since I've felt any meaningful depth in my spiritual walk? Interesting that his book talks about "a life in pursuit of Confucian Christian ideals." Maybe exploring the merits of being a Confucian Christian — to "find my way into flourishing" as he mentioned — could be the ticket. I'm curious to know if reflecting on the *Analects* could also increase and expand my humanity — my humanness on the way. Sounded kind of odd to hear him put it that way, but he's not just a believer — and not just a PhD — but in fact an administrator no less, at my parents' alma mater, right? And yet, as one with 14 years in Japan, I can't help but think how

my Asian pastor would process Prof. Ten Elshof's invitation to "integrate Confucian categories and emphases with Christian commitment."[56] Prof's optimism seems so radically at odds from most of the Asian voices I've heard in my experience. But Prof said reflecting on the *Analects* has aided his pursuit of the Way of Jesus . . . well, why not me too.

The main issue is not whether this has happened or not, but only if Ten Elshof would be concerned over such a scenario. To read his book, one would have to conclude that he would say, "Mission accomplished."

We already have a group made up largely of university professors currently in North America, who have long been proselytizing on behalf of a Confucian ethos. These are called the *New Confucians*. So Confucianism has already being wooing the Blakes of this generation. It's not surprising that such an enticement might not come from beyond the pale, but we must beware that Confucianism might be covertly (or even unintentionally) promoted by ambassadors within the church.[57] For decades, Blake's Japanese pastor has been helping recovering Confucians to place their faith in Christ alone. His concern regarding Blake's email, prompted the following responses:

1. The *I Ching* is a work on divination, which Confucius placed above all other texts, even adding ten appendices (called the

56. Gregg A. Ten Elshof, *Confucius for Christians: What an Ancient Chinese Worldview Can Teach Us about Life in Christ* (Grand Rapids, MI: Eerdmans, 2015). Ten Elshof's motives seem noble, and his work is short and lucid. But if it ever gets translated, it will be interesting to hear the response of Chinese House Church leaders to the premise that Christians should learn at the feet of Confucius.

57. Ten Elshof is not promoting "double belonging," but his thesis would seem to open the door in that direction. A choir of apologists for "double belonging" can be found in Catherine Cornille, ed., *Many Mansions? Multiple Religious Belonging and Christian Identity* (Eugene, OR: Wipf and Stock, 2010). In the introduction, Cornille muses: "In a world of seemingly unlimited choice in matters of religious identity and affiliation, the idea of belonging exclusively to one religious tradition or of drawing from only one set of spiritual, symbolic, or ritual resources is no longer self evident. Why restrict oneself to . . . one religious tradition amid the rich diversity of symbols and rituals presenting themselves to the religious imagination? . . . A heightened and widespread awareness of religious pluralism has presently left the religious person with the choice not only of *which* religion, but also love how many religions she or he might belong to." For attempts to defend "dual-citizenship," see, John H. Berthrong, *All Under Heaven: Transforming Paradigms in Confucian-Christian Dial* (Albany, NY: SUNY Press, 1994), p. 165–186; and Gavin D'Costa and Ross Thompson, *Buddhist-Christian Dual Belonging: Affirmations, Objections, Explorations* (Surrey, UK: Ashgate Publishing, 2015). Compare Han Küng and Julia Ching, *Christianity & Chinese Religions* (New York: Double Day, 1989), p. 273–283.

"Ten Wings"). Is your professor OK with students chewing on these ten wings? Why or why not?

2. When counseling your classmates to plumb Confucius for wisdom, there's so much that goes against Scripture. What standard does your teacher use to disentangle which Confucian tenets to revere and which ones to avoid? Confucius says, "Heaven does no speaking!" How are we helped on *the way* with that?

3. Additionally, does he give clear examples of necessary insights that we can learn from this wisdom tradition that couldn't be garnered from sources in our faith? Is he suggesting that if Confucius had never been born that Christians would in some manner be spiritually or philosophically impoverished?

4. Perhaps he's only intimating that Confucius can be used of the Lord to help unearth our deep-seated cultural or theological biases? Can't that be done without proselytizing for Confucian Christianity?

5. Since key thinkers like Calvin, Luther, and Wesley didn't extol the benefits of sipping at the fount of Southeast Asian thought. Please ask your professor to spell out why it is that his wisdom exceeds theirs.

6. I agree with your professor's counsel to be wary of our cultural blinders. Very wise! But this must cut both ways. Confucius was humanistic and rationalistic to the core — two very serious blinders. You said Ten Elshof has yet to highlight any of the serious weakness in Confucianism. As a former Confucian priest myself, this huge omission is very telling to me.

7. A major focus of your parents' mission here has been to teach that we're all in desperate need of a Savior. Confucius, however, suggested that human nature is basically good, and that we must focus on self-effort, not preoccupied with otherworldly distractions. You're grounded enough to see what's going on here.

8. So many in our congregation here have repented of Confucianism, due to some of its underlying false teachings. They'd be quite concerned to hear that your parents' alma mater is comfortable with the idea that Christians can meditate on

the *Analects*; fashioning these as somehow a handmaiden to theology and Christian devotion.

9. Does your professor arbitrarily stop with Confucius? Why not plunder any humanist for devotional insight? Why not become a Taoist or Buscaglian Christian, or even move to Christian Confucianism with a Whiteheadian emphasis? Where would the quest stop and why?

10. Confucius' words, so often very wise, carry little more authority or inspiration than the obituaries in your local newspaper. Remember, Confucius was just a man. "Thinking Christianly" is our mandate from heaven; thinking otherwise can be dangerous business indeed.

11. Please check your library for the most recent works by Lit-Sen Chang (even Paulos Huang and Abraham Poon) to get another perspective from an Asian sharing something of his own emancipation from Confucianism.

From all I've heard, your favorite prof is a great guy. Please let me know how he responds to the concerns above.

Cordially,

Pastor Taoshiro

Common Ground between Confucianism and Christianity

Common emphases abound between Confucianism and Christianity. One of the more obvious parallels is that both traditions see "ego is a weapon of mass destruction." With this comes an "other centeredness" that both traditions hold as praiseworthy, stemming into other similarities: respect, love, strong morality, centrality of family and tradition, filial piety, justice, leading by example (vs. coercion), and the cultivation of self-discipline, virtue, and wisdom, etc. Such matters and many others have no doubt captured Prof. Elshof's imagination.

Consider also that Confucius' master plan was to train up a small band of young men in virtuous education, sending them out to take leadership positions in and become agents of transformation in their world. Sound familiar?

Moreover, Confucianism has always put a high premium on the importance of education. As with Christianity, understanding accompanies thoughtful study. Taoism's accent toward passivity in educational (and political) processes, on the other hand, is one of many strong contrasts with Confucianism. Confucius' pedagogy and passion attracted many, and he welcomed students from any social background. His greatest student was a commoner, and he was widely known for taking students who could repay him with nothing more than dried meat and gratitude.

The history of the Church boasts similar impulses: that there should be no class distinctions in education; that those of humble means can improve their plight through education and hard work; that meritocracy outweighs entitlement; etc. Confucius deserves accolades for these kinds of things. But man's deepest need is not information or even virtuous modeling, but true heart transformation found in Christ alone. Mere education can't provide that. Education without reformation is vacuous; reformation without transformation is — well — Confucianism. Our greatest need is a redeemed heart that praises, walks, and communes with our Creator.

Last, Christianity strongly concurs with Confucianism that only in community are we fully human. We are not built for isolation; we are built for relation. We can admire Confucius' "five bonds" as the glue for a stable cultural environment. But we lament that he missed the most important relationship a person can have — a personal relationship with God. This "sixth bond" gives a whole different motivation to how the other five relationships are ordered. It is perhaps this single factor that best accounts for the skyrocketing growth of Christianity in China today.

Differences between Confucianism and Christianity

Many more likenesses could be given. But it behooves Christians to discern truth form error. In fact, the similarities above are incidental if not superficial, given that they emanate from radically different origins, and operate with starkly contrasting motives. Some of this can be seen in the following chart showing representative contrasts between Confucianism and Christianity.

Arbitrariness, Inconsistencies, and Weaknesses in Confucianism

Given our investigation so far, the reader can understand why Johnson insists that "Confucian theory is difficult to criticize."[58] Given its broad scope, ambitious humanistic soteriology, "soft supernaturalism," numerous abstractions, toggling between inclusivism and exclusivism, we see why. It

---

58. David Johnson, *A Reasoned Look at Asian Religions* (Minneapolis, MN: Bethany House, 1985), p. 41.

Some Differences between Confucianism and Christianity	
Confucianism	**Christianity**
Main Goal: To have a structured society.	Main Goal: Love God and follow His will
Humans are inherently good	Humans are inherently fallen and sinful
"Sin" is breach of the rule of piety toward a superior, parents, family, or homeland	All have inherited a sin nature. Sins are willful violations of known laws of God
Claims the Way (Dao) has been lost	Jesus said, "I am the way"
One foot in present, the other in the past	One foot in present, the other in the future
Founder wrestled with moral weakness	Founder was sinless
"Earthly salvation" achieved through education behavior modification	Eternal salvation comes in acknowledging Jesus' atoning sacrifice and receiving Him as Savior
An inclusive wisdom tradition	An exclusive worldview
No teaching about redemption for sin	Gospel message: there is redemption for sin
Right doing leads to right being	Right being leads to right doing
Anthropocentric	Theocentric/Christocentric
Silver rule: "Do not do unto others . . ."	Golden rule: "Do unto others . . ."

is difficult to criticize in part because it is hard to grasp. Still, for Christians who find much common ground with Confucianism and Christianity, they should be aware of some of its shortcomings. There are many, but we will mention only eight here.

The Biggie

The early Confucian consensus was that man is good by nature and can be perfected by education. In Confucian terms, each person must "rectify himself," which means he must regulate his own conduct. But as lofty and admirable as this sounds, it only bubbles forth from human thinking, making it entirely arbitrary. Thus, outside of being justified by the Holy One of Israel, there is no eternal hope for those placing any salvific weight in these man-crafted guidelines.[59] Again, the many merits of Confucianism mustn't be allowed to camouflage that it is in large part a failed experiment. The Confucian quest for a perfect utopia never materialized — and never will — simply because it was and remains a human construct.

Human beings cannot make themselves good through sheer act of the will, and "human nature being what it is, the lack of *external* checks and balances on power led to the gradual corruption of dynasties all through history."[60] The notion that man is basically good denies the doctrine of original sin and has made evangelism in Asia very difficult. This biggest weakness latent in Confucianism gives birth to the following remaining shortcomings below.

The Elitist Criticism

Johnson highlights a defect of Confucianism missed by most, one found compelling by those on the right (who embrace democratic principles of social order) and those on the left (like Marxists and Maoists). It relates to Confucianism's "anti-democratic and aristocratic cultivation of a cultural elite."

Recalling our prior mention of the junzi, we noted the strong emphasis Confucianism puts on the development of the "ideal" gentleman — but Johnson highlights the obvious, that not everyone can become a gentleman. Those who "make it" tend to enjoy a privileged and refined life. As he rises up the privileged social ladder, he lacks less and less, finding opportunity to accept or reject things according to his (subjective) inner sense of appropriate behavior.

But doesn't this "refinement and taste" come at the expense of everyone else who cannot attain such position? And this is exactly what happened, as the canyon between an elite (and often corrupt) class and the underprivileged was vast. The former enjoyed a palatial and splendid world, while such blessings never trickled down to those in greatest need. Most people influenced by democratic ideas about equality and the rights of the common man saw something wrong with this Confucian elitism, where a few people are raised "to a level where they are considered to be somehow *better* than others." It's

---

59. A few references suggesting exclusivism are John 14:6; Acts 4:12; 1 Timothy 2:5; 1 Corinthians 15:21–22; Hebrews 9:12.

60. Rob Gifford, *China Road: A Journey into the Future of a Rising Power* (New York: Random House, 2007), p. 104.

no shock that Communists castigated "the scholar gentleman" as representative of all that was "repressive, oppressive, and exploitative about the old system."[61]

The Not-so-Golden Rule

A disciple of Confucius, Zi Gong, asked, "Is there any one word that could guide a person throughout life?" The master replied, "How about [reciprocity]? Do not do unto others what you would not want others to do unto you." This is so similar to Jesus' Golden Rule (Mark 12:31) that some have even suggested Jesus plagiarized Confucius! But this charge lacks punch when noting one key difference. While Confucius (and many religions) frames the rule as a negative, Jesus' states the rule as a positive. Jesus exhorted his disciples to "Do unto others as you would have them do unto you." This is a call to a *higher* degree of service than merely refraining from doing bad things to others.

The Christian rule implicitly challenges us to seek opportunities to do good for others. Yamamoto goes so far as to say that in Confucius' version of the Golden Rule, he was instructing his disciples to focus on *themselves*, and references C. George Fry who contends that the first saving virtue for Confucius was "self love."[62]

Inferiority of Women

In the vast majority of Confucianism's earliest chapters, women are accorded very low status and always ranked below men. He spelled out how to become the "ideal man," but nothing of the ideal woman. He shook the social structure by saying that any *man* could become a junzi and scholar, but females factor in very little in the *Analects*. Confucian teaching, as a whole, did nothing to upend the consensus view that girls were to be subordinate, and essentially servant girls in the making.

Additionally, at temple altars, only the names of male ancestors could be listed. And in the *Book of History*, women seem to only be mentioned when it is to blame them for bad happenings. All this stands in stark contrast to Jesus, whose attitude and compassion toward women was breathtakingly inclusive. You might recall that it was women who were the first bear witnesses to His Resurrection.

---

61. Johnson, *A Reasoned Look at Asian Religions*, p. 41–42.
62. J. Isamu Yamamoto, *Buddhism, Taoism, & Other Far Eastern Religions* (Grand Rapids, MI: Zondervan Publishing House, 1998), p. 59.

We can extend Confucius a modicum of slack, as he certainly didn't create China's patriarchal persona. All of Chinese society was male-centered, and he was a product of his time and culture. Having said that, we are saying that long before the practice of foot binding,[63] Confucian ideology did nothing to loose the psychological fetters women had in being valued less than men.

Consider also the lines from a very famous poem (Book IV, *Odes*, vi)

> Sons shall be born to him:
> They will be put to sleep on couches;
> They will be clothed in robes;
> They will have scepters to play with;
> Daughters shall be born to him:
> They will be put to sleep on the ground;
> They will be clothed with wrappers;
> They will have tiles to play with.

The clear and sad message is that girls are inferior to boys in this religious philosophy.

Note also the yin and yang motif — that famous concept in Asian philosophy where everything in the universe is divided into opposite but complementary elements that interact harmoniously. The male-biased principle of yang is portrayed with positive traits like luminous, fast, moving, and aggressive. The female principle of yin is associated with negative qualities like cold, darkness, graves, death, passivity, ghosts, submission, emptiness, and fear.

The harmony of all things in nature and the mutual relationship between good and evil are often represented with the yin-yang symbol.

Imagine the psychological straitjacketing to millions of women over the centuries, having their gender undeservedly linked with negative things (as was portrayed with the main character in the Disney film *Mulan*). Imagine how this conditioned not just young girls, but also the equal damage of millions of men over the centuries having their gender undeservedly linked with the positive. The long arc of justice is slow but sure, however. With 83 documented generations in Confucius' ancestry, in 2009 women were finally officially recognized in Confucius' family tree.

---

63. This was the constricting of young women's feet to prevent growth, done so as a symbol of beauty and status. The barbaric practice was finally ended in the early 20th century.

God's Word vs. Man's Opinion

Another point bears mention — even though it will only carry force with those who accept the truth claims of Christianity — namely that the claims of Confucius and the Confucianism canon have no grounding in divine revelation. The Confucian classics reveal the vanity of relying on human doctrine without the aid of divine revelation. As such, they carry no more authority than any other man-made proclamations.

Confucius' wisdom is nothing but the opinion of one man. Many moral rubrics espoused in Confucianism can be appreciated and even in part practiced by a Christian, and that may be all that Elshof is suggesting. But it must be constantly borne in mind that the Confucian system is humanistic to the core, and thus large parts of it must be courteously, if not firmly, rejected. Christianity, when properly understood, is not weighed and found in want of something that Confucianism offers. But Confucianism, when properly understood, is weighed and found in great need of what Christianity offers.

Sez Who?

We must make a "typically Western" inquiry here. Confucius' exhorted his followers to make truth a priority in their lives. In the *Analects* VII: 24, he highlighted the priority of "culture, conduct, loyalty, and truthfulness." Consider also some of his famous aphorisms:

> The object of the superior man is truth.

> They who know the truth are not equal to those who love it, and they who love it are not equal to those who delight in it.

> Speak the truth, do not yield to anger; give, if thou art asked for little; by these three steps thou wilt go near the gods.

No one denies that Confucius sincerely promoted virtue, wisdom, morality, and the pursuit of truth. But herein lies a dilemma, according to John Ankerberg. The unstated premise is that all of these lofty standards presuppose an absolute standard; these ideals must be "true for everyone — everywhere and always. Yet, what if these qualities are merely relative concepts, untethered from objective truth? If truth is reduced to mere personal whim — for example by an Emperor Qin type in a power grab — then all the

Confucian ideals are gutted of objective meaning, and thus have no authentic or lasting value.

Presupposing that words have meaning, Ankerberg asks us to consider how Confucius might counsel the *superior man* (i.e., the genuinely virtuous) "to learn truth prudently, with humility and attention to detail."[64] Saying this is one thing, but how exactly do we follow his sagacious advice; how do we learn absolute truth? How do we transcend the wisdom to be found in the routine and practical matters of this earthly life? How do we learn the truth where it matters the most, discovering real answers to the great questions of life that everyone is unavoidably curious about? What about finding the true purpose of life, or how to secure enduring peace and happiness, or knowing what happens when we die, or the nature of ultimate reality? This is where, if we honor Confucius admonition to place truth first in our lives, we discover a dilemma.

But Ankerberg is merely exploiting a philosophical weakness which Arthur Leff calls "The Grand Sez Who?" Why do the rights of the ruler (be he the emperor or Mao) outweigh those of the rice farmer or even the whole country? Leff says that without an objective source of moral authority handing down laws from above, what reason do we have to designate any action or school of thought as "virtuous" as opposed to another?[65]

If a Christian suggests we act more generously to the needy, someone might ask "Sez who?" When she quotes Luke 3:11, it's implicit that she's saying, "Jesus — the Creator and Sustainer and absolute authority in all things! That's who!" Cultured despisers of our faith aren't swayed by this, but that's not the point. We are just saying that this is the *basis* on which we should build our convictions and from which we act.

But think about any exhortation that Confucius ever uttered, or pick any of his pithy proverbs, and immediately ask, "Sez who?" We are not denying that many elements in Confucianism are good, moral, and edifying. We are simply trying to get at the meta-ethical bedrock of what makes the good things *good* that Confucius advocates? For a Christian, the answers come easier than most. Namely, it is the absolute objective moral authority undergirding Christianity — the Almighty God — that permits the Christian to judge elements in Confucianism as good or bad. But anyone should wonder if Confucian precepts should be accepted on

64. https://www.jashow.org/articles/general/the-religions-of-china-and-the-power-of-jesus/.
65. http://www.firstthings.com/article/1993/03/002-nihilism-and-the-end-of-law.

their own ground. Aside from begging the question, we can hear Dr. Leff chime in, "Sez who?"

With Friends Like These

Given China's cyclic anarchy, cruelty, wars, crime, societal discord, government corruption, innumerable manifestations of inhumanity, and collapse of the family in Confucius' day, it is difficult to fathom how Confucius (and Mencius later) could embrace the premise that "mankind is innately good." Mencius agreed. Xun Zi, in the third century B.C., on the other hand, examined the empirical data of life, claiming that man naturally tended toward evil.

Confucians of every stripe, however, were collectively mistaken in thinking that all foibles could be purged through mere education and *self*-cultivation. It was *self*-cultivation, in a sense, that caused all problems in the first place. Mankind has been crippled since that scene played out in the Garden.

The River Elegy

A church leader in central China recently told the author that, "Confucianism buried the Chinese . . . it became the curse on China!" Confucius' philosophy carved out deep ruts that the Chinese slavishly followed for 2,000 years. This observation was from a prominent believer, but it's also a fairly common sentiment on the street that Confucianism has generally held China back.

This exact point was loudly and surprisingly made when CCTV (Chinese state TV) aired a documentary series in 1988 called *River Elegy*, partly blaming Confucianism for China's isolationism and backwardness. It suggested that blindly following traditions had hindered China's modernization. The series brought on a maelstrom, and its proximity to the deadly Tiananmen confrontation a year later should not be missed.

But what of the series title? It refers to the Yellow River, which has come to represent the cradle of Chinese culture and civilization. The earliest written records verify that she was known as the mother river of the nation, and most Mainland Chinese see themselves as offspring of the Yellow River. It has long been called "China's Sorrow" because of its propensity for devastating floods. But now we have reference to an elegy, or "a lament for the dead." Rob Gifford explains why the series title was chosen.

There is an old Chinese saying that "a dipperful of Yellow River water is seven-tenths mud," and *River Elegy* took the silt and sediment of the river as a symbol for the weight of Confucian tradition, clogging up the Chinese mind. The elegy of the title was an aspirational one, a hope that the traditional cultural of China, which has held the country back for so long, might die and be replaced by a more progressive, Western-style way of thinking.[66]

So the suffocating sediments of the Yellow River (in part) symbolized the mud that has suffocated Chinese minds for ages. The creators of *River Elegy* were trying to raise awareness that China's cultural stagnation had many culprits, and Confucianism was a key player.[67] Christians, of course, see a much deeper need here, as this presents an opportunity for the gospel to penetrate Asia's rocky soil. Such, in fact, has already been firmly established in Korea, and missiologists estimate that at present, 22,000 souls turn to Christ every day in China. From river elegy to river of life?

Tips for Redemptive Outreach with Confucians[68]

God-fearing Christians can and do disagree on their approaches to reaching the Confucian soul. Where can we accommodate, and where must we hold firm? Those long-immersed in the Asian world have found some approaches more fruitful than others when sharing Christ with those who are deeply imprinted with Confucian convictions. The author's own parents modeled for him several decades of love for the Asian harvest, and he watched countless souls befriended in his living rooms, seeing questions addressed with biblical truth, barriers come down, and — over time — these souls loved into the Kingdom. The following common sense suggestions can be ignored or adapted according to context, and will often apply just as well when witnessing Buddhists, Taoists, or anyone from a traditional Asian background.

---

66. Gifford, *China Road*, p. 166.
67. Other weaknesses in Confucianism are too numerous to list here. See also, J.N.D. Anderson, ed., *The World's Religions*, 3rd edition (Grand Rapids, MI: Eerdmans, 1955), p. 178–179; and Stuart C. Hackett, *Oriental Philosophy: A Westerner's Guide to Eastern Thought* (Madison, WI: University of Wisconsin Press 1979), p. 140–152.
68. See also "Christian Witness to the Chinese People" at https://www.lausanne.org/content/lop/lop-6, and https://www.lausanne.org/content/lga/2014-11/the-path-to-confuciuss-ideal. Cf. Paulos Huang, "Basic Problems in the Confucian-Christian dialogue," in *Confronting Confucian Understandings of the Christian Doctrine of Salvation* (Leiden, The Netherlands: E.J. Bill, 2009), p. 245–265.

- Spiritual warfare is serious. Begin with prayer! The Holy Spirit has long tilled the soil in Confucian hearts, and will help you.

- To fully comprehend the Chinese psyche it is imperative, as one thinker put it, to "reckon with the long shadow of Confucius." Familiarization with the *Analects* is essential if you are preparing for missions work anywhere with high concentrations of Confucians.

- Huang gives five positives which have increased Confucian receptivity to the gospel: (1) the enthusiasm of Chinese Christian believers; (2) the attractive personalities of many Western missionaries; (3) the respect for, and use of, Confucian classics by many missionaries in their presentation of the Gospel; (4) the dialogical approach that has replaced a more confrontational stance of earlier years; and (5) the employment of natural reasoning by missionaries and Chinese converts, which appeals to the rationalistic bent of Confucianism (i.e., we need the solid grounding in apologetics).[69] This still holds.

- Ancestor worship is not likely to come up in early encounters, but could arise later. Be prepared! How to express deep veneration without worship is not a topic for armchair missionaries. Areas of contextualization at this depth must sometimes be wrestled with for years, to discern which elements Scripture is asking us to adopt, adapt, or abolish.

- Honest seekers have wondered for ages whether they are called to reject their culture when becoming Christian. It's unfortunate and embarrassing that missionaries have botched this so often. Add to this the anti-imperialism mantra of the May Fourth Movement (1919), "One more Christian, one less Chinese," and we get a feel for the psychological warfare that still constricts the Chinese heart. So many Asians continue

---

69. I am indebted to G. Wright Doyle for this tidy summation, as well as drawing my attention to Huang's work, http://www.reachingchineseworldwide.org/blog/reviews/confronting-confucian-understandings-of-the-christian-doctrine-of-salvation. Huang's study should be indispensible reading for anyone serious about the present Confucian-Christian dialogue, and learning how Confucians from the Ricci era to the present have adopted, adapted, or abated the Christian message.

to labor under the illusion that coming to Calvary means betraying family and cultural identity. Be prepared to show how Chinese can be followers of Christ without having to jettison their ethnic identity. Also, anticipate some version of the question as to whether one can be Confucian and Christian.

- Discussing the Father relationship is often helpful as such an exploration can help Confucians form a more accurate concept of our personal God.

- Two Confucian ideals are personified by Jesus — namely the virtues of being (1) junzi, the ideal man, and (2) a son of perfect filiality. Tracing these trajectories for a sensitive seeker is an effective way to find common ground and point to Christ as the perfect image of God.

- Consider adapting this parallel: "China's history is replete with emperors who have utterly failed in their *Mandate* to govern wisely and maintain harmony, But *Shang Di*, the Father, sent His Son of Heaven who sacrificed himself to fulfill his Father's will and usher in reconciliation." To frame things like this is to preemptively address the charge of the gospel being a foreign answer to an indigenous problem, and (again) highlight the Confucian ideal of filial piety.[70]

- Wherever biblically warranted, emphasizing parallels between Christianity and Confucianism in order to evangelize Confucians can be fruitful. But doing so in a way to suggest that becoming a "Confucian Christian" is okay, or that condones "double belonging," is extremely problematic.

- The realization that the Christian message is the missing piece to Confucius' puzzle of the Noble Man could be extremely significant for a cultural Asian considering the claims of Jesus.

- Don't get mired in cherry picking inconsistencies of Confucianism. Such does not fly in Asia. Paint an irresistible narrative of how Christ fulfills the longings of the Confucian heart. Use words as necessary.

70. Adapted from http://rzim.org/just-thinking/jesus-the-path-to-human-flourishing.

- Again, spiritual warfare is serious! The enemy will not easily relinquish territory he's fought millennia to conquer. Pray, pray, pray!

Summary of Confucian Beliefs

Doctrine	Teachings of Confucianism
God	Confucians pursue social ethics, and all traditional Asian cultures see the spiritual realm as carrying the potential for impacting society and all relationships. Deny the God of the Bible, but allowance is made for an impersonal Tian that resembles an ultimate force or ordering principle. Elements of ancestor worship are common.
Authority/ Revelation	Confucius is seen as the pre-eminent leader. The Five Classics, the Four Books form the core Confucian canon. Among these the *Analects* is most revered, and for Confucius himself it was the *I Ching*.
Man	All men are innately good. Only in relation to others can one establish virtuous character. Education, virtuous living, and ritual can create the ideal man. External influences cause moral corruption.
Sin	In early days there was a moral obligation to follow the Mandate of Heaven. To not do so was "sin," but sin was also the result of external corrupting influences or failing to follow *li* or *yi*. Creating disharmony and defying social structures and rites are seen as corruptions of the created order.
Salvation	Man can achieve moral perfection, social harmony and benevolent governing through human effort and proper ritual, including veneration of ancestors. There is no defined concept of an afterlife, or a "reward and punishment" dialectic.
Creation	View the universe as self-existent, so there is no notion of a Creator. Modern adherents may accept various ideas regarding evolution.

Chapter 21

Unitarianism

Roger Patterson

As a writer, I often interact with people on social media platforms who are commenting on my articles or articles from Answers in Genesis. One of the most alarming ideas I encounter from professing Christians is the unitarian view of God.

In articles that talk about the trinitarian God of the Bible, commenters quickly turn to castigating the authors and other commenters for believing in the Trinity. They insist that God has revealed Himself as the "one, true, and living God." "If God is one, how can you say there are three gods?" "The Trinity was invented by Constantine/Council of Nicaea/Roman Catholics." "If you are worshiping the Trinity, you are worshiping false gods."

While these are common responses, they do not reflect the biblical presentation of God. While we must admit that the word "Trinity" does not appear in the Bible, we dare not deny that the concept is presented.[1] This is such an important issue because it is a dividing line between those who know the Father and those who do not. The Apostle John warns the first-century Christians that denying Jesus as God in the flesh is to deny the Father, as well.

> Who is a liar but he who denies that Jesus is the Christ? He
> is antichrist who denies the Father and the Son. Whoever denies

---

1. See Appendix 1, "The Triune God," in volume one of this series for a scriptural validation of the Trinity.

the Son does not have the Father either; he who acknowledges the Son has the Father also (1 John 2:22–23).[2]

The early church had to deal with this question on many occasions. The outcome of every challenge to the doctrine of the Trinity was to denounce the unitarian views of God as heresy — a doctrine that leads to damnation to all who deny the triune God. The fullest summary expression of these trinitarian ideas is contained in the Athanasian Creed. Earlier creeds, like the Nicene and Apostles' Creed, do not have an expressly trinitarian formula that continues to allow non-trinitarian groups to claim allegiance to Christianity through these less-precise creeds.

While these false views are damning, the modern expressions of Unitarianism has moved further away from its historic Christian roots to the point that Dr. Walter Martin has called it "the cult of the intellect."[3] Blending ideas of New Age thinking with rationalism and moral relativism, biblical morality has been abandoned for a truly man-centered view of truth and morality. Within Unitarian Universalism, *man* is truly the measure of all things.

Defining Unitarianism

The term "unitarian" has both a general sense and a more precise theological sense. The focus of this chapter is the religious movement known as Unitarianism and its later expression of Unitarian Universalism, but we will also look at how the term can be applied in a general sense. At its root, a unitarian view of God insists that God is one person and one being. This is practically synonymous with monotheism, believing in one God, but is distinguished from a trinitarian monotheism that believes in one God existing in three persons. The trinitarian distinguishes between the being and the persons of the Godhead while the unitarian denies the distinction in various ways.[4]

In its specific sense, Unitarianism is a system of religious thought that developed in Europe in the mid-16th century. It is characterized by the acknowledgment of one God, denying that Jesus and the Holy Spirit are persons of the Godhead. Jesus is seen as the "son" of God in some sense, and the Holy Spirit is seen as a force or an aspect of God's will in the world.

---

2. Scripture in this chapter is from the New King James Version (NKJV) of the Bible.
3. https://www.youtube.com/watch?v=RVwGaXt4pOk.
4. When referring to the religious movement, Unitarian will be capitalized; when used as an adjective describing the generic view of the nature of God it will be lowercase. The same format will be followed for the use of trinitarian.

Variations on a Theme

Today, we can find many expressions of the unitarian view of God within the broad scope of Christianity. Christadelphians, Jehovah's Witnesses, and others teach a monotheistic unitarian view of God. Additionally, several unitarian groups developed out of trinitarian churches in the US. United Pentecostalism and Oneness Pentecostalism are non-trinitarian groups that teach God is one being manifested in three different modes. This unitarian belief is often referred to as *modalism* and bears strong resemblance to *Sabellianism*, a unitarian view promoted by Sabellius in the third century. Other denominations, some bearing "Church of God" or "Apostolic" in their names, also hold a unitarian view of God while claiming the Bible as an important aspect of their religious views. Judaism and Islam can also be considered unitarian in this general sense, each acknowledging that there is only one God.

There is also a rise in unitarian teaching among groups associated with the modern "Hebrew Roots" movement. Aligning strongly with Judaism, these groups view Jesus as the human Messiah, but deny the Trinity. Similarly, a rise in Biblical Unitarianism in the West has been championed by teachers like Anthony Buzzard, but seeking to distinguish themselves from rational Unitarianism, especially Universal Unitarianism. Biblical Unitarians consider themselves within orthodox Christianity and appeal to the Bible as an authoritative source.

These forms of unitarian religious systems fit within the category of counterfeits of Christianity, the subject of volume one of this series. They are briefly covered here because of the potentially confusing terminology, allowing a clear distinction between unitarian beliefs and the Unitarian movement. At their origin, the Unitarian churches were overtly biblical. In their modern expressions, Unitarianism and Unitarian Universalism can be seen as moralistic religions that draw ideas from many different sources. Both are ultimately grounded in human reasoning and natural law rather than God and His revelation to us in the Bible.

Unitarian History

Unitarian thinking was present in various groups from the beginning of Christianity. As with much of our modern understanding of Christianity, Unitarianism rose out of the Protestant Reformation. You may be familiar with the name Michael Servetus — probably associated with John Calvin — but you may not know why his teaching was being challenged as heresy by both the Roman Catholics and the Protestants. Servetus' views were rejected for good reason — he was openly promoting a unitarian view of God and other false ideas. This ire came to a head in 1531 with the publication of his *Trinitarian Misconceptions*.

Additionally, the Protestants saw him as a dangerous false

Unitarians, including Michael Servetus and Thomas Jefferson, have compared the doctrine of the Trinity to turning the one true God into the three-headed beast, Cerberus.
(Campana Collection, 1861, Louvre Museum, by Eagle Painter, Wikipedia)

teacher because he rejected the biblical teaching of justification by faith alone.[5] He was arrested by Roman Catholics but he escaped. Later, he was arrested in Geneva by Protestants. During his trial in Geneva in 1553, he was questioned on his views of the Trinity, having compared the doctrine of the Trinity to the mythical three-headed Greek beast, Cerberus. Holding a unitarian view of God, he saw the doctrine of the Trinity as unbiblical and denied that Jesus was the eternal Son of God. Unfortunately, Servetus was charged as a heretic and burned at the stake for his heresies by the civil authorities, and much controversy surrounds this event.[6]

Various scholars in Europe continued to study the writings of Servetus, especially in light of his refusal to recant at his martyrdom. While he had not founded a movement, he surely paved the way for a young Italian to do so. Following in the footsteps of his soft-spoken uncle Lelio, Fausto Sozzini would carry Servetus' ideas to the founding of the first unitarian church. While various spellings of his name are found, we often see it presented in its Latin form as Faustus Socinus. It is from this spelling that the anti-Trinitarian view of Socinianism is named.

---

5. Frederick B. Mott, *A Short History of Unitarianism since the Reformation*, 2nd ed. (Boston, MA: Unitarian Sunday-School Society, 1893), p. 15–24, accessed digitally at https://books.google.com/books?id=jHcRAAAAYAAJ.

6. Standford Rives, *Did Calvin Murder Servetus?* (Charleston, SC: BookSurge Publishers, 2008), p. 288–289, accessed digitally at https://books.google.com/books?id=MlPrYQ5srKEC.

Faustus Socinus continued to promote the anti-Trinitarian views of Servetus and began to develop a more robust system of thinking — the system that would ultimately be known as Unitarianism. Beyond teaching against the Trinity, he also promoted an unbiblical view of Christ's sacrifice. Socinus denied that Jesus was a vicarious (substitutionary) sacrifice for sins, but that obedience to God was still necessary.[7]

Rather than Jesus reconciling God to men, the consensus of a majority of the Reformers, Socinus taught that men were reconciled to God through piety, demonstrations of love, and obedience to God — through works. Jesus is seen more as an example for us to follow than a substitute who died in our place having taken upon Himself the penalty for our sins. He also denied the idea of original sin, the pre-existence of Jesus as the Word before His birth, and that God's knowledge of the future is limited to necessary truths.

The Transylvanian and Polish Churches

Socinus was called to Transylvania (in modern-day Romania) to help settle a dispute within the Unitarian Church of Transylvania. Simultaneously in Poland, a Unitarian church was gaining popularity. The Minor Reformed Church, a group who had split from the majority, formed in 1565. Commonly known as the Polish Brethren, this group was banned from Poland in 1656. Many of its members moved to Transylvania, Netherlands, and England, where there had already been considerable Unitarian influence.

Through the writings of Socinus, formal doctrines of Unitarian thought were formulated. Published after his death, the Racovian Catechism provided the platform of Unitarian teaching. Though there were factions that denied miracles and other aspects, these teachings relied heavily on the Bible for their foundation. Though Socinus promoted the use of human reason to validate what the Bible taught (i.e., *man* sitting in judgment over God), it was in England that the secular rationalism of the Scientific Revolution and Enlightenment era would add color to Unitarian thinking.

Spread to England

In 1609, a Latin version of the unitarian Racovian Catechism was produced and eventually banned by the English Parliament, which ordered all of the copies to be burned. Not long after, a version emerged from Amsterdam in

---

7. Mott, *A Short History of Unitarianism since the Reformation*, p. 25–26.

English. Some credit this translation to John Biddle.[8] Biddle had used his own reasoning from the Bible to come to the conclusion that the Trinity was a doctrine foreign to Scripture.

Upon encountering the works of Socinus, Biddle found a kindred spirit and began promoting his ideas in writing and speaking. This promotion of anti-Trinitarian ideas brought the ire of the government who had outlawed anti-Trinitarian teaching as blasphemy, landing him in jail on multiple occasions. Biddle's views also brought condemnation in John Owen's *A Brief Declaration and Vindication of the Doctrine of the Trinity*. Owen specifically targeted the false views of the Trinity and the atonement presented by Biddle and other Socinians.[9] Jonathan Edwards would later argue in a similar manner against John Locke's rationalistic view of Scripture and Socinian views.[10]

Along with the increasing secular humanistic influence of the period before the Enlightenment, Biddle saw human reason as the only appropriate way to interpret Scripture. This influence led Biddle and others to reason that Jesus was not divine, nor was the Holy Spirit a part of the Godhead. The Trinity was deemed irrational by fallible human standards, and they found Bible passages that they twisted to support their ideas. In this, their error is exposed — they used man's fallible reasoning to judge the truth of God's infallible Word. Through the distribution of tracts and preaching in various venues, the application of rationalism to the interpretation of the Scriptures flourished.

This influence is later seen in the writings of John Locke, Isaac Newton, and John Milton. All of these men, though often propped up for their Christian beliefs, denied or questioned the Trinity and the deity of Christ while subjecting the Scriptures to their own rational standards. While acknowledging God's role in the world and even His revelation through Scripture, they used Scripture to support their ideas where it was helpful and set it aside where it was not useful. This rationalistic approach to Scripture would become a hallmark of Unitarianism as it grew in England and spread to America.

---

8. Ibid., p. 28. Also spelled Bidle.
9. John Owen, *A Brief Declaration and Vindication of the Doctrine of the Trinity*, 8th ed., (Glasgow, Scotland: Napier and Khull, 1798), p. viii–xii, accessed digitally at https://books.google.com/books?id=NwM3AAAAMAAJ.
10. J.D. Bowers, *Joseph Priestley and English Unitarianism in America* (University Park, PA: Pennsylvania State University Press, 2007), p. 20.

Because of the strong connection between church and state in 16th- and 17th-century Europe, Unitarians were pushed out of government involvement and generally persecuted for their beliefs by both the Roman Catholic and Protestant regimes. It was not until 1774 that the first Unitarian congregation was established by Theophilus Lindsey. Lindsey was a vicar in the Anglican Church, and you may know him as an early champion of Sunday school. But his rejection of Trinitarian doctrines and subscription to all of the Thirty-Nine Articles of the Anglican Church led him to join a petition to parliament in 1771 to allow the Unitarians and others to remain in the church without holding to the Anglican doctrines in total. After the petition failed, he resigned his vicarage and began teaching at Essex Street Chapel in London. At the dedication of the chapel in April of 1774, Benjamin Franklin made an appearance. Within four years they had purchased more property on Essex Street and a "proper chapel" was built.[11] The headquarters of the British Unitarians remains there to this day.

Lindsey was also a friend of one of the greatest British scientific minds, Joseph Priestley. Priestley took his great analytical mind and applied it to theology. The rational spirit of the age was turning many theists toward deism, though atheism was still socially unacceptable. Mott notes that "Priestley's great help to the growth of Unitarian principles was in the use of shears and pruning-knife. He relentlessly trimmed away conventionalities, the poetry of tradition, and the mystery of accepted faith, and left only the sturdy stock of rational theology, a strong plant for others to cultivate."[12] Priestley's influence stretched beyond his scientific endeavors to philosophy and religious thought.

Other notable Unitarians in England include Josiah Wedgewood, Emma Darwin, John Locke, John Milton, Charles Dickens, and Neville Chamberlain.

Spread to America

Priestley was basically forced out of England for his political and social views. He chose to find a new home in America. Landing there in 1794, he was not the first to bring rationalism and Unitarianism across the Atlantic. As many different groups moved to the English colonies, Unitarian thinkers and teachers were among them, but Priestley unified the movement with his

---

11. Bowers, *Joseph Priestley and English Unitarianism in America*, p. 15.
12. Mott, *A Short History of Unitarianism since the Reformation*, p. 42.

leadership.[13] While the colonies were strongly influenced by biblical Christianity, the rationalism of the Enlightenment blended with the moralism that found its primary basis in the Bible. While many dismissed the miraculous elements of the Bible, it was still an influential book. But as with Biddle and others, reason sat as judge over revelation. Natural law was the standard, and the Bible was used where it was helpful in affirming proverbial wisdom.

Unitarianism as a formal American denomination took root in Boston with the founding of King's Chapel in 1784. Colonial New England was heavily influenced by Calvinist theology, so Socinian ideas denying the divinity of Jesus and substitutionary atonement raised the hackles of the orthodox Christians. However, James Freeman found a sympathetic audience when he arrived at King's Chapel. The congregation was so amenable to his ideas that he reformed the Episcopal liturgy to align with Unitarian doctrines. Being refused ordination as an Episcopal minister, the congregation ordained him as their minister.[14] With the assistance of William Hazlitt and the writings of Priestley and his students, tracts and other writings promoting Unitarian beliefs were distributed, and Unitarianism spread in the fledgling nation.[15]

Unitarian Ideas among the Founding Fathers

If the defining doctrines of Unitarianism are placing reason above Scripture, denying the divinity of Jesus, and rejecting man's sinfulness and need for Christ's atoning blood, its doctrines were broadly accepted even before a church was established. Reading the 18th-century American political discussions, the influence of John Locke cannot be denied. His use of principles from Scripture, acknowledgment of the Divine, and emphasis on reason ring through his work and those who followed his thinking.

While the Bible was revered by many as book of good moral value, even ministers like John Witherspoon taught that reason sat in judgment over revelation. It was his influence that took Princeton from a school training ministers of the gospel to one training rationalists who would greatly influence America's founding period. Dr. Gregg Frazer has dubbed this view "theistic rationalism," documenting how key men involved in writing

---

13. Bowers, *Joseph Priestley and English Unitarianism in America*, p. 2–3.
14. Mott, *A Short History of Unitarianism since the Reformation*, p. 44–46.
15. George Willis Cooke, *Unitarianism in America: A History of Its Origin and Development*, vol. 4 (Boston, Massachusetts: American Unitarian Association, 1902), p. 76–80; Bowers, *Joseph Priestley and English Unitarianism in America*, p. 53.

America's founding documents used biblical principles in the spirit of John Locke's rationalism. While acknowledging God is involved in the affairs of man (acknowledging providence and denying Deism), they looked to their own reason to judge what was useful and true in Scripture.[16]

The influence of Servetus, Priestley, Lindsey, and others seems clear in the writings of Thomas Jefferson who likewise compared the doctrine of the Trinity to Cerberus and promoted Unitarianism as the only rational view of God, though expressing that in public was politically problematic. His view that Trinitarian teaching had corrupted true Christianity and the prominent role of reason are clearly presented in a letter to James Smith from 1822:

> I have to thank you for your pamphlets on the subject of Unitarianism, and to express my gratification with your efforts for the revival of primitive Christianity in your quarter. No historical fact is better established than that the doctrine of one god, pure and uncompounded was that of the early ages of Christianity; and was among the efficacious doctrines which gave it triumph over the polytheism of the ancients, sickened with the absurdities of their own theology. Nor was the unity of the supreme being ousted from the Christian creed by the force of reason, but by the sword of civil government wielded at the will of the fanatic Athanasius. The hocus-pocus phantasm of a god, like another Cerberus, with one body and three heads had its birth and growth in the blood of thousands and thousands of martyrs. And a strong proof of the solidity of the primitive faith is its restoration as soon as a nation arises which vindicates to itself the freedom of religious opinion, and its eternal divorce from the civil authority. The pure and simple unity of the creator of the universe is now all but ascendant in the Eastern states; it is dawning in the West, and advancing towards the South; and I confidently expect that the present generation will see Unitarianism become the general religion of the United States. The Eastern presses are giving us many excellent pieces on the subject, and Priestly's learned writings on it are, or should be in every hand. In fact the Athanasian paradox that one is three, and

---

16. Gregg. Frazer, *The Religious Beliefs of America's Founders: Reason, Revelation, Revolution* (Lawrence, Kansas: University Press of Kansas, 2012).

three but one is so incomprehensible to the human mind that no candid man can say he has any idea of it, and how can he believe what presents no idea. He who thinks he does only, deceives himself. He proves also that man, once surrendering his reason, has no remaining guard against absurdities the most monstrous, and like a ship without rudder is the sport of every wind. With such persons gullibility which they call faith takes the helm from the hand of reason and the mind becomes a wreck.

I write with freedom, because, while I claim a right to believe in one god, if so my reason tells me, I yield as freely to others that of believing in three. both religions I find make honest men, & that is the only point society has any authority to look to — altho' this mutual freedom should produce mutual indulgence, yet I wish not to be brought in question before the public on this or any other subject, and I pray you to consider me as writing under that trust. I take no part in controversies religious or political. at [sic] the age of 80, tranquility is the greatest good of life, and the strongest of our desires that of dying in the good will of all mankind. and [sic] with the assurances of all my good will to Unitarian & Trinitarian, to Whig & Tory accept for yourself that of my entire respect.[17]

Having traveled to England, Benjamin Franklin had been acquainted with Priestley, even offering letters of introduction to his friends in Philadelphia for one of Priestley's students who traveled to America to promote Priestley's writings.[18] While Franklin and Jefferson seem to have gone closer to Deism than Priestley was comfortable doing, the influence and shared ideas are obvious.

In a letter to Jefferson, John Adams wrote of his study of Priestley's writings, the superiority of reason over Scripture, and his denial of the Trinity:

Dear Sir, I owe you a thousand thanks for your favor of August 22d and its enclosures, and for Dr. Priestley's doctrines

---

17. "From Thomas Jefferson to James Smith, 8 December 1822," Founders Online, National Archives, http://founders.archives.gov/documents/Jefferson/98-01-02-3202. Digital copy available through the Library of Congress at https://www.loc.gov/resource/mtj1.053_0578_0579.

18. Bowers, *Joseph Priestley and English Unitarianism in America*, p. 52.

of Heathen Philosophy compared with those of Revelation. . . .
The human understanding is a revelation from its Maker which
can never be disputed or doubted. There can be no skepticism,
Pyrrhonism, or incredulity, or infidelity, here. No prophecies,
no miracles are necessary to prove the celestial communication.

This revelation has made it certain that two and one make
three, and that one is not three nor can three be one. We can
never be so certain of any prophecy, or the fulfillment of any
prophecy, or of any miracle, or the design of any miracle, as we
are form the revelation of nature, I.E., Nature's God, that two
and two are equal to four. Miracles or prophecies might frighten
us out of our wits; might scare us to death; might induce us to
lie, to say that we believe that two and two make five. But we
should not believe it. We should know the contrary.

Had you and I been forty days on Mount Sinai, and been
admitted to behold the divine Shekinah, and there told that one
was three and three one, we might not have had courage to deny
it, but we could not have believed it.[19]

As Adams speaks of revelation, he elevates natural revelation above the
Scriptures, even saying he would deny the Trinity on that basis if God spoke
to him. In the letter, Adams goes on to deny the biblical concept of hell
based on his own reasoning from nature. While these men may not have
been official members of any Unitarian church, the thoughts they express
on religion betray their allegiance to Unitarian doctrines and not orthodox
Christianity. Adams payed homage to Priestley throughout his later writings
and consistently elevated reason above Scripture, even though he acknowledged the Bible's usefulness:

Philosophy, which is the result of reason, is the first, the
original revelation from the Creator to his creature, man. When
this revelation is clear and certain, by intuition or necessary
induction, no subsequent revelation, supported by prophecies
or miracles, can supersede it. Philosophy is not only the love of
wisdom, but the science of the universe and its cause. . . . Phi-

19. "Letter to Thomas Jefferson, September 14, 1813," *The Writings of Thomas Jefferson*, vol.
6 (Washington, DC: Taylor and Maury, 1854), p. 204–207, accessed digitally at https://
books.google.com/books?id=LmMSAAAAYAAJ.

losophy looks with an impartial eye on the terrestrial religions. I have examined all, as well as my narrow sphere, my straitened means, and my busy life would allow me; and the result is, that the Bible is the best book in the world. It contains more of my little philosophy than all the libraries I have seen; and such parts of it as I cannot reconcile to my little philosophy, I postpone for future investigations.[20]

You will note that Adams mentions the Bible as a great book, but only so far as it fits his "little philosophy." Adams has not subjected his thoughts to God's Word, but the reverse. From there, he goes on to extol the virtues of the morality of Zoroaster, Confucius, and the Hindu writings, noting their "sublime" and "transcendent" qualities, offering that there could not "be found theology more orthodox, or philosophy more profound, than in the introduction to the Shasta."[21] As long as a religious writer or philosopher agreed with Adams' perception of the world through his own reasoning, he was obliged to say it was true. Those parts that did not accord with his view of the world were to be set aside for "future investigation." This line of thinking would develop as the fundamental core of Unitarianism, culminating in the eventual emergence of the Unitarian Universal Church of today.

Other notable American Unitarians include John Quincy Adams, Paul Revere, Ralph Waldo Emerson, Susan B. Anthony, Mary Shelley, Alexander Graham Bell, Louis Agassiz, Linus Pauling, and Frank Lloyd Wright.

From Biblical to Universal

Early American Unitarianism, like its English mother, was rooted in the Bible. To varying degrees, the Bible was seen as the source of religious thought and morality. As with Socinus and Servetus, the denial of the divinity of Jesus and the unorthodox view of His death were argued from Scripture mingled with human reason. We should view early (1790–1840) American Unitarianism as a spectrum. Ministers like William Ellery Channing still denied the Trinity but thought of Jesus as more than just a man, as the more liberal Unitarians like Andrews Norton who went beyond Channing in denying the Virgin Birth and

---

20. "Letter to Thomas Jefferson, December 25, 1813," *The Works of John Adams*, vol. 10 (Boston, MA: Little, Brown, and Company, 1856), p. 82–86, accessed digitally at https://books.google.com/books?id=jRXOAwAAQBAJ.
21. Ibid., p. 85.

most of the miracles in the Bible.[22] All shared the elevation of human reasoning above biblical inspiration, but some denied the Trinity and deity of Christ in the form of Arius while others followed Socinus' reasoning.

In 1825, under the initial leadership of Channing, and later Aaron Bancroft, Unitarian congregations in the East joined together to form the American Unitarian Association (AUA). This was the formal denominational structure of Unitarianism in America, holding conferences and publishing various journals and literature. Later, Western Unitarians (e.g., Illinois, Ohio, and Kentucky) joined the association.[23] It was during this period that Unitarianism took hold within Harvard Divinity School and spread to the pulpits supplied with its graduates.[24]

A Transcendental Shift

In the 1830s, a large shift began within the Unitarian movement. Based in the German transcendental philosophy, this shift took Unitarians away from external sources of truth and sought a natural religion that was affirmed by the inner witness of the soul. Much to the consternation of Channing and others, Ralph Waldo Emerson and other young Unitarians continued to move away from Scripture as a foundation, looking to the inner self to define the divine.

Having studied at Harvard and served as a pastor, Emerson eventually came to espouse the transcendental philosophy after travels in Europe. This influence took a strong hold in Unitarian circles, setting personal intuition and inner divinity as the next liberalizing tide. This tide led to the acknowledgment of other religions as valid ways to connect with God, bringing waves of pluralism and syncretism to erode the biblical underpinnings of Unitarianism. As loose as this footing was, it provided little resistance. Unitarianism had become a broadly inclusive religion by the end of the 19th century.[25]

Ralph Waldo Emerson and other transcendentalist writers had a strong influence on the liberalization of Unitarianism in America. (Wikipedia)

22. Cooke, *Unitarianism in America*, p. 92–107.
23. Ibid., p. 127–138.
24. Ibid., p. 108–110.
25. Ibid., p. 412–435.

Influenced by Frederic Hedge and other writers and preachers, Emerson, Henry W. Longfellow, Oliver Wendell Holmes, Louisa May Alcott, and many other poets and writers spread the new form of Unitarianism far and wide. This new era of pluralism was accompanied by the notion of universal salvation on the grounds that every individual was already connected with the Divine — Emerson's Over-Soul — as a part of nature. This had the positive effects of promoting an end to American slavery, supporting various cultural causes, and the enfranchisement of women, but a detrimental effect on the spiritual health of the nation's population. Additionally, an increasing acceptance of materialistic science colored the teaching of the AUA as humanism was advancing within its ranks.

A Humanist Manifesto

Moving forward to the early 20th century,[26] there was a controversy within the association between those who wanted to promote humanism and those who wanted to maintain a theistic view. In 1921, this controversy came up at a national conference as John Dietrich gave a speech that swayed the core of AUA principles from "faith in God, into faith in the Commonwealth of Man." It was from this point that the full "rejection of divine revelation and the affirmation of reason and the scientific method" was solidified in the AUA.[27]

Desiring to have a summary of the beliefs of the Humanist Fellowship, Roy Wood Sellars was asked to draft such a document. With the help of Edwin Wilson, Raymond Bragg, and Curtis Reese, all Unitarian ministers, the document was prepared for publication in 1933. It was widely distributed after being signed by 34 prominent men, creating another wave of controversy with the AUA theists.[28] The first Humanist Manifesto, often called Humanist 1 since there have been more recent versions, promoted the idea that outdated religions should be replaced with a view that is based on "man's larger understanding of the universe."

The document denies God as Creator, appeals to evolution, and generally points to man as the hope for the betterment of society and mankind.[29]

---

26. For a brief overview of the history of Unitarianism, see Walter Martin, *The Kingdom of the Cults*, ed. Ravi Zacharias (Minneapolis, MN: Bethany House, 2003), p. 339–342.

27. William R. Murry, *Reason and Reverence: Religious Humanism for the 21st Century* (Boston, MA: Skinner House Books, 2007) p. 40–43, accessed digitally at https://books.google.com/books?id=pTnDxlHvEj0C.

28. Ibid., p. 43.

29. "Humanist Manifesto I," American Humanist Association, accessed February 17, 2016, http://americanhumanist.org/humanism/humanist_manifesto_i.

The later, and much expanded, Humanist Manifesto II was signed by several Unitarian ministers, as was the current third version. These manifestos have been signed by influential people like John Dewey, Isaac Asimov, Francis Crick, Alan Guttmacher, B.F. Skinner, and Richard Dawkins.

A Parallel Universalism

At the same time Unitarian thought was developing in America, there was also a universalist form of Christianity. The first Universalist church was started by John Murray in Gloucester, Massachusetts, in 1774, though he was preceded by preaching and writing from people like James Relly (Welsh) and Adams Streeter.[30] In 1866, the Universal General Convention formed as a denominational entity teaching the universal salvation of all of mankind through Jesus. While there have been universalist teachings since soon after Christ's death, this American expression was born out of the rationalistic views popular in 19th-century theology.

Seal of the Universal General Convention (Wikipedia)

Using ideas from the Bible and combining them with natural arguments against eternal punishment for men who were considered generally moral, these churches taught that all men will ultimately receive salvation because of what Christ had accomplished. These churches changed their organizational name to the Universalist Church of America in 1942. Beginning in the late 1940s, there was a move toward a very pluralistic religious ideal. The definition of universalism changed from one of salvation to one of universal religion.[31]

The shift from merely a universal view of salvation in Jesus to one of pluralism makes perfect sense. If you begin from the point that Jesus' death satisfied the debt of all of mankind's sin, it is not long on your journey before you step off of the bus at the base of the mountain where all paths lead to God. This was true of both the Unitarians and the Universalists.

---

30. Richard Eddy, *Universalism in America: A History*, vol. 1 (Boston, MA: Universalist Publishing House, 1884), p. 107–142, accessed digitally at https://books.google.com/books?id=_X4AAAAAYAAJ.

31. Martin, *Kingdom of the Cults*, p. 341.

Unitarian Universalism

Two streams that both began with the Bible as their reservoir had been flowing in channels created by denying biblical truths and adding man's own ideas to the supply. These two streams found a common pit to fill in 1961 when the Unitarian Universalist Association (UU) was formed from the union of the AAU and UCA. Picking and choosing which parts of Scripture to believe combined with setting man's own natural reasoning above God's written revelation turned these streams into a stagnant and lifeless pool rather than a vibrant spring of refreshing, life-giving water.

The UUA symbol of a burning chalice encircled by two rings is generally believed to represent holy oil burning on an altar. A chalice is often lit during UU worship services.

These groups both neglected to consider the corrupted nature of mankind. Although man was created upright, Adam's sin has brought corruption to not only our actions but also our faculties of reasoning. Assuming that man can use his God-given reason to examine the world and determine what is true is a fatal flaw found in both groups. Adding to that the corrupted state of the natural world itself, the ideas of humanism and naturalism have no hope of discerning the true state of reality. Because they have forsaken God's Word, Universalist Unitarians (UUs) have sought the wisdom of the world and pursed a pluralism that is almost unimaginable.

UU Beliefs

UUs claim that they follow no creed and have no dogma. Rather, they hold to seven principles and six sources as affirmations:

> Unitarian Universalist congregations affirm and promote seven Principles, which we hold as strong values and moral guides. We live out these Principles within a "living tradition" of wisdom and spirituality, drawn from sources as diverse as science, poetry, scripture, and personal experience.[32]

---

32. "Our Unitarian Universalist Principles," Unitarian Universalist Association, accessed February 18, 2016, http://www.uua.org/beliefs/what-we-believe/principles.

The seven principles are:

1. The inherent worth and dignity of every person

2. Justice, equity, and compassion in human relations

3. Acceptance of one another and encouragement to spiritual growth in our congregations

4. A free and responsible search for truth and meaning

5. The right of conscience and the use of the democratic process within our congregations and in society at large

6. The goal of world community with peace, liberty, and justice for all

7. Respect for the interdependent web of all existence of which we are a part[33]

From these principles, the pluralistic nature of this religious system should be quite obvious. While a Christian can generally agree with these ideas, their true expression can only be met while resting on the authority of the Bible and the person regenerated in Christ. Apart from a standard, these principles ae merely the arbitrary views of the collective wisdom of UUs — each of whom are creatures with a sinful, fallen nature.

> Our faith is not interested in saving your soul — we're here
> to help you unfold the awesome soul you already have.[34]

Of each of these principles, we can ask, "By what standard?" From the Bible, we know that each individual has inherent worth because they are made in the image of God. In denying God as the Creator (a dogma that cannot be affirmed), UUs may pick from any source to affirm their ideas but have no consensus on the reason. Sadly, the persons in the womb are not seen as having inherent dignity. Under the ironic banner of "Reproductive Justice," UUs work to support the murder of the unborn. Among advice given to UU members is celebrating the history of *Roe v. Wade* and the following points:

---

33. Ibid.
34. Andrea Lerner, in Peter Morales, ed., *The Unitarian Universalist Pocket Guide*, 5th edition (Boston, MA: Skinner House Books, 2012), p, 7.

- Volunteer with and/or provide financial support to organizations that provide reproductive health services at little or no cost, abortion clinics, women's shelters, and child and family community support centers.

- Support reproductive health/abortion clinics that are experiencing intimidation and spiritual or physical violence.

- Accompany anyone wanting support (e.g., while seeking government assistance, in making decisions for their families about pregnancy and adoption, during abortions, and during childbirth).

- Advocate for comprehensive reproductive health services, including contraception, prenatal care, abortion, and infertility treatment.[35]

Under the banner of "Standing on the Side of Love,"[36] UU members actively advocate for legal abortion, showing their lack of love for the unborn. While claiming to welcome all views, the acceptance is true "only to a point." As an example, when a pro-life group interrupted a UU worship service to share the view that abortion is murder, they were asked to leave with the sentiment "You are welcome to your beliefs and behaviors. Now please take them outside the threshold of our church."[37]

I will leave you to consider the arbitrary nature and inconsistencies that follow from each of the affirmations, but principle five can serve as an example. If each person is to determine what is right based on their conscience, there can be no determination of right and wrong in an absolute sense. This creates a system of thought in which true contradictions can exist — showing the illogical nature of the worldview. When each person does what is right in their own eyes, sin reigns over all.

A Big Umbrella

To guide UUs in their understanding of the world and the seven principles, they look to six sources:

---

35. "Reproductive Justice," Unitarian Universalist Association, accessed February 18, 2016, http://www.uua.org/statements/reproductive-justice.
36. "Homepage," Standing on the Side of Love, accessed February 18, 2016, http://www.standingonthesideoflove.org.
37. Darcy Baxter, "All Are Welcome, to a Point," UU World, September 15, 2014, http://www.uuworld.org/articles/all-are-welcome.

"Standing on the Side of Love" is a public advocacy program of the UUA which promotes abortion, immigration, racial issues, and other social justice issues from a liberal and anti-biblical perspective. They aim to "harness love's power to stop oppression," but do not call sinners to repentance and trust in Christ — the truly loving act.

1. Direct experience of that transcending mystery and wonder, affirmed in all cultures, which moves us to a renewal of the spirit and an openness to the forces which create and uphold life

2. Words and deeds of prophetic women and men which challenge us to confront powers and structures of evil with justice, compassion, and the transforming power of love

3. Wisdom from the world's religions which inspires us in our ethical and spiritual life

4. Jewish and Christian teachings which call us to respond to God's love by loving our neighbors as ourselves

5. Humanist teachings which counsel us to heed the guidance of reason and the results of science, and warn us against idolatries of the mind and spirit

6. Spiritual teachings of earth-centered traditions which celebrate the sacred circle of life and instruct us to live in harmony with the rhythms of nature

Again, the pluralism in these sources of wisdom indicates how far from Servetus and Socinus Unitarianism has come. Though these men devalued certain parts of Scripture, they still saw the Bible as a revelation from God and submitted to its authority to some degree.

The UU will affirm that truth is not found in any single source, but spread among all of the religious ideas from around the globe. This mentality is the ultimate expression of the religious buffet where each person fills his spiritual plate with whatever catches their eye and delights their tongue. In this list of sources you can find everything from personal visions and insights to interpretations of the Bible or Hindu Vedas to the oral traditions of the Cherokee Indians. Within UU spirituality, studies in particle physics and evolutionary relationships are just as valid for understanding reality as are mystical Eastern practices of meditation and yoga. In this sense, UU is simply a moralistic religion that allows each individual to determine what is moral — right and wrong are a matter of preference.

The most obvious problem with this view is that it cannot be internally consistent. The UU will respond to this concern by suggesting that life is so complex that truth can't be limited to one culture or one religious tradition. But how can they be absolutely sure this claim is true?

Here we see an allusion to the broad path that Jesus warned leads only to eternal destruction. Those on the broad path look around and see everyone far to their right and far to their left. They consider all of those around them, reasoning in their hearts that there are so many on this path headed in the same direction that it couldn't possibly be taking them in the wrong direction. But this reasoning is folly. It abandons the call of Jesus Christ to follow Him through the narrow gate — He is the way, the truth, and the life who leads to the Father.

> There is a way that seems right to a man, but its end is the way of death (Proverbs 14:12).

Unitarian Universalists can be agnostics, atheists, theists, deists, animists, pagans — there is no firm concept of God within the association. God can be seen as anything from something that resembles the biblical Creator, to oneself, to a "unifying force," to the spirit of humanity that binds us together.

Similarly, Jesus is not viewed as God, though many would consider Him a good teacher or example to follow. However, others may arbitrarily consider

Him immoral for calling people to repent of their sin or for His judgmental words. How are these people to come to any agreement? Without an authority higher than each individual's view, there can only be a false unity based on shifting opinions as each person "journeys" to find the truth. "That may be true for you, but it's not true for me" is an ideology that can only lead to destruction for all as it denies the Creator of truth.

Under the UU umbrella you can find the UU Humanist Association, UUs for Polyamory Awareness, UUs for Jewish Awareness, UU Buddhist Fellowship, UU Christian Fellowship, Unitarian Baha'i Fellowship, BDSM Awareness, Covenant for UU Pagans, and others, each promoting their views within the broader UU fellowship and its local expressions. Religious services are typically held on Sundays, and would look much like a Protestant worship service with hymns, prayers, a sermon, and other related activities. All of these activities would use inclusive language and could invoke Buddhist meditation, pagan circle dances, or chanting Jewish prayers.

While UUs speak openly about promoting tolerance, they don't tolerate those who hold to exclusive views and dogmatic statements (e.g., Jesus is the only way of salvation). The rhetoric becomes, "You are accepted in our group as long as you affirm every view. If you do not affirm all views, we will not affirm your views." I trust you can see the absurdity of such an idea. This demonstrates that the UU worldview is not able to live up to its own standard of accepting all views as valid and is self-refuting.

From a biblical perspective, God has prescribed what is good, beautiful, and true. It is by *His standard* that we can make judgments, not on our own authority. We can know what it means to reflect the image of God because Jesus Christ has demonstrated that for us. We should not look inside of ourselves to recognize the divine within us,[38] but to Christ to save us from Adam within us.

What Is Man?

While there are variations, UU teaching generally acknowledges the evolutionary progression in the formation of the universe and life on earth. This teaching begins with children's materials and continues to adults. One curriculum promoted on the UUA website, "Riddle and Mystery," promotes

---

38. When people look to worship the inner divine of humanity, they are worshiping the fact that they are made in the image of God instead of worshiping the God who created us in His image.

evolutionary ideas to grade 6 students as a better way to understand the world than religious "myths." Of course, they fail to teach that evolution can be considered a religious myth, following the religion of scientism. Falsely pitting *myth against science*, students are led along a path from the big bang to human consciousness, with the teacher repeating "riddle and mystery" where there are chasms cutting across the evolutionary path.[39] In the Unitarian tradition, modern UUs value personal reason above God's revelation. In light of this humanistic philosophy, evolutionary processes, from theistic to atheistic, are seen as the best explanation available and advocated within the association.

UUs view humanity as basically good, each soul a part of the journey of truth. Many would adopt John Locke's *tabula rasa* concept — each person is born as a blank slate and is influenced by parents, culture, education, and all of life's experiences. Each person is influenced for good or bad (whatever those terms might mean) by their surroundings and influences.

Contrary to the biblical teaching, they would deny the dogmatic idea that sin has corrupted every human being. It is hard to find any notion or definition of sin within their writings since there is such a broad base of beliefs. With the explicit endorsement of all forms of sexual expression and the refusal to be dogmatic about what actually constitutes immoral behavior, UUs have no foundation for defining right and wrong. A probing question that exposes the inconsistency in this view would ask the UU how the first people who did evil learned how to do evil if they were the first to do so. Additionally, how can they ever call any act good or bad, right or wrong, without a standard? The Bible offers us the only true explanation for the corrupted condition of mankind — our inherited sin nature and personal choice to act on that nature — and the only true standard of right and wrong. The truths in the Bible reflect the perfect character of God. Because of this absolute standard, we can discern truth from error and good from evil.

In the *Unitarian Universalist Pocket Guide*, published by the UUA, one member summarizes his journey. Having been disillusioned with the Christianity of his youth, he was reading a book on Protestant denominations. When he read the UU chapter, the ideals resonated within him.

---

39. Richard S. Kimball, "Riddle and Mystery; Session 5: Out of Nothing," Unitarian Universalist Association, accessed February 18, 2016, http://www.uua.org/re/tapestry/children/riddle/session5.

I realized that I was a Unitarian Universalist and had been for a long time. The words came to me like manna from heaven and I ate every one. Newton's lyrics arose in my mind: "Amazing grace how sweet the sound that saved a wretch like me." Soon after that experience, I found a Unitarian Universalist church that was exactly what I expected — warm, friendly, and open. I was home. Here I wasn't weird. Here I was fully human, fully accepted, and fully loved. I found a place that gave credence to who I was at my core. . . . Being found means, in the words of Unitarian Walt Whitman, that "you shall listen to all sides and filter them from yourself." Being found is not a destination but a journey.[40]

While Christians should affirm that all are welcome and consider what all sides say, we must not determine truth from within ourselves. This is nothing more than a validation of the self (Proverbs 16:2, 26:12; Isaiah 2:22). From the Christian worldview, this is a foolish practice that leads to the denial of sin and its consequences. It is only by the work of the Holy Spirit that one can recognize his own sinfulness and recognize that, at our core, we are sinners in need of salvation from God's wrath (Romans 8:7–8; John 16:8–11). If all we seek is others to affirm our unregenerate nature, then the destination of our journey will be hell and God's just punishment. Jesus calls us to repent and believe the gospel, not to look for affirmation of the self.

Is There an Afterlife?

While there are no affirmative ideas about the afterlife, the one thing that all UUs would reject is the idea of any judgment or punishment after death. Here the metaphor of all of the various religious paths leading up a mountain to the place of God's residence is fitting (whatever "god" might mean). Because of the broad influence of Eastern thought, biblical ideas, pagan myths, and atheism, opinions will vary from a heaven-like state to no existence after death (Daniel 12:1–3; Matthew 25).

Many UUs may be quite unsure of what they believe. For this reason, discussions of final judgment after death are likely to elicit strong reactions from the typical UU. Wisdom and prayerful consideration of how to address

---

40. Morales, *The Unitarian Universalist Pocket Guide*, p. 13–15

the issue is warranted. Asking questions about what they believe happens after someone dies can open up the opportunity to share the truth that all men are appointed to die and face God's just and holy judgment.

Sharing Hope with Unitarians

When you encounter someone who professes to be a unitarian, the first thing you must establish is what they mean by that identification. Simply asking, "What do you mean by 'unitarian'?" is a great place to start. It opens a line of communication and establishes that you are interested in what they believe. If you hear someone claim to be unitarian and begin persuading them that the Bible is true and the miracles in it are real, thinking they are UU, they will know you do not understand what they believe.

While you should never shy away from speaking the truth, you must first understand what their disagreements with Christianity are and proceed from there. Regardless of their concerns, they need to hear of their sinful condition before God and the remedy that Christ provides, calling them to repent and put their trust in Him alone.

Regardless of which unitarian position they hold, they need to acknowledge the truths contained in the God-breathed revelation of the Bible. Rather than sitting in judgment over the Word of God, picking and choosing what they believe, they need to submit to its truths as authoritative. This is where you must pray for each individual, asking God to open blinded eyes and unstop deaf ears — that more would come to know Him and worship around His throne forever.

Summary of Unitarian Universalist Beliefs

Doctrine	Teachings of Universal Unitarianism
God	Reject the biblical teaching on God, especially Trinitarianism. Have no official beliefs on the existence of specific deities. Views range from atheistic to pantheistic to pagan.
Authority/ Revelation	There are no authoritative texts or revelations, but each individual draws from all of human learning and myth to determine their own version of reality.
Man	Man is born as a blank slate. Man is likely the product of evolutionary processes.

Sin	Sin is generally viewed as bringing harm to self and others rather than an individual affront to a holy God. There is no concept of original sin. Biblical morality is denied, with diverse sexuality promoted as normal.
Salvation	There are various views, but generally no view of a judgment in the afterlife. Many believe existence ends at death.
Creation	Various views from atheistic evolution to incorporating various mythical or biblical ideas with evolutionary processes.

Chapter 22

The Gospel and World Religions

Simon Turpin

The world is flooded with a mixture of religions, but where do they come from and how does the Bible view them?[1] These are important questions for Christians to consider in our desire to share the gospel with those from other religions.

Where Does Religion Come From?

If we want to know the meaning of anything we have to understand its origin. The origin of religion began in the Garden of Eden when God clearly revealed himself to Adam. However, Adam and Eve rejected that revelation and chose to believe a falsehood about Him.[2] Their sin was that they wanted to be gods themselves (Genesis 3:4–5). In this act of disobedience, Adam chose to follow Satan's worldview over God's worldview.

Adam's disobedience had consequences for the rest of his descendants, as it affected how they viewed God and creation.[3] This can be seen at the event

---

1. By the term *religion*, I mean a system of belief that is a person's ultimate standard for reality — their worldview.
2. The falsehood was that they chose to disbelieve what God had said and instead chose to accept Satan's lie.
3. The New Testament uses various words to describe the ruin of humanity's intellect: futile (Romans 1:21); debased (Romans 1:28); deluded (Colossians 2:4); darkened (Ephesians 4:18).

of the Tower of Babel, which was the beginning of religious diversity.[4] At the Tower of Babel, monotheism devolved into polytheism, pantheism, and the worship of anything other than the one true living God. When the people were dispersed at Babel, they would have taken with them a hybrid of the truth of the true and living God mixed with the twisting and distorting of the truth of that revelation about Him (Romans 1:18–32). Religion then is first of all a response to God's revelation — it is either in faith or rebellion.

How Does the Bible View other Religions?

This is an important question since how we answer it will determine how we engage people of other religions with the gospel.

From Paul's teaching in Romans 1:18–20 we can understand that religious consciousness is a product of two things: 1) God's revelation, and 2) suppression of that revelation. Because God has clearly revealed himself in creation, there is no one who is "without excuse" for not believing in His existence. However, because of mankind's fallen nature, the truth of God's revelation of His eternal power and divine nature is held down and suppressed. The suppression of that revelation ultimately expresses itself in idolatry. In an attempt to capture the essence of human fallenness, John Calvin wrote that man is a maker of idols:

> Hence we may infer, that the human mind is, so to speak, a perpetual forge of idols. . . . The human mind, stuffed as it is with presumptuous rashness, dares to imagine a God suited to its own capacity.[5]

Idolatry is exchanging the glory of God for the image of the creature, which is ultimately "the de-godding of God."[6] In this exchange, idolatry is a subjective response to objective divine revelation, which only has negative consequences: sin → suppression of the truth → exchange for idolatry → darkness → guilt = God's wrath (Romans 1:18–32).

---

4. The Bible links false religion with Babylon (Revelation 17:5). For an exposition of the Tower of Babel as the origin of religious diversity, see James Montgomery Boice, *Genesis Volume 1; Creation and Fall* (Genesis 1–11) (Grand Rapids, MI: Baker Books, 1998), p. 420–426.

5. John Calvin, *Institutes of the Christian Religion*, trans. H. Beveridge, 2nd ed. (Peabody, MA: Hendrickson Publishers, 2009), p. 55.

6. D.A. Carson, *Christianity and Culture Revisited* (Grand Rapids, MI: W.B. Eerdmans, 2008), p. 46.

Since the "gods" of the nations are idols (Jeremiah 10:1–11), it is only God's special revelation through the gospel that turns people from their idolatry to trust in the living and true God (1 Thessalonians 1:5, 9).

The Gospel and World Religious

Once we realize that misdirected religion is an idolatrous response to God's revelation, it will help us think about communicating the gospel to those of other religions.

Paul's speech to the Greeks of the Areopagus in Acts 17:16–34 is the classic text for guiding us in sharing the gospel with those from different religious backgrounds. At his arrival in Athens, Paul was so "provoked"[7] at seeing the idolatry in the city that he was moved to preach the gospel in the marketplace.[8] It was because Paul was preaching Jesus and the Resurrection (Acts 17:18–19) that some Epicurean (those who were indifferent to the gods) and Stoic (those who were pantheistic) philosophers invited Paul to the Areopagus (on Mars Hill) in order to know more of what he was teaching. These two philosophies had a different worldview from Paul's. For example, the Epicureans were indifferent to the gods, as they believed them to be too removed to be objects of concern. The Epicureans were basically like today's agnostic secularists.[9] The Stoics, on the other hand, were pantheists who argued for the unity of humanity and relationship with the divine.[10] Both the Epicureans and Stoics were essentially materialists who, unlike Paul, did not believe in one God who created the world and was sovereign over it (Acts 17:24–26; cf. 14:16).

Since Paul understood the people he was preaching to and their religious background, he knew the topics he needed to speak on. For instance, in seeing the idol to an "Unknown God," Paul uses it as a springboard for explaining who God is. Paul began by explaining that God is the Creator of the heavens and earth and that He created mankind from one man.[11] This idea contradicted the Athenians, who believed that they originated from the

---

7. New Testament scholar Darrell Bock states: "The verb παροξύνω (*paroxuno*) means "provoke" (Deut. 31:20 LXX; Ps. 73:10 LXX [74:10 Eng.]). It is used of God's anger at idolatry." Darrell L. Bock, *Acts: BECNT* (Grand Rapids, MI: Baker Academic, 2007), p. 560.
8. Paul would have understood the idolatry in Athens as evidence of the suppression of truth (Romans 1:18–20).
9. Bock, *Acts*, p. 561.
10. Ibid.
11. The "one man" Paul has in mind is clearly a reference to Adam (Romans 5:12–19; 1 Corinthians 15:21–22, 45).

soil of the ground.[12] His mention of the Resurrection and future judgment is also important since in the Athenian view, death was seen as immaterial, as the "body is not restored in any form."[13]

Paul started with who God is because he knew that the idols present in Athens were not there by virtue of their ignorance but by virtue of the suppression of the truth in unrighteousness.[14]

Paul then connected the truth of who the Creator God is with the truth that God had already given to them by way of natural revelation. He did this by quoting Greek poets to these Athenian philosophers.[15] Paul used these Greek poets as a part of his defense and persuasion of the gospel. By taking what they already knew and bringing it in to his defense, Paul then used God's revelation in nature to persuade them of what they already knew to be true. He connected that inner knowledge to who God is, adding explicitly Christian content to it.

In this way, the gospel can be seen as subversively fulfilling world religions. The gospel is subversive as it stands as the contradiction and confrontation to all manifestations of world religions. It makes a call of repentance from idolatry to the true and living God (Acts 17:30). But it also is the fulfillment of what these false religions seek. Since idols are counterfeits of the one true God, the metaphysical and epistemological questions that other religions ask (but ultimately cannot answer) are answered by the triune God.[16]

This connection with the knowledge of God that the Athenians already had led to a bridge for Paul to share the gospel.

Paul tells the Athenians that God has overlooked the ignorance of the nations[17] who find themselves in need of repentance and reconciliation to God through Christ. However, unlike the Stoics, who had a cyclical view of the world, Paul concludes that there will be a definitive judgment on the

---

12. Ben Witherington III, *The Acts of the Apostles: A Socio-Rhetorical Commentary* (Grand Rapids, MI: W.B. Eerdmans, 1998), p. 526.

13. Bock, *Acts*, p. 571. This is why by the cultural standard of wisdom the Cross was foolishness to the Greeks (1 Corinthians 1:23).

14. In Acts 17:24–25 there is an allusion to Isaiah 42:5, which is in the context of an anti-idol polemic.

15. The quotation "In him we live and move and have our being" is probably from Epimenides of Crete. The quote "For we are indeed his offspring" is from Aratus' poem "Phainomena."

16. See Daniel Strange, *For Their Rock Is Not As Our Rock: An Evangelical Theology of Religions* (Nottingham: Apollos, 2014), p. 237–273.

17. God in his mercy has not judged the idolatry of the nations as severely as he might have (see Romans 3:25).

world by Christ so it is incumbent of all men to repent of their sin and turn to Him in faith.

Conclusion

World religions are a rebellious, idolatrous response to God's revelation of Himself in creation. Because God has made himself known to every person, we need to communicate the fullness of the truth of the gospel in such a way that it connects with the truth that God has already communicated by way of natural revelation. The good news is that God is now redeeming people from false religions throughout the earth and uniting them into one people of God through the gospel of Jesus Christ.

Appendix 1

Tools for Engaging People from Other Religions

Roger Patterson

If you are a Christian reading this book series, you are probably doing so with a desire to be a more effective ambassador of Jesus Christ. Knowing the basic foundations and doctrines of different religious views is wise. If you are meeting for lunch with a Muslim coworker and you order a ham sandwich or invite a Mormon to a coffee house, you could be placing an unnecessary stumbling block in the path of sharing the gospel. While we must trust God's sovereignty in salvation, we are also responsible to represent Jesus Christ and share the gospel in a way that is filled with grace and truth (Colossians 4:2–6).

Don't Divorce Evangelism, Apologetics, and Discipleship

The classic verses used to inform us about evangelistic and apologetic encounters are often disconnected from one another, but we should think about evangelism and apologetics as two sides of the same coin. And then, we must not forget about the connection to discipleship. When we consider 1 Peter 3:15, the classic apologetics passage, we often forget the context of verses 13–17. When we give a defense or reason for the hope that is in us, we have to remember that our hope is in the person and work of Jesus Christ, not tearing down human evolution or telling people how dinosaurs and humans were created on the same day. While we may use those topics as we discuss the truthfulness of Christianity, we must remember that Christ and the hope of salvation He offers is the focal point of Christianity.

Likewise, in Matthew 28:18–20 we often focus on the "go and make disciples" aspect — evangelism — and forget the "teaching them to observe all things that I have commanded you" aspect — discipleship. Once someone has confessed Christ as Lord and Savior, we now have the opportunity and privilege of helping them grow to be more like Christ as disciples who are being sanctified (Romans 8:28–30) — remembering that we are always growing in our discipleship too.

Our evangelistic encounters should naturally flow into a discipleship relationship.[1] Whether we do this personally in our own local church or help the person connect to a local church body that teaches the Bible, we would be negligent to divorce evangelism and discipleship.[2] In summary, evangelism, apologetics, and discipleship should all be in view as we share the gospel message with those who are not yet children of God (John 1:9–13).

Know Your Own Beliefs Better Than the Counterfeits

In understanding the various religious philosophies, there is a danger to be aware of. Spending too much time studying false views may lead to spiritual dangers. It is not advisable or necessary for every Christian to know every doctrine of every religion and its various cults and sects. First, you will not likely encounter people from all of those views, making your time studying the details a "waste."

Second, if you spend too much time studying the false you will have less time for studying the truth of the Bible. Third, there are other Christians in your own local church or in other areas who have studied the details and are serving the Body of Christ with those gifts and knowledge. This book, and other resources, can give you a summary of the views and a starting point for discussions without being immersed in the falsehoods. Christians who have come out of false religions can be a great source of information and wisdom

---

1. Since this book series focuses primarily on making converts of those who are from other religions, we will not discuss the role of discipleship of young children in a home with Christian parents (or other similar situations).
2. However, in the instance of using tracts, books, or audio/visual forms of communicating the gospel, we can trust that the Holy Spirit's work in the person's heart will direct them to finding a local church. Including contact information on these types of gospel tools is always advisable.

and encouragement. Also, if there is a dominant religious group in the area you live (e.g., Mormonism in the states around Utah), you may want to spend more time understanding those views than a specific cult view you are unlikely to encounter. It's not every day you bump into a Wiccan.

Rather than exhaustively studying all of the counterfeits, you would do much better to know the truth God has revealed to us in the 66 books of the Bible. Knowing the truth in a deep and intimate way will be much more profitable than studying all of the false views. While understanding some basic differences can be very helpful, the strategy of asking wise questions can help you learn about a person's beliefs even if you don't know much about their religion.

Additionally, there are many sects and denominations within religious systems. It is not wise to accuse the person you are speaking to of holding a doctrinal view that they may not hold. If a Muslim told you that they could never believe like you do and pray to Mary, you would dismiss them as igno-rant since you don't pray to Mary as most Roman Catholics do. Likewise, if in speaking to a Mormon you ask them why they believe the Heavenly Father had sexual relations with Mary, they might tell you they don't believe that (as some Mormons have never been taught that particular point of doctrine or don't accept it).

Ask Good Questions

Rather than telling others what they believe — or what you assume they believe because of the religion they identify with — ask questions. "Counsel in the heart of man is like deep water, but a man of understanding will draw it out" (Proverbs 20:5; NKJV). Learning how to ask questions about what others believe is an invaluable strategy for learning what a person thinks about the meaning of life and the future after death.

For example, if you encounter a man on a plane coddling his Buddhist prayer beads, open a conversation by asking him what the beads mean to him and why he uses them. Ask him what he thinks happens when people die. Ask him how he knows what is right and wrong. Ask him if it is hard to work and strive for his own future state. Ask him . . . okay, you get the point.

As you are asking and showing genuine interest in the person, be listen-ing for ways his worldview is different from the Bible, and then be prepared to tell him what the Bible teaches. But to do that you need to know more about the Bible, who God is, and what Jesus has done for us than you know about the Buddhist Eightfold Path to enlightenment. Being filled with the truths of the Bible allows those truths to flow from your heart to your lips and to offer the good news of salvation in Christ. Being filled with love and thankfulness for your own salvation and all Christ has done for you will flow out of your heart into words and actions that will demonstrate your hope in Christ (1 Peter 3:13–17).

Point Them to Rest in Christ

It may be a bit cliché, but it has been noted that all the other religions in the world are based on what a person must *do* to achieve the ultimate state (nirvana, exaltation, paradise, oneness of being, etc.) while Christianity is a religion that is based on what has been *done* for us in Jesus Christ. *Do* vs. *Done*. In pursuing their own righteousness or concept of perfection, people will become weary and discouraged — and rightly so! But there has only been one person who has lived a life of perfection — Jesus Christ.

Jesus knew the weariness of perfectly obeying God. He saw those He walked with striving to please God but falling short (Romans 3:23). Rather than encouraging people to try harder, Jesus called them to find rest in Him, to take His easy yoke rather than striving to do more (Matthew 11:25–30). As we point people to resting in Christ, we can remind them of their own sinfulness, their accumulating debt of sin (Romans 2:5–11), and the fact that Christ bore the wrath of God for sin in His body upon the Cross (1 Peter 2:23–25). We can ask them to trust that their sin is placed on Christ and they can receive His righteousness — the great exchange that makes peace with God and resting in Christ possible (Isaiah 61:10; Titus 3:3–7).

Take Out Your Sword and Use It

As you interact with others in your evangelistic and apologetic discussions, never be afraid to open the Bible and use it — draw your sword! Even if the person claims not to believe in the Bible, it is still the only source of absolute truth God has revealed to us. Just as a soldier would be foolish to set aside his sword in a battle if his enemy said he didn't believe in swords, a Christian is foolish to set aside the most powerful weapon God has given us (Hebrews 4:11–13; Ephesians 6:14–20).

Rather than providing your own opinion, appeal to the authority of the God of the universe who created all things and rules over all things. Declare the true history of the universe and the nature of mankind and explain how the triune God who has revealed Himself in the Bible is the only source of existence, truth, and hope.

Following the analogy, we must know how to wield the sword as an effective weapon. A basic familiarity with what the Bible teaches and the ability to accurately report that truth requires some training and attention to the Holy Spirit at work in you. If they disagree, it is not with your opinion, but with what God has proclaimed. As you faithfully proclaim the truth from God's Word, it will accomplish the purpose He has sent it for (Isaiah 55:10–13). The Word of God is your powerful weapon that the Holy Spirit will use to bring conviction, not the wisdom of men in persuasive words (1 Corinthians 1:17–2:16).

Don't Be Like the Fool

In Proverbs 26:4–5, we are given a basic strategy for dealing with those who are foolishly denying God's existence or pursuing false gods to serve and worship. Rather than following along with the fool and arguing from his beliefs, we should show him how his views lead to foolishness (absurdity), as they are not founded in the truth of God and His Word. We can then present the biblical worldview and the message of the gospel, calling them to submit to God and acknowledge Jesus as Lord and Savior.[3]

As we listen to what people believe and try to understand them, we should not spend an inordinate amount of time arguing fine points of doctrine and debating evidences back and forth. It can take time and patience to continue to witness to people in our lives who deny the gospel, but we need to move beyond secondary issues to deal with the root of their false worldview. As an analogy, we should not spend time trying to pluck nails and boards from their house hoping that it will fall, but take a jackhammer to the foundation and expose the fact that their house is standing on nothing.

As they recognize their need for a true foundation, invite them into the household of God to be adopted as His child. Apart from God and a submission to the truth of the Bible, there is no consistent foundation upon which we can build a worldview (Matthew 7:24–27). Apart from Christ, there is no Creator and Savior. Jesus Christ is the foundation upon which we *must* build our worldview (Ephesians 2:19–22; 1 Peter 2:1–10).

---

3. For a fuller explanation of this presuppositional apologetics view, see Jason Lisle, *The Ultimate Proof of Creation* (Green Forest, AR: Master Books, 2009); for a condensed explanation, see Jason Lisle "Fool-Proof Apologetics," *Answers*, January–March, 2009, p. 66–69, available online at https://answersingenesis.org/apologetics/fool-proof-apologetics.

While exposing the faulty foundation of someone's worldview is no guarantee that they will drop to their knees, repent, and turn to Christ for salvation, it may give them pause and a means by which the Spirit can work in their hearts to bring conviction of sin. While we do our part to be faithful ambassadors, planting seeds and watering those that have been planted, it is God who brings the growth resulting in a harvest of righteousness. The fear of the Lord is the beginning of wisdom (Proverbs 9:10). All the treasures of wisdom and knowledge are found in Jesus Christ (Colossians 2:1–10). Let us embrace the truth and proclaim it boldly to the glory of God.

Questions to Use in Evangelistic Encounters

Doctrinal Questions

- Why do you wear that pendant/head covering/emblem/tattoo?

- Where and how do you worship?

- What is the ultimate goal in your religion?

- How do you achieve the ultimate state?

- How do you know when you have done enough?

- How are you doing in your progress to that goal?

- How did you decide which sect/denomination to follow?

- Who is the leader or main authority that informs your religious views?

- How do you understand the beginning of the universe/world/mankind?

- Is mankind basically good or bad in its nature? Why?

- What writings do you study to help you grow in your faith?

- What is the source/object of your faith?

- How do you view God? How do you know what He is like?

- What do you think happens when someone dies? What will happen to you?

Ultimate Questions

- How do you know what is right and wrong or good and evil?

- How does your worldview account for truth/reality?

- Is it possible that you are wrong about the way you see the world?

- How do you know what the purpose of mankind/your life is?

- If God judged you by your own actions/sins, would you deserve to spend eternity in heaven?

- If you stood before God and He asked you why you should be allowed to spend eternity with Him, what would you say?

- Why do you deny that Jesus Christ is the only Savior of the world?

- The Bible says that everyone knows that God exists based on His attributes displayed in creation, so why do you suppress what you know to be true?

- If there is more than one god, how do you know which god is the right one to obey?

- If the universe/being is an impersonal force, how does it interact with the material world?

- If you believe that matter and energy are all that exist, how do you account for transcendent immaterial entities (logic, numbers, morality, laws of nature)? Do you have a soul?

- How does your worldview account for morality, uniform laws of nature, reasoning, logic?

- Is it possible that you are wrong about everything you believe?

- What would the consequences be if you were wrong?

- How do you know that is true?

- Since your worldview contradicts the Bible's teaching, how do you know you are right and the Bible is wrong?

- Jesus said He was the way, the truth, and the life, and that no one would get to heaven apart from Him. Why do you deny His claims?

- Who do you say Jesus is?

Appendix 2

The Irrationality of Atheism, Polytheism, Deism, and Unitarianism

Timothy McCabe

Abstract

Ultimately, all possibility of rational thought is grounded in the Trinitarian Christian God. This appendix will offer an internal analysis of atheistic, polytheistic, deistic, and unitarian systems. It will find that each of these four systems, by its own nature and according to its own claims, denies mankind all possible grounds for justified conclusions, thereby eliminating all possibility of human rationality. By comparison, it will also offer an internal analysis of Trinitarian Christianity and will find that the problems inherent in the other four systems are refreshingly absent.

Definitions

Throughout this appendix, *atheism* will refer to any claim or set of claims rejecting the existence of a sovereign, rational author of the universe; *polytheism* will refer to any claim or set of claims that there are many sovereign, rational authors of the universe who are equally ultimate; *deism* will refer to any claim in which a sovereign, rational author of the universe exists but has no ongoing involvement with what is created apart from the initial act of creation itself; and *unitarianism* will refer to any claim in which a sovereign author of the universe exists, continues to be involved with the created realm, and whose divinity is not shared in any sense.

These views will each be contrasted with *Trinitarian Christianity*, or *Trinitarianism*, in which one sovereign and rational author of the universe exists, is involved with what is created today, and yet whose divinity is effectively shared between *God the Father* and the *Image of God, the Son*.[1]

Starting Points

From the moment we begin to draw conclusions as individual human beings, we already know how to learn. Knowledge of the basic and fundamental process of learning is already well established in our minds before we begin using it to draw conclusions. Before we learn anything at all, we assume (or presuppose) a method of learning. This initial knowledge of how to learn is not itself learned, rather, acceptance of the method is a precondition of our usage of it. Accepting a method for judging truth claims is common to humanity as one of our starting points. We begin life under the assumption or presupposition that the ways we learn things will actually produce accurate conclusions about the world around us.

When we begin drawing conclusions, when we first start learning things, we do so with certain presupposed assumptions or "first principles." For example:

> Nothing can both be and not be at the same time and in the same way.

This is known as the law of non-contradiction. Before we can learn anything at all, we must first presuppose this rule of thought. Evidence, assertions, conclusions, and thinking itself would all be completely meaningless to us if we did not initially grant that all of reality is non-contradictory.

That we have this initial assumption is true for all humans from the time we begin to think. The infant knows that milk is milk. Milk is not non-milk. If the infant allowed the possibility that milk were non-milk, he would have

---

1. It is not my intent to suggest that these definitions are the only correct definitions of these terms. For example, *Trinitarian Christianity* was often designated as *atheism* by the ancient Romans because Christians rejected the entire pantheon of Roman gods and refused to worship the emperor. I will not be defining atheism as the rejection of Roman gods, but rather, as a rejection of a sovereign, rational author of the universe. As a second example, a hypothetical view may assert that the universe was never created at all but has existed forever, and many gods exist: a god of the sea, a god of the sun, a god of the moon, a god of fire, etc. Typically, such a view would be as *polytheistic*. However, in the course of this appendix, it will be referred to as *atheistic*, since it denies a sovereign rational author of the universe. My intent is not to be militant about "proper" definitions for these terms, but rather to be internally consistent throughout this appendix in my usage of them in the hopes that the discussion itself will be easier to understand.

no reason to believe that he had received what he had been crying for, even as it fills his mouth. The infant simply grants or assumes — the infant *knows* — that the law of non-contradiction is universal and invariant.

It is not my claim that the infant can *articulate* the law of non-contradiction, or *teach* it, or *defend* it, but rather that he inherently *believes* and operates in accordance with the law even if he has never consciously pondered it.

And so do you.

Further, every single correct conclusion the infant ever comes to, and every single correct conclusion the adult ever comes to, is based upon this assumption that the law of non-contradiction is universally valid, both now and forever. We not only start off *believing* it without ever actually *learning* it, but everything we ever conclude is founded on or grounded in that initial assumption.

But what if we're wrong? Is that initial assumption *justified*? Is there a good reason for us to hold to it? Is it a blind invention of random chance? Is the author of our initial assumptions rational? Is this universal truth claim merely an unfounded, dogmatic assertion made by someone without authority over the entire universe such that the universe is not bound to fulfill his dogmatic claims? Could the law of non-contradiction fail to work in some parts of the universe? And what connects our own thoughts with our environment? Why should there be any similarity at all between our own internally presupposed rules of thought and the way that our external environment behaves?

If genuine contradictions could actually exist, it would be impossible for anyone to know anything at all. If contradictions were viable, then even if a conclusion were accurate, it may not be accurate. Assertions would not necessarily be any different than their exact negations. Even if it were true that you are reading this, it may not be true that you are reading this.

That last sentence is completely meaningless and impossible to understand because it asserts a *contradictory proposition*. If it were possible for reality itself to be contradictory, like that sentence, reality itself would be equally impossible to understand. It would not be possible to know anything at all. But this is not the case. We all automatically believe that reality is not contradictory.

Rational Thought Requires Rational Justification

In order for an idea to be *rational*, holding the belief must be *rationally justified*. Even if a belief happened be accurate or factual, this alone is not enough to make that belief *rational*. The process by which the person came to hold that belief is actually more important than the belief's truth value in terms of whether or not the belief is *rationally* held. A belief may be true, yet still be irrational.

For example, any wishful thinker may assert without grounds that there are exactly 501,043 pink flying unicorns on a planet in the next galaxy. For that individual to believe such a thing would be irrational, because they themselves have asserted it groundlessly or without reason. Even if this bizarre, groundless assertion happened to be true, its factuality would not make belief in the assertion any more *rational*, since it was asserted *groundlessly* — without justification or reason.

On the other hand, a belief may be false while being perfectly rational. For example, consider the man who believes that pushing the brake pedal in his car will slow the car and eventually bring it to a complete stop. He believes this because he has been told this is true by his parents and friends, and he tested their claims on thousands of occasions. One hundred percent of the time, the car behaved exactly as he expected. But then one day it didn't, and the man died.

He was wrong to believe his car would stop when he pushed the brakes on that day, but nonetheless, based on all of the evidence, he held to this false belief *rationally*. He had testimony from multiple witnesses, observations, and lots of experience upon which he grounded his belief. It was *rationally justified* in spite of being incorrect.

Now, is our belief that all reality is non-contradictory *rationally justified*? Or are we irrationally, without reason, holding to an idea that is only asserted groundlessly?

Rationally Justifying Rational Justification

While it is true that some beliefs may be rationally justified while being completely false, the same cannot be said of every belief. Consider, for example, the following assertion:

> *Rational justification is possible.*

In addition to the law of non-contradiction, the assertion above is another one of our initial starting points, our "first principles." As humans, we begin the learning process *already believing* that this assertion is true, that *rational justification is possible*. But note that this statement can only be rationally justified if it is also true; if it is false, nothing can be rationally justified, including the statement itself.

The idea that *"rational justification is possible"* must itself be true in order for it to be rationally justified. For any worldview to allow for rational human thought, it must not only allow for our initial assumptions about the non-contradictory nature of the universe to be true, but it must also allow for *the possibility of rational justification itself.* It *must* allow for a mechanism whereby *rational justification is possible.*

Atheism

Atheism *prohibits every imaginable mechanism* whereby rational justification is possible. Truth claims from atheists demand that there is no sovereign rational author of the universe. No one exists who has authority over the universe. No one exists who is justified in claiming that the entire universe is, and always will be, non-contradictory. No person can guarantee these things. Therefore, by whatever random mechanism the bizarre and groundless notion of a non-contradictory universe got into our heads to begin with, that initial assumption of ours is necessarily irrational. All of our conclusions are based upon this rationally unjustified starting point, making all of our conclusions rationally unjustified, or irrational.

If our initial assumptions about reality don't find their origin in a rational sovereign author of the universe, they are rationally unjustified. In other words, if there is no sovereign rational author of the universe, if the claims of atheism are accurate, then all human conclusions are irrational or without reason.[2]

"But what about observable evidence?" one may ask. In the example of the man hitting the brake pedal, he couldn't absolutely guarantee that it would work, yet he was rationally justified in believing it would. Here, no one can guarantee that the universe is non-contradictory, but can't we still be rationally justified in believing that it is, just like the man with the brake pedal?

Surely, even if we initially believe in the complete universality of the law of non-contradiction without having any rational justification for our initial

---

2. While the argument above deals with all worldviews that deny a rational, sovereign Creator, an additional argument against the possibility of rational thought can be offered against materialistic naturalism, a popular atheistic religion that denies that immaterial things exist. Reason, truth, knowledge, logic, and so forth cannot be adequately explained within this atheistic format since they are not material. By the very foundational beliefs of materialistic naturalism, logic and reason are an impossibility.

belief (a claim no atheist could rationally dispute), our present-day usage of that belief can be justified after-the-fact by observing the world around us and recognizing the non-contradictory nature of things, can't it? The more we observe non-contradictory behavior, surely the more justification we have for asserting the universality of the rule.

This inductive argument could be described as follows:

1. We would expect that in a non-contradictory universe we would never find any true contradiction.

2. Thus far, we have never found any true contradiction.

3. Therefore, we rationally conclude that *the universe is most probably non-contradictory.*

But note that points (1) and (2) can only be meaningfully accepted if we first presuppose that the universe is invariantly non-contradictory, making the argument wholly circular in all its points. While circular arguments can be perfectly valid, this one is still founded upon an indisputably irrational starting point, the unjustified initial assumption of non-contradiction. The admitted irrationality of the foundation upon which the circular argument is built negates all possibility of rationality in the conclusion.

The man with the faulty brake pedal believed what he believed *as a result of* meaningful experience, and was therefore justified. On the other hand, we consider our experiences meaningful *as a result of* our belief in the law of non-contradiction, not the other way around. It is the *exact reverse* of the brake pedal example.

The atheist has put the cart before the horse. To see what I mean, let's assume for a moment that the universe is *not* bound by the law of non-contradiction. Let's assume that contradictions are perfectly acceptable statements of truth. There would then be no reason to reject the following argument:

1. We would expect that in a non-contradictory universe we would never find any true contradiction.

2. Thus far, we have never found any true contradiction.

3. Therefore, we rationally conclude that *the universe is full of contradictions.*

"Wait, that doesn't make any sense!" you shout. *The conclusion contradicts the premises — it can't be right!*

Remember, when we formulated the above argument we assumed contradictions could be acceptable statements of truth. The only way the conclusion above could possibly be meaningfully rejected is if we presuppose that the universe is non-contradictory before we even attempt the argument, and since, under atheistic premises, we have absolutely no rational justification for making that initial assumption about the universe before observing it, the entire process, and indeed inductive inference itself, is reduced to meaningless irrationality.

There is, under atheism, no greater reason to prefer the coherent conclusion than to prefer the incoherent one. They are equally unjustified. In short, the absence of any universal and invariant rational authority under atheistic premises demands a lack of rational justification for any kind of universal or invariant claim.

If God doesn't exist, we simply cannot think.

This nonsense can be described via the following deductive syllogism:

1. Conclusions are irrational if they are built upon unjustified premises.

2. Under atheism, all of our conclusions are built upon unjustified initial premises.

3. Under atheism, all of our conclusions are irrational.

This, of course, does not mean that everything an atheist says is wrong or false; rather, it means that his worldview cannot justify *rationality*. When we say that atheism renders everything meaningless, we are not simply referring to some kind of greater purpose in life that appears to be lacking under atheism, or some kind of eternal value that we hope and wish humans had that seems absent without some kind of God. No, indeed, atheism renders every sentence meaningless. Every word. Every thought. Absolutely every concept.

Polytheism

Polytheism, likewise, *prohibits every imaginable mechanism* whereby rational justification is possible. Polytheistic claims, as I am defining them, mandate that there are many sovereign, rational authors of the universe who are equally ultimate.

As these multiple sovereign authors of the universe create our reality, try to imagine what our reality would be like if they disagreed. One god decides certain trees will have abundant green leaves on its branches, but the other god decides these same trees will not have any leaves at all under any circumstances whatsoever. The question we as humans are then faced with is *do these trees have abundant green leaves, or do they not?*

The answer, of course, is that both options are completely and wholly true and both are also completely and wholly false. The trees have leaves and it is not the case that the trees have leaves. At the same time. And in the same way. Not only does this make our reality incoherent and incomprehensible; not only does this make our presupposed universality and invariance of the law of non-contradiction invalid (though if it is invalid it may also be valid at the same time and in the same way); but this also points out an interesting fact about exactly what the gods themselves, the ultimate authorities over our reality, each individually hold to be correct.

Our first god who is sovereignly authoring the universe determines that these certain trees have abundant leaves. Therefore, he knows that those trees do in fact have abundant leaves. However, even though he is right, *he is also wrong.* Even if this sovereign god directly informed us that the universe he created was non-contradictory, his personal opinion on the matter would not be trustworthy given the presence of the other equally authoritative god. Indeed, this first god cannot authoritatively guarantee *anything at all* for his created humans, so he cannot be trusted to present us with an accurate view of his very own creation.

To misappropriate an old saying, if everyone is sovereign, no one is.

If the law of non-contradiction is an untrustworthy test of truth, as it would necessarily be with multiple sovereign gods who are equally ultimate, then, just as under atheism, it is not possible to guarantee any kind of meaning for anything at all. Things may mean what they don't mean. Arguments may prove what they disprove. Assertions and their negations may be equivalent. No one, not even the gods, could be justifiably certain of anything at all. Rational thought, dependent upon the universality and invariance of the law of non-contradiction, would be nonexistent.

Under such a scenario, the very concept of rational justification (which here may entail what it doesn't entail) becomes meaningless. Since there is then no such thing as rational justification, it is therefore impossible to rationally justify anything at all, and thus, every belief is irrational, or without reason.

In short, the equally ultimate sovereignty of polytheistic gods leads to a lack of rational justification for any and every claim.[3]

This nonsense can likewise be described via the same deductive syllogism as was used to describe atheistic epistemology:

1. Conclusions are irrational if they are built upon unjustified premises.

2. Under polytheism, all of our conclusions are built upon unjustified initial premises.

3. Under polytheism, all of our conclusions are irrational.

Deism

Deism, too, *prohibits every imaginable mechanism* whereby rational justification is possible. Deistic claims demand that a sovereign author of the universe exists but has no ongoing involvement with what is created apart from the initial act of creation itself. Such a god cannot justifiably guarantee anything about any moment beyond creation.

The unfolding of time is independent of the deistic god. Future moments are not created by him. Somehow, both future moments and therefore time itself exist autonomously, independently, and apart from his sovereignty. If this were not the case, every moment would depend upon him for its existence, in which case he would by definition continue to be intimately involved with his creation, even today.

If anything is independent of the deistic god, he cannot authoritatively guarantee that it will behave according to his expectations or deterministic decrees. This means that his expectations or truth claims may not be valid. Indeed, if time is independent of god, even if we tried to believe that god himself were perfectly rational, time could hypothetically behave in a completely irrational manner. Logical contradictions could become perfectly viable — or perhaps they always have been.

The deistic god cannot guarantee anything about those things he has no control over. Even if he has caused humans to reproduce in such a fashion that each successive generation assumes that the law of non-contradiction is always valid, without variation — even if our initial beliefs somehow had his

---

3. According to Plato's *Four Dialogues*, Socrates made this same case against the conflicting sovereignty of the Greek pantheon of gods in *Euthyphro*, but restricted his argument in his particular discourse to moral facts. Here, I have merely expanded Socrates' argument to all facts.

own mark of authority on them and were not randomly produced — then, since our assumptions were determined by one who had *no authority to make such claims*, we are not rationally justified in accepting our own assumptions. With absolutely all of our conclusions being based solely upon his ultimate authority, authority that is lacking, we are then never rationally justified in holding to any of them.

"But couldn't the deistic god observe time for a while and see how it behaved?" you ask. "And then, based upon this observable evidence, cause humans to believe that it is non-contradictory? Even if he were wrong, wouldn't we still be rationally justified in trusting our initial assumptions based on god's careful consideration of the evidence?" Actually, no.

As demonstrated when we discussed atheism, the use of probability and evidentiary claims is meaningless without the establishment first of the universality and invariance of the law of non-contradiction, which the deistic god simply cannot establish. Evidential inference is subject to the law of non-contradiction, not the other way around. The deist, just like the atheist, has put the same cart before the same horse.

Yet again, just as in atheism and polytheism, our initial assumptions about reality are arbitrary and unjustified in a deistic framework. They have come from a being that cannot guarantee their accuracy, since time is an influence on both us and on our universe and time is not under his control.

Deism, like atheism and polytheism, prohibits us from being justified in believing that the law of non-contradiction is valid, thereby denying the possibility of rational justification. In short, the deistic god's lack of authority over time (and over time's functionality) dictates a lack of sufficient justification for trusting our starting assumptions today.

If our initial premises are unjustified, it is irrational for us to believe any conclusions based upon them. We see that the same syllogism properly applies to deism:

1. Conclusions are irrational if they are built upon unjustified premises.

2. Under deism, all of our conclusions are built upon unjustified initial premises.

3. Under deism, all of our conclusions are irrational.

Unitarianism

Finally, unitarianism (e.g., the god of the Jehovah's Witnesses, Unitarian Universalism's concept of god, or the Islamic god) also *prohibits every imaginable mechanism* whereby rational justification is possible.[4]

Unitarian claims demand that a sovereign author of the universe exists and continues to be involved with the created realm. Further, the unitarian holds that his god's divinity is not shared in any sense. A unitarian god's beliefs, conclusions, actions, decisions, purposes, intentions, preferences, and decrees, etc., would then be both unjustified and unjustifiable, making every such god irrational.

Yes that was a bold claim, but let me explain. Under our definition of unitarianism, and from within a unitarian perspective, the one creator god himself is, in the ultimate sense, the only reason for anything at all. He alone is the originator of all things other than himself. According to unitarianism, he is the reason they exist. He is the reason things are the way they are. Otherwise, things would not be under his control, and he would have no justification for making universal claims about them, as we have already seen above with three other worldviews. As a supposedly rational being, he would necessarily reflect upon his reason for his beliefs, his reason for his conclusions, his reason for his actions, his reason for his decisions, his reason for his decrees, and so forth. And, of course, in reflecting upon his reason, he is reflecting upon himself, because ultimately, he is his own reason. As he reflects upon himself, however, he himself is reflected.

To grant unitarianism the benefit of the doubt, the unitarian god must know himself perfectly, or else he would not be able to guarantee what he himself will do, and we would then have no rational justification for trusting his assertions about the non-contradictory nature of anything under his control. Because the unitarian god knows himself perfectly, when he reflects upon himself, his reflection, the image that he holds of himself, has all of the same attributes that he knows himself to have, with the exception, of course, of those attributes that necessarily differentiate anything from its reflection.[5]

---

4. For definition sake, monotheism is not necessarily unitarian. While all unitarians are monotheists, biblical Christianity is monotheistic trinitarianism, which holds to one God existing in three co-equal and co-eternal persons — the Father, the Son, and the Holy Spirit.

5. As Jonathan Edwards writes in *An Unpublished Essay on the Trinity*, "The knowledge or view which God has of Himself must necessarily be conceived to be something distinct from His mere direct existence. There must be something that answers to our own reflection. The reflection as we reflect on our own minds carries something of imperfection in it.

As the unitarian god himself is eternal, so his image of himself, that is, his reason, is likewise eternal. As he himself is consistent, so his image of himself is consistent. His conception of himself must eternally be the exact representation of himself, sharing divine sovereignty, since this conception is the reason for everything that occurs.[6] This presents the problem in unitarianism, which denies that divine sovereignty is shared in any manner, though we have seen that it must be for the sovereign creator to be rational.

Since any rational author of reality could have no reason other than Himself, and as the *unitarian god does not have a divine conception of himself, the unitarian god, if he is the author of reality, cannot be said to be rational.* Whatever his ultimate reason is, it is either nonexistent, since he alone is the self-existent one, or it is an attribute of himself rather than himself. Therefore, it is not ultimate in the fullest sense.

The unitarian god's rationality is thus insufficient to provide us with universal and invariant guarantees about reality. Understanding this, we now see that unitarianism could actually fall under our definition of atheism, since under atheism there is no sovereign *rational* author of the universe, and while the unitarian god (under unitarianism) is the sovereign author of the universe, he is certainly not rational. Remember, if our initial assumptions about reality don't find their origin in a rational sovereign author of the universe, they are rationally unjustified — completely without reason.

In short, the faulty thinking of the unitarian god dictates a lack of sufficient justification for trusting any and all of his claims. Under unitarianism, then, every human's initial assumption, given to us by the god who created us, that the universe is invariantly non-contradictory, is therefore unjustified. Yet again, we see the same syllogism applied to unitarianism.

However, if God beholds Himself so as thence to have delight and joy in Himself He must become his own object. There is God and the idea (the λόγος) of God. Therefore as God with perfect clearness, fullness and strength, understands Himself, views His own essence, that idea which God hath of Himself is absolutely Himself. This representation of the Divine nature and essence is the Divine nature and essence again: so that by God's thinking of the Deity must certainly be generated. Hereby there is another person begotten, there is another Infinite Eternal Almighty and most holy and the same God, the very same Divine nature. And this Person is the second person in the Trinity, the Only Begotten and dearly Beloved Son of God; He is the eternal, necessary, perfect, substantial and personal idea which God hath of Himself; and that it is so seems to me to be abundantly confirmed by the Word of God." http://www.ccel.org/ccel/edwards/trinity/files/trinity.html.

6. As the Nicene Creed states in its modern wording, "We believe in one Lord, Jesus Christ, the only son of God, eternally begotten of the Father, God from God, Light from Light, true God from true God, begotten, not made, of one being with the Father."

1. Conclusions are irrational if they are built upon unjustified premises.

2. Under unitarianism, all of our conclusions are built upon unjustified initial premises.

3. Under unitarianism, all of our conclusions are irrational.

Woe Is Me

Thus far, every worldview we've examined has collapsed in upon itself. Each of these four religious concepts (atheism, polytheism, deism, and unitarianism) have exhibited a lack of a rational and permanent authority behind the universe, making it impossible for human beings to rationally justify anything at all. Our prospects of ever actually being rational, of ever having good reasons for what we think and what we do, are looking dimmer by the minute. Must we now conclude that there is no reason to hold to any idea at all? That every assertion is just as rational as its negation? That truth, if it exists at all, is completely unknowable?

Before we give up on thinking entirely, we do have one more worldview to consider.

Trinitarian Christianity

Unlike atheism, which has no one in authority to guarantee the universality and invariance of the law of non-contradiction, Trinitarian Christianity holds that there is a sovereign author of the universe.

In the beginning God created the heavens and the earth (Genesis 1:1).[7]

All things were made through Him, and without Him nothing was made that was made (John 1:3).

For by Him all things were created that are in heaven and that are on earth, visible and invisible, whether thrones or dominions or principalities or powers. All things were created through Him and for Him (Colossians 1:16).

You are worthy, O Lord, to receive glory and honor and power; for You created all things, and by Your will they exist and were created (Revelation 4:11).

---

7. In this chapter, all Scripture is from the New King James Version (NKJV) of the Bible.

> By faith we understand that the worlds were framed by the word of God, so that the things which are seen were not made of things which are visible (Hebrews 11:3).

Unlike the gods of polytheism, the monotheistic God of the Bible exists as one God, yet three persons — Father, Son, and Holy Spirit. The persons of the trinitarian God, since they are the same God, are guaranteed to always agree with one another, obey one another, and to be perfectly consistent with one another, never denying Himself as one God. God even claims that His existence directly corresponds to His existence rather than ever being contrary to it.

> If we are faithless, He [God] remains faithful; He cannot deny Himself (2 Timothy 2:13).

> Father, if it is Your will, take this cup away from Me [Jesus]; nevertheless not My will, but Yours [the Father], be done (Luke 22:42).

> And being found in appearance as a man, He [Jesus] humbled Himself and became obedient to the point of death, even the death of the cross (Philippians 2:8).

> Then Jesus answered and said to them, "Most assuredly, I say to you, the Son can do nothing of Himself, but what He sees the Father do; for whatever He does, the Son also does in like manner" (John 5:19).

> And God said to Moses, "I AM WHO I AM." And He said, "Thus you shall say to the children of Israel, 'I AM has sent me to you' " (Exodus 3:14).

Unlike deism, the Trinitarian God is the author of time, sustaining His creation every moment, Himself being both eternal and omnitemporal.

> And He is before all things, and in Him all things consist (Colossians 1:17).

> Declaring the end from the beginning, and from ancient times things that are not yet done, saying, "My counsel shall stand, and I will do all My pleasure" (Isaiah 46:10).

Now to the King eternal, immortal, invisible, to God who alone is wise, be honor and glory forever and ever. Amen (1 Timothy 1:17).

I am the Alpha and the Omega, the Beginning and the End, the First and the Last (Revelation 22:13).

For a thousand years in Your sight are like yesterday when it is past, and like a watch in the night (Psalm 90:4).

And finally, unlike unitarianism, the Trinitarian God is wise enough to genuinely understand what the only possible rational justification, or reason, for all things is — namely, Himself.

For My own sake, for My own sake, I will do it; For how should My name be profaned? And I will not give My glory to another (Isaiah 48:11).

This people I have formed for Myself; they shall declare My praise (Isaiah 43:21).

Jesus said to him, "I am the way, the truth, and the life. No one comes to the Father except through Me. If you had known Me, you would have known My Father also; and from now on you know Him and have seen Him." Philip said to Him, "Lord, show us the Father, and it is sufficient for us." Jesus said to him, "Have I been with you so long, and yet you have not known Me, Philip? He who has seen Me has seen the Father; so how can you say, 'Show us the Father'?" (John 14:6–9).

He is the image of the invisible God, the firstborn over all creation (Colossians 1:15).

God . . . has in these last days spoken to us by His Son . . . who being the brightness of His glory and the express image of His person . . . sat down at the right hand of the Majesty on high, having become so much better than the angels, as He has by inheritance obtained a more excellent name than they (Hebrews 1:1–4).

But even if our gospel is veiled, it is veiled to those who are perishing, whose minds the god of this age has blinded, who do not believe, lest the light of the gospel of the glory of Christ, who is the image of God, should shine on them (2 Corinthians 4:3–4).

Let this mind be in you which was also in Christ Jesus, who, being in the form of God, did not consider it robbery to be equal with God, but made Himself of no reputation, taking the form of a bondservant, and coming in the likeness of men (Philippians 2:5–7).

But of Him you are in Christ Jesus, who became for us wisdom from God — and righteousness and sanctification and redemption — that, as it is written, "He who glories, let him glory in the LORD" (1 Corinthians 1:30–31).

For Jews request a sign, and Greeks seek after wisdom; but we preach Christ crucified, to the Jews a stumbling block and to the Greeks foolishness, but to those who are called, both Jews and Greeks, Christ the power of God and the wisdom of God (1 Corinthians 1:22–24).

In the beginning was the Word, and the Word was with God, and the Word was God. . . . And the Word became flesh and dwelt among us, and we beheld His glory, the glory as of the only begotten of the Father, full of grace and truth (John 1:1–14).

Conclusion

By standing on the Bible and the God it professes as the absolute authority, it is perfectly rational for the Trinitarian Christian to assert the premises of rationality, like the permanent universality of the law of non-contradiction, to proclaim these premises and uphold them. He may also use them as an unfailing standard for judging and discerning truth claims. The same cannot be said for the unitarian, the deist, the polytheist, or the atheist. For these groups, it is inconsistent to assert the premises of rationality as an unfailing standard for judging truth claims since, according to their own worldviews, rationality is not within the domain of human capability.

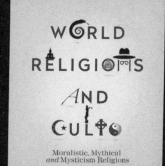